Reading STREET

Program Authors

Peter Afflerbach

Camille Blachowicz

Candy Dawson Boyd

Elena Izquierdo

Connie Juel

Edward Kame'enui

Donald Leu

Jeanne R. Paratore

P. David Pearson

Sam Sebesta

Deborah Simmons

Alfred Tatum

Sharon Vaughn

Susan Watts Taffe

Karen Kring Wixson

PEARSON

Glenview, Illinois • Boston, Massachusetts
Chandler, Arizona • Upper Saddle River, New Jersey

We dedicate Reading Street to
Peter Jovanovich.

His wisdom, courage,
and passion for education
are an inspiration to us all.

This work is protected by the United States copyright laws and is provided *solely for the use of teachers and administrators* in teaching courses and assessing student learning in their classes and schools. Dissemination or sale of any part of this work (including the World Wide Web) will destroy the integrity of the work and is *not* permitted.

ISBN-13: 978-0-328-47047-1
ISBN-10:   0-328-47047-3
2 3 4 5 6 7 8 9 10 V003 14 13 12 11 10
CC1

Any Path, Any Pace

"Welcome to Reading Street! Bienvenidos too."

PEARSON

Find Your Place on Reading Street!

T 61419

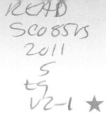

Who said so?

The Leading Researchers,

Program Authors

Peter Afflerbach, Ph.D.
Professor
Department of Curriculum
and Instruction
University of Maryland
at College Park

Camille L. Z. Blachowicz, Ph.D.
Professor of Education
National-Louis University

Candy Dawson Boyd, Ph.D.
Professor
School of Education
Saint Mary's College of California

Elena Izquierdo, Ph.D.
Associate Professor
University of Texas at El Paso

Connie Juel, Ph.D.
Professor of Education
School of Education
Stanford University

Edward J. Kame'enui, Ph.D.
Dean-Knight Professor of Education and Director
Institute for the Development of
Educational Achievement and
the Center on Teaching and Learning
College of Education
University of Oregon

Donald J. Leu, Ph.D.
John and Maria Neag Endowed Chair in Literacy and Technology Director, The New Literacies Research Lab
University of Connecticut

Jeanne R. Paratore, Ed.D.
Associate Professor of Education
Department of Literacy and
Language Development
Boston University

P. David Pearson, Ph.D.
Professor and Dean
Graduate School of Education
University of California, Berkeley

Sam L. Sebesta, Ed.D.
Professor Emeritus
College of Education
University of Washington, Seattle

Deborah Simmons, Ph.D.
Professor
College of Education and
Human Development
Texas A&M University

Alfred W. Tatum, Ph.D.
Associate Professor and Director of the UIC Reading Clinic
University of Illinois at Chicago

Sharon Vaughn, Ph.D.
H. E. Hartfelder/Southland Corporation Regents Professor Director, Meadows Center for Preventing Educational Risk
University of Texas

Susan Watts Taffe, Ph.D.
Associate Professor in Literacy
Division of Teacher Education
University of Cincinnati

Karen Kring Wixson, Ph.D.
Professor of Education
University of Michigan

Consulting Authors

Jeff Anderson, M.Ed.
Author and Consultant
San Antonio, Texas

Jim Cummins, Ph.D.
Professor
Department of Curriculum,
Teaching and Learning
University of Toronto

Lily Wong Fillmore, Ph.D.
Professor Emerita
Graduate School of Education
University of California, Berkeley

Georgia Earnest García, Ph.D.
Professor
Language and Literacy Division
Department of Curriculum
and Instruction
University of Illinois at
Urbana-Champaign

George A. González, Ph.D.
Professor (Retired)
School of Education
University of Texas-Pan American,
Edinburg

Valerie Ooka Pang, Ph.D.
Professor
School of Teacher Education
San Diego State University

Sally M. Reis, Ph.D.
Board of Trustees Distinguished Professor
Department of Educational
Psychology
University of Connecticut

Jon Scieszka, M.F.A.
Children's Book Author Founder of GUYS READ Named First National Ambassador for Young People's Literature 2008

Grant Wiggins, Ed.D.
Educational Consultant
Authentic Education
Concept Development

Lee Wright, M.Ed.
Pearland, Texas

Practitioners, and Authors.

Consultant

Sharroky Hollie, Ph.D.
Assistant Professor
California State University
Dominguez Hills, CA

Teacher Reviewers

Dr. Bettyann Brugger
*Educational Support Coordinator–
Reading Office*
Milwaukee Public Schools
Milwaukee, WI

Kathleen Burke
K–12 Reading Coordinator
Peoria Public Schools, Peoria, IL

Darci Burns, M.S.Ed.
University of Oregon

Bridget Cantrell
District Intervention Specialist
Blackburn Elementary School
Independence, MO

**Tahira DuPree Chase,
M.A., M.S.Ed.**
*Administrator of Elementary
English Language Arts*
Mount Vernon City School District
Mount Vernon, NY

Michele Conner
Director, Elementary Education
Aiken County School District
Aiken, SC

Georgia Coulombe
*K–6 Regional Trainer/
Literacy Specialist*
Regional Center for Training and
Learning (RCTL), Reno, NV

Kelly Dalmas
Third Grade Teacher
Avery's Creek Elementary, Arden, NC

Seely Dillard
First Grade Teacher
Laurel Hill Primary School
Mt. Pleasant, SC

Jodi Dodds-Kinner
Director of Elementary Reading
Chicago Public Schools, Chicago, IL

Dr. Ann Wild Evenson
District Instructional Coach
Osseo Area Schools, Maple Grove, MN

Stephanie Fascitelli
Principal
Apache Elementary, Albuquerque
Public Schools, Albuquerque, NM

Alice Franklin
*Elementary Coordinator, Language
Arts & Reading*
Spokane Public Schools, Spokane, WA

Laureen Fromberg
Assistant Principal
PS 100 Queens, NY

Kimberly Gibson
First Grade Teacher
Edgar B. Davis Community School
Brockton, MA

Kristen Gray
Lead Teacher
A.T. Allen Elementary School
Concord, NC

Mary Ellen Hazen
State Pre-K Teacher
Rockford Public Schools #205
Rockford, IL

Patrick M. Johnson
Elementary Instructional Director
Seattle Public Schools, Seattle, WA

Theresa Jaramillo Jones
Principal
Highland Elementary School
Las Cruces, NM

Sophie Kowzun
*Program Supervisor, Reading/
Language Arts, PreK-5*
Montgomery County Public Schools
Rockville, MD

David W. Matthews
Sixth Grade Teacher
Easton Area Middle School
Easton, PA

Ana Nuncio
Editor and Independent Publisher
Salem, MA

Joseph Peila
Principal
Chappell Elementary School
Chicago, IL

Ivana Reimer
Literacy Coordinator
PS 100 Queens, NY

Sally Riley
Curriculum Coordinator
Rochester Public Schools
Rochester, NH

Dyan M. Smiley
Independent Educational Consultant

Michael J. Swiatowiec
Lead Literacy Teacher
Graham Elementary School
Chicago, IL

Dr. Helen Taylor
Director of English Education
Portsmouth City Public Schools
Portsmouth, VA

Carol Thompson
Teaching and Learning Coach
Independence School District
Independence, MO

Erinn Zeitlin
Kindergarten Teacher
Carderock Springs Elementary School
Bethesda, MD

Any Path, Any Pace

UNIT 2

Doing the Right Thing

In this Teacher's Edition Unit 2, Volume 1

WEEK 1 · At the Beach

WEEK 2 · Hold the Flag High

WEEK 3 · The Ch'i-lin Purse

In the First Stop on Reading Street

GO Digital!

See It!

- Big Question Video

- Concept Talk Video

- Envision It! Animations

Hear It!

- eSelections

- eReaders

- Grammar Jammer

- Leveled Reader Database

Do It!

- Vocabulary Activities

- Story Sort

- 21st Century Skills

- Online Assessment

- Letter Tile Drag and Drop

UNIT 1

Meeting Challenges

Key
- **SI** Strategic Intervention
- **OL** On-Level
- **A** Advanced
- **ELL** ELL

Volume 1

Volume 2

What kinds of challenges do people face and how do they meet them?

UNIT 2

Doing the Right Thing

Key
SI Strategic Intervention
OL On-Level
A Advanced
ELL ELL

Volume 1

UNIT 3

Inventors and Artists

Volume 1

Volume 2

UNIT 4

Adapting

Volume 1

Volume 2

How do people and animals adapt to different situations?

UNIT 5

Adventurers

Volume 1

WEEK 1 • The Skunk Ladder

WEEK 2 • The Unsinkable Wreck of the R.M.S. *Titanic*

WEEK 3 • Talk with an Astronaut

Volume 2

WEEK 4 • Journey to the Center of the Earth

WEEK 5 • Ghost Towns of the American West

WEEK 6 • Interactive Review

Who goes seeking adventure and why?

UNIT 6

The Unexpected

Volume 1

Volume 2

UNIT 2

Skills Overview

Key
T Tested Skill
🔁 Target Skill

WEEK 1

At the Beach
Realistic Fiction pp. 182–193

The Eagle and the Bat
Legend pp. 198–199

WEEK 2

Hold the Flag High
Literary Nonfiction pp. 208–219

How to Fold the American Flag
Web Site pp. 224–227

Get Ready to Read

	WEEK 1	WEEK 2
Question of the Week	Why is honesty important?	What are the risks in helping others?
Amazing Words	*integrity, frank, honorable, moral, oath, principled, candid, guilt, justice, deceit*	*poses, officers, unwavering, maneuver, cooperation, nation, trembling, sacrifice, audacity, brazen*
Word Analysis	Spanish Word Origins	French Word Origins
Literary Terms	Imagery	Foreshadowing
Structure/Features	Conflict	Climax

Read and Comprehend

	WEEK 1	WEEK 2
Comprehension	T 🔁 **Skill** Compare and Contrast 🔁 **Strategy** Visualize **Review Skill** Author's Purpose	T 🔁 **Skill** Sequence 🔁 **Strategy** Inferring **Review Skill** Compare and Contrast
Vocabulary	T 🔁 **Skill** Unfamiliar words algae, concealed, driftwood, hammocks, lamented, sea urchins, sternly, tweezers	T 🔁 **Skill** Unknown words quarrel, union, confederacy, rebellion, glory, canteen, stallion
Fluency	Expression	Accuracy

Language Arts

	WEEK 1	WEEK 2
Writing	Description Trait: Vary Sentence Beginnings	Informal Letter Trait: Voice
Conventions	Regular and Irregular Plural Nouns	Possessive Nouns
Spelling	Digraphs *th, sh, ch, ph*	Irregular Plurals
Speaking/Listening	Talk Show	Speech
Research Skills	Reference Book	Parts of a Book

The Big Question
What makes people want to do the right thing?

WEEK 3	WEEK 4	WEEK 5	WEEK 6
The Ch'i-lin Purse Folk Tale pp. 236–249 **The Story of Phan Ku** Myth pp. 254–255	**A Summer's Trade** Realistic Fiction pp. 264–277 **Thunderbird and Killer Whale** Myth pp. 282–285	**The Midnight Ride of Paul Revere** Poem pp. 294–307 **The Heroic Paul Revere** Drama pp. 312–315	**Interactive Review**
What are the rewards in helping others?	Why do people make sacrifices for others?	How can people promote freedom?	Connect the Question of the Week to the Big Question
stranded favor, panic, distress, praise, nurture aid, selflessness, social worker, victim	*committed, consequences, donated, underprivileged, gratifying, charitable, forfeit, relinquish, altruism, noble*	*battlefield, freedom, beloved, battle, vote, acquire, representation, revolution, liberty, government*	**Review** Amazing Words for Unit 2
Suffixes *-tion, -ion*	Spanish Word Origins	Word Families	
Symbolism	Point of View	Rhyme, Rhythm, and Cadence	
Resolution	Conflict	Sequence	
T ⏺ **Skill** Compare and Contrast ⏺ **Strategy** Story Structure **Review** **Skill** Sequence	T ⏺ **Skill** Author's Purpose ⏺ **Strategy** Monitor and Clarify **Review** **Skill** Compare and Contrast	T ⏺ **Skill** Author's Purpose ⏺ **Strategy** Background Knowledge **Review** **Skill** Theme and Setting	**Review** Compare and Contrast, Sequence, Author's Purpose
T ⏺ **Skill** Greek and Latin Roots astonished, behavior, benefactor, distribution, gratitude, procession, recommend, sacred, traditions	T ⏺ **Skill** Unfamiliar Words Navajo, mesa, jostled, turquoise, bandana, hogan, bracelet	T ⏺ **Skill** Endings *-s, -ed, -ing* fate, fearless, glimmer, lingers, magnified, somber, steed	**Review** Unfamiliar Words, Unknown Words, Greek and Latin Roots, Inflected Endings
Expression	Appropriate Phrasing	Rate	**Review** Fluency for Unit 2
Poem Trait: Organization/Poetic Structure	Personal Narrative Trait: Word Choice	Historical Fiction Trait: Word Choice: Sensory Details	Quick Write for Fluency
Action and Linking Verbs	Main and Helping Verbs	Subject-Verb Agreement	**Review** Unit 2 Conventions
Vowel Sounds with *r*	Final Syllables *-en, -an, -el, -le, -il*	Final Syllables *er, ar, or*	**Review** Unit 2 Spelling Patterns
Reader's Theater	Panel Discussion	Media Literacy: Documentary	
Textbook/Trade Book	Electronic Media	Illustration/Caption	

UNIT 2

Monitor Progress

Don't Wait Until Friday! SUCCESS PREDICTOR	WEEK 1	WEEK 2	WEEK 3	WEEK 4
WCPM **Fluency**	Expression 110–116 WCPM	Accuracy 110–116 WCPM	Expression 110–116 WCPM	Appropriate Phrasing 110–116 WCPM
Oral Vocabulary **Oral Vocabulary/ Concept Development** (assessed informally)	integrity frank honorable moral oath principled candid guilt justice deceit	poses officers unwavering maneuver cooperation nation trembling sacrifice audacity brazen	stranded favor panic distress praise nurture aid selflessness social worker victim	committed consequences donated underprivileged gratifying charitable forfeit relinquish altruism noble
Lesson Vocabulary	T algae T concealed T driftwood T hammocks T lamented T sea urchins T sternly T tweezers	T quarrel T union T confederacy T rebellion T glory T canteen T stallion	T astonished T behavior T benefactor T distribution T gratitude T procession T recommend T sacred T traditions	T Navajo T mesa T jostled T turquoise T bandana T hogan T bracelet
Retelling **Text Comprehension**	T **Skill** Compare and Contrast **Strategy** Visualize	T **Skill** Sequence **Strategy** Inferring	T **Skill** Compare and Contrast **Strategy** Story Structure	T **Skill** Author's Purpose **Strategy** Monitor and Clarify

Key	
T	Tested Skill
↻	Target Skill

WEEK 5 / WEEK 6

R E V I E W

WEEK 5
Rate
110–116 WCPM
battlefield
freedom
beloved
battle
vote
acquire
representation
revolution
liberty
government
T fate
T fearless
T glimmer
T lingers
T magnified
T somber
T steed
T ↻ **Skill** Author's Purpose
↻ **Strategy** Background Knowledge

Online Classroom

Manage Data

- Assign the Unit 2 Benchmark Test for students to take online.

- Online Assessment records results and generates reports by school, grade, classroom, or student.

- Use reports to disaggregate and aggregate Unit 2 skills and standards data to monitor progress.

- Based on class lists created to support the categories important for AYP (gender, ethnicity, migrant education, English proficiency, disabilities, economic status), reports let you track adequate yearly progress every six weeks.

Group

- Use results from Unit 2 Benchmark Tests taken online through Online Assessment to measure whether students have mastered the English-Language Arts Content Standards taught in this unit.

- Reports in Online Assessment suggest whether students need Extra Support or Intervention.

Individualized Instruction

- Assessments are correlated to Unit 2 tested skills and standards so that prescriptions for individual teaching and learning plans can be created.

- Individualized prescriptions target instruction and accelerate student progress toward learning outcome goals.

- Prescriptions include remediation activities and resources to reteach Unit 2 skills and standards.

Select a Class: Reading 101

Make Assignments	View Reports and Logs
Assign Tests Search by: Unit ▸ GO!	**Class Reports** View by: Standard ▸ GO!
	Assignment Log View by: Entire Class ▸ GO!

Other Resources and Information

Certificates Motivate your students with printable certificates.

The User's Guide and Quick Start Guide get you the help you need fast. Learn how to make the most of the Reading Success Tracker System with our simple to use guides.

UNIT 2

Assessment and Grouping
for Data-Driven Instruction

4-Step Plan for Assessment
1 Diagnose and Differentiate
2 Monitor Progress
3 Assess and Regroup
4 Summative Assessment

STEP 1 Diagnose and Differentiate

Baseline Group Tests

Diagnose

To make initial grouping decisions, use the Baseline Group Test, the *Texas Primary Reading Inventory (TPRI),* or another initial placement test. Depending on student's ability levels, you may have more than one of each group.

Differentiate

If... student performance is then... use the regular instruction and the daily **Strategic Intervention** small group lessons.

If... student performance is then... use the regular instruction and the daily **On-Level** small group lessons.

If... student performance is then... use the regular instruction and the daily **Advanced** small group lessons.

Small Group Time

SI Strategic Intervention

- Daily small group lessons provide more intensive instruction, more scaffolding, more practice, and more opportunities to respond.
- Reteach lessons in the *First Stop on Reading Street* provide more instruction with target skills.
- Leveled readers build background and provide practice for target skills and vocabulary.

OL On-Level

- Explicit instructional routines teach core skills and strategies.
- Daily On-Level lessons provide more practice and more opportunities to respond.
- Independent activities provide practice for core skills and extension and enrichment options.
- Leveled readers provide additional reading and practice for core skills and vocabulary.

A Advanced

- Daily Advanced lessons provide instruction for accelerated learning.
- Leveled readers provide additional reading tied to lesson concepts and skills.

Additional Differentiated Learning Options

Reading Street Response to Intervention Kit

- Focused intervention lessons on the five critical areas of reading: phonemic awareness, phonics, vocabulary, comprehension, and fluency

My Sidewalks on Reading Street

- Intensive intervention for struggling readers

STEP 2 Monitor Progress

Use these tools during lesson teaching to **monitor student progress.**

- **Skill and Strategy** instruction during reading

- **Don't Wait Until Friday** boxes to check retelling, fluency, and oral vocabulary

- **Weekly Assessment** on Day 5 checks comprehension and fluency

- **Reader's and Writer's Notebook** pages at point of use

- **Weekly Tests** assess target skills for the week

- **Fresh Reads** for Fluency and Comprehension

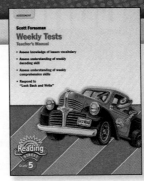

Weekly Tests

Fresh Reads for Fluency and Comprehension

STEP 3 Assess and Regroup

Use these tools during lesson teaching to **assess and regroup.**

- **Weekly Assessments** Record results of weekly assessments in retelling, comprehension, and fluency to track student progress.

- **Unit Benchmark Test** Administer this assessment to check mastery of unit skills.

- **Regroup** We recommend the first regrouping to be at the end of Unit 2. Use weekly assessment information and Unit Benchmark Test performance to inform regrouping decisions. Then regroup at the end of each subsequent unit.

Unit Assessment Charts in First Stop

Group					
Baseline →	Regroup →	Regroup →	Regroup →	Regroup →	**End of Year**
Group Test	Units 1 and 2	Unit 3	Unit 4	Unit 5	
Weeks 1-6	Weeks 7-12	Weeks 13-18	Weeks 19-24	Weeks 25-30	Weeks 31-36

Outside assessments, such as *TPRI, DRA,* and *DIBELS,* may recommend regrouping at other times during the year.

STEP 4 Summative Assessment

Use these tools after lesson teaching to **assess students.**

- **Unit Benchmark Tests** Use to measure a student's mastery of each unit's skills.

- **End-of-Year Benchmark Test** Use to measure a student's mastery of program skills covered in all six units.

Unit and End-of-Year Benchmark Tests

Concept Launch

Understanding By Design

*Grant Wiggins, Ed. D.
Reading Street Author*

❝The big idea connects the dots for the learner by establishing learning priorities. As a teacher friend of ours observed, they serve as 'conceptual Velcro'— they help the facts and skills stick together and stick in our minds!❞

Doing the Right Thing

Reading Street Online

www.ReadingStreet.com
• Big Question Video
• eSelections
• Envision It! Animations
• Story Sort

THE BIG ?

What makes people want to do the right thing?

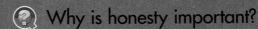

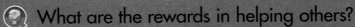

Theme Launch **xxi**

UNIT 2

Small Group Time
Flexible Pacing Plans

5 Day Plan

DAY 1
- Reinforce the Concept
- Read Leveled Readers Concept Literacy Below-Level

DAY 2
- Comprehension Skill
- Comprehension Strategy
- Revisit Main Selection

DAY 3
- Vocabulary Skill
- Revisit Main Selection

DAY 4
- Practice Retelling
- Read/Revisit Paired Selection

DAY 5
- Reread for Fluency
- Reread Leveled Readers

4 Day Plan

DAY 1
- Reinforce the Concept
- Read Leveled Readers Concept Literacy Below-Level

DAY 2
- Comprehension Skill
- Comprehension Strategy
- Revisit Main Selection

DAY 3
- Vocabulary Skill
- Revisit Main Selection

DAY 4
- Practice Retelling
- Read/Revisit Paired Selection
- Reread for Fluency
- Reread Leveled Readers

3 Day Plan

DAY 1
- Reinforce the Concept
- Read Leveled Readers Concept Literacy Below-Level

DAY 2
- Comprehension Skill
- Comprehension Strategy
- Revisit Main Selection

DAY 3
- Practice Retelling
- Read/Revisit Paired Selection
- Reread for Fluency
- Reread Leveled Readers

ELL

5 Day Plan

DAY 1
- Frontload Concept
- Preteach Skills
- Conventions/Writing

DAY 2
- Review Concept/Skills
- Frontload and Read Main Selection
- Conventions/Writing

DAY 3
- Review Concept/Skills
- Reread Main Selection
- Conventions/Writing

DAY 4
- Review Concept/Skills
- Read ELL or ELD Reader
- Conventions/Writing

DAY 5
- Review Concept/Skills
- Read ELL or ELD Reader
- Conventions/Writing

4 Day Plan

DAY 1
- Frontload Concept
- Preteach Skills
- Conventions/Writing

DAY 2
- Review Concept/Skills
- Frontload and Read Main Selection
- Conventions/Writing

DAY 3
- Review Concept/Skills
- Reread Main Selection
- Conventions/Writing

DAY 4
- Review Concept/Skills
- Read ELL or ELD Reader
- Conventions/Writing

3 Day Plan

DAY 1
- Frontload Concept
- Preteach Skills
- Conventions/Writing

DAY 2
- Review Concept/Skills
- Frontload and Read Main Selection
- Conventions/Writing

DAY 3
- Review Concept/Skills
- Read ELL or ELD Reader
- Conventions/Writing

This Week's ELL Overview

ELL Handbook

- Maximize Literacy and Cognitive Engagement
- Research Into Practice
- Full Weekly Support for Every Selection

At the Beach
- Multi-Lingual Summaries in Five Languages
- Selection-Specific Vocabulary Word Cards
- Frontloading/Reteaching for Comprehension Skill Lessons
- ELD and ELL Reader Study Guides

- Transfer Activities
- Professional Development

Daily Leveled ELL Notes

ELL notes appear throughout this week's instruction and ELL Support is on the DI pages of your Teacher's Edition. The following is a sample of an ELL note from this week.

English Language Learners

Beginning Have students pick one or two nouns and change them into plural nouns.

Intermediate Assist students as they identify whether they are regular or irregular.

Advanced Have students change each word into a plural noun. Ask students to identify if the plural noun is regular or irregular and to explain their choice.

Advanced High Have students make a list of items in their desk, locker, and backpack. Then have them change each noun to its plural form and write a check by each irregular plural noun.

ELL by Strand

The ELL lessons on this week's Support for English Language Learners pages are organized by strand. They offer additional scaffolding for the core curriculum. Leveled support notes on these pages address the different proficiency levels in your class. See pages DI•16–DI•25.

ELL Guy
Dr. Jim Cummins

The Three Pillars of ELL Instruction

ELL Strands	Activate Prior Knowledge	Access Content	Extend Language
Vocabulary pp. DI•17–DI•18	Preteach	Reteach	Leveled Writing Activities
Reading Comprehension p. DI•22	Frontloading	Sheltered Reading	After Reading
Phonics, Spelling, and Word Analysis p. DI•20	Preteach	Model	Leveled Practice Activities
Listening Comprehension p. DI•19	Prepare for the Read Aloud	First Listening	Second Listening
Conventions and Writing pp. DI•24–DI•25	Preteach	Leveled Practice Activities	Leveled Writing Activities
Concept Development p. DI•16	Activate Prior Knowledge	Discuss Concept	Daily Concept and Vocabulary Development

This Week's Practice Stations Overview

Six Weekly Practice Stations with Leveled Activities can be found at the beginning of each week of instruction. For this week's Practice Stations, see pp. 176h–176i.

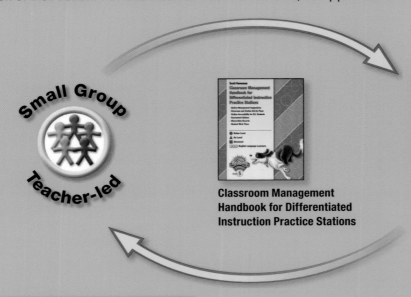

Practice Stations

Classroom Management Handbook for Differentiated Instruction Practice Stations

Daily Leveled Center Activities

Below   Advanced
On-Level   E L L

Practice Stations Flip Charts

	Word Wise	Word Work	Words to Know	Let's Write	Read for Meaning	Get Fluent
Objectives	• Spell common contractions.	• Identify and write contractions.	• Distinguish between meanings of multiple-meaning words.	• Write an expository composition.	• Understand cause and effect in expository text.	• Read aloud with accuracy.
Materials	• *Word Wise* Flip Chart Activity 6 • Teacher-made word cards • paper • pencils	• *Word Work* Flip Chart Activity 6 • Teacher-made word cards • paper • pencils	• *Words to Know* Flip Chart Activity 6 • Teacher-made word cards • paper • pencils	• *Let's Write* Flip Chart Activity 6 • paper • pencils	• *Read for Meaning* Flip Chart Activity 6 • Leveled Readers • paper • pencils	• *Get Fluent* Flip Chart Activity 6 • Leveled Readers

This Week on Reading Street!

Question of the Week
Why is honesty important?

Daily Plan

Don't Wait Until Friday

Whole Group

- ◉ Compare and Contrast
- ◉ Unfamiliar Words
- • Fluency/Expression
- • Research and Inquiry

MONITOR PROGRESS	Success Predictor		
Day 1 Check Oral Vocabulary	Days 2–3 Check Retelling	Day 4 Check Fluency	Day 5 Check Oral Vocabulary

Small Group

Teacher-Led

- • Reading Support
- • Skill Support
- • Fluency Practice

Practice Stations

Independent Activities

Customize Literacy More support for a balanced literacy approach, see pp. CL•1–CL•47

Customize Writing More support for a customized writing approach, see pp. CW•1–CW•10

Whole Group

- • Writing: Description
- • Conventions: Regular and Irregular Plural Nouns

Assessment

- • Weekly Tests
- • Day 5 Assessment
- • Fresh Reads

You Are Here!
Unit 2 Week 1

This Week's Reading Selections

Main Selection
Genre: **Realistic Fiction**

Paired Selection
Genre: **Legend**

Leveled Readers

ELL and ELD Readers

Resources on Reading Street!

	Build Concepts	**Comprehension**
Whole Group	 Let's Talk About pp. 176–177	Envision It! Skills/ Strategies  Comprehension Skills Lesson pp. 178–179
Go Digital	• Concept Talk Video	• Envision It! Animations • eSelections
Small Group and Independent Practice	 At the Beach pp. 182–183 ELL and ELD Readers Leveled Readers	 At the Beach pp. 182–183 ELL and ELD Readers Leveled Readers Envision It! Skills/ Strategies Reader's and Writer's Notebook Practice Station Flip Chart
Go Digital	• eReaders • eSelections	• Envision It! Animations • eSelections • eReaders
Customize Literacy	• Leveled Readers	• Envision It! Skills and Strategies Handbook • Leveled Readers
Go Digital	• Concept Talk Video • Big Question Video • eReaders	• Envision It! Animations • eReaders

Question of the Week
Why is honesty important?

Vocabulary

Envision It!
Vocabulary
Cards

Vocabulary Skill Lesson
pp. 180–181

- Envision It! Vocabulary Cards
- Vocabulary Activities

Envision It!
Vocabulary
Cards

At the Beach
pp. 182–183

Practice
Station
Flip Chart

Context Clues
Words!

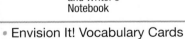
Reader's
and Writer's
Notebook

- Envision It! Vocabulary Cards
- Vocabulary Activities
- eSelections

- Envision It! Vocabulary Cards

- Vocabulary Activities

Fluency

Let's Learn It!
pp. 200–201

- eSelections
- eReaders

At the Beach
pp. 182–183

Practice
Station
Flip Chart

Leveled
Readers

ELL and ELD
Readers

- eSelections
- eReaders

- Leveled Readers

- eReaders

Conventions and Writing

Let's Write It! pp. 196–197

- Grammar Jammer

Reader's
and Writer's
Notebook

At the Beach
pp. 182–183

Practice
Station
Flip Chart

- Grammar Jammer

- Reader's and Writer's Notebook

- Grammar Jammer

You Are
Here!
Unit 2
Week 1

My 5-Day Planner for Reading Street!

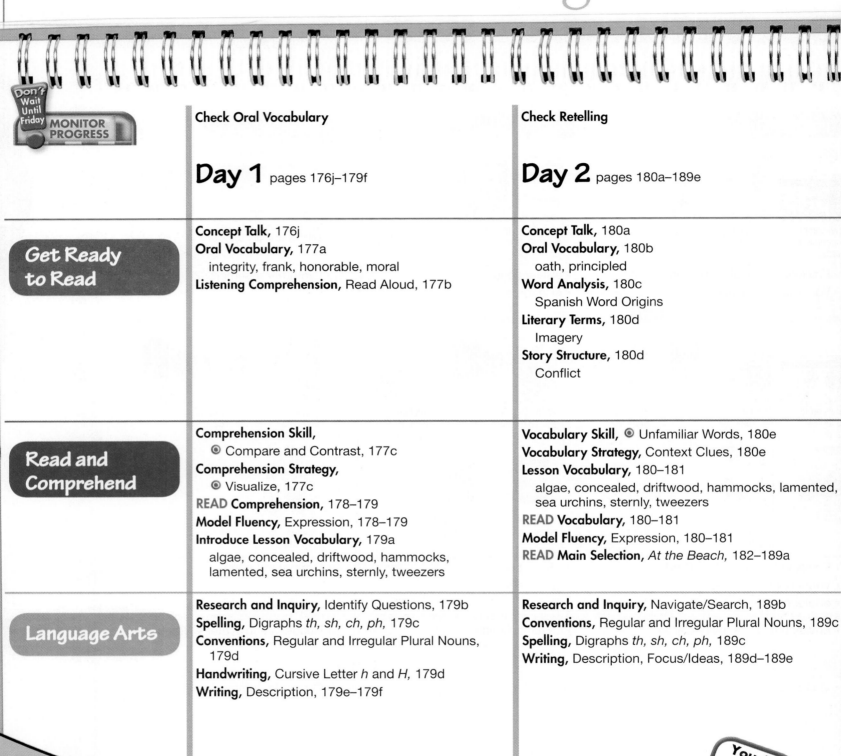

	Check Oral Vocabulary **Day 1** pages 176j–179f	**Check Retelling** **Day 2** pages 180a–189e

Get Ready to Read	**Concept Talk,** 176j
	Oral Vocabulary, 177a
	   integrity, frank, honorable, moral
	Listening Comprehension, Read Aloud, 177b
		Concept Talk, 180a
		Oral Vocabulary, 180b
		   oath, principled
		Word Analysis, 180c
		   Spanish Word Origins
		Literary Terms, 180d
		   Imagery
		Story Structure, 180d
		   Conflict

Read and Comprehend	**Comprehension Skill,**
	   ◉ Compare and Contrast, 177c
	Comprehension Strategy,
	   ◉ Visualize, 177c
	READ Comprehension, 178–179
	Model Fluency, Expression, 178–179
	Introduce Lesson Vocabulary, 179a
	   algae, concealed, driftwood, hammocks,
	   lamented, sea urchins, sternly, tweezers
		Vocabulary Skill, ◉ Unfamiliar Words, 180e
		Vocabulary Strategy, Context Clues, 180e
		Lesson Vocabulary, 180–181
		   algae, concealed, driftwood, hammocks, lamented,
		   sea urchins, sternly, tweezers
		READ Vocabulary, 180–181
		Model Fluency, Expression, 180–181
		READ Main Selection, *At the Beach,* 182–189a

Language Arts	**Research and Inquiry,** Identify Questions, 179b **Spelling,** Digraphs *th, sh, ch, ph,* 179c **Conventions,** Regular and Irregular Plural Nouns, 179d **Handwriting,** Cursive Letter *h* and *H,* 179d **Writing,** Description, 179e–179f	**Research and Inquiry,** Navigate/Search, 189b **Conventions,** Regular and Irregular Plural Nouns, 189c **Spelling,** Digraphs *th, sh, ch, ph,* 189c **Writing,** Description, Focus/Ideas, 189d–189e

You Are Here!
Unit 2
Week 1

Question of the Week
Why is honesty important?

Check Retelling	Check Fluency	Check Oral Vocabulary
Day 3 pages 190a–197c	**Day 4** pages 198a–201e	**Day 5** pages 201f–201q

Concept Talk, 190a
Oral Vocabulary, 190b
  candid, guilt
Comprehension Check, 190c
Check Retelling, 190d
	Concept Talk, 198a
	Oral Vocabulary, 198b
	  justice, deceit
	Genre,
	  Legend: Genre Elements, 198c
		Concept Wrap Up, 201f
		Check Oral Vocabulary, 201g
		  integrity, frank, honorable, moral,
		  oath, principled, candid, guilt,
		  justice, deceit
		Amazing Ideas, 201g
		Review ◉ Compare and Contrast, 201h
		Review ◉ Unfamiliar Words, 201h
		Review Word Analysis, 201i
		Review Literary Terms, 201i

READ Main Selection, *At the Beach,* 190–193a
Retelling, 194–195
Think Critically, 195a
Model Fluency, Expression, 195b
Research and Study Skills, Reference Books, 195c
	READ Paired Selection, "The Eagle and the Bat," 198–199a
	Let's Learn It! 200–201a
	  Fluency: Expression
	  Vocabulary: Unfamiliar Words
	  Listening and Speaking:
	  Talk Show
		Fluency Assessment,
		  WCPM, 201j–201k
		Comprehension Assessment,
		  ◉ Compare and Contrast, 201l–201m

Research and Inquiry, Analyze, 195d **Conventions,** Regular and Irregular Plural Nouns, 195e **Spelling,** Digraphs *th, sh, ch, ph,* 195e **Let's Write It!** Description, 196–197a **Writing,** Description, Descriptive Language, 197b–197c	**Research and Inquiry,** Synthesize, 201b **Conventions,** Regular and Irregular Plural Nouns, 201c **Spelling,** Digraphs *th, sh, ch, ph,* 201c **Writing,** Description, Revising, 201d–201e	**Research and Inquiry,** Communicate, 201n **Conventions,** Regular and Irregular Plural Nouns, 201o **Spelling Test,** Digraphs *th, sh, ch, ph,* 201o **Writing,** Description, Plural Nouns and Quotations, 201p–201q **Quick Write for Fluency,** 201q

Grouping Options for Differentiated Instruction
Turn the page for the small group time lesson plan.

Planning Small Group Time on Reading Street!

SMALL GROUP TIME RESOURCES

Look for this Small Group Time box each day to help meet the individual needs of all your students. Differentiated Instrucion lessons appear on the DI pages at the end of each week.

DAY 1

Teacher Led

SI Strategic Intervention	**OL** On-Level	**A** Advanced
Teacher Led	**Teacher Led**	**Teacher Led**
• Reinforce the Concept	• Expand the Concept	• Extend the Concept
• **Read** *Concept Literacy* or *Below-Level Reader*	• **Read** *On-Level Reader*	• **Read** *Advanced Reader*

ELL Place English language learners in the groups that correspond to their reading abilities in English.

Practice Stations	**Independent Activities**
• Read for Meaning	• Concept Talk Video
• Get Fluent	• Reader's and Writer's Notebook
• Word Work	• Research and Inquiry

ELL

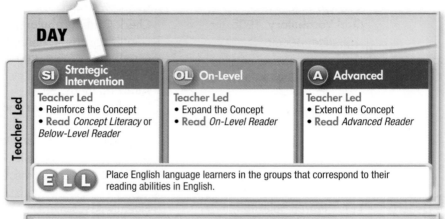

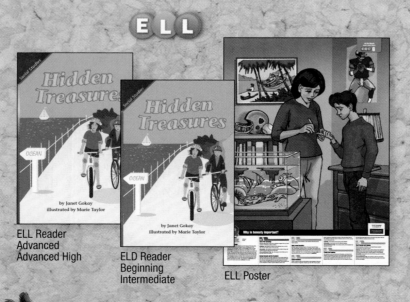

ELL Reader
Advanced
Advanced High

ELD Reader
Beginning
Intermediate

ELL Poster

You Are Here!
Unit 2 Week 1

Day 1

SI Strategic Intervention	Reinforce the Concept, DI•1–DI•2 Read **Concept Literacy Reader** or **Below-Level Reader**	
OL On-Level	Expand the Concept, DI•7 Read **On-Level Reader**	
A Advanced	Extend the Concept, DI•12 Read **Advanced Reader**	
ELL English Language Learners	DI•16–DI•25 **Frontload Concept Preteach Skills Writing**	

Reading Street Response
to Intervention Kit

Reading Street
Practice Stations Kit

Question of the Week
Why is honesty important?

SI Strategic Intervention

OL On-Level

A Advanced

Below-Level
Reader

Concept Literacy Reader

On-Level Reader

Advanced
Reader

At the Beach pp. 182–183

The Eagle and the Bat pp. 198–199

Small Group Weekly Plan

Day 2	Day 3	Day 4	Day 5
Reinforce Comprehension, DI•3 **Revisit Main Selection**	**Reinforce Vocabulary,** DI•4 **Read/Revisit Main Selection**	**Reinforce Comprehension,** Practice Retelling DI•5 Genre Focus **Read/Revisit Paired Selection**	**Practice Fluency,** DI•6 **Reread Concept Literacy Reader** or **Below-Level Reader**
Expand Comprehension, DI•8 **Revisit Main Selection**	**Expand Vocabulary,** DI•9 **Read/Revisit Main Selection**	**Expand Comprehension,** Practice Retelling DI•10 Genre Focus **Read/Revisit Paired Selection**	**Practice Fluency,** DI•11 **Reread On-Level Reader**
Extend Comprehension, DI•13 **Revisit Main Selection**	**Extend Vocabulary,** DI•14 **Read/Revisit Main Selection**	**Extend Comprehension,** Genre Focus DI•15 **Read/Revisit Paired Selection**	**Practice Fluency,** DI•15 **Reread Advanced Reader**
DI•16–DI•25 **Review Concept/Skills Frontload Main Selection Practice**	DI•16–DI•25 **Review Concept/Skills Reread Main Selection Practice**	DI•16–DI•25 **Review Concept Read ELL/ELD Readers Practice**	DI•16–DI•25 **Review Concept/Skills Reread ELL/ELD Reader Writing**

Practice Stations for Everyone on Reading Street!

Word Wise
Common contractions

Objectives
• Spell common contractions.

Materials
• *Word Wise* Flip Chart Activity 6
• Teacher-made word cards
• paper • pencils

Differentiated Activities

⬤ Choose five word cards. Write the words in a list. Write the two words that form each contraction. Write sentences using your contractions.

▲ Choose seven word cards, and write the words in a list. Write the two words that form each contraction. Write sentences using each contraction.

◼ Choose ten word cards, and write the words in a list. Write the two words that form each contraction. Write sentences for each of your contractions.

Technology
• Online Dictionary

Word Work
Contractions

Objectives
• Identify and write contractions.

Materials
• *Word Work* Flip Chart Activity 6
• Teacher-made word cards
• paper • pencils

Differentiated Activities

⬤ Choose six word cards. Write the words in a list. Quietly say each word to yourself. Think of other contractions you know. Add them to your list.

▲ Choose nine word cards, and write the words in a list. Quietly say the words to yourself. Write sentences using the contractions.

◼ Choose twelve word cards, and write the words in a list. Quietly say each word to yourself. Write sentences using the contractions.

Technology
• Modeled Pronunciation Audio CD

Words to Know
Multiple-meaning words

Objectives
• Distinguish between meanings of multiple-meaning words.

Materials
• *Words to Know* Flip Chart Activity 6
• Teacher-made word cards
• paper • pencils

Differentiated Activities

⬤ Choose three word cards. Write the words in a list. Use the dictionary to find two meanings for each word. Write two sentences for each word to show its multiple meanings.

▲ Choose five word cards, and write the words in a list. Use the dictionary to find two meanings for each word. Write two sentences for each word to show its multiple meanings.

◼ Choose seven word cards, and write the words in a list. Use the dictionary to find two meanings for each word. Write two sentences for each word to show its multiple meanings.

Technology
• Online Dictionary

You Are Here!
**Unit 2
Week 1**

Key

● Below-Level Activities
▲ On-Level Activities
■ Advanced Activities

Practice Station Flip Chart

Let's Write!
Expository composition

Objectives
• Write an expository composition.

Materials
• *Let's Write!* Flip Chart Activity 6
• paper • pencils

Differentiated Activities

● Think of a solution somebody had to a problem. Write a short composition that tells about the problem. Explain what the solution to the problem was. Include details and facts.

▲ Many inventions have made people's lives easier. Write a short composition describing a problem that existed before an invention. Explain how the invention helped solve the problem.

■ Write a short composition describing a problem that an invention helped solve. Give details about the problem, and explain how the invention was the solution. Organize your writing into paragraphs.

Technology
• Online Graphic Organizers

Read for Meaning
Cause and effect

Objectives
• Understand cause and effect in expository text.

Materials
• *Read for Meaning* Flip Chart Activity 6
• Leveled Readers
• paper • pencils

Differentiated Activities

● Choose a book from those your teacher provided. Think about something that happens in the book. What caused this to happen? Write one sentence that tells about an effect. Write one sentence that tells what caused the effect.

▲ Choose a book from those your teacher provided. Think about the causes and effects the author writes about. Write sentences telling about two causes. Then write sentences stating the effects.

■ Choose a book from those your teacher provided. As you read, think about the causes and effects the author describes. Explain three causes in the selection. Then describe the effects.

Technology
• Leveled Reader Database

Get Fluent
Practice fluent reading.

Objectives
• Read aloud with accuracy.

Materials
• *Get Fluent* Flip Chart Activity 6
• Leveled Readers

Differentiated Activities

● Work with a partner. Choose a Concept Literacy Reader or Below-Level Reader. Take turns reading a page from the book. Use the reader to practice accuracy. Provide feedback as needed.

▲ Work with a partner. Choose an On-Level Reader. Take turns reading a page from the book. Use the reader to practice accuracy. Provide feedback as needed.

■ Work with a partner. Choose an Advanced Reader. Take turns reading a page from the book. Use the reader to practice accuracy. Provide feedback as needed.

Technology
• Leveled Reader Database
• Leveled Reading Street Readers CD-ROM

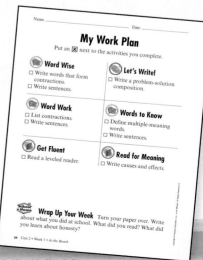

My Weekly Work Plan

Week 1

Objectives
- Introduce the weekly concept.
- Develop oral vocabulary.

Today at a Glance

Oral Vocabulary
Integrity, frank, honorable, moral

Comprehension
◉ Compare and contrast
◉ Visualize

Reading
"Ryan and Jonah"

Fluency
Expression

Lesson Vocabulary
Tested vocabulary

Research and Inquiry
Identify questions

Spelling
Digraphs *th, sh, ch, ph*

Conventions
Regular and irregular plural nouns

Handwriting
Cursive *k* and *K*

Writing
Description

Concept Talk

Question of the Week
Why is honesty important?

Introduce the concept

To further explore the unit concept of Doing the Right Thing, this week students will read, write, and talk about why it is important to be honest. Write the Question of the Week on the board.

ROUTINE **Activate Prior Knowledge** **Team Talk**

 Think Have students think about times when it takes courage to be honest.

 Pair Have pairs of students discuss the Question of the Week. Remind them to consider each other's suggestions.

 Share Call on a few students to share their ideas with the group. Guide the discussion and encourage elaboration with prompts such as:

- Can you describe a character in a story or a movie who chose to be honest in a difficult situation?

- What are some examples of ways people can be honest?

Routines Flip Chart

Anchored Talk

Develop oral vocabulary

Have students turn to pp. 176–177 in their Student Editions. Look at each of the photos. Then, use the prompts to guide discussion and create the *Honesty* concept map.

- What is the woman in the courtroom doing? (She is taking an oath to promise that she will tell the truth.) A trial depends on people being honest so that justice can be done. Let's add *Honest person* to the concept map.

- Why is it important to be honest if you talk to a police officer? (The officer needs to know the truth.) If a police officer does not know the truth, she cannot do her job and stop crime.

Student Edition pp. 176–177

Oral Vocabulary

Let's Talk About

Honesty
- Share opinions about the importance of being honest.
- Listen to a classmate's ideas about honesty.
- Determine your classmates' main and supporting ideas about honesty.

READING STREET ONLINE
CONCEPT TALK VIDEO
www.ReadingStreet.com

Objectives
- Listen to and interpret a speaker's messages and ask questions.
- Identify the main ideas and supporting ideas in the speaker's message.

You've learned **0 5 0** Amazing Words so far this year!

Amazing Words

You've learned **0 5 0** words so far

You'll learn **0 1 0** words this week!

integrity	oath
frank	candid
honorable	guilt
moral	justice
principled	deceit

Writing on Demand

Writing fluency
Ask students to respond to the photos on pp. 176–177 by writing as well as they can and as much as they can about why honesty is important.

- What might a dishonest person do during a test? **(They might look at another student's paper.)** Let's add *Dishonest person* to the concept map.

- After discussing the photos, ask: Why is honesty important?

```
              Honesty
             /        \
   Honest person    Dishonest
                     person
```

Connect to reading

Tell students that this week they will be reading about why honesty is important. Throughout the week, encourage students to add concept-related words to this week's concept map.

ELL Preteach Concepts Use the Day 1 instruction on ELL Poster 6 to assess and build background knowledge, develop concepts, and build oral vocabulary.

ELL

English Language Learners
ELL support Additional ELL support and modified instruction is provided in the *ELL Handbook* and in the ELL Support lessons on pp. DI•16–DI•25.

Listening comprehension
English learners will benefit from additional visual support to understand the key terms in the concept map. Use the pictures on pp. 176–177 to scaffold understanding.

Frontload for Read Aloud Use the modified Read Aloud on p. DI•19 of the ELL Support lessons to prepare students to listen to "Bullseye" (p. 177b).

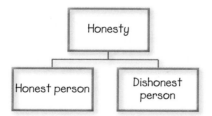

ELL Poster 6

Objectives
- Develop listening comprehension.
- Develop oral vocabulary.

— **Check Oral Vocabulary**
SUCCESS PREDICTOR

Oral Vocabulary
Amazing Words

Introduce Amazing Words

"Bullseye" on page 177b is about a boy who learns a lesson about honesty from his grandfather. Tell students to listen for this week's Amazing Words—*integrity, frank, honorable,* and *moral*—as you read.

Model fluency

As you read "Bullseye," model appropriate expression by adjusting your voice to demonstrate a lively, fluent reader.

Teach Amazing Words

Amazing Words ⭐ Oral Vocabulary Routine

| integrity |
| frank |
| honorable |
| moral |

1 **Introduce** Write the word *integrity* on the board. Have students say the word with you. In "Bullseye," what word does Grandpa say that has a similar meaning to the word *integrity*? (*honesty*) Supply a student-friendly definition. Someone with *integrity* is honest and has good morals.

2 **Demonstrate** Have students answer questions to demonstrate understanding. How can a person show *integrity* when he or she makes a mistake?

3 **Apply** Ask students to give personal examples of *integrity*.
See p. OV•1 to teach *frank, honorable,* and *moral*.

Routines Flip Chart

Apply Amazing Words

To build oral language, lead the class in a discussion about the meanings of the Amazing Words.

MONITOR PROGRESS Check Oral Vocabulary

During discussion, listen for students' use of the Amazing Words.

If... students are unable to use the Amazing Words to discuss the concept,

then... use Oral Vocabulary Routine in the Routines Flip Chart to demonstrate words in different contexts.

Day 1	Days 2–3	Day 4	Day 5
Check Oral Vocabulary	Check Retelling	Check Fluency	Check Oral Vocabulary

Bullseye

Mikey kept firing the baseball at the black-and-white bullseye his grandfather had painted on the concrete wall—and missing.

Mikey's grandfather watched from the kitchen window. Grandpa was about to call Mikey in for dinner when Mikey tossed another wild pitch. This one went sailing over the wall. The ball toppled the neighbors' recycling bin, sending bottles and cans flying into the alley.

Grandpa watched as Mikey threw his glove down and stomped on it, raising an angry dust cloud. Grandpa waited for Mikey to do the right thing. Instead, Mikey headed for the house.

When Mikey arrived, he was all smiles. "Wow, Grandpa, you should've seen me out there."

Grandpa stirred the chicken stew. "Oh?"

"Remember how you told me, 'Practice makes perfect'?" Mikey asked. "I hit the bullseye with every pitch. What do you think about that?"

"I think we need to talk, Mikey."

"Sure, Grandpa. What about?"

"Integrity," Grandpa said. "It's like honesty, remember?"

Mikey shrugged nervously. "The stew smells great," he said. "And boy, am I starving."

Grandpa held up a hand until Mikey sat back down. "I was watching you out there," he said.

"Wasn't I terrific?" Mikey asked.

"May I be frank with you, Mikey?" Grandpa said. "You were wild, Mikey."

"Me? Wild? Well, maybe a teeny bit," Mikey admitted.

"Your pitching will improve," Grandpa said. "But it's not your pitching that concerns me, Mikey. It's your integrity. Even more than seeing my grandson take the mound at Dodger Stadium, I would like to see him grow up to be an honorable man. A wise and moral man who knows what it means to do the right thing and does not hesitate to do it. A man who . . . cleans up his own messes. Do you know what I mean?"

Mikey looked down a moment and frowned. "Uh, Grandpa, there's something I forgot I need to do before we eat." Mikey started toward the door, then turned back. "I didn't really forget to do it," Mikey admitted. "The truth is, I just plain didn't do it. But I'm going to do it right now." Mikey walked outside.

(continued on p. 201s)

Oral Vocabulary

Success Predictor

Objectives

◎ Compare and contrast to aid comprehension.

◎ Visualize to aid comprehension.

• Read grade-level text with expression.

Skills Trace

◎ **Compare and Contrast**

Introduce U2W1D1; U2W3D1; U6W3D1

Practice U2W1D2; U2W1D3; U2W3D2; U2W3D3; U6W3D2; U6W3D3

Reteach/Review U2W1D5; U2W3D5; U2W4D2; U2W4D3; U6W3D5

Assess/Test Weekly Tests U2W1; U2W3; U6W3 Benchmark Tests U2

KEY:
U=Unit   W=Week   D=Day

Reader's and Writer's Notebook p. 109

Skill ↔ Strategy
◎ Compare and Contrast
◎ Visualize

Student Edition p. El•6

Introduce compare and contrast

When you compare and contrast, you tell how things are alike and different. The second bullet says that an author might use clue words. Name some clue words. *(same, unlike, but, although)* What types of things can you compare and contrast as you read? (settings, characters, and parts of the plot) Have students turn to p. El•6 in the Student Edition to review compare and contrast. Then read "Ryan and Jonah" with students.

Model the skill

Think Aloud

In today's story, Ryan tells two different stories about what happened to Jonah. Have students follow along as you reread paragraph 3 of "Ryan and Jonah." What two stories does Ryan tell? (First, he says that Jonah is cold and wet because Ryan tried to clean his clothes. Then he tells the truth: that Jonah fell into the pool when Ryan was not watching.) How are these stories different? (The first is a lie and the second is the truth.)

Guide practice

Have students finish reading "Ryan and Jonah" on their own. After they read, have them use a graphic organizer like the one on p. 178 to compare and contrast Ryan's actions in the passage.

Strategy check

Visualize Remind students that if they have difficulty comparing and contrasting, they can use the strategy of visualizing. Model the strategy of visualizing sensory images to monitor and adjust understanding.

Model the strategy

Think Aloud

As I think about the events in the story, I imagine how cold and wet Jonah looks after he falls in the pool. I have been nervous to tell the truth before, so I know how nervous Ryan must be as he talks to his mother. I can understand why Ryan changed his story and told the truth. Have students review the strategy of visualizing on p. El•25 of the Student Edition.

Student Edition p. El•25

On their own

Use p. 109 in the *Reader's and Writer's Notebook* for additional practice with compare and contrast.

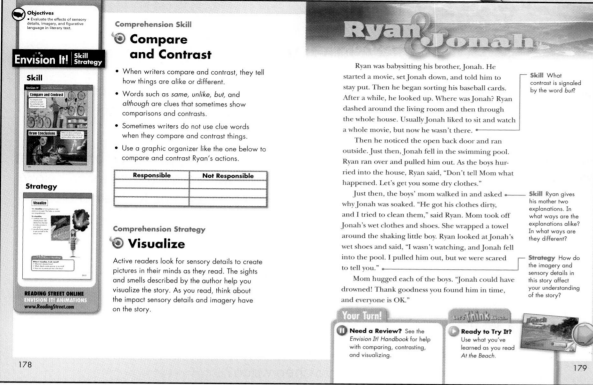

Objectives
● Evaluate the effects of sensory details, imagery, and figurative language in literary text.

Envision It! Skill Strategy

Skill
Compare and Contrast

Draw Conclusions

Strategy
Visualize

READING STREET ONLINE
ENVISION IT! ANIMATIONS
www.ReadingStreet.com

178

Comprehension Skill

Compare and Contrast

- When writers compare and contrast, they tell how things are alike or different.
- Words such as *same, unlike, but,* and *although* are clues that sometimes show comparisons and contrasts.
- Sometimes writers do not use clue words when they compare and contrast things.
- Use a graphic organizer like the one below to compare and contrast Ryan's actions.

Responsible	Not Responsible

Comprehension Strategy

Visualize

Active readers look for sensory details to create pictures in their minds as they read. The sights and smells described by the author help you visualize the story. As you read, think about the impact sensory details and imagery have on the story.

Ryan & Jonah

Ryan was babysitting his brother, Jonah. He started a movie, set Jonah down, and told him to stay put. Then he began sorting his baseball cards. After a while, he looked up. Where was Jonah? Ryan dashed around the living room and then through the whole house. Usually Jonah liked to sit and watch a whole movie, but now he wasn't there.

Then he noticed the open back door and ran outside. Just then, Jonah fell in the swimming pool. Ryan ran over and pulled him out. As the boys hurried into the house, Ryan said, "Don't tell Mom what happened. Let's get you some dry clothes."

Just then, the boys' mom walked in and asked why Jonah was soaked. "He got his clothes dirty, and I tried to clean them," said Ryan. Mom took off Jonah's wet clothes and shoes. She wrapped a towel around the shaking little boy. Ryan looked at Jonah's wet shoes and said, "I wasn't watching, and Jonah fell into the pool. I pulled him out, but we were scared to tell you."

Mom hugged each of the boys. "Jonah could have drowned! Thank goodness you found him in time, and everyone is OK."

Skill What contrast is signaled by the word *but*?

Skill Ryan gives his mother two explanations. In what ways are the explanations alike? In what ways are they different?

Strategy How do the imagery and sensory details in this story affect your understanding of the story?

Your Turn!

🕐 **Need a Review?** See the *Envision It! Handbook* for help with comparing, contrasting, and visualizing.

▶ **Ready to Try It?** Use what you've learned as you read *At the Beach.*

179

Student Edition pp. 178–179

Model Fluency
Expression

Model fluent reading

Have students listen as you read paragraphs 3 and 4 of "Ryan and Jonah" with appropriate expression. Explain that you will adjust your voice level to emphasize words, phrases, and questions.

ROUTINE **Paired Reading**

1. **Select a passage** For "Ryan and Jonah," read the entire passage.

2. **Reader 1** Students read the passage, switching readers after paragraph 2.

3. **Reader 2** Partners reread the passage. This time the other student begins.

4. **Reread** For optimal fluency, have partners continue to read three or four times.

5. **Corrective Feedback** Provide feedback about students' expression and encourage them to adjust their voice levels.

Routines Flip Chart

Academic Vocabulary

compare to tell how two or more things are alike

contrast to tell how two or more things are different

visualize to use imagery and sensory details to create a picture in your mind as you read

Skill The word *but* shows the contrast between what Jonah usually does and what he is doing today.

Skill First, Ryan tells his mother that Jonah is wet because they tried to clean his clothes. Then, he admits that Jonah fell into the pool when Ryan wasn't watching. Both explanations tell why Jonah might be wet, but the second is the truth—that this is Ryan's fault.

Strategy The description of how Jonah was soaked and shaking helps the reader understand why Ryan told the truth.

ELL

English Language Learners
Compare and contrast Display a reference book and a trade book. Ask students to describe how the books are alike and different. Use a T-chart or a Venn diagram to record students' responses.

Objectives
- Activate prior knowledge of words.
- Identify questions for research.

Vocabulary
Tested Vocabulary

Lesson vocabulary

Use the following question-and-answer activity to help students acquire word knowledge by using context clues to determine or clarify the meaning of a word.

Activate prior knowledge

Display the selection words. Give students the opportunity to share what they know about these words. Then ask oral questions like those below. Students should respond *yes* or *no* and give reasons for their choice.

- Would you want to take a nap in a *hammock*?
- Would you find *driftwood* at the beach?
- Are other people happy with your behavior when you are *punished*?
- If something is *concealed,* is it easy to find?
- Would you see *algae* at the beach?
- Is a *sea urchin* as big as a whale?
- Would you use *tweezers* to chop wood?
- Would you *lament* the loss of your favorite pet?

Word origin

Use the word *algae* to point out that some words have Latin origins. (The word *alga* has the same meaning.) Ask students how knowing the Latin word could help them determine the meaning of the English word.

By the end of the week, students should know the lesson vocabulary. Students can use lesson vocabulary to write *yes* and *no* questions for classmates to answer.

Preteach Academic Vocabulary

 Academic Vocabulary Write the following words on the board:

compare and contrast	legend
visualize	imagery
realistic fiction	irregular plural nouns

Have students share what they know about this week's Academic Vocabulary. Use the students' responses to assess their prior knowledge. Preteach the Academic Vocabulary by providing a student-friendly description, explanation, or example that clarifies the meaning of each term. Then ask students to restate the meaning of the Academic Vocabulary term in their own words.

Research and Inquiry
Identify Questions

INTERNET GUY
Don Leu

21st Century Skills	
Weekly Inquiry Project	
Day 1	Identify Questions
Day 2	Navigate/Search
Day 3	Analyze
Day 4	Synthesize
Day 5	Communicate

Teach

Discuss the Question of the Week: *Why is honesty important?* Tell students they will conduct research on careers that require a great deal of honesty. On Day 5, they will create a table that lists reasons why each career requires honesty.

Model

Think Aloud I know that honesty is important for every job. But some jobs require a great deal of integrity every day. I think a doctor would need to be very honest with himself and his or her patients. Some possible questions could be: *Why does a doctor need to be honest? Why do people depend on their doctor to be honest?*

Guide practice

After students have brainstormed careers and open-ended inquiry questions, explain that tomorrow they will research their questions. Help students think of reliable, useful texts such as encyclopedias and reference books so they can plan their research.

On their own

Have students work individually, in pairs, or in small groups to write an inquiry question. Encourage them to consult with other students as they write their question.

Small Group Time

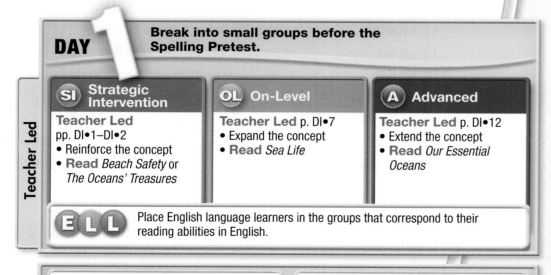

DAY 1

Break into small groups before the Spelling Pretest.

SI Strategic Intervention

Teacher Led pp. DI•1–DI•2
• Reinforce the concept
• **Read** *Beach Safety* or *The Oceans' Treasures*

OL On-Level

Teacher Led p. DI•7
• Expand the concept
• **Read** *Sea Life*

A Advanced

Teacher Led p. DI•12
• Extend the concept
• **Read** *Our Essential Oceans*

ELL Place English language learners in the groups that correspond to their reading abilities in English.

Practice Stations
• Read for Meaning
• Get Fluent
• Word Work

Independent Activities
• Concept Talk Video
• *Reader's and Writer's Notebook*
• Vocabulary Activities

English Language Learners
Multilingual Vocabulary
Students can apply knowledge of their home languages to acquire new English vocabulary by using Multilingual Vocabulary Lists (*ELL Handbook* pp. 431–444).

Objectives
- Spell words with digraphs *th, sh, ch, ph.*
- Use and understand regular and irregular plural nouns.
- Write cursive capital *H* and lowercase *h.*

Spelling Pretest
Digraphs *th, sh, ch, ph*

Introduce Tell students to think of words with the digraphs *th (think), sh (shin), ch (chase)* and *ph (phone).* Tell them to look for spelling patterns with the digraphs. This week we will spell words with digraphs *th, sh, ch,* and *ph.*

Pretest Use these sentences to administer the spelling pretest. Say each word, read the sentence, and repeat the word.

1. **shovel**	Tom dug a hole with the **shovel**.
2. **southern**	The **southern** states have a warmer climate.
3. **northern**	Maine is **northern** state.
4. **chapter**	Read the book's first **chapter**.
5. **hyphen**	Use a **hyphen** to divide the word.
6. **chosen**	Al was **chosen** for our team.
7. **establish**	Let's **establish** a plan for getting the work done.
8. **although**	**Although** it was cold, we had fun.
9. **challenge**	I **challenge** you to a race.
10. **approach**	Never **approach** a wild animal.
11. **astonish**	Did the surprise **astonish** you?
12. **python**	A **python** crawled down the trail?
13. **shatter**	The glass will **shatter** if you drop it.
14. **ethnic**	Each **ethnic** group has special customs.
15. **shiver**	The icy rain made us **shiver**.
16. **pharmacy**	The doctor sent us to the **pharmacy**.
17. **charity**	A **charity** helps people in need.
18. **china**	Some dishes are made of fine **china**.
19. **attach**	Can you **attach** the nametag with a pin?
20. **ostrich**	An **ostrich** is a bird that cannot fly.

Challenge words

21. **emphasis**	The writer underlined the word for **emphasis.**
22. **sophomore**	A high school **sophomore** is in the tenth grade.
23. **athlete**	The **athlete** trained daily after school.
24. **phenomenal**	Gary is a **phenomenal** speller.
25. **chimpanzee**	A **chimpanzee** is a member of the primate family.

Self-correct After the pretest, you can either display the correctly spelled words or spell them orally. Have students self-correct their pretests by writing misspelled words.

Let's Practice It!
TR DVD•62

On their own For additional practice, use *Let's Practice It!* p. 62 on the *Teacher Resources DVD-ROM.*

Conventions
Regular and Irregular Plural Nouns

Teach
Display Grammar Transparency 6, and read aloud the explanations and examples in the box. Point to one sample of each type of regular and irregular plural nouns.

Model
Model writing the correct plural form of the nouns to complete numbers 1 and 2. Apply the rules for plural nouns to show how you determined the correct form.

Guide practice
Guide students to complete items 3–10. Remind them to study the spelling of each word to determine how to make it plural. Record the correct responses on the transparency.

Daily Fix-It
Use Daily Fix-It numbers 1 and 2 in the right margin.

Connect to oral language
Have students read sentences 11 to 15 on the transparency and write the correct form of each regular or irregular noun.

Grammar Transparency 6, TR DVD

Handwriting
Cursive Letter *h* and *H*

Model letter formation
Display the capital and lowercase cursive *h* and *H*. Follow the stroke instruction pictured to model letter formation.

Model smoothness
Explain that writing legibly means letters are the correct size, form, and slant. Focus on letter formation by having students write this sentence: *Harry hears humming birds.* Make sure the letters aren't too light, dark, or jagged.

Guide practice
Have students write these sentences: *Hannah has hives as she hikes in the Himilayas. He is happy about his new hat.* Circulate around the room, guiding students.

Daily Fix-It

1. Students put their sack lunchs in a row on the tabel. *(lunches; table)*
2. Does the cafeteria serves hot food. *(serve; food?)*

 ELL

English Language Learners
Language Production: Regular and Irregular Plural Nouns Review the difference between regular and irregular nouns as defined on Grammar Transparency 6. Provide additional instruction for students based on their own proficiency levels. Begin by writing this list of words: *table, orange, leaf, octopus, potato.*

Beginning Have students pick two nouns and change them into plural nouns.

Intermediate Have students pick two nouns, change them into plural nouns, and then write whether they are regular or irregular.

Advanced Have students change each word into a plural noun. Ask students to identify if the plural noun is regular or irregular and have them orally explain their choices.

Handwriting: Letter Formation
To provide practice in cursive letter formation, have students write *h* and *H* in cursive ten times each.

Writing—Description
Introduce

MINI-LESSON

5 Day Planner
Guide to Mini-Lessons

DAY 1	Read Like a Writer
DAY 2	Focus on Description
DAY 3	Using Sensory Words
DAY 4	Revising Strategy: Consolidating
DAY 5	Proofread for Plural Nouns and Quotations

MINI-LESSON

Read Like a Writer

■ **Introduce** This week you will write a narrative composition in the form of a description. A description uses sensory words that relate to the five senses: smell, touch, taste, sight, and hearing.

Prompt   Think about a time in which you learned something important. Write a description of that moment, using your senses of smell, touch, taste, sight, and hearing to make the memory vivid.

Trait   Sentences/Vary sentence beginnings

Mode   Narrative

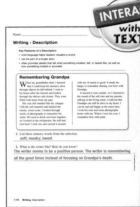

Reader's and Writer's Notebook p. 110

■ **Examine Model Text** Let's read an example of a description. Have students read "Remembering Grandpa" on p. 110 of their *Reader's and Writer's Notebook.* The writer's grandfather has died, and the writer is recalling the memory of going to his house.

■ **Key Features** Descriptions **help readers visualize a scene.** Have students read through the selection and then discuss where the writer is and what the weather is like outside. Talk about what the mood might be like inside the house.

Descriptions use sensory words that provide details about how something **smelled, tasted, looked, sounded, or felt.** Have students list three sensory words that appear in the description.

Descriptions can **sometimes be a part of a longer story.** They often can tell information about the writer by the way the writer has chosen to describe something. We are seeing the world through the writer's eyes only. **Have students describe the characteristics of the writer based on what they read.**

Review key features

Review the key features of a description with students. You may want to post the key features in the classroom for students to refer to as they work on their descriptions.

Key Features of a Description

- vivid language helps readers visualize a scene
- can be part of a longer story
- often provides details that tell what something smelled, felt, or tasted like, as well as how something looked or sounded

ROUTINE

Quick Write for Fluency   **Team Talk**

1. **Talk** Have pairs discuss the key features of a description.
2. **Write** Each person writes a short paragraph about how the five senses are used in descriptions, including examples of each type.
3. **Share** Partners read one another's writing.

Routines Flip Chart

Wrap Up Your Day

✔ **Build Concepts** What did you learn about doing the right thing?

✔ **Oral Vocabulary** Have students use the Amazing Words they learned in context sentences.

✔ **Homework** Send home this week's Family Times Newsletter on *Let's Practice It!* pp. 63–64 on the *Teacher Resources DVD-ROM.*

Let's Practice It!
TR DVD•63–64

Write Guy
Jeff Anderson

Nice, Big, Long, Pointless, Listy Adjective Strings

As children learn to write, many love to "improve" sentences with adjectives—big adjectives, little adjectives, many adjectives. We don't want to encourage strings of adjectives. On the other hand, this is a problem that can correct itself. Show a sample of a sentence with too many adjectives (not written by the student). Ask which one adjective might be unnecessary.

ELL

English Language Learners
Examine model text Read the writing model aloud. Remind students that descriptions create a picture of a person, place, or thing. Have students draw an important person in their lives. Then have them orally describe the person.

Preview DAY 2

Tell students that tomorrow they will read about a boy who learns about honesty.

Objectives
- Expand the weekly concept.
- Develop oral vocabulary.

Today at a Glance

Oral Vocabulary
principled, oath

Word Analysis
Spanish word origins

Literary Terms
Imagery

Story Structure
Conflict

Lesson Vocabulary
◉ Unfamiliar words

Reading
"My Special Island"
At the Beach

Fluency
Expression

Research and Inquiry
Navigate/Search

Spelling
Digraphs *th, sh, ch, ph*

Conventions
Regular and irregular plural nouns

Writing
Description

Concept Talk

? Question of the Week
Why is honesty important?

Expand the concept

Remind students of the weekly concept question. Tell students that today they will begin reading *At the Beach.* As they read, encourage students to think about why honesty is important.

Anchored Talk

Develop oral vocabulary

Use the photos on pp. 176–177 and the Read Aloud, "Bullseye," to talk about the Amazing Words: *integrity, frank, honorable,* and *moral.* Add these words to the concept map to develop students' knowledge of the topic. Break into groups. Have students discuss the following questions, considering suggestions from other group members.

- When might it be important for friends and family members to show *integrity?*

- Think about a time when you needed to be *frank.* What was the situation?

- Why is it necessary for elected officials to be *honorable* and *moral?*

Oral Vocabulary
Amazing Words

Amazing Words

integrity	oath
frank	candid
honorable	guilt
moral	justice
principled	deceit

Teach Amazing Words

Amazing Words **Oral Vocabulary Routine**

1. **Introduce** Write the Amazing Word *principled* on the board. Have students say it aloud with you. Relate *principled* to the photographs on pp. 176–177 and "Bullseye." What would a *principled* person do if he or she saw someone cheating? What values does a *principled* person like Mikey's grandpa have? Have students determine the definition of the word. A *principled* person shows honor and integrity.

2. **Demonstrate** Have students answer questions to demonstrate understanding. In "Bullseye," how did Grandpa show that he was *principled*? How did Mikey show that he was learning to be *principled*?

3. **Apply** Have students apply their understanding. Name a person that you know who is *principled*. Explain.

See p. OV•1 to teach *oath*.

Routines Flip Chart

Apply Amazing Words

As students read "My Special Island" on p. 181, have them decide whether the narrator of the story is *principled*. Discuss whether principled students daydream in class. Then ask students whether a world-famous scientist might take an *oath* not to harm any living creatures.

Connect to reading

Explain to students that they will read about a young boy's experience at the beach. As they read, they should think about how the Question of the Week and the Amazing Words *principled* and *oath* apply to the story.

ELL **Reinforce Vocabulary** Use the Day 2 instruction on ELL Poster 6 to teach lesson vocabulary and the lesson concept.

ELL Poster 6

DAY 2 Get Ready to Read

Objectives

- Use Spanish origins to determine the meanings of English words.
- Understand how imagery enhances a story.
- Understand how conflict is used to advance a story.

Word Analysis
Spanish Word Origins

Teach Spanish word origins

Tell students that Spanish words can give them clues about the meanings of English words. Have students choose an English word from the first column and match it with a similar Spanish word in the second column.

Model the skill

I will choose the word *hammock* from the first column. The Spanish word *hamaca* is similar. The word *hammock* means "a hanging bed made of netting, canvas, or cord."

English word	Spanish word
hammock	hamaca
canyon	armadillo
armadillo	estampida
stampede	montaña
Montana	cañón

Guide practice

Have students match words from both columns and give a definition for each English word.

On their own

Have students check a dictionary entry for each word to confirm its meaning and origin. Then follow the Strategy for Multisyllabic Words to teach the word *hammock*.

ROUTINE Strategy for Multisyllabic Words

1. **Look for recognizable word parts** When I see a word I don't know, first I look for meaningful parts. If I don't recognize any parts, I break the word into chunks and use sound-spellings to read the chunks.

2. **Connect to sound-spelling** Write *hammock.* I don't recognize any parts, so I'll break it into chunks. The chunk at the beginning is *ham.* For the second chunk, I'll use the sound for short *o* and blend the *ck* sound: *mock.*

3. **Read the word** Have students blend the syllables to read *hammock.* I say each chunk slowly: *ham mock.* I say the chunks quickly to make a whole word: *hammock.* It's a real word that I know.

Continue the Routine with *canyon, armadillo, stampede,* and *Montana.*

Routines Flip Chart

Literary Terms
Imagery

Teach imagery

Tell students that imagery is the use of words that help the reader imagine in his or her mind the way things look, sound, taste, smell, or feel. An image is a detail that stimulates the senses or the imagination.

Model imagery

 Think Aloud Let's look at "My Special Island" on page 181. What examples of imagery can you find in the first paragraph? (wild driftwood shapes, polished by the waves and sun) How do you know this is imagery? (I can imagine how it looks, so this appeals to my sense of sight.)

Guide practice

Ask students to find an example of imagery in paragraphs 2 and 3 of "My Special Island." Have them explain which senses are stimulated by each description.

On their own

Have students brainstorm other examples of imagery that could be added to "My Special Island" (descriptions of fish or crabs, the sound of the waves).

Story Structure
Conflict

Teach story structure

There is usually conflict, or a struggle between opposing forces, in realistic fiction. Major events and actions affect the way conflict develops. The conflict is directly confronted at the climax of the story. Then the conflict is resolved.

Model the strategy

Think Aloud There are four different types of conflict in a story. Conflict can be between two characters or groups, between a character and the laws of society, between a character and a force of nature, or between a character's conflicting feelings or temptations.

Guide practice

Remind students of the Read Aloud, "Bullseye," that you shared with them on Day 1 (see Teacher's Edition, p. 177b). Discuss the type of conflict found in "Bullseye," (person against person). Have students explain how they know.

On their own

Have students preview the illustrations in *At the Beach.* Ask them to predict how the conflict in "Bullseye" foreshadows events in *At the Beach.*

Academic Vocabulary

imagery the use of words that help the reader imagine the way things look, sound, taste, smell, or feel

realistic fiction tells about events that could really happen in a setting that seems real and with realistic characters

Objectives

◎ Use context clues to determine the meanings of unfamiliar words.

• Read grade-level text with expression.

Vocabulary Strategy for
↻ Unfamiliar Words

Student Edition p. W•7

Teach unfamiliar words

Envision It!

Tell students that when they encounter an unfamiliar word, they can use the strategy of looking for context clues in nearby sentences and phrases to determine or clarify its meaning. Explain how words in the sentence often mean similar things or give hints about meaning. Refer students to *Words!* on p. W•7 in the Student Edition for additional practice.

Model the strategy

Think Aloud Write on the board: *My mother's voice was firm as she sternly told me how to cross the street with my little sister.* I don't know the meaning of the word *sternly.* A good strategy is to look for context clues or in-sentence restatement. In this sentence, the phrase *my mother's voice was firm* is related to the word *sternly.* I determine that the word *sternly* means "with a firm voice." I can also infer that the mother was serious and strict because she wants her children to be careful about crossing the street. If I substitute the words "seriously" or "firmly" in the sentence, it makes sense.

Guide practice

Write this sentence on the board: *I concealed the present under my bed so that my sister wouldn't find it.* Have students use context clues to determine the meaning of *concealed*, and have them identify the clue words. *(wouldn't find it)* If students need further clarification, have them look up the word *concealed* in a thesaurus to find alternate word choices. *(hidden, invisible, disguised)* For additional support, use *Envision It! Pictured Vocabulary Cards* or *Tested Vocabulary Cards.*

On their own

Read "My Special Island" on p. 181. Have students use context clues to determine the meaning of the word *driftwood.* ("wood polished by the waves and sun") For additional practice, use *Reader's and Writer's Notebook* p. 111.

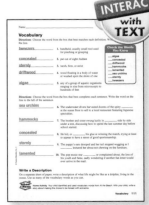

Reader's and Writer's Notebook p. 111

Objectives
● Determine the meanings of unfamiliar words or multiple-meaning words by using the context of the sentence.

Envision It! | Words to Know

driftwood

hammocks

tweezers

algae
concealed
lamented
sea urchins
sternly

READING STREET ONLINE
VOCABULARY ACTIVITIES
www.ReadingStreet.com

180

Vocabulary Strategy for
Unfamiliar Words

Context Clues As you read, you may see a word you don't know. Often you can use context to determine the meaning of a new word. *Context* means "the words and sentences near an unfamiliar word or words."

Choose one of the *Words to Know* and follow these steps.

1. Reread the sentence with the unfamiliar word. The author may include a synonym or other context clue to the word's meaning.

2. If you need help, read the surrounding sentences for context clues.

3. Think about the clues and then decide on the meaning of the word.

4. Check to see that this meaning makes sense in the sentence.

Read "My Special Island" on page 181. Use context clues to help you determine the meanings of unfamiliar words.

Words to Write Reread "My Special Island." Imagine you are at the beach. Write a paragraph about what you see, hear, taste, smell, and touch. Use words from the *Words to Know* list.

My Special Island

I like to daydream about my special island. It has the most beautiful beach for exploring. I walk along the sand and admire the wild driftwood shapes, polished by the waves and sun. I pause beside a tidal pool and watch crabs, sea urchins, and other strange animals.

Standing in the water, I look at a forest of algae stretching as far as I can see. I wonder what strange and beautiful creatures lie concealed in that underwater forest. In my dream I am a world-famous scientist. Armed with my microscope, tweezers, and diving equipment, I learn all the secrets of the ocean world.

After a long day of amazing discoveries, I head for one of the hammocks under the palm trees. There I store my treasures and lie down, letting a gentle breeze rock me to sleep.

"Martin!" Ms. Smith says sternly. "Wake up and get to work!" Oh, well. Back to arithmetic. I have often lamented my bad habit of daydreaming during classes!

Your Turn!

⏸ **Need a Review?** For additional help with using context clues to determine the meanings of unfamiliar words, see *Words!*

▶ **Ready to Try It?** Read *At the Beach* on pp. 182–193.

181

Student Edition pp. 180–181

Reread for Fluency
Expression

Model fluent reading

Read paragraphs 3 and 4 of "My Special Island" aloud, using changes of voice level for emphasis. Point out that when you read dialogue, you imitate how you think the characters would sound.

ROUTINE Paired Reading

① **Select a passage** For "My Special Island," use the whole passage.

② **Reading 1** Students read the selected text, switching readers after paragraph 2.

③ **Reading 2** Partners reread the passage. This time the other student begins.

④ **Reread** For optimal fluency, have students read three or four times.

⑤ **Corrective feedback** Tell students to emphasize the dialogue in the last paragraph and the descriptive words throughout.

Routines Flip Chart

Lesson Vocabulary

algae a group of living things, mostly found in water, that can make their own food

concealed put out of sight; hidden

driftwood wood carried along by water, or washed ashore by the water

hammocks hanging beds or couches made of canvas, cord, or other material

lamented felt or showed grief

sea urchins small, round sea animals with spiny shells

sternly strictly; firmly

tweezers small pincers for picking up small objects

Differentiated Instruction

SI Strategic Intervention
Have students find the compound word (*driftwood*) from this week's lesson vocabulary. Talk about how the two separate words provide context clues for the word's meaning. Compare the compound word, *driftwood,* and the two-word phrase, *sea urchins.*

ELL

English Language Learners
Build Academic Vocabulary
Use the lesson vocabulary pictured on p. 180 to teach the meanings of *driftwood, hammocks,* and *tweezers.* Call on pairs to write the words on sticky notes and use them to label images of the words on the ELL Poster.

At The **Beach**
Abuelito's Story

by Lulu Delacre
paintings by Michael Sterinagle

Genre **Realistic fiction** deals with characters and actions that seem real but come from the author's imagination. As you read, notice how the author uses words to paint a realistic picture of Guanabo Beach.

Question of the Week
Why is honesty important?

Let's **Think** About **Reading!**

182

Student Edition pp. 182–183

Build Background

Discuss the beach

Team Talk Have students turn to a partner and discuss the Question of the Week and these questions about the beach. Remind students to elicit suggestions from their partners and identify points of agreement.

- Why do people usually go to the beach?
- What are some things that people need to watch out for at the beach?
- Why might the children in the story have to be honest?

Connect to selection

Have students discuss their answers with the class. Possible responses: People usually go to the beach to relax, enjoy the sun and weather, and participate in activities or sports. People need to watch out for changing weather conditions and fish or other animals that might be dangerous. If someone else is injured at the beach, the children will need to be honest about how it happened. For additional opportunities to build background, use the Background Building Audio.

Prereading Strategies

Genre Explain that **realistic fiction** tells about events or experiences that could happen in real life. The fictional characters act and talk in realistic ways.

Preview and predict Have students preview the illustrations in *At the Beach.* As students look at pp. 182–183, explain that *abuelito* means "grandfather." Ask students what the illustrations show about the story's setting and events.

Set purpose Prior to reading, have students establish their own purpose for reading this selection. To help students set a purpose, ask them to think about why honesty is important and why it might be important in this story.

Strategy Response Log

Have students use their prior knowledge to visualize what they think *At the Beach* will be about. Have them write their responses on p. 12 in the *Reader's and Writer's Notebook.*

Small Group Time

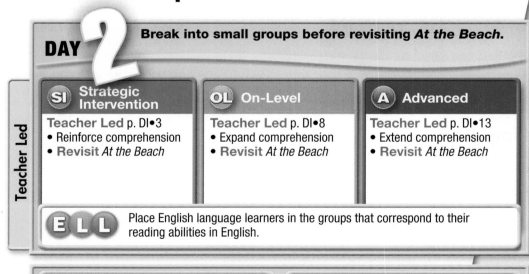

Break into small groups before revisiting *At the Beach.*

DAY 2

Teacher Led

SI Strategic Intervention
Teacher Led p. DI•3
• Reinforce comprehension
• Revisit *At the Beach*

OL On-Level
Teacher Led p. DI•8
• Expand comprehension
• Revisit *At the Beach*

A Advanced
Teacher Led p. DI•13
• Extend comprehension
• Revisit *At the Beach*

ELL Place English language learners in the groups that correspond to their reading abilities in English.

Practice Stations
• Words to Know
• Get Fluent
• Word Wise

Independent Activities
• Background Building Audio
• *Reader's and Writer's Notebook*
• Research and Inquiry

Differentiated Instruction

SI Strategic Intervention
Work with students to set a purpose for reading, or if time permits, have students work with partners to set purposes.

A Advanced
Have students find out what life was like in Cuba during the 1940s and 1950s. Have them talk about their findings.

Multidraft Reading

For **Whole Group** instruction, choose one of the reading options below. For each reading, have students set the purpose indicated.

Option 1
Day 2 Read the selection. Use Guide Comprehension to monitor and clarify understanding.
Day 3 Reread the selection. Use Extend Thinking to develop higher-order thinking skills.

Option 2
Day 2 Read the first half of the selection, using both Guide Comprehension and Extend Thinking instruction.
Day 3 Read the second half of the selection, using both Guide Comprehension and Extend Thinking instruction.

English Language Learners
Build background To build background, review the selection summary in English (*ELL Handbook* p. 61). Use the Retelling Cards to provide visual support for the summary.

Objectives

◎ Visualize to aid comprehension.

OPTION 1 Guide Comprehension Skills and Strategies

Teach Visualize

🔍 **Visualize** Write this sentence on the board: *All I could think about was the soft white sand, the warm foamy water, and Mami's delicious tortilla.* Ask students to identify which senses these words appeal to. (touch: *soft, warm, foamy;* sight: *white, water;* taste: *delicious tortilla*) Have students generate other words that describe the beach. (*salty water, warm sun, sounds of children playing*) Ask students why Fernando is excited to go.

Corrective Feedback

If... students are unable to visualize as they read,
then... model using background knowledge to create images.

Student Edition pp. 184–185

OPTION 2 Extend Thinking Think Critically

Higher-Order Thinking Skills

🔍 **Visualize • Evaluation** Reread paragraph 1 on page 185 and visualize how Papi's car looked, felt, and sounded. Explain how sensory details and background knowledge help you understand the text. **Possible response:** The car must have been very crowded, with nine people, several children squeezed in the back, and *the clutter of pots and plates, food and bags, towels and blankets and hammocks.* It was probably loud and hot too. I have been in a crowded car before, so I can imagine that drive was not very comfortable.

Model the Strategy

Think Aloud We can use our background knowledge to create sensory images. How would the white sand feel between your toes? (soft, warm, squishy, grainy)

I remember those evenings well when I was a young boy in Cuba, those balmy island nights before a trip to Guanabo Beach. The spicy aroma of *tortilla española* that Mami had left to cool would waft through the house as I lay in my bed. But I was always too excited to sleep. All I could think about was the soft white sand, the warm foamy water, and Mami's delicious tortilla. Ahhh. A day at the beach. It was full of possibilities.

One Saturday in May, I was awakened at the crack of dawn by sounds of laughter. My aunts, Rosa and Olga, had arrived with hammocks, blankets, and an iron kettle filled with Aunt Rosa's steaming *congrí*. And best of all, they had arrived with my cousins: Luisa, Mari, and little Javi. Uncle Toni had come too.

Let's Think About...

From what you have read so far, visualize Cuba, the setting. Is this like or unlike where you live?
🔍 **Visualize**

184 ❶

Let's Think About...

❶ This is unlike where I live. We don't have hammocks and I don't live on a beach.

❷ Fernando is telling the story. I can tell that Fernando is surrounded by family and loves to go to the beach.

How would warm, foamy ocean water look and feel? (turquoise; comfortable and relaxing; good for swimming) How would a tortilla taste and smell? (spicy; like flour or corn) Do you understand now why Fernando is so excited to go to the beach? (yes)

On Their Own

Have students find more sensory details on pp. 184–185. (*sounds of laughter, clutter of pots and plates, cool morning breeze, salty skin*)

Differentiated Instruction

 Strategic Intervention

Point of view Ask students to identify the narrator of this story (Fernando). If students have difficulty, direct them to paragraphs 3 and 4 on p. 185. Point out that Luisa asks Fernando if his skin is salty. Then the narrator realizes: *She was right. My skin tasted salty.* Help students understand how this exchange tells the reader that Fernando is the narrator.

Connect to Social Studies

In the 1930s, a group of physicians asked car manufacturers to develop a restraining device to promote auto safety. Some doctors even developed their own seat belts. It was not until the 1950s that seat belts started to become more common.

When we were ready to leave, Papi, the only one in the family who owned a car, packed his Ford woody wagon with the nine of us. No one cared that we children had to squeeze into the back along with the clutter of pots and plates, food and bags, towels and blankets and hammocks. Soon the engine turned, and the car rumbled down the road into the rising sun.

Along the way, we drove past sugarcane fields and roadside markets. My cousins and I shouted warnings to the barking dogs and laughed at the frightened hens that scurried in every direction at the sight of our car. It seemed like a long time until the cool morning breeze that blew into the windows turned warm. And the growing heat made the aroma of Mami's tortilla all the more tempting.

"Lick your skin, Fernando," my older cousin Luisa told me. "If it tastes salty, that means we'll be there any time now."

She was right. My skin tasted salty. And soon—almost magically—the turquoise ocean appeared as we rounded a bend in the road. Papi pulled into the familiar dirt lot and parked under the pine trees. While the grown-ups unloaded the car, we eagerly jumped out and ran toward the sea, peeling off our clothes along the way.

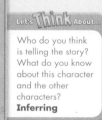
Let's Think About...
Who do you think is telling the story? What do you know about this character and the other characters? **Inferring**

185

Genre • Analysis This story is realistic fiction. How do you think the characters will act and talk? Describe their relationships to each other. Possible response: Since the story is realistic fiction, the characters will act like a real family. They might argue or tease each other, but they are all trying to have a good time together.

Compare and Contrast • Synthesis How does the breeze change as Fernando's family drives to the beach? What can you infer from this comparison? Possible response: Fernando compares the cool morning breeze and the warm air. This change shows that it is now midday instead of morning, so it must have been a long drive to the beach.

ELL

English Language Learners
Activate prior knowledge Have students use the illustrations and the text to discuss what the beach looks like. Have students write descriptive words from the text on the board and point to illustrations that help them visualize the beach.

Objectives
- Understand the author's purpose to aid comprehension.

Student Edition pp. 186–187

OPTION 1 Skills and Strategies, continued

Teach Author's Purpose

Review Author's Purpose Ask students to describe how Fernando is dishonest. (Fernando and his cousins go to explore the reef even though they are not supposed to go that far.) Ask students to infer why the author included dialogue about this act. (It foreshadows the theme and events in the plot.)

Corrective Feedback

If... students are unable to determine the author's purpose,

then... model how to infer to find an author's purpose.

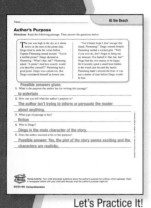

Let's Practice It!
TR DVD•66

Model the Skill

Think Aloud What do Mami and Aunt Olga say at the top of page 187? ("Don't go too far.") Does Fernando disobey? (yes) Why? (He thinks the adults will not notice, and he knows the way.)

186

Let's **Think** About...
3 It's probably not safe.

OPTION 2 Think Critically, continued

Higher-Order Thinking Skills

Imagery • Analysis What imagery did the author include in paragraph 3 on page 187? How do these words help you visualize? Possible response: Words such as *splashed, swallowed the stinging seawater,* and *chased* help me imagine how the children looked and felt as they played. This imagery and my background knowledge helped me understand that the kids were having a lot of fun.

The selections in this unit are about doing the right thing. Why did the author include dialogue about Fernando being dishonest? (This dialogue probably foreshadows other events in the story since it has to do with the theme of honesty.)

On Their Own

Ask students to find another example of Fernando being dishonest. (In paragraph 4 on p. 187, he considers sneaking a bite of Mami's tortilla.) Ask why the author included this detail. For additional practice, use *Let's Practice It!* p. 66 on the *Teacher Resources DVD-ROM.*

Differentiated Instruction

 **Strategic Intervention**

Imagery Remind students that imagery is the use of sensory details to help the reader experience the way things look, sound, smell, taste, or feel. Have partners find examples of imagery in the story that help them use their senses to create mental pictures. If necessary, point out the following words: *clear water, schools of tiny fish, stinging seawater, marbled rocks, shady spot.*

---

emember, don't go too far!" Mami and Aunt Olga warned ternly from the distance. I turned to see them picking ur scattered clothing.

When we reached the edge of the ocean, the water felt d. I waded farther in and went under to warm up quickly. en I emerged I saw Luisa, Mari, and little Javi, all standing in the clear water. They were watching the schools of gold-and-black striped fish rush between their legs. n they swam over to join me, and together we rode the waves.

Later, Uncle Toni came in to play shark with us. We shed and swallowed the stinging seawater as he chased bove and under the waves. But after a while, we tired out, and he went back to sit with the grown-ups.

I was getting very hungry, and for a moment I thought eturning with him to sneak a bite of Mami's tortilla. But 1 I had a better idea.

et's explore the reef!" I said.

Sí!" everyone agreed. "Let's go!"

We all splashed out of the water and ran, dripping wet, ss the sand. High above, the sun beat down on us.

When we got to the marbled rocks, Luisa looked erned. "Our moms told us not to come this far," she said. I know the way well," I replied. "Besides, nobody will ce. They're too busy talking."

I looked in the distance and saw Mami and my two s in the shady spot they had picked. They had set up a camp. The hammocks were tied to the pine trees; the kets were spread over the fine sand. Papi and Uncle Toni ed dominoes, while they sipped coffee and shared the *rucho de maní* they had purchased from the peanut lor. They were having fun. No one would miss us for a ; time.

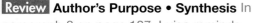

Let's **Think** About...

Why do you think Mami and Aunt Olga warned the children not to go too far? **Inferring**

3

187

Review **Author's Purpose • Synthesis** In paragraph 8 on page 187, Luisa reminds Fernando that their mothers told them not to go to the reef. Why did the author include this dialogue? Think about the story's theme. Possible response: The author wants to foreshadow future plot events and the theme about honesty. The author uses Luisa's reminder to let the reader know that Fernando is aware that he should not go to the reef. Yet he convinces his cousins to go to the reef anyway.

Foreshadowing • Analysis At the end of page 187, the children splashed away from their parents and ended up far in the reef. Does the change of setting foreshadow how the story might change? **Possible response:** We know that the children aren't supposed to go to the reef. The setting change foreshadows that the reef might be dangerous and the children may have a problem.

 English Language Learners

Vocabulary: Verbs Direct students to verbs on p. 187, such as *waded, splashed, chased, looked,* and *sipped.* Tell students that these verbs, or action words, help us make a picture in our mind. Have students act out the verbs and use the words in sentences.

Activate prior knowledge Discuss why Mami tells the children not to go too far. Ask: Have people in your family ever given you a warning? Why?

Objectives

◎ Compare and contrast to aid comprehension.

Teach Compare and Contrast

◎ **Compare and Contrast** Have students reread paragraph 1 on p. 188. Ask them to contrast how Luisa and Mari walked with how Javi walked. (Luisa and Mari were careful, but Javi was distracted.)

Corrective Feedback

If... students are unable to contrast, **then...** model finding differences.

Let's Practice It!
TR DVD•65

Model the Skill

Think Aloud Let's reread paragraph 1 aloud and listen for words that tell us how the children walked. **Reread paragraph 1 chorally.** What words describe how Luisa and Mari walked? *(They were careful to only step on the rocks I stepped on.)*

"Watch out for sea urchins!" I warned as I led the group on our climb. The spiny black sea urchins hid inside the crevices and crannies of the rough boulders. It was very painful if you stepped on one. Luisa and Mari followed behind me. They were careful to only step on the rocks I stepped on. Little Javi came last. He stopped constantly to look at the *cobitos,* the tiny hermit crabs that scurried around on the rocks, and at the iridescent tropical fish that were concealed in the deepest tide pools. I had to keep checking behind me to make sure he didn't stray from our path.

Just then, I turned around to watch helplessly as Javi slipped on an algae-covered rock. *"¡Cuidado!"* I warned. But it was too late.

Let's Think About...

Picture the children playing on the rocks. Why do you think Javi stopped so often to look at the crabs and fish?
◎ **Visualize**

4

188

Student Edition pp. 188–189

Higher-Order Thinking Skills

◎ **Compare and Contrast • Synthesis** Reread paragraph 4 on page 189. Think of a time when you were in a difficult situation. Did you or another person react like Luisa did? **Possible response: I have gotten in an argument with my brother before, and like Luisa, I blamed him when we got caught.**

Let's Think About...

4 I think Javi was fascinated with the crabs and fish.

5 Fernando and his cousins decide to explore the reef. Javi steps on a sea urchin. Fernando and Luisa try to remove it themselves.

◎ **Visualize • Analysis** How does Fernando's description help you visualize what a sea urchin looks like? How does this help you adjust your understanding of what happens next? **Possible response: Fernando describes a sea urchin as spiny and black, and he says it is painful to step on one.**

What words describe how Javi walked? *(He stopped constantly to look at cobitos. I had to keep checking behind me to make sure he didn't stray.)* How are the children acting differently? (The girls are walking carefully, but Javi is distracted.)

"*¡Ay!*" he shrieked, and then began to cry uncontrollably.

Cautiously, we all hurried back to help Javi. Luisa and Mari crouched down to examine his foot.

"He stepped on a sea urchin!" Mari cried. "Now what are we going to do?"

"We should have never followed you," Luisa lamented. "We'll all be punished."

At that moment I did not want to think of what the punishment would be. What if we couldn't have any of Mami's tortilla? All I knew was that we had to help Javi right away. I looked around and found a piece of driftwood.

"Luisa," I ordered. "Hold his leg still while I remove the urchin from his foot."

Let's **Think** About...

What's happened to Javi and the cousins so far? **Summarize**

5

189

On Their Own

Have students compare and contrast the children's reactions after Javi's accident. Ask students to explain what they learned about each character's role from his or her reaction to the conflict. For additional practice, use *Let's Practice It!* p. 65 on the *Teacher Resources DVD-ROM.*

I can imagine that these sharp black spines could stick in someone's foot and make the foot bleed. It also helps me understand why Javi shrieked, cried, and needed help.

Background Knowledge • Analysis • Text to World How would it feel to have a spiny sea urchin stuck in your foot? What do you think could happen to Javi if his foot isn't fixed soon? Use your background knowledge to help you understand.

Possible response: I have stepped on something sharp before, but never something that sharp. I can imagine it would hurt a lot. If the children do not fix it soon, the cut could become infected.

Check Predictions Have students look back at the predictions they made earlier and discuss whether they were accurate. Then have students preview the rest of the selection and either adjust their predictions accordingly or make new predictions.

Differentiated Instruction

SI Strategic Intervention

Compare and contrast Have groups choose two characters in the story, such as Luisa and Fernando. Have them tell how the characters are alike and different. (Luisa keeps the rules in mind but panics when something goes wrong. Fernando is daring and breaks the rules, but he is logical and smart when Javi steps on the sea urchin.)

A Advanced

Ask students to think of other actions the children might have taken to help Javi. Have students write a paragraph to share their ideas.

ELL

English Language Learners

Vocabulary Point to the word *stray* in paragraph 1 on p. 188. Here, *stray* means "leave" or "lose the path." Have students think of a time when a child or animal they knew strayed from what they were supposed to do or where they were supposed to go. Have students tell what happened.

Compare and contrast Luisa agreed to go to the reef. How did her feelings change after the accident? Why? (She was sorry about Javi's accident, and she was afraid of being punished.)

If you want to teach this selection in two sessions, stop here.

Objectives
- Find pertinent information in print reference sources.
- Recognize and correctly use regular and irregular plural nouns.
- Practice correctly spelling words with *th, sh, ch, ph*.

Research and Inquiry
Navigate/Search

Teach

After students have written an inquiry question about a career in which honesty is important, have them investigate a variety of reference texts to find information about the career. Have them follow the research plan to collect data from encyclopedias, career guides, and other print references. Point out that they will assemble their findings into a numbered table, and encourage them to take notes as they begin their research.

Model

Think Aloud I will use the index in each of the reference texts to help me find information. My inquiry is about why honesty is important for a doctor. In the library I can look up entries such as doctor training, medical school, or I can research the legal requirements for becoming a doctor. I will start with an encyclopedia, but I am also going to look for information about medical schools and the training doctors receive.

Guide practice

Have students continue their review of print references they identified. Tell students to evaluate the relevance, validity, and reliability of each source. Discuss how most reference texts are valid and reliable, but some entries may not be relevant to the research topic. Tell students to look up related entries or keywords if necessary.

On their own

Have students make a list of honesty-related requirements in their notes as they prepare to assemble a numbered table to present on Day 5.

Conventions
Regular and Irregular Plural Nouns

Teach

Write these words on the board: *baby/babies* and *car/cars.* Point out that *baby* has an irregular plural noun form while *car* has a regular plural noun form.

Guide practice

Say these verbs. Have students write and say the plural noun form.

tomato/tomatoes	beach/beaches
wife/wives	computer/computers

Daily Fix-It

Use Daily Fix-It numbers 3 and 4 in the right margin.

Connect to oral language

Have students look for and read aloud regular and irregular plural nouns in *At the Beach.* (*nights*, p. 184; *pots*, p. 185; *dominoes*, p. 187; *crannies*, p. 188; *pools*, p. 188)

On their own

For additional practice, use the *Reader's and Writer's Notebook* p. 112.

Reader's and Writer's Notebook, p. 112

Spelling
Digraphs *th, sh, ch, ph*

Teach

Remind students of the rule that consonant digraphs consist of two letters that together stand for one sound. They can use this spelling pattern to spell this week's words.

Guide practice

Write *ostrich,* replacing the *ch* with two blank lines. Say the word. What is the sound represented by the missing letters? (/ch/) What two letters make the sound /ch/? (*c* and *h*) Fill in the missing letters. Together, *c* and *h* form a consonant digraph that represents the sound /ch/. Have students write the remaining spelling words and underline the digraphs *th, sh, ch,* and *ph.*

On their own

For additional practice, use the *Reader's and Writer's Notebook* p. 113.

Reader's and Writer's Notebook, p. 113

Daily Fix-It

3. The children wor warm coats and scarfs. (*wore; scarves*)
4. That cold wind make me siver. (*makes; shiver*)

English Language Learners

Conventions To provide students with practice on regular and irregular plural nouns, use the modified grammar lessons in the *ELL Handbook* and the Grammar Jammer online at: www.ReadingStreet.com

Language transfer: Plural nouns Plural nouns can be challenging because they are formed differently in English than in many other languages, yet they occur frequently in everyday situations. Model forming plural nouns by selecting objects from around the classroom (*one eraser*) and saying and writing the plural form of the object (*two erasers*). Ask students to choose items and say and write the plural form of the noun.

DAY 2 Language Arts

Objectives
- Organize ideas to prepare for writing a description.
- Use a concept web.

Writing—Description
Writing Trait: Focus/Ideas

Introduce the prompt

Review the key features of a description. Remind students that they should think about these features as they plan their writing. Then explain that today they will begin the writing process for a narrative composition in the form of a description. Read aloud the writing prompt.

> ### Writing Prompt
>
> Think about a time in which you learned something important. Write a description of that moment, using your senses of smell, touch, taste, sight, and hearing to make the memory vivid.

Select a topic

 Think Aloud To help choose a topic, let's make a list of times when we learned important information. **Display a T-Chart.** I know that I need to list events and what I learned from them. My trip to the dentist was memorable because I learned about taking care of my teeth. **Add the information to the T-Chart. Ask students to name additional memorable times and why they were important.**

Gather information

Remind students that they can discuss the topic with one another and ask questions to help remember memorable times in their lives.

Memorable Time	Important Information I Learned
Trip to the dentist	How to take care of my teeth
First day of school	Making friends can be hard work
Day I got a puppy	Having pets is a serious responsibility

Corrective feedback

Circulate around the room as students discuss important events in their lives and choose a topic to write about. Conference briefly with students who are having difficulty choosing topics. Ask each struggling student guiding questions, such as *When did you meet your best friend?*

MINI-LESSON

Focus on Description

■ To stay focused on description, let's make a concept web. Display a simple concept web with one circle in the middle and five smaller circles connected to it. In the center circle write "First Day of School." In each smaller circle, let's list only the most vivid and interesting images and feelings that come to mind when we think about the first day of school. Complete this concept web with students. Some examples of images might include *hot and humid weather, desks arranged in a circle,* and *musty smell of books.* Have students begin their own concept webs using the form on p. 114 of their *Reader's and Writer's Notebook.* Explain that they will fill out the web with images and feelings that relate to their chosen topics.

ROUTINE   Quick Write for Fluency   [Team Talk]

1. **Talk** Have pairs discuss memorable times in their lives.

2. **Write** Each student writes two sentences describing what they remember most about it.

3. **Share** Each partner reads their own writing to the other. Then each partner asks the other one question about the special time.

Routines Flip Chart

Wrap Up Your Day

✔ **Build Concepts** Have students discuss honesty.

✔ **Compare and Contrast** What did you compare and contrast in *At the Beach*?

✔ **Visualize** How did visualizing the sights and sounds of a beach help you experience the story?

Differentiated Instruction

A Advanced

Elaborating Challenge students to create spin-off web bubbles with even more sensory words that connect to their chosen images and feelings.

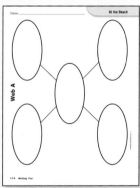

Reader's and Writer's Notebook p. 114

Teacher Tip

Provide dictionaries and thesauruses for students to use while they make their concept webs, or show students how to access these tools online. Encourage students to use these tools to find descriptive sensory words.

Preview DAY 3

Tell students that tomorrow they will read about what happens to Fernando.

Objectives
- Expand the weekly concept.
- Develop oral vocabulary.

Today at a Glance

Oral Vocabulary
candid, guilt

Comprehension Check/ Retelling
Discuss questions

Reading
At the Beach

Think Critically
Retelling

Fluency
Expression

Research and Study Skills
Reference Books

Research and Inquiry
Analyze

Spelling
Digraphs *th, sh, ch, ph*

Conventions
Regular and irregular plural nouns

Writing
Description

Concept Talk

Question of the Week
? Why is honesty important?

Expand the concept
Remind students of the weekly concept question. Discuss how the question relates to *At the Beach.* Tell students that today they will read about Fernando's honorable decision. Encourage students to think about how Fernando shows he is principled.

Anchored Talk

Develop oral vocabulary
Use the illustrations and dialogue to review pp. 182–189 of *At the Beach.* Discuss the Amazing Words *principled* and *oath*. Add these words to the concept map. Use the following questions to develop students' understanding of the concept.

- Sometimes young people learn how to be *principled* through their experiences. Think about a character in a movie or story that learned what it meant to be honest and truthful. How did that person's behavior change?

- Think about an *oath* that a person might take to show that he or she is *principled.* When might a person take such an *oath*?

Oral Vocabulary
Amazing Words

Amazing Words **Oral Vocabulary Routine**

Teach Amazing Words

1 **Introduce** Write the word *candid* on the board. Have students say it with you. Luisa was *candid* when she told Fernando that they shouldn't go to the reef. Have students use context to determine a definition of *candid*. (Being *candid* means saying what you really think or feel.)

2 **Demonstrate** Have students answer questions to demonstrate understanding. Was Luisa being *candid* when she said, "We never should have followed you"? (yes)

3 **Apply** Have students apply their understanding. In what types of situations would it be important to be *candid*?

See p. OV•1 to teach *guilt*

Routines Flip Chart

Apply Amazing Words

As students read pp. 190–193 of *At the Beach,* have them think about what the Amazing Words *candid* and *guilt* have to do with the decision that Fernando makes.

Connect to reading

Explain that today students will discover what Fernando says when the children see their parents. As they read, students should think about how this week's Question of the Week and the Amazing Words *candid* and *guilt* apply to Fernando's actions.

Amazing Words

integrity	oath
frank	candid
honorable	guilt
moral	justice
principled	deceit

ELL **Expand Vocabulary** Use the Day 3 instruction on ELL Poster 6 to help students expand vocabulary.

ELL Poster 6

Objectives

◎ Use compare and contrast to aid comprehension.

◎ Use visualization to aid comprehension.

◎ Use context clues for unfamiliar words to define new vocabulary.

Comprehension Check

Have students discuss each question with a partner. Ask several pairs to share their responses.

☑ **Genre • Analysis**

How does the author make the story realistic? **Possible response: The characters act and talk like people in real life. The many physical details included by the author made me feel as if I were there watching it happen.**

☑ **Compare and Contrast • Synthesis**

The setting of *At the Beach* is an important part of the story. Compare the sensory images of this setting to beaches you have experienced in real life or seen in movies. **Possible response: I have seen a beach with beautiful sand, water, and palm trees like the beach in the story. The beach I visited did not have a reef with sea urchins.**

☑ **Visualize • Analysis**

How does the author use sensory details to help you visualize parts of the story? **Possible response: The author uses words that describe sounds and smells at the beach. I can imagine the sound of the waves and the smell of the air.**

☑ **Unfamiliar words • Synthesis**

Use context clues in this sentence to define the word *foamy:* I saw the white sand and the warm, foamy water as the waves crashed on the beach. **Possible response: The words *sand, warm water,* and *waves* relate to the ocean. I know that the tops of waves look bubbly. I think *foamy* means *bubbly.* When I substitute that word in the sentence, it makes sense.**

☑ **Connect text to self**

The narrator of the story, Fernando, enjoys spending time with his family. Do you think this is an important value? Why or why not? **Possible response: I think it is an important value. We learn more about our families when we spend time together. When we do fun things together, we have memories that we can look back on.**

Strategy Response Log

INTERACT with TEXT

Have students use p. 12 in the *Reader's and Writer's Notebook* to revise and refine their mental pictures of *At the Beach* based on what they have read so far.

Check Retelling

Have students retell the first part of *At the Beach.*
Encourage students to paraphrase the selection in their
retellings.

Corrective feedback

If... students leave out important details,
then... have students look back through the illustrations in the
selection.

Small Group Time

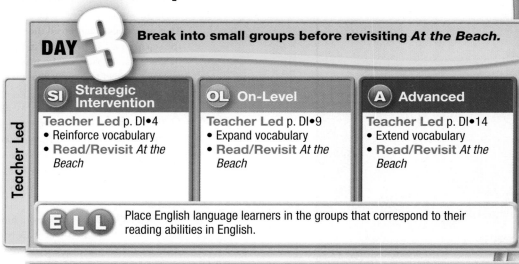

DAY 3 — Break into small groups before revisiting *At the Beach.*

Teacher Led

SI Strategic Intervention
Teacher Led p. DI•4
• Reinforce vocabulary
• **Read/Revisit** *At the Beach*

OL On-Level
Teacher Led p. DI•9
• Expand vocabulary
• **Read/Revisit** *At the Beach*

A Advanced
Teacher Led p. DI•14
• Extend vocabulary
• **Read/Revisit** *At the Beach*

ELL Place English language learners in the groups that correspond to their reading abilities in English.

Practice Stations
• Let's Write
• Get Fluent
• Word Work

Independent Activities
• AudioText of *At the Beach*
• *Reader's and Writer's Notebook*
• Research and Inquiry

ELL

English Language Learners
Check Retelling To support retelling, review the multilingual summary for *At the Beach* with the appropriate Retelling Cards to scaffold understanding.

Objectives
⦿ Use context clues to determine the meaning of unfamiliar words.

Teach Unfamiliar Words

🔍 **Unfamiliar Words** Have students use context clues to determine the meaning of the word *dislodge* on p. 190, paragraph 4. (to remove something that is stuck)

Corrective Feedback

If... students are unable to figure out the meaning of *dislodge*,

then... model how to figure out the meaning of the word *dislodge.*

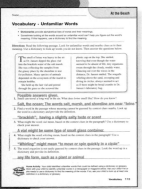

Reader's and Writer's
Notebook p. 115

Model the Skill

Think Aloud When I read the word *dislodge*, I am not sure what it means. I will reread paragraphs 2 and 3 for clues. In paragraph 2, I see that the urchin is stuck and won't budge.

Luisa held Javi's leg still as Mari held his hand and tried to comfort him. But Javi's desperate cries were now drowning out the sound of the sea.

I pulled and tugged, but the urchin wouldn't budge. It was stuck to Javi's foot by the tips of its spines. Javi was scared and in pain. And we were too far from our parents to ask for help. What if we couldn't get Javi back? I struggled relentlessly until I was finally able to remove the spiny creature from his foot.

Gently, Luisa poured some seawater over Javi's foot. That was when she noticed there was still a piece of the sea urchin's spine lodged in it. Javi wasn't going to be able to walk back, and he was much too heavy for us to carry. We had to remove that piece of spine so that he could walk on his own.

The sun burnt our backs as we all took turns trying to dislodge the sea urchin's spine.

"I have an idea," said Luisa suddenly. She removed her hair barrettes and held them like tweezers. Then, with the smallest movement, she pulled the broken spine out. With that solved, we started back.

I helped Javi walk on his sore foot. He wept and limped with every step. Our walk back seemed endless. As we got closer I realized that we would have to explain how it was that we went to the reef in the first place. I would surely end up with no tortilla if we told the truth.

"What will we do now?" Mari asked.

"We'll have to tell our parents what happened," said Luisa matter-of-factly.

"No!" I said emphatically. "We'll be punished for sure

190

Double Day Reads! Multidraft Reading

If you chose...

Option 1 Return to Extend Thinking instruction starting on p. 184–185.
Option 2 Read pp. 190–193.
Use the Guide Comprehension and Extend Thinking instruction.

Student Edition pp. 190–191

Higher-Order Thinking Skills

🔍 **Unfamiliar Words • Analysis** Use context clues to find the meaning of the word *relentlessly* in paragraph 2 on page 190. Ask students to look up the word *relentlessly* in a dictionary to confirm the meaning. Possible response: Fernando was pulling and tugging hard, and he finally got the sea urchin out of Javi's foot. I think the word *relentlessly* means "trying hard without giving up." When I look up the word in a dictionary, I see that *relentlessly* means "harsh or unyielding."

Let's Think About...

❻ The children are no longer happy and excited. They feel bad about what happened to Javi. Javi is in pain.

🔍 **Compare and Contrast • Evaluation** Read paragraph 4 on page 191. How does Fernando's story of Javi's injury compare with what really happened? Possible response: Fernando's story was similar to what really happened because Javi did step on the sea urchin. However, Fernando told a lie when he said it happened on the beach instead of the reef.

In paragraph 3, the children want to remove the sea urchin. If they want to dislodge the sea urchin, they must want to remove it, since it is stuck. What does *dislodge* mean? **(to remove something that is stuck)**

We walked the rest of the way in silence. The sound of crashing waves, children playing, and seagulls' calls became a background drone to Javi's cries.

When we finally reached our parents, Javi was crying louder than ever. Aunt Olga took one look at him and gasped. *"¡Niños!* Children! What's happened to Javi?"

Mari looked at Luisa. Luisa looked at me. Javi cried even louder.

"Well...," I hesitated. By now everyone was staring at me. "We were walking along the beach looking for cockles and urchin shells," I began, "when I found a live sea urchin attached to a piece of driftwood. So I called the others. Javi came running so fast that he stepped on it by accident."

Luisa and Mari stared at me in disbelief. I didn't think they liked my story.

"Let me see your foot, Javi," Aunt Olga said, kneeling next to her son.

Let's **Think** About...
Picture the cousins walking back to the beach. How is the mood different from earlier in the day?
🔵 **Visualize**

6

191

On Their Own

Have students figure out the meaning of the word *emphatically* in paragraph 9 on p. 190. (in a forceful, passionate way) Make sure they identify context clues, such as the exclamation point. Ask students how Fernando is feeling as he speaks. For additional practice, use *Reader's and Writer's Notebook* p. 115.

Inferring • Synthesis Why did Fernando hesitate before telling his story? Why did Luisa and Mari stare in disbelief? Tell how you think the characters felt. Possible response: Fernando probably hesitated and felt uncomfortable because he was about to tell a lie. Luisa and Mari knew he was lying, and they were probably surprised and disappointed.

Sensory Details • Evaluation Evaluate the author's use of sensory details to enrich the story. Support your answer. **Possible response:** Throughout the story, the author gives sensory details to help the reader visualize the beach and the events in the story. For example, in paragraph 1 on p. 191, the author describes several noises: *crashing waves* and *seagulls' calls.* These details help me understand what Fernando is hearing, seeing, and feeling.

DAY 3 Read and Comprehend

OPTION 1 Skills and Strategies, continued

Teach Author's Purpose

Review **Author's Purpose** Remind students that an author's purpose can be to persuade, to inform, to entertain, or to express. Ask students why they think Lulu Delacre wrote *At the Beach*. (to inform readers about Cuban culture; to entertain with a realistic story; to express a theme) Ask students to identify the theme. (honesty)

Corrective Feedback

If... students are unable to identify the author's purpose,

then... use the model to help them determine the author's purpose.

Student Edition pp. 192–193

OPTION 2 Think Critically, continued

Higher-Order Thinking Skills

Review **Author's Purpose • Synthesis** Understanding the author's purpose helps you know what to look for as you read. If you read *At the Beach* again, what would you pay attention to? Explain why. Possible response: Since the author wants to inform, I would look for details about Cuban culture and the Spanish words. Since the author wants to entertain, I would pay attention to Fernando's feelings and surroundings so I could put myself in his place. Since the author wants to express a message about honesty, I would look for Fernando's dishonest actions.

Model the Skill

Think Aloud I don't think the author was trying to persuade me to think a certain way. However, *At the Beach* entertained me by letting me imagine being in Fernando's shoes.

Mami and Aunt Rosa looked on as Aunt Olga examined Javi's foot closely. Then she gave him a big h■ and a kiss. "He's fine," she said at last. "It looks like the children were able to pull it out."

And at this good news, Javi's tears disappeared and were replaced by a big broad smile. "I'm hungry," he sa■

"Then let's have lunch," Aunt Olga suggested.

I was dumbfounded. Not only had they believed m■ but we were also going to eat Mami's tortilla!

The men went back to their domino game. The women went back to their conversation as they busied themselves serving everybody. No one but me seemed ■ notice how quiet Luisa and Mari had grown.

Mami handed me a plate filled with my favorite foo■ The tortilla smelled delicious. But I was unable to eat. I looked up at Luisa and Mari who were quietly picking ■ their food. I watched Mami as she served herself and sa■

192

Let's  About...

7 The tortillas tasted good because Fernando felt better about telling the truth, and now he was able to enjoy them.

Monitor and Clarify • Synthesis Imagine that Fernando never told Mami the truth about what happened. How do you think he would have felt? Possible response: He might have felt guilty and might not have been able to enjoy himself for the rest of the day.

It informed me about the foods in Cuban culture and how people lived many years ago. It also made me think about honesty and dishonesty. I think the theme is that honesty is always best.

---

ext to my aunts. I looked at my plate again. How could enjoy my food when I knew I had done something wasn't supposed to do? There was only one thing I ould do now. I stood up, picked up my plate, and went ght over to Mami.

"What's wrong, Fernando?" Mami asked.

I looked back at Luisa and Mari and swallowed ard. Then, I handed Mami my untouched plate.

"You wouldn't have given me this if I had told you he truth," I said.

Mami looked puzzled. The whole group grew silent nd watched me struggle. I was very embarrassed.

"It was my fault," Luisa said. "I should have opped them."

"And I went along," said Mari.

"No, no, it was my idea to go to the reef," I said. Then told everyone about our adventure at the reef. When was finished, Mami looked at me with tear-filled eyes.

"You are right, Fernando," she said. "I should unish you for doing something you knew not to do. omebody could have been seriously hurt."

"I know," I whispered, "and I'm sorry." But then he glimmer of a smile softened Mami's expression. he slid her arm over my shoulders as she said, "You now, Fernando, anyone can make a mistake. But not veryone has the courage to admit it. *Gracias*. Thank ou for telling the truth."

That afternoon, under the shade of the pine trees, he nine of us sat down on the old blankets for lunch. Ve had congrí, bread, and Mami's famous tortilla spañola. And do you know something? That day it sted better than it ever had before.

Let's Think About...

Why do you think the tortillas tasted so good to the narrator? **Inferring**

7

193

On Their Own

Ask students to think of another story that was written to express a theme about honesty. ("Ryan and Jonah"; "Bullseye") Have students compare the themes and moral lessons of these works of fiction.

Differentiated Instruction

SI **Strategic Intervention**
Author's purpose On the board, create a word web with the words *Inform, Entertain,* and *Express.* Help students scan the text to find examples of each. Have students work with partners.

A **Advanced**
Theme Remind students that this story is told by Lulu Delacre's *abuelito* (grandfather), Fernando. Ask partners to think about what Fernando would say to his grandchildren about the importance of honesty. If time allows, have them act out a conversation for the class.

Six Pillars of Character
Trustworthiness

Trustworthiness is being honest, reliable, and loyal. Is Fernando trustworthy? Why or why not?

ELL

English Language Learners
Vocabulary: Context clues Reread the first sentence in paragraph 4 on p. 192. Model determining the meaning using context clues: I wonder what *dumbfounded* means. The next sentence gives me a clue. Fernando is really surprised that they were able to eat the tortilla. I think *dumbfounded* means "really surprised." I will try the words *really surprised* in the sentence: I was *really surprised*. It makes sense, so this is probably the correct meaning for *dumbfounded*.

Comprehension Check

Spiral Review

Summarize • Synthesis Summarize the text, maintaining meaning and logical order. **Possible response:** Fernando and his family go to the beach. Mami and Aunt Olga tell the children not to stray far. Fernando and his cousins venture out to the reef. Javi steps on a sea urchin. The cousins pull the urchin out of Javi's foot, and they help him walk back. Fernando lies about the accident. Finally, Fernando has the courage to tell the truth.

Inferring • Analysis Why do you think Luisa and Mari offered to share the blame with Fernando? Possible response: They followed Fernando, even though they knew they were disobeying.

Check Predictions Have students look back at the predictions they made earlier and confirm whether they were accurate.

Objectives
• Provide evidence from text to support understanding. • Read independently for a sustained period of time and paraphrase the reading, including the order in which events occur.

Envision It! Retell

Think Critically

1. Imagine that you are Fernando. How would you feel if you were responsible for someone getting hurt? Why do you think you would feel this way? Text to Self

2. Think about the setting of the story. Find examples to show how the author helps readers imagine the sight, feel, and taste of things at the beach. Think Like an Author

3. Both the grown-ups and the children are partly responsible for Javi getting hurt. Compare and contrast the ways the two groups are partly responsible.
 Compare and Contrast

4. Pick the moment in the story that you remember best. Close your eyes and visualize it. Then describe it. Afterward, reread that scene to see how accurate your mental picture was. Visualize

5. **Look Back and Write** Look back at page 193. Explain in your own words what led Fernando to confess.

TEST PRACTICE Extended Response

READING STREET ONLINE
STORY SORT
www.ReadingStreet.com

194

Meet the Author

Lulu Delacre

Lulu Delacre grew up in Puerto Rico and is the daughter of two professors. Today she lives in Maryland and writes and illustrates books about Latin America.

For her story "At the Beach," Ms. Delacre says, "I wanted to write about an adventure at the beach. When I was a child, I went to the beach with my father and sister most weekends. One of my fondest memories is walking carefully on the big boulders, sidestepping sea urchins to reach the deepest pools where colorful fish hid." Like the boy in the story, Ms. Delacre has actually stepped on a sea urchin! "It is indeed very painful," she says.

"Growing up on the island was a fun-filled experience, where climbing up a *tamarindo* tree with a friend to eat its fruit was as commonplace as hunting for tiny brown lizards. I used to gently open their mouths and hang them from my earlobes as earrings!"

Here are other books by Lulu Delacre.

Salsa Stories

Arroz con Leche: Popular Songs and Rhymes from Latin America

Use the Reader's and Writer's Notebook to record your independent reading.

195

Student Edition pp. 194–195

Retelling

Envision It!

Have students work in pairs to retell the selection, using the Envision It! Retelling Cards as prompts. Remind students that they should accurately describe the plot and characters and use key vocabulary in their retellings. Encourage students to use sensory details in their retellings to monitor and adjust their comprehension of the selection.

Scoring rubric

Top-Score Response A top-score response makes connections beyond the text, describes the plot and characters using accurate information, and draws conclusions from the text.

Plan to Assess Retelling

☑ **This week assess Strategic Intervention students.**

☐ **Week 2** Assess Advanced students.

☐ **Week 3** Assess Strategic Intervention students.

☐ **Week 4** Assess On-Level students.

☐ **Week 5** Assess any students you have not yet checked during this unit.

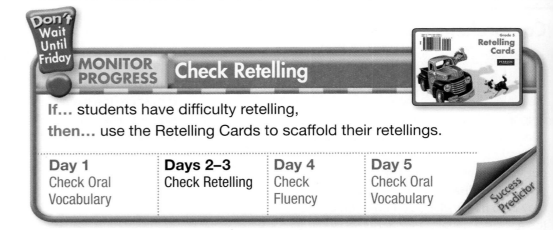

Don't Wait Until Friday

MONITOR PROGRESS Check Retelling

Grade 5 Retelling Cards PEARSON

If... students have difficulty retelling,

then... use the Retelling Cards to scaffold their retellings.

Day 1	Days 2–3	Day 4	Day 5
Check Oral Vocabulary	Check Retelling	Check Fluency	Check Oral Vocabulary

Success Predictor

Think Critically

Text to self

1. Possible response: I would feel guilty because I would realize that I made a bad decision.

Think like an author

2. Responses will vary but should include sensory details about the beach.

Compare and contrast

3. Possible response: The children and the grown-ups were irresponsible. The grown-ups were not watching the children closely. The children went to a place they were not supposed to go.

**Visualize**

4. Possible response: I can visualize different people trying to take the sea urchin out of Javi's foot.

Writing on Demand

5. **Look Back and Write** To build writing fluency, assign a 10–15 minute time limit.

Suggest that students use a prewriting strategy, such as brainstorming or using a graphic organizer, to organize their ideas. Remind them to establish a topic sentence and support it with facts, details, or explanations. As students finish, encourage them to reread their responses, revise for organization and support, and proofread for errors in grammar and conventions.

Scoring rubric

Top-Score Response A top-score response uses details and an understanding of character to explain Fernando's actions.

A top-score response should include:

- Fernando realized that he did something wrong.
- Fernando's cousins knew they disobeyed their parents.
- Fernando felt guilty because he deserved a punishment.

Differentiated Instruction

 Strategic Intervention

Have partners retell the ending of the story. Ask them to explain why Fernando lost his appetite and how they might feel if they had been in a similar situation.

Meet the Author

Have students read about author Lulu Delacre on p. 195. Ask them how her own life experiences helped her to write *At the Beach*.

Independent Reading

After students read independently for a sustained period of time, have them enter their independent reading information into their Reading Logs. Then have them summarize what they have read. Remind students that a summary should be no more than a few sentences about the main idea of a text.

E L L

English Language Learners
Retelling Use the Retelling Cards to summarize the selection with students. Then have partners describe each scene or setting shown on the cards.

Retelling

Success Predictor

Objectives
- Read grade-level text with expression.
- Reread for fluency.
- Understand how to use print reference sources.

Model Fluency
Expression

Model fluent reading

Have students turn to p. 189 of *At the Beach.* Have students follow along as you read the first four paragraphs. Tell them to listen to the expression of your voice as you read dialogue. Adjust your voice level to stress important words and phrases.

Guide practice

Have students follow along as you read paragraphs 1–4 again. Then have them reread the passage as a group without you until they read with the right expression and with no mistakes. Ask questions to make sure students comprehend the text. Continue in the same way as you read the rest of p. 189.

Reread for Fluency

Corrective feedback

If... students are having difficulty reading with the right expression, **then...** prompt:

- Which word is a problem? Let's read it together.
- Read the sentence again to be sure you understand it.
- Tell me the sentence. Now read it as if you are speaking to me.

ROUTINE Paired Reading

1. **Select a Passage** For *At the Beach*, use p. 189.
2. **Reading 1 Begins** Students read the selected text, switching readers after paragraph 4.
3. **Reading 2 Begins** Partners reread. This time the other student begins.
4. **Reread** For optimal fluency, have partners continue to read three or four times.
5. **Corrective Feedback** Listen to students read and provide corrective feedback. Tell students that their voices should reflect the frantic, worried feelings that Fernando and Luisa have at this point in the story.

Routines Flip Chart

Research and Study Skills
Reference Books

Teach

Ask students to name different types of reference books. Students may mention encyclopedias, dictionaries, manuals, or handbooks. Discuss how these reference books are alike and different.

- An **encyclopedia** gives information on specialized areas of knowledge. Some encyclopedias, such as the *Encyclopedia of Careers and Vocational Guidance*, focus on one particular area.

- A **handbook** is usually a small reference book that gives information about a particular subject.

- A **manual** is a book that explains how to do something.

- A **dictionary** is a large book that lists words in alphabetical order and explains their meanings.

Have groups go to the library and use reference books to find out more about personal and professional traits needed for a specific career. Have each group make a list of these traits and discuss the reference books they used to collect their data.

Guide practice

Discuss these questions:

Suppose you wanted to find out about education needed for a certain career. Which book might be most helpful? Why? (An occupation handbook would give information about training and education.)

How might an encyclopedia be helpful to find out about traits needed for a career? (An encyclopedia might provide information about a particular career.)

After groups describe their findings, ask specific questions about their lists.

On their own

Have students complete pp. 116–117 of the *Reader's and Writer's Notebook*.

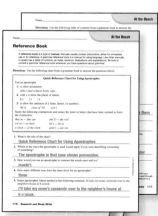

Reader's and Writer's
Notebook pp. 116–117

English Language Learners
ELL Professional Development: What ELL experts say about sheltering instruction "English language learners benefit when teachers shelter, or make comprehensible their literacy instruction. One way to do this is to use consistent, simplified, clearly enunciated, and slower-paced oral language to explain literacy concepts or activities."
—Dr. Georgia Ernest García

Reference books Display each type of reference book mentioned in the class discussion. Ask specific questions about each book and help students find examples to answer the questions.

Research and Inquiry
Analyze

Teach

Explain to students that today they will analyze their findings and decide if they need to change the focus of their inquiry question. When they look at what they have found, they may want to refine their research question.

Model

Think Aloud At first I thought I would explore doctors and honesty. Part of my research was to look in reference books to see if I could find information about training for doctors and personal traits that are necessary for a good doctor. I also talked to a local doctor. She thought that honesty was just as important for nurses. I will refocus my inquiry question to include other people in the medical profession. Now my inquiry question is *Why is it important for doctors and nurses to be honest?*

Guide practice

Have students analyze their findings. Remind students to ask you or ask other students for advice if they have trouble refining their research question.

Encourage students to use reference books to find additional information or to check facts. Since they will be producing tables, have them study the tables in the reference books to use as models for their own tables. Make sure they can interpret other tables accurately.

On their own

Have partners share their findings. Have them explain to one another why honesty is important for the career they are researching. Partners should ask each other questions or clarify points when necessary. Encourage them to help one another assemble numbered lists that can be turned into tables.

Conventions
Regular and Irregular Plural Nouns

Review

Remind students that this week they learned about regular and irregular plural nouns:

- Plural nouns name more than one person, place, or thing.
- Nouns ending in *ch, sh, x, z, s,* and *ss* add *-es.* Nouns ending in consonant *-y,* change the *y* to *i* and add *-es.*
- Nouns with irregular plurals change spelling or have the same singular and plural forms.

Daily Fix-It

Use Daily Fix-It numbers 5 and 6 in the right margin.

Connect to oral language

Have students say the proper plural form of each noun.

> **person, self, hand, plant, shelf, paper, family** *(people, selves, hands, plants, shelves, papers, families)*

On their own

For additional practice, use *Let's Practice It!* p. 67 on the *Teacher Resources DVD-ROM.*

Let's Practice It!
TR DVD•67

Spelling
Digraphs *th, sh, ch, ph*

Frequently misspelled words

The words *which, they,* and *thought* are words that students often misspell. Remember to use the spelling patterns to spell these words. I'm going to read a sentence. Choose the right word to complete the sentence and then write it correctly. Provide students with dictionaries to check their spellings.

1. _____ of these books do you want to buy? **(Which)**
2. Jane _____ that the food tasted delicious. **(thought)**
3. I think _____ need a break. **(they)**

On their own

For additional practice, use the *Reader's and Writer's Notebook* p. 118.

Reader's and Writer's
Notebook p. 118

Differentiated Instruction

 Strategic Intervention

Flashcards Have partners use a dictionary to locate ten new regular and irregular plural nouns. Then have them test each other with the flashcards to identify the correct plural forms.

Daily Fix-It

5. A butterflys wings astonis me. (*butterfly's; astonish*)
6. The migrating insects travel thousands of mile to a suthern country. (*miles; southern*)

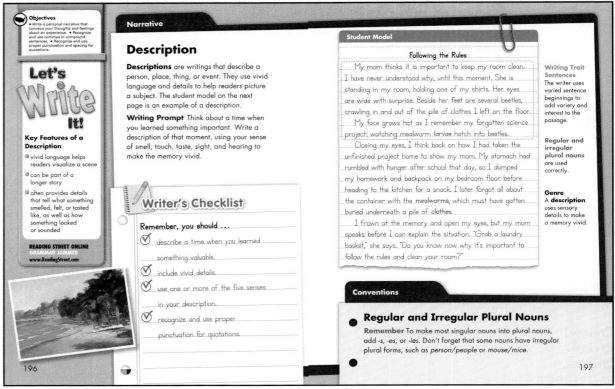

Student Edition pp. 196–197

Let's Write It!
Description

Teach

Use pp. 196–197 in the Student Edition. Direct students to read the key features of a description, which appear on p. 196. Remind students that they can refer to the information in the Writer's Checklist as they write their own descriptions.

Read the student model on p. 197. Point out the sensory words in the model and how the writer varies the beginnings of sentences to add variety.

Connect to conventions

Remind students that nouns can have regular or irregular forms. Point out the correct use of regular and irregular nouns in the model. Also point out and discuss the correct use of proper punctuation and spacing for quotations. Have students write some examples of sentences using quotations, showing the correct punctuation and spacing.

Writing—Description
Writing Trait: Descriptive Language: The Five Senses

Display rubric Display Scoring Rubric 6 from the *Teacher Resources DVD* and go over the criteria for each trait under each score. Then, using the model in the Student Edition, choose students to explain why the model should score a 4 for one of the traits. If a student offers that the model should score below 4 for a particular trait, the student should offer support for that response. Remind students that this is the rubric that will be used to evaluate the descriptions they write.

Write Guy
Jeff Anderson

What Do You Notice?

When students are examining the model text, ask, "What do you notice?" By giving students the responsibility of commenting on what they find effective in the text, they build self-confidence and often begin to notice features of the writing they might not have otherwise. Eventually they will start trying them in their writing. Relish students' movement toward correctness and beauty.

Scoring Rubric: Description

	4	3	2	1
Focus/Ideas	Clear focus on description	Fairly clear focus on description	No focus on description	No description
Sentences	Clear use of varied sentence beginnings	Mostly varied sentence beginnings	Very little variety in sentence beginnings	No attempt at variety in sentence beginnings
Word Choice	Strong use of sensory words	Some sensory words	Little attempt to use sensory words	No sensory words
Voice	Writing is personal and conveys the writer's emotions	Writing is mostly personal and conveys some of the writer's emotions	Writing is not very personal and conveys very few emotions	Writing is not personal and conveys no emotions
Organization	Description easy to follow	Description generally easy to follow	Description sometimes difficult to follow	Description lacks focus
Conventions	Few errors; strong understanding of regular and irregular plural nouns	Several minor errors; adequate understanding of regular and irregular plural nouns	Many errors; no understanding of regular and irregular plural nouns	Numerous errors; no attempt at correct regular and irregular plural nouns

Concept web Have students get out the concept webs they worked on yesterday. If their webs are not complete, have them use the Internet and print resources to gather information, take notes, and complete their webs.

Write You will be using your concept web as you write the draft of your description. When you are drafting, don't worry if your description does not sound exactly as you want it. You will have a chance to revise it tomorrow.

Objectives
- Write a first draft of a description.
- Use sensory words.

Writing, continued
Writing Trait: Descriptive Language

MINI-LESSON

Using Sensory Words

■ **Introduce** Review the key features of a description. Remind students that sensory words relate to the five senses: touch, taste, hearing, sight, and smell. Display the drafting tips for students. Remind them that the focus of drafting is to get their ideas down in an organized way by building on ideas they used while brainstorming. Then display Writing Transparency 6A.

Brothers and Baseball

I play baseball on a little league team. I am the pitcher, and I'm pretty good. One Sunday, my little brother asked me if he could practice with me. We decided to play catch.

My little brother is three years younger than me. My little brother couldn't catch the ball at all! My little brother threw the ball all over the place. I got mad. I kept diving to chase the Baseball. I yelled at him, "You are so bad!" He started to cry. He made some whimpering sounds and ran away.

I had a big game. The weather was really hot. I could smell delicious hot dogs and salty, fresh popcorn coming from the stands. I could hear the fans were cheering loudly for both teams. I was pitching really well. But then the sun started to set. The bright, orange sun seemed to pierce my eyes. Sweat poured down my face. My eyes stung. I started pitching terribly.

My brother was sitting in the stands. Even though I could barely make my pitchs, he still cheered for me. "Hooray!" he shouted. "That's my big brother". I felt really bad about yelling at him earlier in the day. It turns out that I'm not the best baseball player, either. I learned that day to have patience with other people. I learned our familys can teach us the most important lessons of our lifes. I also learned that I make mistakes, too.

Unit 2 · At the Beach   Writing: Model 6A

Writing Transparency 6A, TR DVD

Drafting Tips

✔ To get started, create a concept web to generate images and feelings related to your topic.

✔ Close your eyes and visualize the setting of where you learned an important lesson. Focus on the senses. Write down some words that come to mind.

✔ Don't worry about grammar and mechanics when drafting. Get down ideas now because you can proofread later.

 Think Aloud I'm going to write a description about when I learned an important lesson from my little brother. When I draft, I develop my ideas. I don't worry about revising or proofreading, because those tasks come later. I will add sensory words to make my description more vivid.

Direct students to use the drafting tips to guide them in writing their drafts. Remind them to make sure that they are using descriptive words for each of the five senses.

ROUTINE Quick Write for Fluency — Team Talk

1. **Talk** Pairs talk about making the choice to do the right thing in a difficult situation from their pasts.

2. **Write** Each person writes a brief paragraph about learning how to do the right thing using correct regular and irregular plural nouns.

3. **Share** Pairs read their own writing to their partners and then each checks his or her partner's writing for correct use of regular and irregular plural nouns.

Routines Flip Chart

Wrap Up Your Day

✔ **Build Concepts** What did you learn from Fernando about honesty?

✔ **Compare and Contrast** How did comparing Fernando and Luisa help you understand their actions?

✔ **Visualize** What details about the beach did you use to visualize?

Differentiated Instruction

SI Strategic Intervention
Visualizing Work one-on-one with students. Ask them guiding questions to help them visualize, such as *What sounds do you hear? What are the colors you see?*

Preview DAY 4

Tell students that tomorrow they will read an origin myth about why mice live in holes.

Objectives
- Expand the weekly concept.
- Develop oral vocabulary.

Today at a Glance

Oral Vocabulary
deceit, justice

Genre
Legend: Genre elements

Reading
"The Eagle and the Bat"

Let's Learn It!
Fluency: Expression
Vocabulary: Unfamiliar words
Listening and Speaking: Talk show

Research and Inquiry
Synthesize

Spelling
Digraphs *th, sh, ch, ph*

Conventions
Regular and irregular plural nouns

Writing
Description

Concept Talk

Question of the Week
Why is honesty important?

Expand the concept

Remind students that this week they have read about Fernando's decisions to be dishonest and then truthful about what happened to Javi. Tell students that today they will read a legend about a dishonest character.

Anchored Talk

Develop oral vocabulary

Have students use the illustrations to review pp. 190–193 of *At the Beach*. Discuss the Amazing Words *candid* and *guilt*. Add these and other concept-related words to the concept map. Use the following questions to develop students' understanding of the concept. Have students break into groups and identify points of agreement before telling their ideas.

- Fernando decided to be *candid* when he told the truth. Do you think it is important to be *candid*? Why or why not?
- Fernando felt *guilt* when he lied to his family. Can a feeling of *guilt* sometimes help a person to do the right thing? Explain your answer. (Yes; A feeling of guilt can encourage a person to tell the truth.)

Strategy Response Log

INTERACT with TEXT

Have students complete p. 12 in the *Reader's and Writer's Notebook.* Then have students write a descriptive summary of the selection.

Oral Vocabulary
Amazing Words

Amazing Words

frank	candid
honorable	guilt
moral	deceit
principled	justice
oath	

Teach Amazing Words

Amazing Words **Oral Vocabulary Routine**

1 **Introduce** Write the Amazing Word *deceit* on the board. Have students say it aloud with you. In *At the Beach,* Fernando acted with *deceit* when he lied to Mami and Aunt Olga. What context clue helps you determine the meaning of *deceit? (lied)* Have students determine the meaning of *deceit.* (*Deceit is* a dishonest act or statement.)

2 **Demonstrate** Have students answer questions to demonstrate understanding. Did Fernando and the others act with *deceit*? Explain. (Yes; They snuck away even though their mothers had told them not go that far.)

3 **Apply** Have students apply their understanding. Name a synonym and an antonym for the word *deceit.* (synonyms: *dishonesty, cheating, trickery, lying;* antonyms: *honesty, integrity, morals*)

See p. OV•1 to teach *justice.*

Routines Flip Chart

Apply Amazing Words

Help students establish a purpose for reading as they read "The Eagle and the Bat" on pp. 198–199. Have them think about the consequences of acting with *deceit* and how a dishonest person can be brought to *justice.*

Connect to reading

As students read today's legend, have them think about how the Question of the Week and the Amazing Words *deceit* and *justice* apply to the moral of the story.

ELL **Produce oral language** Use the Day 4 instruction on ELL Poster 6 to extend and enrich language.

ELL Poster 6

Objectives
• Introduce legends.

Let's Think About Genre
Legend: Genre Elements

Introduce the genre

Explain to students that what we read is structured differently depending on the author's reasons for writing and what kind of information he or she wishes to convey. Different types of texts are called genres. Tell them that a legend is one type of genre.

Discuss the genre

Discuss stories that tell about the great deeds of a hero. Explain: A legend is a story usually told by word of mouth. Usually a legend has a lesson, or moral, at the end. The stories might be about heroes, animals, or historical characters, such as King Arthur or George Washington. Legends about historical figures are based on the characters but not on facts about their lives.

On the board, draw a word web like the one below. Ask the following questions:

• Why do you think people like to tell legends? **Possible response: Legends explain a moral in an interesting context that people can understand easily.**

• Who are usually the characters in legends? **Possible responses: animals, heroes, historical figures**

• Why could there be several versions of the same legend? **Possible response: Since legends are usually told orally, the characters, settings, or plots may change.**

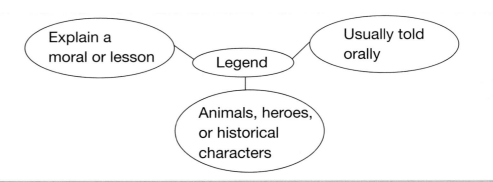

Guide practice

Have students work in small groups to make a list of legends that they have heard or read from various cultures. Ask them to include in their lists the main characters and moral or theme of each legend. Tell groups to select two of the legends from their lists and make a T-chart that compares and contrasts the themes and moral lessons.

Connect to reading

Tell students that they will now read a legend about a bat who learns about honesty. Ask volunteers to think of other legends or tales that share this lesson.

Small Group Time

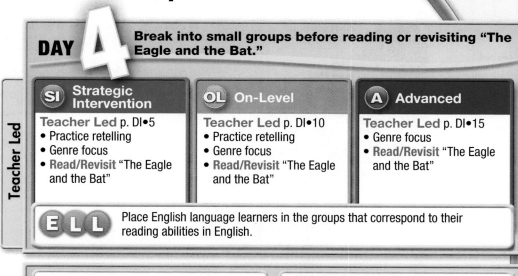

DAY 4 Break into small groups before reading or revisiting "The Eagle and the Bat."

Teacher Led

SI Strategic Intervention

Teacher Led p. DI•5
• Practice retelling
• Genre focus
• **Read/Revisit** "The Eagle and the Bat"

OL On-Level

Teacher Led p. DI•10
• Practice retelling
• Genre focus
• **Read/Revisit** "The Eagle and the Bat"

A Advanced

Teacher Led p. DI•15
• Genre focus
• **Read/Revisit** "The Eagle and the Bat"

ELL Place English language learners in the groups that correspond to their reading abilities in English.

Practice Stations
• Read for Meaning
• Get Fluent
• Words to Know

Independent Activities
• AudioText: "The Eagle and the Bat"
• *Reader's and Writer's Notebook*
• Research and Inquiry

Objectives

• Understand the elements of legends.

Student Edition pp. 198–199

Guide Comprehension
Skills and Strategies

Teach the genre

Legend: Genre Elements Have students preview "The Eagle and the Bat" on pp. 198–199. Have them look at the illustration and note the characters and the setting of the story. Then ask: Since this story is from a book of legends, what features can you expect from the story?

Corrective feedback

If... students are unable to explain the features of a legend,
then... use the model to help them identify the features.

Model the genre

Think Aloud Most legends are told orally. I can tell this is true because the author is listed as "told by." Often legends have animals as characters. This legend is about a bat and an eagle. As with most legends, the purpose is to teach the reader something, probably a lesson or a moral.

On their own

Have students work with partners to explain the moral of this legend. Have them write a brief paragraph about how the lesson compares and contrasts to their own lives.

 **eSelection**

Extend Thinking
Think Critically

Higher-order thinking skills

Compare and Contrast • Evaluation Think about the character traits of the bat and the eagle. Compare the two characters. Which character is more admirable and why? Possible response: The bat was clever and dishonest because he tried to trick the other animals. The eagle was clever and honorable because he taught a lesson to the bat.

Visualize • Analysis What words or phrases in paragraph 3 help you visualize the eagle and the bat? Possible response: "little bat popped up from out of the plumes on the top of Wanblee's head, flapping its puny leather wings…."

Let's Think About…

From "the Eagle and the Bat," I learned that trickery is a form of dishonesty. Everyone makes mistakes, but it takes courage to be honest and tell the truth.

Reading Across Texts

Have students discuss what happens to each character who lies in *At the Beach* and "The Eagle and the Bat." Use that information to determine the lessons taught in each selection. Then ask students to compare and contrast those lessons with ones taught in other stories they have read.

Writing Across Texts

Have students discuss their paragraphs as they develop them. Circulate among students and offer suggestions when necessary.

Differentiated Instruction

SI Strategic Intervention
Story Structure Have students make a story map to show the setting, characters, and plot of the legend. Then help them to explain the theme of the story in a few sentences.

A Advanced
Storytelling Have partners orally retell the legend to each other. Encourage them to use expressive voices and details to add interest. Students may wish to make a recording of their stories.

Academic Vocabulary

legend a traditional story that has been passed down through spoken language

English Language Learners
Leveled support: Digraphs
Supply students with these words to practice the digraphs *th* and *ch* at their own language level:
beneath, chin
leather, which
together, couch

DAY 4 Read and Comprehend

Objectives

- Read with fluency and comprehension.
- ◎ Use context clues to understand the meanings of unfamiliar words.
- Conduct an interview on a talk show.

Check Fluency WCPM
SUCCESS PREDICTOR

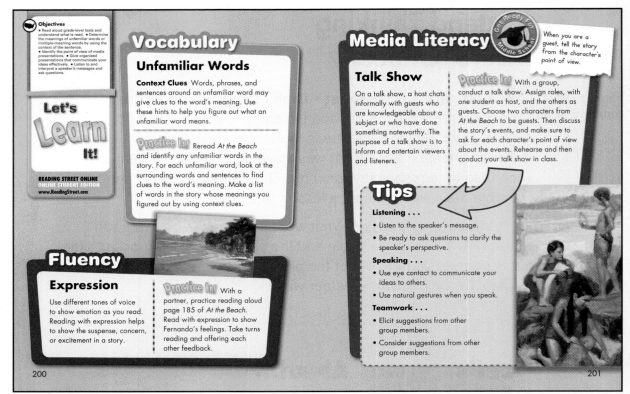

Objectives
• Read aloud grade-level texts and understand what is read. • Determine the meanings of unfamiliar words or multiple-meaning words by using the context of the sentence.
• Identify the point of view of media presentations. • Give organized presentations that communicate your ideas effectively. • Listen to and interpret a speaker's messages and ask questions.

Let's Learn It!

READING STREET ONLINE
ONLINE STUDENT EDITION
www.ReadingStreet.com

Vocabulary

Unfamiliar Words

Context Clues Words, phrases, and sentences around an unfamiliar word may give clues to the word's meaning. Use these hints to help you figure out what an unfamiliar word means.

Practice It! Reread *At the Beach* and identify any unfamiliar words in the story. For each unfamiliar word, look at the surrounding words and sentences to find clues to the word's meaning. Make a list of words in the story whose meanings you figured out by using context clues.

Fluency

Expression

Use different tones of voice to show emotion as you read. Reading with expression helps to show the suspense, concern, or excitement in a story.

Practice It! With a partner, practice reading aloud page 185 of *At the Beach*. Read with expression to show Fernando's feelings. Take turns reading and offering each other feedback.

Media Literacy

Talk Show

On a talk show, a host chats informally with guests who are knowledgeable about a subject or who have done something noteworthy. The purpose of a talk show is to inform and entertain viewers and listeners.

Practice It! With a group, conduct a talk show. Assign roles, with one student as host, and the others as guests. Choose two characters from *At the Beach* to be guests. Then discuss the story's events, and make sure to ask for each character's point of view about the events. Rehearse and then conduct your talk show in class.

When you are a guest, tell the story from the character's point of view.

Tips

Listening . . .
- Listen to the speaker's message.
- Be ready to ask questions to clarify the speaker's perspective.

Speaking . . .
- Use eye contact to communicate your ideas to others.
- Use natural gestures when you speak.

Teamwork . . .
- Elicit suggestions from other group members.
- Consider suggestions from other group members.

200

201

Student Edition pp. 200–201

Fluency
Expression

Guide Practice

Use the Student Edition activity as an assessment tool. Make sure the reading passage is at least 200 words in length. As students read aloud with partners, walk around to make sure their expression is appropriate and that it changes to enhance the meaning of what they are reading.

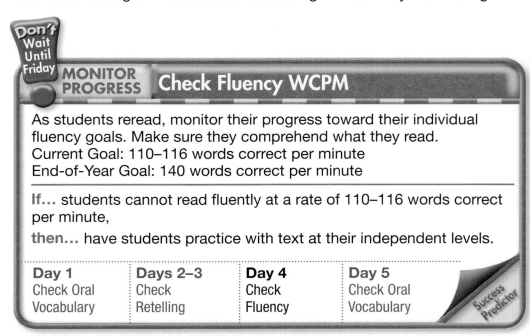

Don't Wait Until Friday

MONITOR PROGRESS | Check Fluency WCPM

As students reread, monitor their progress toward their individual fluency goals. Make sure they comprehend what they read.
Current Goal: 110–116 words correct per minute
End-of-Year Goal: 140 words correct per minute

If... students cannot read fluently at a rate of 110–116 words correct per minute,

then... have students practice with text at their independent levels.

Day 1	Days 2–3	Day 4	Day 5
Check Oral Vocabulary	Check Retelling	Check Fluency	Check Oral Vocabulary

Success Predictor

Vocabulary
Unfamiliar Words

Teach unfamiliar words

Context Clues Write this sentence on the board: *I used tweezers to pick up the very small beads.* Have students identify the words in the sentence that provide context clues for the meaning of the word *tweezers* (*pick up, very small beads*). Have students clarify the meaning of the word *tweezers* in a dictionary.

Guide practice

Write this sentence: *I enjoyed napping and swinging in a hammock as I rested at the beach.* Have students use context clues such as *napping, swinging, rested,* and *beach* to figure out the meaning of the word *hammock.*

On their own

Have students come up with sentences that provide context clues for each of the unfamiliar words students identified. Ask them to switch sentences with each other and name the words that act as context clues before they define the unfamiliar word. Encourage them to check the meanings in a dictionary or glossary.

Listening and Speaking
Talk Show

Teach

Point out that everyone needs to work together to ensure success for the talk show. The host needs to plan relevant, interesting questions that she or he will ask. After students agree on the roles, each person should think about the character's feelings and point of view. Students should elicit suggestions from other group members and identify points of agreement.

Guide practice

Observe and guide students to ask thought-provoking questions so that the guests will be able to respond with accuracy and emotion. Make sure that the student playing the talk show host pays attention to the guest's emotions, perspectives, and expressions so that they can ask relevant questions. Remind students that it is important for a talk show host to interpret their guest's comments and direct the interview accordingly.

On their own

Have small groups conduct the talk show for others. Encourage students in the audience to give constructive feedback that will improve enunciation, volume, speaking rate, and grammar.

Talk Show

Remind students that they should be aware of everyone's role so that one person does not dominate the discussion. Encourage students to use rehearsal techniques, such as taking breaths or videotaping, to prepare for the presentation.

English Language Learners

Practice pronunciation Assist pairs of students by modeling the correct pronunciation of the words from the glossary, then having students repeat after you. Have students with mixed language proficiencies work together to practice pronunciation and employ self-corrective techniques.

Fluency

Success Predictor

Objectives

- Synthesize information from various sources into a table.
- Recognize and correctly use regular and irregular plural nouns.
- Spell words with *th, sh, ch, ph.*

Research and Inquiry
Synthesize

Teach

Have students synthesize information by combining the most important pieces of information from the reference books that they used. Have them assemble their information in a table with reasons why honesty is important in their chosen career. The tables should be numbered so that the audience can easily interpret the information.

Guide practice

If students have not collected sufficient information, direct them to revisit more reference books or to check online references such as electronic encyclopedias. Then have students use a word processing program to prepare for their presentations on Day 5. As students prepare their tables, help them choose font styles, sizes, colors, and formatting that will make their lists easy to read. They should paste the list onto a poster board.

On their own

Have students prepare for their presentations by explaining their tables to a family member or friend.

Conventions
Regular and Irregular Plural Nouns

Test practice

Remind students that grammar skills, such as regular and irregular plural noun forms, are often assessed on important tests.

- Plural nouns name more than one person, place, or thing.

- Most plural nouns are formed by adding *-s.* For nouns ending in *ch, sh, x, z, s,* and *ss,* add *-es* to form the plural. For nouns ending in consonant *-y,* change the *y* to *i* and add *-es.*

- Nouns with irregular plurals change spelling or have the same singular and plural forms

Reader's and Writer's Notebook p. 119

Daily Fix-It

Use Daily Fix-It numbers 7 and 8 in the right margin.

On their own

For additional practice, use the *Reader's and Writer's Notebook* p. 119.

Spelling
Digraphs *th, sh, ch, ph*

Practice spelling strategy

Have students work in pairs to create a word search puzzle in which at least ten spelling words fit into a block of grid paper. Tell students that the words can be spelled forward, backward, up, down, or diagonally. Suggest that they first write the spelling words onto the grid and then fill in the blank spaces with extra letters. In addition to the ten correctly spelled spelling words, suggest students also include misspelled spelling words as decoys. They can exchange puzzles with other pairs and solve each other's puzzles. Tell students to use dictionaries to check their work.

Let's Practice It! TR DVD•68

On their own

For additional practice, use *Let's Practice It!* p. 68 on the *Teacher Resources DVD-ROM.*

Daily Fix-It

7. The story is a chater from a longer book about a migrent family. (*chapter; migrant*)

8. Francisco have trouble at school because him does not speak English. (*has; he does*)

E L L

English Language Learners

Leveled Support: Digraphs *th, sh, ch, ph* Creating a word search puzzle may be too difficult for English Language Learners. Provide instruction for students based on their proficiency levels.

Beginning Have students locate and write all the spelling words that begin with *sh.* Then have them echo: /sh/ *shovel;* /sh/ *shatter.*

Intermediate Have students locate and write all the spelling words that end with *sh* and *ch.* Have them echo the digraph sounds along with the words.

Advanced Have students write the spelling words two at a time in a word search puzzle format, such as connecting *shovel* and *southern* by the *s.* Then have them read the pairs aloud.

Objectives
- Revise a draft of a description.
- Apply revising strategy of consolidating.

Writing—Description
Revising Strategy

MINI-LESSON

Revising Strategy: Consolidating

■ Yesterday we wrote descriptions about an important lesson. Today we will revise our drafts.

■ Display Writing Transparency 6B. Remind students that revising does not include corrections of grammar and mechanics. Then introduce the revising strategy Consolidating.

Writing Transparency 6B, TR DVD

■ When you revise, ask yourself *Have I used a variety of sentence beginnings?* The revising strategy Consolidating is the process by which we consolidate, or combine, words and sentences so that our sentences begin in a variety of ways. Let's look at the draft from yesterday. More than one sentence starts with *I learned.* I will change these sentences to begin in a different way. This will add more variety to my writing. Reread your composition for places where you might want to add more information so that the reader will want to read on.

Tell students that as they revise, not only should they look for places where they might add information to clarify meaning and enhance style, but they should also make sure that they have a topic sentence and supporting details.

Revising Tips

✔ Read each sentence, taking note of how each begins.

✔ Look for consecutive sentences that begin with the same words or phrases.

✔ Find ways to consolidate words, phrases, or sentences in order to have more variety in the way sentences begin.

Peer conferencing

Peer Revision Have pairs of students exchange papers for peer revision. Students should write three questions about the partner's writing. Tell students that their questions should focus on where their partner could revise by adding information to make the writing clearer and more informative. Refer to the *Reader's and Writer's Notebook* for more information about peer conferencing.

Circulate around the room to monitor pairs and have conferences with students as they revise. Remind students correcting errors that they will have time to edit tomorrow. They should be working on sensory content and organization today.

> **ROUTINE** **Quick Write for Fluency** **Team Talk**
>
> 1. **Talk** Pairs discuss the lesson Fernando learned about telling the truth.
>
> 2. **Write** Each person writes a paragraph about what Fernando did wrong.
>
> 3. **Share** Partners read one another's writing and then check their partner's writing for words that appeal to the senses.

Routines Flip Chart

Wrap Up Your Day

✔ **Build Concepts** What did you learn about origin myths?

✔ **Oral Vocabulary** Monitor students' use of oral vocabulary as they respond: In "The Eagle and the Bat," did the bat act in an honorable way, or did he act with deceit?

✔ **Text Features** Discuss how the illustrations in "The Eagle and the Bat" and *At the Beach* helped students understand the text.

Teacher Tip
If students have trouble writing their compositions, then suggest that they respond orally to the prompt.

English Language Learners
Leveled Support: Revising
Provide sentences about *At the Beach* for the students to revise.

Beginning Students add two sensory words to one sentence.

Intermediate Students add two sensory words to two sentences.

Advanced Students add sensory words to a short paragraph

Preview DAY 5

Remind students to think about why honesty is important.

Objectives
- Review the weekly concept.
- Review oral vocabulary.

Today at a Glance

Oral Vocabulary

Comprehension
◉ Compare and contrast

Lesson Vocabulary
◉ Unfamiliar words

Word Analysis
Spanish word origins

Literary Terms
Imagery

Assessment
Fluency
Comprehension

Research and Inquiry
Communicate

Spelling
Digraphs *th, sh, ch, ph*

Conventions
Regular and irregular plural nouns

Writing
Description

Check Oral Vocabulary
SUCCESS PREDICTOR

Concept Wrap Up

Question of the Week
Why is honesty important?

Review the concept
Have students look back at the reading selections to find examples that demonstrate why it is important to be honest.

Review Amazing Words
Display and review this week's concept map. Remind students that this week they have learned ten Amazing Words related to honesty. Have students use the Amazing Words and the concept map to answer the Question of the Week, *Why is honesty important*?

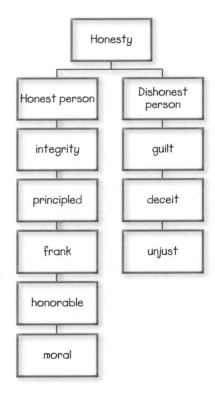

Honesty
├── Honest person
│   ├── integrity
│   ├── principled
│   ├── frank
│   ├── honorable
│   └── moral
└── Dishonest person
    ├── guilt
    ├── deceit
    └── unjust

ELL **Check Concepts and Language** Use the Day 5 instruction on ELL Poster 6 to monitor students' understanding of the lesson concept.

ELL Poster 6

Amazing Ideas

Connect to the Big Question

Have groups of students discuss how the Question of the Week connects to the Big Question: *What makes people want to do the right thing*? Tell groups to use the concept map and what they have learned from this week's Anchored Talks and reading selections to form an Amazing Idea—a realization or "big idea" about honesty. Have students consider each other's suggestions. Then ask each group to share its Amazing Idea with the class.

Amazing Ideas might include these key concepts:

- Honesty is important because it is a basic part of moral behavior.
- Honesty is the foundation of integrity.
- Honesty is important because it shows that a person is principled.

Write about it

Have students write a few sentences about their Amazing Idea, beginning with "This week I learned …"

Amazing Words

integrity	oath
frank	candid
honorable	guilt
moral	justice
principled	deceit

 It's Friday

MONITOR PROGRESS | **Check Oral Vocabulary**

Have individuals use this week's Amazing Words to describe honesty. Monitor students' abilities to use the Amazing Words and note which words you need to reteach.

If… students have difficulty using the Amazing Words,

Then… reteach using the Oral Vocabulary Routine, pp. 177a, 180b, 190b, 198b, OV•1.

Day 1	Days 2–3	Day 4	Day 5
Check Oral Vocabulary	Check Retelling	Check Fluency	Check Oral Vocabulary

Success Predictor

ELL

English Language Learners
Concept map Work with students to add new words to the concept map.

Oral Vocabulary | Success Predictor

Objectives
◎ Review compare and contrast.
◎ Review unfamiliar words.
• Review Spanish word origins.
• Review imagery.

Comprehension Review
↻ Compare and Contrast

Student Edition p. EI•6

Teach compare and contrast

Envision It!

Review the definitions of compare and contrast on p. 178. Remind students that when they compare and contrast, they look for ways that things, people, or situations are alike and different. For additional support, have students review p. EI•6 on compare and contrast.

Guide practice

Tell students that comparing and contrasting can deepen their understanding of the characters in a story. Have them work in pairs to compare and contrast two of the characters in *At the Beach*. Have students use details from the story to explain how the characters are alike and different. Compare and contrast how each character responds to the conflict in the story.

On their own

For additional practice with compare and contrast, use *Let's Practice It!* p. 69 on the *Teacher Resources DVD-ROM*.

Let's Practice It! TR DVD•69

Vocabulary Review
↻ Unfamiliar Words

Teach unfamiliar words

Remind students to use clues to help them understand the meanings of unfamiliar words.

Guide practice

Write this sentence on the board: *We concealed the gift under the bed so that Dad wouldn't find it*. Review with students how to use context clues to determine the meaning of the word *concealed*. ("hidden so it can't be found") Then have students identify the context clues. (*under the bed, so that Dad wouldn't find it*)

On their own

Have partners work together to write sentences using this week's lesson vocabulary words. Partners can trade sentences and identify the context clues that help them determine each word's meaning.

Word Analysis Review
Spanish Word Origins

Teach Spanish word origins

Remind students that many English words have their origins in other languages. Write the word *mesa* and explain that it is a Spanish word meaning "table."

Guide practice

Display the following words: *mesa, banana, canoe.* Use the Strategy for Multisyllabic Words to teach the word *mesa.*

ROUTINE   **Strategy for Multisyllabic Words**

1. **Look for recognizable word parts** When I see a word I don't know, I look for meaningful parts. If I don't see any parts, I chunk the word and use sound-spellings to read the parts.

2. **Connect to sound-spelling** Write *mesa.* I don't recognize any parts, so I'll chunk it. The chunk at the beginning is *me.* The second part is *sa.* I say each chunk slowly: *me sa.* I say the chunks fast to make a whole word: *mesa.* I think the *e* sounds like long *a* in this word, because it has Spanish origins.

3. **Blend** Have students blend the word parts to read *mesa.*

Routines Flip Chart

On their own

Have students use a dictionary to check the pronunciation and find the meanings of *mesa, banana,* and *canoe.*

Literary Terms Review
Imagery

Teach imagery

Remind students that imagery is the use of words that help the reader experience the way things look, sound, smell, taste, or feel.

Guide practice

Have students find an example of imagery in "The Eagle and the Bat," pp. 198–199. Discuss how imagery enriches the story and which senses are stimulated by the details.

On their own

Have students choose one of the animals from "The Eagle and the Bat." Have them write a description of the animal using imagery.

Lesson Vocabulary

algae a group of living things, mostly found in water, that can make their own food

concealed put out of sight; hidden

driftwood wood carried along by water, or washed ashore by the water

hammocks hanging beds or couches made of canvas, cord, or other material

lamented felt or showed grief

sea urchins small, round sea animals with spiny shells

sternly strictly; firmly

tweezers small pincers for picking up small objects

ELL

English Language Learners
Imagery To help students understand how to use sensory language, provide visual and auditory examples. Have students tell what these sentences help them see or hear.

Visual: Water from the dog's tangled, wet coat dripped into small puddles.

Auditory: The sharp crack of thunder rattled the dishes on the shelf.

Objectives
- Read grade-level text with fluency.

Plan to Assess Fluency

☑ **This week assess Advanced students.**

☐ **Week 2** Assess Strategic Intervention students.

☐ **Week 3** Assess On-Level students.

☐ **Week 4** Assess Strategic Intervention students.

☐ **Week 5** Assess any students you have not yet checked during this unit.

Set individual goals for students to enable them to reach the year-end goal.

- Current Goal: 110–116 WCPM
- Year-End Goal: 140 WCPM

Assessment

Check words correct per minute

Fluency Make two copies of the fluency passage on p. 201k. As the student reads the text aloud, mark mistakes on your copy. Also mark where the student is at the end of one minute. To figure words correct per minute (WCPM), subtract the number of mistakes from the total number of words read in one minute. Make sure students comprehend what they read by having them retell what was read.

Corrective feedback

If... students cannot read fluently at a rate of 110–116 WCPM,
then... make sure they practice with text at their independent reading levels. Provide additional fluency practice by pairing nonfluent readers with fluent readers.

If... students already read at 140 WCPM,
then... have them read a book of their choice independently.

Small Group Time

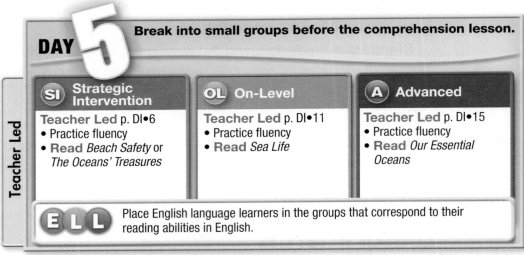

DAY 5 Break into small groups before the comprehension lesson.

SI Strategic Intervention	**OL On-Level**	**A Advanced**
Teacher Led p. DI•6 • Practice fluency • **Read** *Beach Safety* or *The Oceans' Treasures*	Teacher Led p. DI•11 • Practice fluency • **Read** *Sea Life*	Teacher Led p. DI•15 • Practice fluency • **Read** *Our Essential Oceans*

Teacher Led

ELL Place English language learners in the groups that correspond to their reading abilities in English.

Practice Stations	**Independent Activities**
• Words to Know • Get Fluent • Read for Meaning	• Grammar Jammer • Concept Talk Video • Vocabulary Activities

Name _____

The Right Change

My cousin Leah and I each had a ten-dollar bill that we could spend at   15

the school carnival. For weeks we had talked about the big day and what we   30

would do.   32

Leah had said, "I will spend two dollars on cotton candy, and two dollars   46

on a strawberry shake."   50

I knew that Leah would spend the remaining six dollars on carnival rides.   63

I would spend my ten dollars in the same way except that I would have a   79

peach shake instead of strawberry. I could almost taste the creamy sweetness   91

as Leah and I planned our day.   98

On the big day, Leah and I walked over to the park and went straight   113

to the fruit-shake man. Leah paid for her strawberry shake, took the change,   126

and walked over to the Bumper Boats while she waited for me. The peach   140

shake was cold in my hand as I gave the man my ten-dollar bill. He gave me   157

change and I began to walk away. Before stuffing the bills into my pocket, I   172

caught a quick glimpse of one. I should have had a five-dollar bill and three   187

one-dollar bills after paying for my two-dollar shake. But instead I had a ten-   201

dollar bill and three one-dollar bills. The shake man had given me too much   214

change. I began to think of all the things I could buy with the extra money.   230

I could ride even more rides and maybe take a chance on the Ring Toss   245

Game.   246

I took a sip of my shake and felt an ache in my stomach. I walked back   263

to the shake man and got the right change.   275

MONITOR
PROGRESS   • Check Fluency

Objectives
- Read grade-level text with comprehension.

Assessment

Check compare and contrast

◉ **Compare and Contrast** Use "Upside Down Under" on p. 201m to check students' understanding of compare and contrast.

1. How does the narrator think life in upstate New York will compare with life in Australia? Use evidence to support your answer. **Possible response: The narrator thinks that life will be boring compared to life in New York. The narrator plays with friends around a lake each summer; in Australia, the narrator thinks there will be nothing to do in the desert except watching dust blow.**

2. Compare the father and sister's reactions to the narrator's demonstration of the cowboy falling off the Earth. **Possible response: The father knows that the narrator is aware of gravity and is just trying to get out of moving to Australia; the sister believes the demonstration and becomes afraid that she will fall off the Earth.**

3. Describe the narrator's sister when she thinks she is too small and will fall off the Earth. How is she different by the end of the story? **Possible response: She is pale and screaming as she thinks about her doom; she calms down because she is going to learn about gravity and why she won't fall off the Earth.**

Corrective feedback

If... students are unable to answer the comprehension questions, **then...** use the Reteach lesson in the *First Stop* book.

Upside Down Under

I spent the first ten years of my life living in upstate New York. My friends and I enjoyed summer days splashing in the lake, finding driftwood, and napping in hammocks. That changed the day my dad told us we were moving. He had accepted a job in some desert in Australia. What would I do there? Watch the dust blow? I felt my life turn upside down.

Really! I showed my dad my world globe. "We'll fall off!" I protested. I held a toy cowboy's feet on the green space that was Australia. His head pointed down and out into unknown space.

"Ever heard of gravity?" my dad asked. "The cowboy won't fall off and neither will you. But nice try!"

My only hope was to get my little sister stirred up into a huge fit. I showed her the globe and the cowboy. "See," I demonstrated. "Up here in New York we can stand up." I moved the cowboy down to our new home. "See, down here…." I let the cowboy drop to the floor and then shook my head slowly. "The rest of us might make it because we're heavier. But you're so small, there's no hope!" Her scream was all that I dreamed of and more.

"What did you tell her?" my dad asked. But he knew when he saw my sister. She was pale and screaming, standing next to the globe with the doomed cowboy at her feet.

She calmed down when my dad told her that at dinner I would explain gravity to her. For the next two hours I sat in my room writing a three-page report on gravity. I also had to include a poster that explained why we wouldn't fall off the Earth.

MONITOR PROGRESS   • Compare and Contrast

Objectives
- Communicate inquiry results.
- Take spelling test.
- Review regular and irregular plural nouns.

Research and Inquiry
Communicate

Present ideas Have students share their inquiry results with the class. Have students display and explain the tables they created on Day 4. Encourage them to give organized presentations that follow the numbered reasons they have included in their tables.

Listening and speaking Remind students how to be good speakers and how to communicate effectively with their audience.

- Keep eye contact with audience members.
- When appropriate, gesture at the numbers on the poster board.
- Speak clearly, loudly, and at an appropriate rate (not too fast or too slow).
- Use good grammar and use language appropriate for your audience.
- Respond to questions using evidence from your research.

Remind students to follow these tips for being a good listener.

- Listen to and interpret all of the speaker's messages, both verbal and nonverbal.
- Wait until the speaker has finished before raising your hand to ask a question.
- Be polite, even if you disagree.

Spelling Test
Digraphs *th, sh, ch, ph*

Spelling test   To administer the spelling test, refer to the directions, words, and sentences on p. 179c.

Conventions
Extra Practice

Teach   Remind students that nouns can have regular or irregular plural forms. Regular verbs end in *-s,* but irregular verbs can have many different endings.

Guide practice   Have students work with a partner to underline the nouns in these sentences. Then have them identify whether the nouns are regular or irregular.

> The <u>cars</u> move quickly down the <u>streets</u>. (regular, regular)
>
> There are <u>deer</u> and <u>butterflies</u> in the meadow. (irregular, irregular)

Daily Fix-It   Use Daily Fix-It numbers 9 and 10 in the right margin.

On their own   Write these sentences. Have students look back in *At the Beach* to find the correct regular and irregular plural nouns to fill in the blanks. Remind students to look at the spelling of the noun to determine its plural form.

> 1. **Along the way, we drove past sugarcane _____ and roadside _____.** (fields, markets)
>
> 2. **When we got to the marbled _____, Luisa looked concerned.** (rocks)
>
> 3. **The sound of crashing _____, children playing, and seagulls' _____ became a background drone to Javi's _____.** (waves, calls, cries)
>
> 4. **"It looks like the _____ were able to pull it out."** (children)
>
> 5. **Mami handed me a plate filled with my favorite _____.** (foods)

Students should complete *Let's Practice It!* p. 70 on the *Teacher Resources DVD-ROM.*

Daily Fix-It

9. Did the girls wipe there feets? *(their feet)*

10. Curtis and adam plays football at recess. *(Adam; play)*

Let's Practice it!
TR DVD • 70

Objectives
- Proofread revised drafts of descriptions, focusing on plural nouns and quotations.
- Create and present a final draft.

Writing—Description
Plural Nouns and Quotations

Review revising

Remind students that yesterday they revised their descriptions, paying particular attention to varying their sentences and consolidating the text. Today they will proofread their descriptions.

MINI-LESSON

Proofread for Plural Nouns and Quotations

- **Teach** When we proofread, we look closely at our work, searching for errors in mechanics such as spelling, capitalization, punctuation, and grammar. Today we will focus on proofreading for correct use of plural nouns as well as correct punctuation and spacing in quotations.

Writing Transparency 6C, TR DVD

- **Model** Let's look at the last paragraph we revised yesterday. Display Writing Transparency 6C. Point out that *stands* is a regular plural noun that should end in *-s* instead of *-es*. Help students find other errors regarding plural nouns. Then examine the two quotations closely. Help students recognize the extra spacing in the first quotation and the incorrect placement of punctuation in the second quotation. Explain to students that they should reread their composition multiple times. Each time, they should check for errors in spelling, punctuation, capitalization, and grammar.

Proofread

Display the Proofreading Tips. Ask students to proofread their compositions, using the Proofreading Tips and paying particular attention to sentence beginnings. Circulate around the room answering students' questions. When students have finished editing their own work, have pairs proofread one another's descriptions.

Proofreading Tips

- ✔ Be sure that all regular and irregular plural nouns are spelled correctly.
- ✔ Check for correct punctuation and spacing for any quotations.
- ✔ Begin postwriting only after you have completed the drafting, revising, and editing stages.

Present Have students incorporate revisions and proofreading edits into their descriptions to create a final draft.

Have pairs work together to create a booklet about important lessons they have learned. Have students create art and other graphics to accompany their writing. Remind pairs to create a cover and a table of contents in their booklets. Pairs can trade booklets to learn new important life lessons. When students have finished, have each complete a Writing Self-Evaluation Guide.

ROUTINE **Quick Write for Fluency** Team Talk

1. **Talk** Pairs discuss what they learned about important life lessons this week.

2. **Write** Each student writes a few sentences summarizing what they learned.

3. **Share** Partners read their summaries to one another.

Routines Flip Chart

Teacher Note

Writing Self-Evaluation Guide
Make copies of the Writing Self-Evaluation Guide on p. 39 of the *Reader's and Writer's Notebook* and hand out to students.

ELL

English Language Learners
Support editing Help students identify quotation errors by sharing examples of quotations from newspaper and magazine articles. Point out the proper use of punctuation and spacing in each example.

Poster preview Prepare students for next week by using Week 1, ELL Poster 7. Read the Poster Talk-Through to introduce the concept and vocabulary. Ask students to identify and describe objects and actions in the art.

Selection summary Send home the summary of *Hold the Flag High,* in English and in the students' home languages, if available, from the ELL Handbook. Students can read the summary with family members.

Preview NEXT WEEK

What are the risks in helping others? Tell students that next week they will read about one of the first black regiments in the Civil War and how those soldiers took risks for their country.

Weekly Assessment

Use pp. 39–46 of *Weekly Tests* to check:

✔ **Word Analysis** Spanish Word Origins

✔ ◉ **Comprehension Skill** Compare and Contrast

✔ Review **Comprehension Skill** Author's Purpose

✔ **Lesson Vocabulary**

algae	lamented
concealed	sea urchins
driftwood	sternly
hammocks	tweezers

Weekly Tests

Advanced

Differentiated Assessment

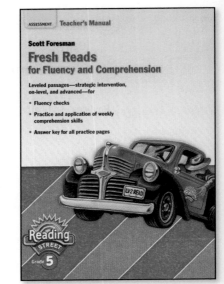

OL
On-Level

Use pp. 31–36 of *Fresh Reads for Fluency and Comprehension* to check:

✔ ◉ **Comprehension Skill** Compare and Contrast

✔ Review **Comprehension Skill** Author's Purpose

✔ **Fluency** Words Correct Per Minute

SI
Strategic Intervention

Fresh Reads for Fluency and Comprehension

Managing Assessment

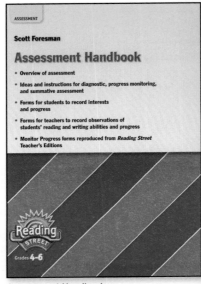

Use *Assessment Handbook* for:

✔ **Weekly Assessment Blackline Masters for Monitoring Progress**

✔ **Observation Checklists**

✔ **Record-Keeping Forms**

✔ **Portfolio Assessment**

Assessment Handbook

"Bullseye"

Continued from p. 177b

Grandpa stood at the window watching his grandson go into the alley, pick up every last loose bottle and can, and put them back into the neighbors' recycling bin. Mikey looked up at the window and Grandpa nodded.

"Now you've hit the bullseye," Grandpa said to himself with a smile.

Small Group Time

Pacing Small Group Instruction

5-Day Plan

DAY 1	• Reinforce the concept • Read Leveled Readers Concept Literacy Below Level
DAY 2	• Compare and Contrast • Visualize • Revisit Student Edition pp. 182–189
DAY 3	• Unfamiliar Words • Revisit Student Edition pp. 190–193
DAY 4	• Practice Retelling • Read/Revisit Student Edition pp. 198–199
DAY 5	• Reread for fluency • Reread Leveled Readers

3- or 4-Day Plan

DAY 1	• Reinforce the concept • Read Leveled Readers
DAY 2	• Compare and Contrast • Visualize • Revisit Student Edition pp. 182–189
DAY 3	• Unfamiliar Words • Revisit Student Edition pp. 190–193
DAY 4	• Practice Retelling • Read/Revisit Student Edition pp. 198–199 • Reread for fluency • Reread Leveled Readers

3-Day Plan: Eliminate the shaded box.

SI *Strategic Intervention* **DAY 1**

Build Background

■ **Reinforce the Concept** Discuss the weekly question *Why is honesty important?* This week's concept is *honesty*. What do you think *honesty* means? *(possible answers: telling the truth; keeping your promises; admitting mistakes; respecting yourself and others)* Honest people tell the truth and do the right thing, even when it is difficult. Why do you think that honesty is important? *(possible answers: so people can trust each other; without it, people don't know what the real situation is)* Discuss the words on the concept map on pp. 176–177 in the Teacher Edition.

■ **Connect to Reading** Discuss with students a time when they or someone they know did something wrong and then decided not to tell the truth about it. What were the conditions that made them want to take that risk? What did they fear that led them to lie? Sometimes we think that by lying we can save ourselves from being punished. We forget about our own conscience. This week you will read about someone in *At the Beach* who makes this same mistake.

Objectives
• Interpret a speaker's messages (both verbal and nonverbal).

 Strategic Intervention

DAY 1

For a complete literacy instructional plan and additional practice with this week's target skills and strategies, see the **Leveled Reader Teaching Guide.**

Concept Literacy Reader

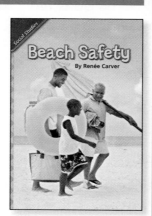

- **Read** *Beach Safety*

- **Before Reading** Preview the story with students, focusing on key concepts and vocabulary. Then have them set a purpose for reading.

- **During Reading** Read the first two pages of the story aloud while students track the print. Then have students finish reading the story with a partner.

- **After Reading** After students finish reading the story, connect it to the weekly question *Why is honesty important?*

Below-Level Reader

- **Read** *The Oceans' Treasures*

- **Before Reading** Use a picture walk to guide students through the text, focusing on key concepts and vocabulary. Then have students set a purpose for reading.

- **During Reading** Do a choral reading of the first two pages. If students are able, have them read and discuss the remainder of the book with a partner. Have partners discuss the following questions:

  - What are coral reefs made of? *(the skeletons of dead stony corals)*

  - Why do coral reefs need to be protected? *(because it takes thousands of years for a large reef to be built up)*

- **After Reading** Have students look at and discuss the concept map. Connect the Below-Level Reader to the weekly question *Why is honesty important?* *(Doing the right thing is necessary to protect our oceans and the life in them.)*

MONITOR PROGRESS

If... students have difficulty reading the selection with a partner,

then... have them follow along as they listen to the Leveled Readers DVD-ROM.

If... students have trouble understanding how some sea creatures stay alive along the coasts,

then... reread pp. 4–6 and discuss the information together.

Objectives
- Interpret a speaker's messages (both verbal and nonverbal).

Small Group Time

Student Edition p. EI•6

More Reading

Use additional Leveled Readers or other texts at students' instructional levels to reinforce this week's skills and strategies. For text suggestions, see the Leveled Reader Database or the Leveled Readers Skills Chart on pp. CL 24–CL 29.

SI Strategic Intervention — **DAY 2**

Reinforce Comprehension

◉ **Skill Compare and Contrast** Review with students *Envision It!* p. EI•6 on Compare and Contrast. Then use p. 178 to review the definition.

When you compare and contrast, you are showing how things are alike or different. You can visualize as you read to help you compare and contrast.

◉ **Strategy Visualize** Review the definition of visualize. Remind students to form pictures in their minds to help them compare and contrast people and events in the story. If students have trouble visualizing, suggest they look closely at the existing illustrations. For additional support, refer students to *Envision It!* p. EI•25.

Revisit *At the Beach* on pp. 182–189. Have students begin reading the story aloud with a partner. As they read, have them apply the comprehension skill and strategy to the story.

- Contrast what the countryside looks like with what the beach looks like. *(countryside: sugarcane fields, roadside markets, barking dogs and chickens; beach: sand, waves, fish, hot sun)*

- What is the difference between what Luisa wants to tell the adults and what the narrator wants to tell them? *(She wants to tell the truth, that they strayed too far. Fernando wants to lie so they won't be punished.)*

- How does Fernando feel about the tortilla when Mami first gives it to him, compared to how he felt before? *(He was really hungry for the tortilla before, but after he tells a lie, he feels too guilty to eat.)*

Use the During Reading Differentiated Instruction for additional support for struggling readers.

MONITOR PROGRESS

If... students have difficulty reading along with the group,
then... have them follow along as they listen to the AudioText.

Objectives
- Compare and contrast ideas and information.
- Evaluate the impact of imagery in literary text.

SI Strategic Intervention

DAY **3**

Reinforce Vocabulary

👁 **Unfamiliar Words/Context Clues** Say the term *sea urchin* as you write it on the board. Then model how to use context clues to figure out the meaning of an unfamiliar word.

First, I read the rest of the paragraph. From the name, I think a sea urchin lives in the ocean. I notice that the second sentence says that sea urchins are "spiny" and "black" and that they "hide." The third sentence says they are "painful" to step on, probably because of the spines. So I put all the clues together and figure that a sea urchin is "an animal that lives in the ocean and hides from other animals; it is black with sharp spines to protect itself and is painful to step on."

Revisit *At the Beach* on pp. 190–193. Review *Words!* on p. W•7. As students finish reading *At the Beach*, encourage them to use context clues to figure out the meaning of any unfamiliar words.

• Point out the words *hammocks, sternly, algae, lamented, driftwood,* and *tweezers* from the story.

• Read paragraph 5 on p. 190. Look at the word *tweezers*. What are some context clues that can help you figure out the meaning of *tweezers*? *(Luisa used her barrette to pull the sea urchin's spine out of Javi's foot. So* tweezers *must be something with two prongs that you can pinch together to pull something out.)* Have students look for context clues to the other unfamiliar words to figure out their meanings.

Use the During Reading Differentiated Instruction for additional support for struggling readers.

Student Edition p. W•7

More Reading

Use additional Leveled Readers or other texts at students' instructional levels to reinforce this week's skills and strategies. For text suggestions, see the Leveled Reader Database or the Leveled Readers Skills Chart on pp. CL 24–CL 29.

MONITOR PROGRESS

If... students need more practice with the lesson vocabulary,
then... use *Envision It! Pictured Vocabulary Cards.*

Objectives
• Use context to determine the meaning of unfamiliar words.

Small Group Time

Practice Retelling

■ **Retell** Have students work in pairs and use the Retelling Cards to retell *At the Beach.* Monitor their retellings and prompt students as needed. For example, ask:

• Tell me what this story is about in a few sentences.

• What did you learn from this story?

If students struggle, model a fluent retelling.

Genre Focus

■ **Before Reading or Revisiting** "The Eagle and the Bat" on pp. 198–199, read aloud the genre information about legends on p. 198. "The Eagle and the Bat" is a fictional story that, like all legends, explains how something in nature came to be and teaches a life lesson.

Then have students preview "The Eagle and the Bat." Ask:

• What pictures, words, and features do you see? *(the word "legend," large title, picture of a large eagle with a tiny bat above it, opening line like a fairy tale)*

• What clue does the picture of the eagle and bat give you about the story? *(eagle probably plays a big part; bat will play a smaller part)*

Then have students set a purpose for reading based on their preview.

■ **During Reading or Revisiting** Have students do a choral reading of the legend. Point out that the legend gives a fictional explanation of how mice came to be and why owls catch them.

■ **After Reading or Revisiting** Have students share their reactions to the legend. Then guide them through the Reading Across Texts and Writing Across Texts activities.

> **MONITOR PROGRESS**
>
> **If...** students have difficulty retelling the selection,
> **then...** have them review the story using the illustrations.

> **Objectives**
> • Compare themes or moral lessons of several works of fiction from various cultures.

 **SI** Strategic Intervention

DAY 5

For a complete literacy instructional plan and additional practice with this week's target skills and strategies, see the **Leveled Reader Teaching Guide.**

Concept Literacy Reader

■ **Model** Model the fluency skill of expression. Ask students to listen carefully as you read aloud two pages of *Beach Safety*. Have students notice how you read with expression, adjusting as you read to reflect changes in tone or to emphasize important parts.

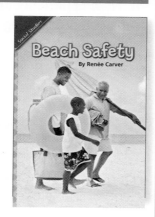

■ **Fluency Routine**

1. Have students reread passages from *Beach Safety* with a partner or individually.

2. For optimal fluency, students should reread three to four times.

3. As students read, monitor fluency and provide corrective feedback. Discuss how stressing important words creates a more natural rhythm.

See *Routines Flip Chart* for more help with fluency.

■ **Retell** Have students retell *Beach Safety*. Prompt as necessary.

● What happens in this part?

● Summarize the selection in a few sentences.

Below-Level Reader

■ **Model** Ask students to listen carefully as you read aloud two pages of *The Oceans' Treasures*. Have students notice how you read with expression, raising your voice slightly to emphasize important names or details and speaking more quickly for lists.

■ **Fluency Routine**

1. Have students reread passages from *The Oceans' Treasures* with a partner or individually.

2. For optimal fluency, students should reread three to four times.

3. As students read, monitor fluency and provide corrective feedback. Discuss how adjusting reading speed and volume can make the reading more interesting.

See *Routines Flip Chart* for more help with fluency.

■ **Retell** For additional practice, have students retell *The Oceans' Treasures* page-by-page, using the illustrations. Prompt as necessary.

● What did you learn in this part of the Reader?

● How did the author organize the Reader? *(according to location in the ocean)*

MONITOR PROGRESS

If... students have difficulty reading fluently,

then... provide additional fluency practice by pairing nonfluent readers with fluent ones.

Objectives
● Read aloud grade-level stories with fluency.

Small Group Time

Pacing Small Group Instruction

5-Day Plan

DAY 1	• Expand the concept • Read On-Level Reader
DAY 2	• Compare and Contrast • Visualize • Revisit Student Edition pp. 182–189
DAY 3	• Unfamiliar Words • Revisit Student Edition pp. 190–193
DAY 4	• Practice Retelling • Read/Revisit Student Edition pp. 198–199
DAY 5	• Reread for fluency • Reread On-Level Reader

3- or 4-Day Plan

DAY 1	• Expand the concept • On-Level Reader
DAY 2	• Compare and Contrast • Visualize • Revisit Student Edition pp. 182–189
DAY 3	• Unfamiliar Words • Revisit Student Edition pp. 190–193
DAY 4	• Practice Retelling • Read/Revisit Student Edition pp. 198–199 • Reread for fluency • Reread On-Level Reader

3-Day Plan: Eliminate the shaded box.

OL On-Level ------------------------------------ **DAY 1**

Build Background

■ **Expand the Concept** Connect the weekly question *Why is honesty important?* and expand the concept. How is honesty important for maintaining the health of our planet? *(possible answers: disposing of toxic waste in legal ways, not polluting the environment, not wasting resources)* Discuss the meaning of the words on the concept map on pp. 176–177 in the Teacher Edition.

On-Level Reader

For a complete literacy instructional plan and additional practice with this week's target skills and strategies, see the **Leveled Reader Teaching Guide.**

■ **Before Reading** *Sea Life,* have students preview the On-Level Reader by looking at the title, cover, and pictures in the book. Ask:

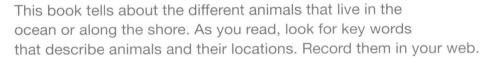

• What is the topic of this book? *(creatures that live in the ocean)*

• In which parts of the ocean do the animals in the photographs live? *(coast, reef, deeper waters)*

Have students create a concept web with the label *Sea Life.*

This book tells about the different animals that live in the ocean or along the shore. As you read, look for key words that describe animals and their locations. Record them in your web.

■ **During Reading** Read aloud the first four pages of the book as students follow along. Then have them finish reading the book on their own. Remind students to add words to their web as they read.

■ **After Reading** Have partners compare the words on their web.

• Which animals live in which locations in the sea?

• What new technologies have helped scientists research sea life?

• How can people "do the right thing" to help protect life in the oceans?

Objectives
• Interpret a speaker's messages (both verbal and nonverbal).

OL On-Level

DAY **2**

Expand Comprehension

👁 **Skill Compare and Contrast** Use p. 178 to review the definitions of comparing and contrasting. For additional review, see p. EI•6 in the *Envision It!*

👁 **Strategy Visualize** Review the definition of visualize. Encourage students to form mental pictures of the scenes and action to help them compare and contrast as they read. For further support, refer students to the Extend Thinking questions or *Envision It!* p. EI•25.

Revisit *At the Beach* on pp. 182–189. As students begin reading, have them apply the comprehension skill and strategy to the story.

- What are some differences between Fernando and Luisa? *(She is older and knows more than he does. She is more likely to follow the adults' rules.)*

- How does visualizing help you identify differences between the scenery on the car trip and at the beach? *(Readers can picture the characters driving past sugarcane fields and roadside markets, frightening dogs and chickens. Readers can also picture the clear water and colorful fish, smell the salt, and feel the hot sun.)*

- After Javi is injured, how are Fernando and Luisa's actions alike? *(They are both calm and clever enough to help him.)*

Student Edition p. EI•6

More Reading

Use additional Leveled Readers or other texts at students' instructional levels to reinforce this week's skills and strategies. For text suggestions, see the Leveled Reader Database or the Leveled Readers Skills Chart on pp. CL 24–CL 29.

Objectives
- Compare and contrast ideas and information.
- Evaluate the impact of imagery in literary text.

OL On-Level   DAY 3

Expand Vocabulary

Student Edition p. W•7

More Reading

Use additional Leveled Readers or other texts at students' instructional levels to reinforce this week's skills and strategies. For text suggestions, see the Leveled Reader Database or the Leveled Readers Skills Chart on pp. CL 24–CL 29.

⦿ **Unfamiliar Words/Context Clues** Tell students that context clues can help them figure out unfamiliar words. Then write the following sentence from the selection on the board: "Camouflage helps scorpion fish and stonefish stay concealed among the corals." Underline *camouflage* and *concealed*.

Revisit *At the Beach* on pp. 190–193. Point out that *camouflage* and *concealed* might be unfamiliar words. Students can use context clues in the paragraph to help them figure out what both words mean. Ask:

- What is the passage about? *(how animals adapt to survive in their ocean environment)*

- Besides running way, what is another way for animals to avoid predators? *(They can hide.)*

- Based on the context clues, what might the word *camouflage* mean? *(protective coloring or shapes that help animals hide from predators)*

- How does this word help you understand the meaning of *concealed?* *(Something that is camouflaged is hidden, so* concealed *must mean "hidden.")*

Have students finishing reading *At the Beach.* Encourage them to apply the strategy as they read.

Objectives
• Use context to determine the meaning of unfamiliar words.

 OL On-Level

DAY 4

Practice Retelling

■ **Retell** To assess students' comprehension, use the Retelling Cards. Monitor retelling and prompt students as needed.

Genre Focus

■ **Before Reading or Revisiting** "The Eagle and the Bat" on pp. 198–199, read aloud the genre information about legends on p. 198. Have students preview "The Eagle and the Bat" and set a purpose for reading. Ask:

- What features do you see here that are different from those in most short stories you read? *(The legend is a very short story. Also, the first sentence is like a fairy tale.)*

■ **During Reading or Revisiting** Have students read along with you while tracking the print.

- How do you know in the first paragraph that this is not a true story? *(The birds can talk.)*

- What lesson does the bat learn in this legend? *(not to be a trickster)*

■ **After Reading or Revisiting** Have students share their reactions to the legend. Then have them pick an animal and write a brief legend explaining how the animal came to look or act the way it does (for example, how cats acquired tails or why cockroaches hate light).

Objectives
• Compare themes or moral lessons of several works of fiction from various cultures.

Small Group Time

On-Level Reader

■ **Model** Model the fluency skill of expression for students. Ask students to listen carefully as you read aloud the first two pages of *Sea Life*. Have students note how you read with expression, for example, slowing down and raising your voice to emphasize important information.

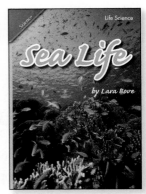

■ **Fluency Routine** Discuss how varying volume and pace creates expression.

1. Have students reread passages from the On-Level Reader *Sea Life* with a partner.

2. For optimal fluency, students should reread passages three to four times.

3. As students read, monitor fluency and provide corrective feedback. Point out that varying volume and pace makes the information more interesting. Also, discuss how stressing important words or statements can help the listener understand the text better.

See the *Routines Flip Chart* for more help with fluency.

■ **Retell** For additional practice, have students use headings and photographs as a guide to retell *Sea Life*. Prompt as necessary.

• What is this selection mostly about?

• What is the most interesting thing you learned from this selection?

Objectives
• Read aloud grade-level stories with fluency.

eReaders

Differentiated Instruction

A Advanced

A Advanced

DAY 1

Build Background

Our Essential Oceans
by J. F. Culbertson

■ **Extend the Concept** Discuss the weekly question *Why is honesty important?* Scientists help us know more about the environment and how people can harm or help the planet. Why do you think honesty in scientific work is so important? *(Possible answer: Governments and other groups use scientific work to make important decisions about our environment. If scientists are not honest, it is harder for people to do the right thing.)*

Advanced Reader

For a complete literacy instructional plan and additional practice with this week's target skills and strategies, see the **Leveled Reader Teaching Guide.**

■ **Before Reading** *Our Essential Oceans.* Prepare students to read. Today you will read about how important ocean resources are and some ideas for using them more wisely. Have students use the illustrations to predict what they will learn about Earth's oceans. Then have students set a purpose for reading.

■ **During Reading** Have students read the Advanced Reader independently.

Encourage them to think critically. For example, ask:

• How does the writer present an honest view about the ways that people have used ocean resources? *(talks about abuses, pollution, and overfishing as well as the benefits people have gained)*

• How might people use the oceans differently to conserve resources? *(reduce pollution, fish more wisely)*

■ **After Reading** Have students review the concept map and explain how *Our Essential Oceans* helps students answer the weekly question *Why is honesty important?* Prompt as necessary.

• What problems did you learn about from this selection?

• What has your family done to help conserve Earth's resources?

■ **Now Try This** Assign "Now Try This" at the end of the Advanced Reader.

Objectives
• Interpret a speaker's messages (both verbal and nonverbal).

Pacing Small Group Instruction

15–20 mins.

5-Day Plan

DAY 1	• Extend the concept • Read Advanced Reader
DAY 2	• Compare and Contrast • Visualize • Revisit Student Edition pp. 182–189
DAY 3	• Unfamiliar Words • Revisit Student Edition pp. 190–193
DAY 4	• Legend • Read/Revisit Student Edition pp. 198–199
DAY 5	• Reread for fluency • Reread Advanced Reader

3- or 4-Day Plan

DAY 1	• Extend the concept • Advanced Reader
DAY 2	• Compare and Contrast • Visualize • Revisit Student Edition pp. 182–189
DAY 3	• Unfamiliar Words • Revisit Student Edition pp. 190–193
DAY 4	• Legend • Read/Revisit Student Edition pp. 198–199 • Reread for fluency • Reread Advanced Reader

3-Day Plan: Eliminate the shaded box.

Small Group Time

More Reading

Use additional Leveled Readers or other texts at students' instructional levels to reinforce this week's skills and strategies. For text suggestions, see the Leveled Reader Database or the Leveled Readers Skills Chart on pp. CL 24–CL 29.

Extend Comprehension

Skill Compare and Contrast Tell students that classifying is a form of comparing and contrasting where students can sort things into different categories. For example, they can classify Fernando and Luisa's statements into the categories of *True statements* versus *Lies*.

Strategy Visualize Review the definition of visualize and remind students to form mental images of the scenes and action as they read the rest of *At the Beach*. This strategy can help them classify features of the story. During reading, use the Extend Thinking questions and the During Reading Differentiated Instruction for additional support.

■ **Revisit** *At the Beach* on pp. 182–189. Have students apply the comprehension skill and strategy as they begin reading.

- What other things from *At the Beach* can you classify into different categories? *(possible answers: children versus adults, beach versus countryside, having fun versus getting hurt; punishment versus forgiveness)*

- How can classifying things help you understand the story? *(Classifying helps show the differences and similarities among different people, statements, landscapes, and other things in the story.)*

■ **Critical Thinking** Encourage students to think critically as they read.

- Why do you think all the children follow Fernando, even though some disagree with him?

- If you were Fernando's friend, would you have tried to stop him? Why or why not?

Objectives
- Compare and contrast ideas and information.
- Evaluate the impact of imagery in literary text.

DAY 3

Extend Vocabulary

◉ **Unfamiliar Words/Context Clues** Remind students that they can use context clues to help them understand unfamiliar words. Read the following sentence from the selection, emphasizing *compounds*: "Fish is high in both protein and certain compounds that nutritionists believe may contribute to having a healthy heart."

- What context clues can you find in the sentence to help you figure out the meaning of *compounds*? *("protein," "nutritionists," "contribute," "healthy heart")*

- What do you think the word *compounds* means? *(something that is needed for good health, such as vitamins and minerals)*

■ **Revisit** *At the Beach* on pp. 190–193. Remind students to use the strategy to figure out the meaning of such words such as *iridescent, relentlessly,* and *emphatically* as they read.

■ **Critical Thinking** Have students recall what happened in the selection. Encourage them to think critically. For example, ask:

- Should Fernando's mother have forgiven him? Why or why not?

- What do you think would have happened if Fernando had told the truth right away?

More Reading

Use additional Leveled Readers or other texts at students' instructional levels to reinforce this week's skills and strategies. For text suggestions, see the Leveled Reader Database or the Leveled Readers Skills Chart on pp. CL 24–CL 29.

Objectives
• Use context to determine the meaning of unfamiliar words.

Small Group Time

A Advanced · DAY **4**

Genre Focus

■ **Before Reading or Revisiting** *"The Eagle and the Bat"* on pp. 198–199, remind students that legends are usually traditional stories that teach a lesson. Then have students reread *"The Eagle and the Bat"* on their own.

■ **During Reading or Revisiting** Tell students that a symbol is something that stands for something beyond itself. Ask:

- What does the bat symbolize in the story? *(Possible answer: The bat symbolizes people who are tricksters or sneaky. Adults told young people the legend to teach them not to be tricksters like the bat.)*

■ **After Reading or Revisiting** Have students discuss Reading Across Texts. Then have them do Writing Across Texts independently. For example, they might write the last page of a short story in which the bat learns his lesson, like Fernando.

Objectives
- Compare themes or moral lessons of several works of fiction from various cultures.

A Advanced · DAY **5**

■ **Reread For Fluency** Have students silently reread passages from the Advanced Reader *Our Essential Oceans*. Then have them reread aloud with a partner or individually. As students read, monitor fluency and provide corrective feedback. If students read fluently on the first reading, they do not need to reread three to four times. Assess the fluency of students in this group using p. 201j.

■ **Retell** Have students summarize the main idea and key details from the Advanced Reader *Our Essential Oceans*.

■ **Now Try This** Have students complete their projects. You may wish to review their work to see if they need additional ideas. Have them share their finished work with classmates.

Objectives
- Read aloud grade-level stories with fluency.

The ELL lessons are organized by strands. Use them to scaffold the weekly curriculum of lessons or during small group time instruction.

Academic Language

Students will hear or read the following academic language in this week's core instruction. As students encounter the vocabulary, provide a simple definition or concrete example. Then ask students to suggest an example or synonym of the word and identify available cognates.

Skill Words	compare (*comparar*) contrast (*contrastar*) compound words	regular irregular plural (*plural*)
Concept Words	honesty truth	important (*importante*)

Spanish cognates in parentheses

Concept Development

 Why is honesty important?

■ **Preteach Concept**

- **Prior Knowledge** Have students turn to pp. 176 –177 in the Student Edition. Call attention to the picture of the children taking a test and tap into students' knowledge of test taking. Why is it important not to look at anyone else's paper when you are taking a test? What could happen if you looked at your neighbor's paper?

- **Discuss Concept** Elicit students' knowledge and experience of honesty. Why should people tell the truth? What can happen if people don't tell the truth? Who is in the picture with the boy and the bicycle? What do you think happened? Supply background information as needed.

- **Poster Talk-Through** Read the Poster Talk-Through on ELL Poster 6 aloud and work through the Day 1 activities.

■ **Daily Concept and Vocabulary Development** Use the daily activities on ELL Poster 6 to build concept and vocabulary knowledge.

Objectives
- Use prior knowledge and experiences to understand meanings in English.
- Use accessible language and learn new and essential language in the process.
- Speak using grade-level content area vocabulary in context to internalize new English words and build academic language proficiency.

Content Objectives
- Use concept vocabulary related to hontesty.

Language Objectives
- Express ideas in response to art and discussion.
- Learn new expressions.

Daily Planner

DAY 1	• **Frontload Concept** • **Preteach** Comprehension Skill, Vocabulary, Phonics/Spelling, Conventions • **Writing**
DAY 2	• **Review** Concept, Vocabulary, Comprehension Skill • **Frontload Main Selection** • **Practice** Phonics/Spelling, Conventions/Writing
DAY 3	• **Review** Concept, Comprehension Skill, Vocabulary, Conventions/Writing • **Reread Main Selection** • **Practice** Phonics/Spelling
DAY 4	• **Review Concept** • **Read ELL/ELD Readers** • **Practice** Phonics/Spelling, Conventions/Writing
DAY 5	• **Review** Concept, Vocabulary, Comprehension Skill, Phonics/Spelling, Conventions • **Reread ELL/ELD Readers** • **Writing**

See the ELL Handbook for ELL Workshops with targeted instruction.

Concept Talk Video

Use the Concept Talk Video Routine (*ELL Handbook*, p. 477) to build background knowledge about honesty.

Language Opportunity

Use the unit opener to discuss a saying: *Do the right thing*. What does it mean to do the right thing? In what instances in school would students need to think about doing the right thing?

Support for English Language Learners

Language Objectives

- Understand and use basic vocabulary.
- Learn meanings of grade-level vocabulary.
- Write using content-based vocabulary.

Language Opportunity: Writing

Have students use the lesson words for writing. They might use the words to write a journal entry about a trip to the beach or a story about the fate of the crew of a boat on a deserted island.

Basic Vocabulary

■ **High-Frequency Words** Use the vocabulary routines and the high-frequency word list on p. 448 of the *ELL Handbook* to systematically teach newcomers the first 300 sight words in English. Students who began learning ten words per week at the beginning of the year are now learning 51–60 words.

Lesson Vocabulary

■ **Preteach** Use the following routine to introduce the Lesson Vocabulary:

1. Distribute copies of this week's Word Cards *(ELL Handbook,* p. 59).

2. Display ELL Poster 6 and reread the Poster Talk-Through.

3. Using the poster illustrations, model how a word's meaning can be expressed with other similar words: The fish *concealed,* or hid, itself behind the rock.

4. Use these sentences to reveal the meaning of the other words.

   - Mila found some *driftwood* on the beach. (wood washed ashore by water)

   - Amy saw the sharp spines on the *sea urchins* in the aquarium. (small, spiny creatures)

   - Mario noticed green *algae* growing on the pond. (tiny organisms that grow in water; seaweeds are a type of algae)

   - The mother used the *tweezers* to pull out the splinter. (metal holder used to grab small things)

   - Matteo likes to take naps in a *hammock.* (netting tied between two trees)

   - Mama spoke *sternly* to Lucas when he broke a window. (firmly)

   - Sarah *lamented* the loss of her goldfish. (mourned)

Objectives

- Use visual and contextual support and support from peers and teachers to read grade-appropriate content area text, enhance and confirm understanding, and develop vocabulary, grasp of language structures, and background knowledge needed to comprehend increasingly challenging language.

 E L L English Language Learners

■ **Reteach** Read these statements and have students answer "true" or "false" to check their understanding of the vocabulary.

- If you speak to someone *sternly*, you speak softly. **(false)**

- *Concealed* means out in the open. **(false)**

- *Driftwood* is a piece of wood. **(true)**

- A sea *urchin* is an animal you find on land. **(false)**

- You can look for *algae* in your desk. **(false)**

- The word *lamented* means the same as "grieved" or "mourned." **(true)**

- You can take a nap in a *hammock*. **(true)**

- *Tweezers* are used to grab big things. **(false)**

Have students use the strategy of naming synonyms to remember the word meanings. Students may say such pairs as *algae/seaweed, hammock/bed, sternly/firmly,* and *lamented/mourned*. Have them use the words and synonyms in sentences.

■ **Writing** Place students into mixed proficiency groups. Provide each group with a set of Word Cards. Provide practice for students at the various language proficiency levels.

Leveled LS Support

Beginning Display a variety of sentence frames for students to complete with the Word Cards. Have students copy the sentences.

I found a piece of _____ on the beach. (driftwood)

There were blue-green _____ in the fish tank. (algae)

We slept in _____ on the beach. (hammocks)

Intermediate Ask students to choose a Word Card and write a sentence using that word.

Advanced/Advanced High Have students generate and write sentences using all of the Word Cards. Invite students to share them with the class.

Language Objectives

- Produce drawings, phrases, and short sentences to show understanding of Lesson Vocabulary.

- Speak using the strategy of naming synonyms.

ELL Teacher Tip

For English learners who have developed emergent writing skills in their home languages, build on these skills by occasionally having them write in both languages. Short sentences and picture labels written both in a home language and in English help students with writing and English acquisition.

Objectives

- Expand and internalize initial English vocabulary by learning and using high-frequency English words necessary for identifying and describing people, places, and objects, by retelling simple stories and basic information represented or supported by pictures, and by learning and using routine language needed for classroom communication.

Support for English Language Learners

Content Objectives

- Monitor and adjust oral comprehension.

Language Objectives

- Discuss oral passages.
- Use a graphic organizer to take notes.
- Use linguistic support to understand spoken languages.

ELL Teacher Tip

As you read the story, have students act out what Mikey is doing.

Language Opportunity: Essential Language

Use the accessible language of the Read Aloud to teach the students essential language, such as *honest, Grandpa, forget,* and *smiles.* Have students use these words orally in original sentences to be sure they know their meanings.

ELL English Language Learners

Listening Comprehension

Always Do the Right Thing

Mikey is practicing throwing baseballs outside. His grandfather has painted a bull's eye on the wall. A bull's eye is a circle inside a circle inside a circle. Mikey throws balls at the bull's eye to see if he can hit it.

Grandpa watches as Mikey throws the ball. The ball goes over the wall. It crashes into the yard next door. The ball has knocked over a bin that contains bottles and cans. Grandpa waits for Mikey to pick them up. But instead Mikey stomps on his glove and then comes into the house.

Mikey is smiling. He tells Grandpa that he hit the bull's eye every time. Grandpa talks about to Mikey about being honest.

Mikey admits that he was a little bit wild. But Grandpa is more concerned that Mikey was not honest. Mikey looks down and frowns. He says, "Grandpa, I need to do something that I forgot to do." Mikey walks to the door but turns back. He says, "I did not forget to do it. I just did not do it. But I am going to do it right now."

Grandpa watches as Mikey picks up all the bottles and cans that he knocked over and puts them back into the bin. Grandpa nods at Mikey and smiles.

Prepare for the Read Aloud The modified Read Aloud above prepares students for listening to the oral reading "Bullseye" on p. 177b.

- **First Listening: Listen to Understand** Write the title of the Read Aloud on the board. This is a story about a boy who does something wrong. What does the boy do wrong? After reading the first time, provide linguistic support to understand the spoken language of the Read Aloud.

- **Second Listening: Listen to Check Understanding** Make a Venn diagram to compare and contrast the characters of Mikey and Grandpa. Now listen again to make sure you included all the ways that the characters are alike and different.

Objectives

- Demonstrate listening comprehension of increasingly complex spoken English by following directions, retelling or summarizing spoken messages, responding to questions and requests, collaborating with peers, and taking notes commensurate with content and grade-level needs.

Phonics and Spelling

■ **Digraphs *ch, sh*** Use Sound-Spelling Cards 34 and 47 to teach the sounds, pronunciations, and spellings of *ch* and *sh*.

• Display Card 34 to teach *ch*. Have students practice producing sounds in English. This is a *chair*. The beginning sound is /ch/. When you say /ch/, your lips are open and your teeth are close together. Say it with me: /ch/. Point to the letters *ch*. The sound /ch/ is spelled *ch*. Have students say /ch/ several times as you point to *ch* so students learn the relationship between sounds and letters. What is the sound for these letters? Write *chin* on the board and model blending. Say each sound individually. Then run your hand under *chin* as you blend the whole word: /ch/ /i/ /n/, *chin*.

• Follow the routine above to teach *sh* (Sound-Spelling Card 47). Say words with both sounds for students to distinguish between them. Students can then write the words with the correct letter combinations.

For more practice pronouncing these sounds, use the Modeled Pronunciation Audio CD Routine (*ELL Handbook,* p. 477). Have students use the CD as a model for their own oral language. They can work with partners to listen for words pronounced correctly.

Word Analysis: Compound Words

■ **Preteach and Model** Write *seawater* on the board. *Seawater* is made up of two words: *sea* and *water.* Seawater is water that comes from the sea. This is how I read a compound word. First, I figure out the first word. **Cover *water* and read *sea*.** Then I read the second word. **Cover *sea* and read *water*.** Then I read the two parts together. **Run your hand under the word parts and read.**

■ **Practice** Write these words on the board: *sugarcane, roadside, driftwood, homework, backpack, classroom, doghouse.*

Beginning/Intermediate Read the words aloud with students. Then have students come to the board and draw a line between the two words.

Advanced/Advanced High Have partners work together to write sentences for the words. Have volunteers share their sentences.

Content Objectives
• Identify and define words in compound words.
• Identify digraphs *ch* and *sh*.

Language Objectives
• Apply phonics and decoding skills to vocabulary.
• Discuss meanings of compound words.
• Monitor and self-correct.
• Distinguish sounds of English.
• Practice producing sounds.

 Transfer Skills

The consonant digraphs /ch/ and /sh/ may sound alike to some English language learners. Have students practice holding the /sh/ sound: /shhhh/. Point out that with /ch/ they cannot hold the sound: /ch/.

Content Objectives

- Identify the difference between compare and contrast.

Language Objectives

- Speak using connecting words.
- Give information in a speaking assignment.
- Compare and contrast a character in a reading.
- Write comparisons and contrasts about a character in a reading.

Language Opportunity: Speaking

Tell students that comparisons and contrasts are often joined by connecting words, such as *similarly, likewise, still, like* (comparisons) and *although, instead of,* and *more than* (contrasts).

ELL English Language Learners

Comprehension
Compare and Contrast

■ **Preteach** To compare is to tell how things are the same. To contrast is to tell how things are different. Have students turn to Envision It! on p. EI•6 in the Student Edition. Read the text aloud together. Have students talk about the similarities and differences between the two bicycles.

■ **Reteach** Distribute copies of the Picture It! (*ELL Handbook,* p. 60). Explain to students how "comparing" and "contrasting" can help us understand the characters and events in a story better. When we compare and contrast the characters and events, we think about things in new ways. We can see how things are connected or how they are different. Read the directions aloud. Explain that charts can help readers organize and compare and contrast information. (Honest: Maria tells her teacher why she did not finish her homework; Her report is in her own words; She does not cheat on tests. Not Honest: Maria doesn't always tell her mother the truth; She blames her brother for things she did; She didn't ask her sister if she could borrow her sweater.)

Beginning/Intermediate Reread the paragraphs aloud as students read along. Guide them as they compare and contrast Maria's behavior. Then have them write this information on the chart.

Advanced/Advanced High Have students reread the paragraphs, looking at the chart as they read. Then have them fill in the chart with as many details as possible.

MINI-LESSON

Give Information

Have students give information in a speaking assignment by comparing and contrasting. Have them compare and contrast with familiar topics, such as two kinds of plants, animals, weather systems, or rocks. As they speak, they should use the words that signal comparisons and contrasts.

Objectives

- Understand the general meaning, main points, and important details of spoken language ranging from situations in which topics, language, and contexts are familiar to unfamiliar.

ELL English Language Learners

Reading Comprehension
At the Beach

Student Edition pp. 182–183

- **Frontloading** Read the title aloud. Explain that the story is about honesty. Discuss what honesty is. Ask students why it is important to be honest. Guide students on a picture walk through *At the Beach*. Ask students to predict what happens to the characters in the story. During reading, pause and invite students to adjust their predictions. Provide students with a two-column chart to fill out as they read the selection. Supply these headings: *What might happen? What did happen?*

Sheltered Reading Ask questions to guide students' comprehension:

- p. 184: Where was the family going? (to Guanabo Beach)

- p. 187: What warning did Mami and Aunt Olga give to the children? (not to go too far)

- p. 188: What happened to Javi? (He slipped on algae-covered rock and stepped on a sea urchin.)

- p. 193: What did Mami say after Fernando told her the truth? (She told him that she should punish him, but she wouldn't because he had the courage to tell the truth.)

- **Fluency: Read with Expression** Remind students that reading with expression means to read like you are speaking when you talk to a friend. Read the paragraph on p. 187 that starts with *I was getting very hungry* and end with the second to last paragraph. Model the excitement in your voice when you read, *Let's explore the reef!* The exclamation point gives a clue about how to read expressively. Have pairs choose a paragraph on p. 188. Have students read as their partners listen and offer feedback. For more practice, use the Fluency: Oral Reading Routine (*ELL Handbook,* p. 474).

After Reading Help students retell the story in order with the Retelling Cards. Ask questions that prompt students to correctly order the details of the story.

Content Objectives
- Monitor and adjust comprehension.
- Make and adjust predictions.

Language Objectives
- Read grade-level text with expression.
- Summarize text using visual support.

Audio Support
Students can prepare for reading *At the Beach* by using the eSelection or the AudioText CD. See the AudioText CD Routine (*ELL Handbook,* p. 477).

Language Opportunity: Speaking and Listening
Turn to p. 201 of the Student Edition and read the directions aloud for students. Students should use the directions to create a talk show with their groups. Have groups listen to each other and retell what they have learned to show comprehension.

Support for English Language Learners

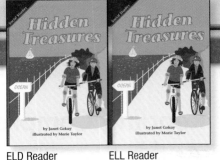

ELL *English Language Learners*

For additional leveled instruction, see the **ELL/ELD Reader Teaching Guide.**

Comprehension
Hidden Treasures

■ **Before Reading** Distribute copies of the ELL and ELD Readers, *Hidden Treasures,* to students at their reading level.

• **Preview** Read the title aloud with students. This is a story about two girls who find hidden treasures on the beach. Invite students to look through the pictures and name what they see. Have them predict what the hidden treasures might be.

• **Set a Purpose for Reading** Let's read to figure out what the hidden treasures are.

■ **During Reading** Follow the Reading Routine for both reading groups.

1. Read the entire Reader aloud slowly.

ELD Reader   ELL Reader

2. Reread pp. 1–9, pausing to build background or model comprehension. Have Beginning students finger-point as you read. Use the questions in the chart to check students' comprehension.

3. Have students reread pp. 1–9 in pairs, taking turns reading alternate pages.

4. Repeat steps 2–3 for pp. 10–12 of the Reader.

■ **After Reading** Use the exercises on the inside back cover of each Reader and invite students to share their writing. In a whole-group discussion, ask students, What were the hidden treasures in this story? Record their answers on the board and invite them to point to pictures in the book to support their answers.

ELD Reader Beginning/Intermediate

• **pp. 2–3** Who is Katie? (Sophie's little sister)

• **pp. 10–11** What do Sophie and Katie do with the wallet? (They mail it back to the woman who owns it.)

Writing What did Sophie and Katie do that shows they are honest? Find the sentence in the book that tells what they did. Copy the sentence. Then read it aloud to your partner.

ELL Reader Advanced/Advanced High

• **pp. 2–3** Why does Sophie want to go to the beach? (to look for driftwood)

• **p. 12** How do Sophie and Katie feel about returning the wallet to Mrs. Porter? (happy and proud)

Study Guide Distribute copies of the ELL Reader Study Guide (*ELL Handbook,* p. 64). Help students look back through the Reader in order to compare and contrast Sophie and Katie and to fill in the graphic organizer. Review their responses together. (See *ELL Handbook,* pp. 209–212.)

Objectives
• Express opinions, ideas, and feelings ranging from communicating single words and short phrases to participating in extended discussions on a variety of social and grade-appropriate academic topics.
• Demonstrate comprehension of increasingly complex English by participating in shared reading, retelling or summarizing material, responding to questions, and taking notes commensurate with content area and grade level needs.

 English Language Learners

Conventions
Regular and Irregular Plural Nouns

■ **Preteach** Remind students that plural nouns tell about more than one person, place, thing, or idea. Explain that regular plural nouns follow these rules:

If a noun ends in *s, x, ch,* or *sh,* you add *-es* to the end. (**toss** = tosses)

If a noun ends in a consonant plus *y,* you change the *y* to *i* and add *-es.* (**fly** = flies)

For most other nouns, just add *s.* (**dog** = dogs)

Explain that irregular plural nouns follow these rules:

If a noun ends with *-fe,* you change the *f* to *v* and add *-s.* (**life** = lives)

If a noun ends with *-o,* add *-es.* (**tomato** = tomatoes)

If a noun ends with *-us,* change the *us* to *i.* (**cactus** = cacti)

Point out that sometimes the singular and plural noun are the same. (**deer** = deer)

■ **Practice** Have students use the following nouns for the exercise below: *girls, shells, fishes, houses, knives, potatoes, sheep.*

Beginning/Intermediate Have students pick two nouns. Guide students in categorizing them as regular or irregular plural nouns.

Advanced/Advanced High Have students categorize all the words above as regular or irregular nouns and explain their choice.

■ **Reteach** Read aloud from the ELL Reader. Ask students to listen for plural nouns during the reading. Display a sentence from the text. Ask students to identify the plural nouns. Have them tell if each noun is regular or irregular.

■ **Practice** Provide students with a list of words: *table, computer, leaf, octopus, potato.*

Beginning/Intermediate Have students pick one or two nouns and change them into plural nouns. Assist students as they identify whether they are regular or irregular.

Advanced/Advanced High Have students change each word into a plural noun. Ask students to identify if the plural noun is regular or irregular and to explain their choice.

Content Objectives
- Decode and use regular and irregular plural nouns.
- Correctly form regular and irregular plural nouns.

Language Objectives
- Speak using the pattern of regular and irregular plural nouns.
- Write regular and irregular plural nouns.

 ## Transfer Skills
Irregular Plurals English learners may add *-s* to irregular nouns in sentences or to nouns for which English uses the singular form for a quantity: *sheeps, mens, clothings.*

Grammar Jammer
For more practice with nouns, use the Grammar Jammer for this target skill. See the Grammar Jammer Routine (*ELL Handbook,* p. 478) for suggestions on using this learning tool.

Objectives
- Speak using a variety of grammatical structures, sentence lengths, sentence types, and connecting words with increasing accuracy and ease as more English is acquired.

At the Beach **DI•24**

Support for English Language Learners

Content Objectives

- Identify descriptive language.
- Understand the purpose of descriptive language in writing.

Language Objectives

- Write sentences using descriptive language.
- Share feedback for editing and revising.

Language Opportunity: Describing

Turn to Student Edition p. 196 and read the prompt. Have students speak and then write a description about learning something important. Tell them that, as they describe, they should use specific details to bring the experience to life for listeners and readers. Prompt them by asking questions that elicit more specific details.

ELL — English Language Learners

Descriptive Language

■ **Introduce** Display the writing model and read it aloud. Writers use descriptive language to help readers form a picture in their minds. Descriptive language often engages all five senses: sight, sound, smell, taste, and touch. Underline the words *salty smell, loud roar,* and *icy water.* These words help you picture the beach in your mind.

Writing Model

I breathed in the salty smell of the ocean. We were finally at the beach! I could not hear anything over the loud roar of the waves. I jumped in. The icy water made me shiver. Brrr!

■ **Practice** Write the following incomplete paragraph on the board. Work with students to fill in the blanks with descriptive language that paints a picture.

We visited an amusement park. There was so much to do there! We saw the _____ as soon as we walked in. Everywhere we heard sounds of _____. I could not wait to taste the _____. Point out that sentences in the model vary in length. The variety makes the writing flow in an interesting way. Have students write sentences of varying length.

■ **Write** Invite students to write a paragraph about a place they have visited. Have them use descriptive language.

Beginning Have students write the name of the place they visited at the top of their paper. Then have them draw details about the place and dictate to you sentences using descriptive language. Write out their sentences and have students copy them.

Intermediate Supply students with sentence frames: *I saw _____. It looked like _____. It sounded like _____.* Have students fill in the sentence frames with as many descriptive words as they can.

Advanced/Advanced High Have students develop their paragraphs independently. Encourage them to use descriptive language in their writing. Then have pairs exchange papers and provide feedback for revising and editing.

Objectives

- Narrate, describe, and explain with increasing specificity and detail as more English is acquired.
- Narrate, describe, and explain with increasing specificity and detail to fulfill content area writing needs as more English is acquired.

This Week's ELL Overview

ELL Handbook

- Maximize Literacy and Cognitive Engagement
- Research Into Practice
- Full Weekly Support for Every Selection

Hold the Flag High

- Multi-Lingual Summaries in Five Languages
- Selection-Specific Vocabulary Word Cards
- Frontloading/Reteaching for Comprehension Skill Lessons
- ELD and ELL Reader Study Guides

- Transfer Activities
- Professional Development

Daily Leveled ELL Notes

ELL notes appear throughout this week's instruction and ELL Support is on the DI pages of your Teacher's Edition. The following is a sample of an ELL note from this week.

English Language Learners

Beginning Help students look up the words *pride, defend,* and *troops.* Use gestures, pictures, or motions to explain the words.

Intermediate Have students look up *performance, bronze,* and *ceremony.* Have them explain the words in short sentences.

Advanced Have students look up *dedicated, impressive,* and *contributed.* Ask them to name synonyms.

Advanced High Have students look up and read definitions for *erect, regiment,* and *memorial.* Ask them to apply the words to the story.

ELL by Strand

The ELL lessons on this week's Support for English Language Learners pages are organized by strand. They offer additional scaffolding for the core curriculum. Leveled support notes on these pages address the different proficiency levels in your class. See pages DI•41–DI•50.

ELL Guy
Dr. Jim Cummins

The Three Pillars of ELL Instruction

ELL Strands	Activate Prior Knowledge	Access Content	Extend Language
Vocabulary pp. DI•42–DI•43	Preteach	Reteach	Leveled Writing Activities
Reading Comprehension p. DI•47	Frontloading	Sheltered Reading	After Reading
Phonics, Spelling, and Word Analysis p. DI•45	Teach	Model	Leveled Practice Activities
Listening Comprehension p. DI•44	Prepare for the Read Aloud	First Listening	Second Listening
Conventions and Writing pp. DI•49–DI•50	Preteach	Leveled Practice Activities	Leveled Writing Activities
Concept Development p. DI•41	Activate Prior Knowledge	Discuss Concept	Daily Concept and Vocabulary Development

This Week's Practice Stations Overview

Six Weekly Practice Stations with Leveled Activities can be found at the beginning of each week of instruction. For this week's Practice Stations, see pp. 202h–202i.

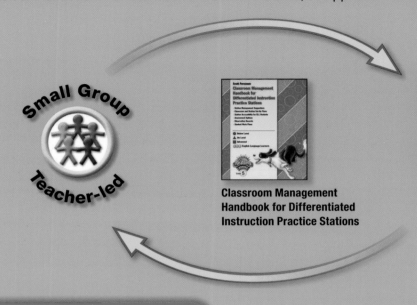

Small Group Teacher-led

Classroom Management Handbook for Differentiated Instruction Practice Stations

Practice Stations

Daily Leveled Center Activities

○ Below   ■ Advanced

△ On-Level   E L L

Practice Stations Flip Charts

	Word Wise	Word Work	Words to Know	Let's Write	Read for Meaning	Get Fluent

Objectives	• Spell words that contain digraphs *th, sh, ch,* and *ph.*	• Identify and write words that contain the digraphs *th, sh, ch,* and *ph.*	• Identify the meaning of unfamiliar words.	• Write a vivid description.	• Compare and contrast.	• Read aloud dialogue with expression.
Materials	• *Word Wise* Flip Chart Activity 7 • Teacher-made word cards • paper • pencils	• *Word Work* Flip Chart Activity 7 • Teacher-made word cards • paper • pencils	• *Words to Know* Flip Chart Activity 7 • Tested Vocabulary Cards • paper • pencils	• *Let's Write* Flip Chart Activity 7 • paper • pencils	• *Read for Meaning* Flip Chart Activity 7 • Leveled Readers • paper • pencils	• *Get Fluent* Flip Chart Activity 7 • Leveled Readers

This Week on Reading Street!

Question of the Week

What are the risks in helping others?

Daily Plan

Don't Wait Until Friday

Whole Group

- ◉ Sequence
- ◉ Unknown Words
- • Fluency/Accuracy
- • Research and Inquiry

MONITOR PROGRESS | **Success Predictor**

Day 1 Check Oral Vocabulary	Days 2–3 Check Retelling	Day 4 Check Fluency	Day 5 Check Oral Vocabulary

Small Group

Teacher-Led

- • Reading Support
- • Skill Support
- • Fluency Practice

Practice Stations

Independent Activities

Customize Literacy More support for a balanced literacy approach, see pp. CL•1–CL•47

Customize Writing More support for a customized writing approach, see pp. CW•1–CW•10

Whole Group

- • Writing: Informal Letter
- • Conventions: Possessive Nouns

Assessment

- • Weekly Tests
- • Day 5 Assessment
- • Fresh Reads

You Are Here!
Unit 2
Week 2

This Week's Reading Selections

Main Selection
Genre: **Literary Nonfiction**

Paired Selection
21st Century Skills

Leveled Readers

ELL and ELD Readers

Resources on Reading Street!

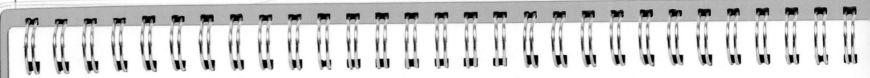

	Build Concepts			**Comprehension**			
Whole Group	 Let's Talk About pp. 202–203			 Envision It! Skills/ Strategies	 Comprehension Skills Lesson pp. 204–205		
Go Digital	• Concept Talk Video			• Envision It! Animations • eSelections			
Small Group and Independent Practice	 Hold the Flag High pp. 208–209	ELL and ELD Readers	Leveled Readers	 Hold the Flag High pp. 208–209	ELL and ELD Readers	Leveled Readers	 Envision It! Skills/ Strategies
				Reader's and Writer's Notebook	Practice Station Flip Chart		
Go Digital	• eReaders • eSelections			• Envision It! Animations • eSelections • eReaders			
Customize Literacy	• Leveled Readers			• Envision It! Skills and Strategies Handbook • Leveled Readers			
Go Digital	• Concept Talk Video • Big Question Video • eReaders			• Envision It! Animations • eReaders			

Question of the Week
What are the risks in helping others?

Vocabulary

Envision It!
Vocabulary
Cards

Vocabulary Skill Lesson
pp. 206–207

- Envision It! Vocabulary Cards
- Vocabulary Activities

Fluency

Let's Learn It!
pp. 228–229

- eSelections
- eReaders

Conventions and Writing

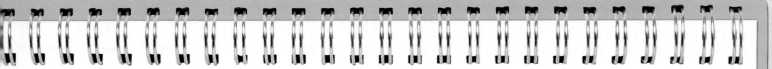

Let's Write It! pp. 222–223

- Grammar Jammer

Envision It!
Vocabulary
Cards

Hold the Flag High
pp. 208–209

Practice
Station
Flip Chart

Words!

Reader's
and Writer's
Notebook

Hold the Flag High
pp. 208–209

Practice
Station
Flip Chart

Leveled
Readers

ELL and ELD
Readers

Reader's
and Writer's
Notebook

Hold the Flag High
pp. 208–209

Practice
Station
Flip Chart

- Envision It! Vocabulary Cards
- Vocabulary Activities
- eSelections

- eSelections
- eReaders

- Grammar Jammer

- Envision It! Vocabulary Cards

- Leveled Readers

- Reader's and Writer's Notebook

- Vocabulary Activities

- eReaders

- Grammar Jammer

You Are Here!
Unit 2
Week 2

My 5-Day Planner for Reading Street!

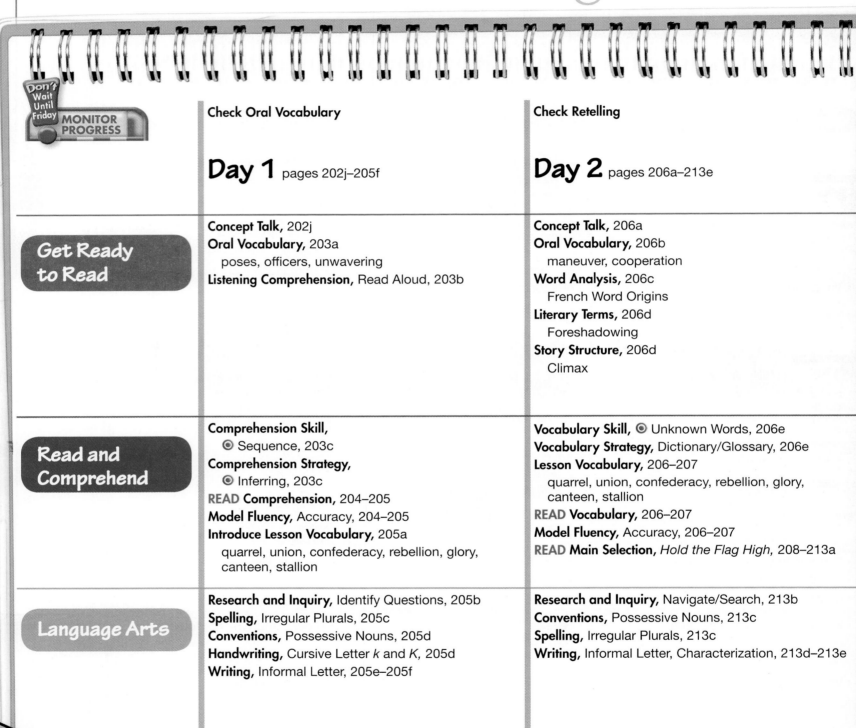

Don't Wait Until Friday

MONITOR PROGRESS

	Check Oral Vocabulary	Check Retelling
	Day 1 pages 202j–205f	**Day 2** pages 206a–213e
Get Ready to Read	**Concept Talk,** 202j **Oral Vocabulary,** 203a poses, officers, unwavering **Listening Comprehension,** Read Aloud, 203b	**Concept Talk,** 206a **Oral Vocabulary,** 206b maneuver, cooperation **Word Analysis,** 206c French Word Origins **Literary Terms,** 206d Foreshadowing **Story Structure,** 206d Climax
Read and Comprehend	**Comprehension Skill,** ◉ Sequence, 203c **Comprehension Strategy,** ◉ Inferring, 203c **READ Comprehension,** 204–205 **Model Fluency,** Accuracy, 204–205 **Introduce Lesson Vocabulary,** 205a quarrel, union, confederacy, rebellion, glory, canteen, stallion	**Vocabulary Skill,** ◉ Unknown Words, 206e **Vocabulary Strategy,** Dictionary/Glossary, 206e **Lesson Vocabulary,** 206–207 quarrel, union, confederacy, rebellion, glory, canteen, stallion **READ Vocabulary,** 206–207 **Model Fluency,** Accuracy, 206–207 **READ Main Selection,** *Hold the Flag High,* 208–213a
Language Arts	**Research and Inquiry,** Identify Questions, 205b **Spelling,** Irregular Plurals, 205c **Conventions,** Possessive Nouns, 205d **Handwriting,** Cursive Letter *k* and *K,* 205d **Writing,** Informal Letter, 205e–205f	**Research and Inquiry,** Navigate/Search, 213b **Conventions,** Possessive Nouns, 213c **Spelling,** Irregular Plurals, 213c **Writing,** Informal Letter, Characterization, 213d–213e

You Are Here! Unit 2 Week 2

Check Retelling	Check Fluency	Check Oral Vocabulary
Day 3 pages 214a–223c	**Day 4** pages 224a–229e	**Day 5** pages 229f–229q

Concept Talk, 214a
Oral Vocabulary, 214b
  nation, trembling
Comprehension Check, 214c
Check Retelling, 214d
	Concept Talk, 224a
	Oral Vocabulary, 224b
	  sacrifice, audacity, brazen
	21st Century Skills,
	  Website, 224c
		Concept Wrap Up, 229f
		Check Oral Vocabulary, 229g
		  poses, officers, unwavering,
		  maneuver, cooperation, nation,
		  trembling, sacrifice, audacity,
		  brazen
		Amazing Ideas, 229g
		Review ⊙ Sequence, 229h
		Review ⊙ Unknown Words, 229h
		Review Word Analysis, 229i
		Review Literary Terms, 229i

READ Main Selection, *Hold the Flag High*, 214–219a
Retelling, 220–221
Think Critically, 221a
Model Fluency, Accuracy, 221b
Research and Study Skills, Parts of a Book, 221c
	READ Paired Selection, "How to Fold the American Flag," 224–227a
	Let's Learn It! 228–229a
	  Fluency: Accuracy
	  Vocabulary: Unknown Words
	  Listening and Speaking: Informational Speech
		Fluency Assessment, WCPM, 229j–229k
		Comprehension Assessment, ⊙ Sequence, 229l–229m

Research and Inquiry, Analyze, 221d **Conventions,** Possessive Nouns, 221e **Spelling,** Irregular Plurals, 221e **Let's Write It!** Informal Letter, 222–223a **Writing,** Informal Letter, Voice, 222b–223c	**Research and Inquiry,** Synthesize, 229b **Conventions,** Possessive Nouns, 229c **Spelling,** Irregular Plurals, 229c **Writing,** Informal Letter, Revising, 229d–229e	**Research and Inquiry,** Communicate, 229n **Conventions,** Possessive Nouns, 229o **Spelling Test,** Irregular Plurals, 229o **Writing,** Informal Letter, Possessive Nouns, 229p–229q **Quick Write for Fluency,** 229q

Week 2

Grouping Options for Differentiated Instruction
Turn the page for the small group time lesson plan.

Planning Small Group Time on Reading Street!

SMALL GROUP TIME RESOURCES

Look for this Small Group Time box each day to help meet the individual needs of all your students. Differentiated Instruction lessons appear on the DI pages at the end of each week.

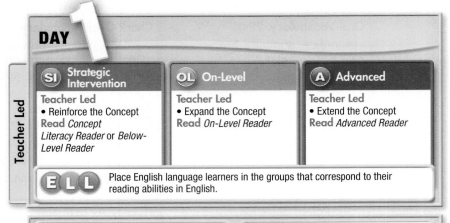

DAY 1

Teacher Led

SI Strategic Intervention

Teacher Led
• Reinforce the Concept
Read *Concept Literacy Reader* or *Below-Level Reader*

OL On-Level

Teacher Led
• Expand the Concept
Read *On-Level Reader*

A Advanced

Teacher Led
• Extend the Concept
Read *Advanced Reader*

ELL Place English language learners in the groups that correspond to their reading abilities in English.

Practice Stations
• Read for Meaning
• Get Fluent
• Word Work

Independent Activities
• Concept Talk Video
• *Reader's and Writer's Notebook*
• Research and Inquiry

ELL Reader
Advanced
Advanced High

ELD Reader
Beginning
Intermediate

ELL Poster

Day 1

SI Strategic Intervention	**Reinforce the Concept,** DI•26–DI•27 **Read Concept Literacy Reader or Below-Level Reader**
OL On-Level	**Expand the Concept,** DI•32 **Read On-Level Reader**
A Advanced	**Extend the Concept,** DI•37 **Read Advanced Reader**
ELL English Language Learners	DI•41–DI•50 **Frontload Concept Preteach Skills Writing**

Reading Street Response
to Intervention Kit

Reading Street
Practice Stations Kit

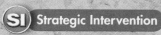 **SI** Strategic Intervention

Below-Level
Reader

*William Carney:
An American Hero*

by Mary Lindeen

Concept Literacy Reader

OL On-Level

A Spy in Disguise

On-Level Reader

A Advanced

The Most Dangerous
Woman in America

Advanced
Reader

HOLD THE FLAG HIGH

Hold the Flag High pp. 208–209

How to Fold the American Flag pp. 224–225

Week 2

Small Group Weekly Plan

Day 2	Day 3	Day 4	Day 5
Reinforce Comprehension, DI•28 **Revisit Main Selection**	**Reinforce Vocabulary,** DI•29 **Read/Revisit Main Selection**	**Reinforce Comprehension,** Practice Retelling DI•30 Genre Focus **Read/Revisit Paired Selection**	**Practice Fluency,** DI•31 **Reread Concept Literacy Reader** or **Below-Level Reader**
Expand Comprehension, DI•33 **Revisit Main Selection**	**Expand Vocabulary,** DI•34 **Read/Revisit Main Selection**	**Expand Comprehension,** Practice Retelling DI•35 Genre Focus **Read/Revisit Paired Selection**	**Practice Fluency,** DI•36 **Reread On-Level Reader**
Extend Comprehension, DI•38 **Revisit Main Selection**	**Extend Vocabulary,** DI•39 **Read/Revisit Main Selection**	**Extend Comprehension,** DI•40 **Read/Revisit Paired Selection**	**Practice Fluency,** DI•40 **Reread Advanced Reader**
DI•41–DI•50 **Review Concept/Skills** **Frontload Main Selection** **Practice**	DI•41–DI•50 **Review Concept/Skills** **Reread Main Selection** **Practice**	DI•41–DI•50 **Review Concept** **Read ELL/ELD Readers** **Practice**	DI•41–DI•50 **Reiew Concept/Skills** **Reread ELL/ELD Readers** **Writing**

Practice Stations for Everyone on Reading Street!

Word Wise
Digraphs *th, sh, ch,* and *ph*

Objectives
- Spell words that contain digraphs *th, sh, ch,* and *ph*.

Materials
- *Word Wise* Flip Chart Activity 7
- Teacher-made word cards
- paper • pencils

Differentiated Activities

⬤ Choose six word cards. Write your words in a list. Circle the digraph. Write sentence for each of the words. Add other words with these spellings to your list.

▲ Choose eight word cards that contain the *th, sh, ch,* or *ph* digraph. Write your words in a list, and circle the digraph. Write sentences for six of your words.

■ Choose ten word cards that contain the *th, sh, ch,* or *ph* digraph. Write your words in a list and circle the digraph. Write sentences for your words. Add other words with these spellings to your list.

Technology
- Online Dictionary

Word Work
Digraphs *th, sh, ch,* and *ph*

Objectives
- Identify and write words that contain the digraphs *th, sh, ch,* and *ph*.

Materials
- *Word Work* Flip Chart Activity 7
- Teacher-made word cards
- paper • pencils

Differentiated Activities

⬤ Use the magazines to find two words or pictures for each of the digraphs *th, sh, ch,* and *ph*. Write the words in a list. Quietly say each word. Circle the digraph in each word.

▲ Use the magazines to find three words or pictures for each of the digraphs *th, sh, ch,* and *ph*. Write the words in a list. Quietly say each word. Circle the digraph in each word.

■ Make a four-column chart using the digraphs *th, sh, ch,* and *ph* as headings. Think of four words for each digraph sound and write them under the correct heading. Quietly say the words.

Technology
- Modeled Pronunciation Audio CD

Words to Know
Unfamiliar words

Objectives
- Identify the meaning of unfamiliar words.

Materials
- *Words to Know* Flip Chart Activity 7
- Tested Vocabulary Cards
- paper • pencils

Differentiated Activities

⬤ Choose four vocabulary cards. Write each word and its definition. Write a sentence for each word that shows its meaning.

▲ Choose six vocabulary cards. Write each word and its definition. Write a sentence for each word that shows its meaning.

■ Choose eight vocabulary cards. Write each word, and provide its definition. Write a paragraph that uses context to demonstrate each word's meaning.

Technology
- Online Dictionary

You Are Here!
Unit 2
Week 2

Use this week's materials from the Reading Street Leveled Practice Stations Kit to organize this week's stations.

Key
● Below-Level Activities
▲ On-Level Activities
■ Advanced Activities

Practice Station Flip Chart

Let's Write!
Description

Objectives
• Write a vivid description.

Materials
• *Let's Write!* Flip Chart Activity 7
• paper • pencils

Differentiated Activities

● Think about a place you have visited. Write a description telling what the place is like. Use sensory details to help your readers imagine the place.

▲ Write a description telling about a place you have visited. Use sensory details to help your readers imagine the place. Describe why this place was memorable. Vary the length of your sentences.

■ Write a paragraph describing a place you have been to. Use sensory language to make your description vivid. Vary sentence length and give details telling why this place is memorable.

Technology
• Online Graphic Organizers

Read for Meaning
Compare and contrast

Objectives
• Compare and contrast.

Materials
• *Read for Meaning* Flip Chart Activity 7
• Leveled Readers
• paper • pencils

Differentiated Activities

● Choose a book from those your teacher provided. Choose two characters from the story. Write one sentence that tells how the characters are alike. Write one sentence that tells how the characters are different.

▲ Choose a book from those your teacher provided. Choose two characters from the story. Write a short paragraph that compares and contrasts the characters. Tell how they are alike and how they are different.

■ Choose a book from those your teacher provided. As you read, think about how two characters are alike and how they are different. Write a short paragraph that compares the characters and a short paragraph that contrasts them.

Technology
• Leveled Reader Database

Get Fluent
Practice fluent reading.

Objectives
• Read aloud dialogue with expression.

Materials
• *Get Fluent* Flip Chart Activity 7
• Leveled Readers

Differentiated Activities

● Work with a partner. Choose a Concept Literacy Reader or Below-Level Reader. Take turns reading a page from the book. Use the reader to practice correct expression. Provide feedback as needed.

▲ Work with a partner. Choose an On-Level Reader. Take turns reading a page from the book. Use the reader to practice correct expression. Provide feedback as needed.

■ Work with a partner. Choose an Advanced Reader. Take turns reading a page from the book. Use the reader to practice correct expression. Provide feedback as needed.

Technology
• Leveled Reader Database
• Reading Street Readers CD-ROM

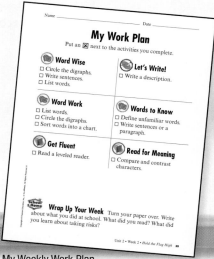

My Weekly Work Plan

Week 2

Objectives
• Introduce the weekly concept.
• Develop oral vocabulary.

Today at a Glance

Oral Vocabulary
poses, officers, unwavering

Comprehension
◉ Sequence
◉ Inferring

Reading
"A Flag Unfurled"

Fluency
Accuracy

Lesson Vocabulary
Tested vocabulary

Research and Inquiry
Identify questions

Spelling
Irregular plurals

Conventions
Possessive nouns

Handwriting
Cursive letters *k* and *K*

Writing
Informal letter

Concept Talk

Question of the Week

What are the risks in helping others?

Introduce the concept
To further explore the unit concept of the risks in helping others, this week students will read, write, and talk about the risks people may take when helping others. Write the Question of the Week on the board.

ROUTINE · Activate Prior Knowledge · Team Talk

1 **Think** Have students think for a minute about the risks of helping others.

2 **Pair** Have pairs of students discuss the Question of the Week. Remind students to elicit and consider each other's ideas.

3 **Share** Call on a few students to share their ideas with the group. Guide discussion and encourage elaboration with prompts such as:
• When have you taken a risk by helping someone else? Why?
• When might helping another person involve a sacrifice?

Routines Flip Chart

Anchored Talk

Develop oral vocabulary
Have students turn to pp. 202–203 in their Student Editions. Look at each of the photos. Then, use the prompts to guide discussion and create the *Risks in helping others* concept map.

• Why is one hiker helping the other? (They need to cooperate to complete the hike.) People often help others in order to accomplish something. Let's add *Motivation* to our concept map.

• The Coast Guard is trying to rescue people from the ocean. What risks do they take? (The winds are dangerous for the helicopter.) Coast Guard rescuers are trained to help in these situations, but the rescuers are still very brave. Let's add *Ways to help* to our concept map.

Objectives
• Listen to and interpret a speaker's messages and ask questions.

Oral Vocabulary

Let's **Talk** About

Taking Risks
⊚ Share ideas about why we must take risks.
⊚ Listen to and interpret a classmate's ideas about taking risks.
⊚ Ask questions about taking risks.

READING STREET ONLINE
CONCEPT TALK VIDEO
www.ReadingStreet.com

• You've learned **0 6 0** Amazing Words so far this year!

202

203

Student Edition pp. 202–203

Amazing Words

You've learned **0 6 0** words so far

You'll learn **0 1 0** words this week!

poses	nation
officers	trembling
unwavering	sacrifice
cooperation	audacity
maneuver	brazen

Writing on Demand ⏱

Writing fluency
Ask students to respond to the photos on pp. 202–203 by writing as well as they can and as much as they can about the risks in helping others.

E L L

English Language Learners
ELL support Additional ELL support and modified instruction is provided in the ELL Handbook and in the ELL Support lessons on pp. DI•41–DI•50

Listening comprehension
English learners will benefit from additional visual support to understand the key terms in the concept map. Use the pictures on pp. 202–203 to scaffold understanding.

Frontload for Read Aloud Use the modified Read Aloud on p. DI•44 of the ELL Support lessons to prepare students to listen to "Number the Stars" (p. 203b).

• These soldiers are on the island of Iwo Jima during World War II. What is their goal? (putting up an American flag) What is the risk? (They are in a vulnerable position and acting brave and patriotic.) Let's add *Qualities* to our concept map.

• After discussing the photos, ask: What are the risks in helping others?

```
          Risks in helping
               others
         ┌───────┼───────┐
    Motivation  Qualities  Ways to help
```

Connect to reading

Tell students this week they will read about people who take risks to help others during war and in other risky situations.

E L L **Preteach Concepts** Use the Day 1 instruction on ELL Poster 7 to assess and build background knowledge, develop concepts, and build oral vocabulary.

E L L Poster 7

Hold the Flag High **202–203**

Objectives
- Develop listening comprehension.
- Develop oral vocabulary.

Check Oral Vocabulary
SUCCESS PREDICTOR

Oral Vocabulary
Amazing Words

Introduce Amazing Words

Number the Stars on p. 203b tells about the risks a family takes to save a Jewish girl during World War II. Have students listen for the Amazing Words—*poses, officers,* and *unwavering*—as you read.

Model fluency

As you read *Number the Stars,* model accuracy with smooth, fluent reading.

Teach Amazing Words

Amazing Words Oral Vocabulary Routine

> poses
> officers
> unwavering

1 Introduce Write the word *unwavering* on the board. Have students say it aloud with you. In *Number the Stars,* the soldier stares at Ellen for an *unwavering* moment. Which words are context clues? *(finally, stared, long)* Supply a student-friendly definition ("steady or resolute; not moving").

2 Demonstrate Break into groups. Have students elicit suggestions from group members to demonstrate understanding. Ask: Would an Olympic swimmer be *unwavering* in pursuit of the finish line?

3 Apply Have students tell about a time when they pursued a goal in an *unwavering* way. Then have students demonstrate an *unwavering* stare.

See p. OV•2 to teach *poses* and *officers.*

Routines Flip Chart

Apply Amazing Words

To build oral language, have students discuss the Amazing Words.

MONITOR PROGRESS **Check Oral Vocabulary**

During discussion, listen for students' use of the Amazing Words.

If... students are unable to use the Amazing Words to discuss the concept,

then... use the Oral Vocabulary Routine in the Routines Flip Chart to demonstrate words in different contexts.

Day 1	**Days 2–3**	**Day 4**	**Day 5**
Check Oral Vocabulary	Check Retelling	Check Fluency	Check Oral Vocabulary

Number the Stars

by Lois Lowry

On September 29, 1943, Jewish people in Denmark were rounded up by Nazi soldiers, and then sent to death camps. In this passage a Jewish girl named Ellen Rosen poses as the sister of her best friend, Annemarie Johansen, as the Nazi soldiers search for Jews.

"Get up!" he ordered. "Come out here!"

Trembling, the two girls rose from the bed and followed him, brushing past the two remaining officers in the doorway, to the living room.

These men were older and their faces were set with anger.

"Your names?" the officer barked.

"Annemarie Johansen. And this is my—"

"Quiet! Let her speak for herself. Your name?" He was glaring at Ellen.

Ellen swallowed. "Lise," she said, and cleared her throat. "Lise Johansen."

The officer stared at them grimly.

"Now," Mama said in a strong voice, "you have seen that we are not hiding anything. May my children go back to bed?"

The officer ignored her. Suddenly he grabbed a handful of Ellen's hair. Ellen winced.

He laughed scornfully. "You have a blond child sleeping in the other room. And you have this blond daughter—" He gestured toward Annemarie with his head. "Where did you get the dark-haired one?"

For a moment no one spoke. Then Annemarie, watching in panic, saw her father move swiftly to the small bookcase and take out a book. She saw that he was holding the family photograph album. Very quickly he searched through its pages, found what he was looking for, and tore out three pictures from three separate pages.

He handed them to the German officer, who released Ellen's hair.

"You will see each of my daughters, each with her name written on the photograph," Papa said. Annemarie knew instantly which photographs he had chosen. The album had many snapshots—all the poorly focused pictures of school events and birthday parties. But it also contained a portrait, taken by a photographer, of each girl as a tiny infant. Mama had written, in her delicate handwriting, the name of each baby daughter across the bottom of those photographs. She realized too, with an icy feeling, why Papa had torn them from the book. At the bottom of each page, below the photograph itself,

(continued on p. 229s)

Oral Vocabulary

Success Predictor

Objectives

◎ Identify sequence to aid comprehension.

◎ Infer to aid comprehension.

• Read grade-level text with accuracy.

Skills Trace

◎ **Sequence**

Introduce U2W2D1; U3W1D1; U6W5D1

Practice U2W2D2; U2W2D3; U3W1D2; U3W1D3; U6W5D2; U6W5D3

Reteach/Review U1W1D2; U2W2D5; U2W3D3; U3W1D5; U6W2D1; U6W5D5

Assess/Test

Weekly Tests U2W2; U3W1; U6W5

Benchmark Tests U2; U6

KEY:

U=Unit   W=Week   D=Day

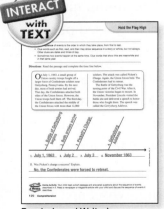

Reader's and Writer's
Notebook, p. 120

Skill ↔ Strategy

 Sequence

 Inferring

Introduce sequence

Envision It!

Sequence is the order in which events take place, from first to last. What clue words may show sequence? (*first, next, then, finally,* dates, times of day) Which clue words tell you that events are occurring at the same time? (*while* and *at the same time*) Have students turn to p. El•13 in the Student Edition to review sequence. Then read "A Flag Unfurled" with students.

Student Edition p. El•13

Model the skill

Think Aloud

Today we're going to read about the American flag. Have students follow along as you read the third paragraph of "A Flag Unfurled." What happened first: Betsy Ross sewed the flag or George Washington visited her shop? (Washington visited her shop.) How do you know? (because George Washington had visited the shop to show Betsy a design) Yes, Washington visited her shop first, even though the author tells about this event after she tells that Betsy Ross sewed the first flag.

Guide practice

Have students read "A Flag Unfurled" on their own. After they read, have them use a graphic organizer like the one on p. 204 and then identify sequence when they read the passage.

Strategy check

Inferring Remind students that if they have trouble understanding "A Flag Unfurled," they can use the strategy of inferring. Model the strategy of making inferences to understand the reading.

Model the strategy

Think Aloud

The second paragraph says that Washington did not want to use the British Union Jack flag for the country. How can you use your background knowledge to infer why not?

Envision It!

(I know that the United States became its own country during the Revolutionary War, so they probably did not want to have a flag that made it seem like they were still under British rule.) Have students review the strategy of inferring on p. El•18 of the Student Edition.

Student Edition p. El•18

On their own

For additional practice with Sequence, use p. 120 in the *Reader's and Writer's Notebook*.

Objectives
- Make inferences about a text and use evidence from the text to support understanding. • Summarize and paraphrase information in a text.

Envision It! | Skill Strategy

Skill

Strategy

READING STREET ONLINE
ENVISION IT! ANIMATIONS
www.ReadingStreet.com

Comprehension Skill

Sequence

- The sequence of events is the order in which events take place, from first to last.
- Clue words such as *first, next, then,* and *finally* may show sequence. Other clues are dates and the times of day.
- *While* and *at the same time* are clues that events are occurring at once.
- Use a graphic organizer like the one below to put the events in sequence. Then write a summary of the events in sequence.

 First Event → **Second Event** → **Third Event** → **Fourth Event**

Comprehension Strategy

Inferring

When you infer, you combine your own knowledge with evidence in the text to come up with an idea about what the author is presenting. Active readers often infer about the ideas, morals, and themes of a written work.

A Flag Unfurled

Do you know how many times the American flag has changed? From 1777 to 1960 Congress has changed the flag more than a dozen times!

In 1776, George Washington needed a symbol for the country. Washington had used the Grand Union during the Revolutionary War. The Grand Union flag had the British Union Jack in the upper left corner. In 1777, the Continental Congress passed the first Flag Act. The Act stated that the flag be made of 13 stripes and 13 stars.

One year earlier, Betsy Ross, a seamstress from Philadelphia, reported that she had sewed the first American flag. As the legend goes, Washington had visited her shop and showed her a flag design. The result was the first "stars and stripes" flag. It had a circle of 13 stars that represented the original 13 colonies.

The "stars and stripes" flag remained in use for several years. Then, in 1791, Vermont was added to the Union. Another star and stripe were added. After that, another star and stripe were added for every new state, until finally, in 1818, Congress decided to keep the number of stripes at 13, and allow the addition of a new star for each new state.

Strategy What inference can you make about the Grand Union flag? Why was it unsuitable for the new Union?

Skill What clue word tells you that the practice of adding stripes to the flag stopped?

Skill What is the earliest event that appears in this article?

Your Turn!

Need a Review? See the *Envision It! Handbook* for additional help with sequence and inferring.

Ready to Try It? Use what you learned about sequence as you read *Hold the Flag High.*

204

205

Student Edition pp. 204–205

Strategy Possible response: The Grand Union flag was unsuitable for the new Union because it had the British Union Jack in the corner. Since the colonists had just separated from Britain, they did not want the British Union Jack on their new flag.

Skill The word *finally* tells the reader that the United States had stopped adding stripes to the flag.

Skill The first event is in 1776, when Washington wanted a flag for his troops.

Academic Vocabulary

Sequence is the order of events in a story.

Model Fluency
Accuracy

Model fluent reading

Have students listen as you read paragraph 2 of "A Flag Unfurled" with accuracy. Explain that as you read about the Revolutionary War, you will try to read each word correctly.

 **Oral Rereading**

1. **Read** Have students read paragraph 2 of "A Flag Unfurled" orally.

2. **Reread** To achieve optimal fluency, students should reread the text three to four times.

3. **Corrective Feedback** Have students read aloud without you. Provide feedback about their accuracy and encourage them to read slowly enough so they can read each word accurately.

Routines Flip Chart

ELL

English Language Learners

Sequence Write these four statements on cards: *The flag changed as new states were added to the Union. Congress passed the first Flag Act. Betsy Ross sewed the first American Flag. Congress decided to keep the number of stripes at 13.* Read the cards to students and have them place them in the correct sequence.

Objectives
- Activate prior knowledge of words.
- Identify questions for research.

Vocabulary
Tested Vocabulary

Lesson vocabulary
Use the following categorizing activity to help students acquire word knowledge.

Activate prior knowledge
Give oral clues that help students think about the categories in which the lesson vocabulary words belong. Display selection words. Have students check a dictionary for the meanings of any unknown words. Read aloud each three-item list below. Ask students to name the word or words that fit in the same category. Discuss reasons.

- can, bottle, thermos (canteen—all of these things hold drinks)
- fight, struggle, conflict (quarrel, rebellion—all are kinds of fights)
- pony, mare, colt (stallion—all are types of horses)
- fame, honor, pride (glory—all are things that you earn by doing something brave or difficult)
- league, alliance, country (confederacy, union—all are groups of people with similar ideals)

Analogies
Tell students that analogies are comparisons between pairs of related words. Incorporate lesson words into oral analogies, as shown below. Have students supply the lesson vocabulary words and explain the relationships. Then have them make their own analogies, using a thesaurus if necessary.

- *Quiet* is to **silence** as *praise* is to **glory**. (synonyms)

Preteach Academic Vocabulary
 Academic Vocabulary Write the following words on the board:

sequence	foreshadowing
dictionary/glossary	voice
literary nonfiction	possessive nouns

Have students share what they know about this week's Academic Vocabulary. Use the students' responses to assess their prior knowledge. Preteach the Academic Vocabulary by providing a student-friendly description, explanation, or example that clarifies the meaning of each term. Then ask students to restate the meaning of the Academic Vocabulary term in their own words.

Research and Inquiry
Identify Questions

Teach

Discuss the Question of the Week: *What are the risks in helping others?* Tell students they will research a famous incident in which people took risks to help others. They will write the table of contents for a book about this incident, and they will share their findings with the class on Day 5.

Model

I'll start by brainstorming famous incidents in which people took risks to help others. For example, the abolitionists who helped slaves escape through the Underground Railroad took many risks. After I choose a person or an event from history, I can write questions that will help me, such as: *How did Harriet Tubman help others? What risks did she take? Why?*

Guide practice

Have students consult with others to choose and refine their topics. Explain that tomorrow they will conduct research using their questions. They should use primary sources such as interviews and autobiographies, as well as secondary sources such as newspaper articles. Help students identify a person and an incident to research.

On their own

Have students work individually, in pairs, or in small groups to write inquiry questions. Encourage them to consult others.

INTERNET GUY
Don Leu

21st Century Skills

Weekly Inquiry Project

Day 1 Identify Questions

Day 2 Navigate/Search

Day 3 Analyze

Day 4 Synthesize

Day 5 Communicate

Small Group Time

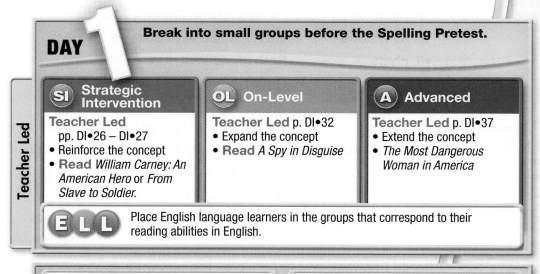

DAY 1

Break into small groups before the Spelling Pretest.

Teacher Led

(SI) Strategic Intervention	(OL) On-Level	(A) Advanced
Teacher Led pp. DI•26 – DI•27 • Reinforce the concept • **Read** *William Carney: An American Hero* or *From Slave to Soldier.*	**Teacher Led** p. DI•32 • Expand the concept • **Read** *A Spy in Disguise*	**Teacher Led** p. DI•37 • Extend the concept • *The Most Dangerous Woman in America*

ELL Place English language learners in the groups that correspond to their reading abilities in English.

Practice Stations
• Read for Meaning
• Get Fluent
• Word Work

Independent Activities
• Concept Talk Video
• *Reader's and Writer's Notebook*
• Vocabulary Activities

English Language Learners
Multilingual vocabulary
Students can apply knowledge of their home languages to acquire new English vocabulary by using Multilingual Vocabulary Lists (*ELL Handbook* pp. 431–444).

DAY 1

30–35 mins.

Spelling Pretest
Irregular Plurals

Introduce

Remind students that most nouns are made plural by adding *-s* or *-es* to the end of the singular form. This week we will spell irregular plurals, or plural nouns that are formed in different ways.

Pretest

Use these sentences to administer the spelling pretest. Say each word, read the sentence, and repeat the word.

1. **staffs**	The **staffs** at both companies went to the party.
2. **ourselves**	We gave **ourselves** plenty of time.
3. **pants**	Both boys tore their **pants** on the fence.
4. **scissors**	All the **scissors** are in that bin.
5. **loaves**	We need two **loaves** of bread.
6. **volcanoes**	Active **volcanoes** can be deadly.
7. **chiefs**	Three fire **chiefs** raced to the fire.
8. **buffalos**	Many **buffalos** once covered the plains.
9. **flamingos**	Pink **flamingos** wade in the pond.
10. **beliefs**	I always try to act on my **beliefs.**
11. **echoes**	The **echoes** grew fainter.
12. **shelves**	The **shelves** are filled with cans.
13. **quizzes**	I have three **quizzes** on Friday.
14. **sheriffs**	Two **sheriffs** worked on the case.
15. **dominoes**	John put the **dominoes** in the box.
16. **thieves**	The **thieves** were soon arrested.
17. **measles**	All the children have **measles.**
18. **avocados**	We need two **avocados** for this dish.
19. **chefs**	Both **chefs** host cooking shows.
20. **pianos**	Grand **pianos** take up lots of space.

Challenge words

21. **bailiffs**	**Bailiffs** help the judge keep the court calm.
22. **wharves**	There are many **wharves** along the seashore.
23. **mosquitoes**	**Mosquitoes** bite my arms.
24. **armadillos**	**Armadillos** live in Texas.
25. **desperadoes**	The Wild West had many **desperadoes.**

Self-correct

After the pretest, you can display the correctly spelled words or spell them orally. Have students self-correct their pretests by rewriting misspelled words correctly.

Let's Practice It!
TR DVD•71

On their own

For additional practice, use *Let's Practice It!* p. 71 on the *Teacher Resources DVD-ROM*.

Conventions
Possessive Nouns

Grammar Transparency 7, TR DVD

Teach

Display Grammar Transparency 7, and read aloud the explanation and examples in the box. Point out the three possessive nouns, *America's flag, the soldiers' uniforms,* and *the men's shoes.*

Model

Model writing the correct form of singular and plural possessive nouns by completing numbers 1 and 11. Apply the rules for possessive nouns to show how you determined the correct form.

Guided practice

Guide students to complete items 2–10 and 12–20. Remind them to place the apostrophe before the -s for singular possessive nouns and after the -s for plural possessive nouns. Remind them that they will have to add an apostrophe and -s for plural nouns that do not end in -s. Record the correct responses on the transparency.

Daily Fix-It

Use Daily Fix-It numbers 1 and 2 in the right margin.

Connect to oral language

Have students read sentences 21 to 25 on the transparency and circle the correct possessive noun to complete each sentence.

Handwriting
Cursive Letter *k* and *K*

Model letter formation

Display the cursive capital letter *K* and lowercase letter *k*. Follow the stroke instruction pictured to model letter formation.

Model letter shape

Explain that writing legibly means letters are the correct size and shape. Point out that while the lowercase *k* has loops, the capital *K* does not. Write the following phrase, *Kelly's kin in Kankakee,* carefully forming the loops of each lowercase *k* and making no loops in each capital *K*.

Guide practice

Have students write these phrases: *Kentucky kid Kevin, Kelly keeps knickknacks,* and *kooky kitten Kiki.* Circulate around the room, guiding students.

Academic Vocabulary

Possessive nouns are nouns that show ownership.

Daily Fix-It

1. The childrens eyes were sad?
   (children's; sad.)
2. Them fled from the nazis.
   (They; Nazis.)

ELL

English Language Learners

Possessive nouns Ask students to name objects in the classroom. Model introducing the owner(s) of each object. For example, say: This is the teacher's desk. That is the boys' coat closet. These are the children's books. Write the sentences on the board and underline the possessive nouns. Have students read aloud each sentence.

Handwriting: Proper nouns
For students who are not accustomed to writing the cursive letters *k* and *K*, provide extra practice with place names such as *Kazakhstan, Kenya, Korea, Kentucky, Kansas, Oakland,* and *Lake Tahoe.*

Objectives
- Understand and identify the features of an informal letter.

Writing—Informal Letter
Introduce

MINI-LESSON

5 Day Planner
Guide to Mini-Lessons

DAY 1	Read Like a Writer
DAY 2	Developing a Story Sequence Chart
DAY 3	Establishing the Tone
DAY 4	Revising Strategy: Subtracting
DAY 5	Proofread for Possessive Nouns

MINI-LESSON

Read Like a Writer

▪ **Introduce** This week you will write an **informal letter.** An informal letter is a casual way to communicate with someone you know.

Prompt Think of a time when you or someone you know had to act with bravery. Write a letter to a friend or family member describing the event.

Trait   Voice

Mode   Narrative

INTERAC with TEXT

Reader's and Writer's Notebook p. 121

▪ **Examine Model Text** Let's read an example of an informal letter that tells how Eric overcame his fear of heights to help a friend. Have students read the sample letter from Eric on p. 121 of their *Reader's and Writer's Notebook.*

▪ **Key Features** An informal letter contains a **date, greeting,** and **closing.** Have students locate, circle, and label the heading, greeting, and closing. Point out the correct use of commas in the address, date, greeting, and closing.

An informal letter has a casual tone. Have students find and share examples of Eric's use of casual language. Discuss his use of humor when sharing his story.

Lastly, an informal letter is usually written to someone you know well. Describe the relationship between Eric and Patrick. Have students underline any words or phrases that help them know that these two people are friends.

Review
key features

Review the key features of an informal letter with students. You may want to post the key features in the classroom for students to refer to as they work on their letters.

Key Features of an Informal Letter

- includes a date, greeting, and closing
- written in an informal tone
- usually written to someone you know
- contains a body, or the paragraphs that make up the main part of the letter

ROUTINE Quick Write for Fluency **Team Talk**

1. **Talk** Have pairs discuss the features of an informal letter.
2. **Write** Each student writes a sentence or two summarizing the key features.
3. **Share** Partners read one another's paragraphs.

Routines Flip Chart

Wrap Up Your Day

✔ **Build Concepts** Have students discuss why helping others might involve taking risks.

✔ **Oral Vocabulary** Have students use the Amazing Words they learned in context sentences.

✔ **Homework** Send home this week's Family Times newsletter on *Let's Practice It!* pp. 72–73 on the *Teacher Resources DVD-ROM.*

Let's Practice It!
TR DVD•72–73

Write Guy
Jeff Anderson

Writing to Learn

When a student writes a sentence, she is writing to learn. Let's provide her with at least one reader so that she learns how her language communicates. That reader may be a partner, a family member, the teacher, or a group of classmates. Writing comes alive and has a purpose when it has an audience. Young writers do as well.

ELL

English Language Learners
Visual learning: Key features of an informal letter Display samples of informal letters and invite students to bring in letters from home. Point out the conventions in each letter and review feature-specific vocabulary terms, such as *date, salutation,* and *closing.* Write each term on a sticky note. Call on students to place the sticky notes next to the features in the letters.

Preview DAY 2

Tell students that tomorrow they will read about the first African American regiment in the Civil War.

Concept Talk

Question of the Week

What are the risks in helping others?

Expand the concept

Remind students of the Question of the Week. Tell students that today they will begin reading *Hold the Flag High.* As they read, encourage students to think about the risks people sometimes have to take to help others.

Anchored Talk

Develop oral vocabulary

Use the photos on pp. 202–203 and the Read Aloud, "Number the Stars," to talk about Amazing Words: *poses, officers,* and *unwavering.* Add these and other concept-related words to the concept map to develop students' knowledge of the topic. Break into groups. Discuss the following questions. Encourage students to elicit suggestions from others.

- Why might an *officer* scare people like the Johansen family? (Commanding *officers* told him to do it. He also may have believed he was helping his nation, Germany.)

- Is it better to stand up for what you believe in with an *unwavering* or a trembling attitude? (an *unwavering* attitude)

- In "Number the Stars," why did the Johansen family help Ellen Rosen *pose* as their daughter? (They wanted to save her life. They did not want the officers to send her away.)

Oral Vocabulary
Amazing Words

Amazing Words

Amazing Words

poses	nation
officers	trembling
unwavering	sacrifice
cooperation	audacity
maneuver	brazen

Amazing Words **Oral Vocabulary Routine**

Teach Amazing Words

1 Introduce Write the Amazing Word *cooperation* on the board. Have students say it aloud with you. Relate *cooperation* to the photographs on pp. 202–203 and the context of "Number the Stars." How do the activities in the photographs require *cooperation?* (The people must all work together to help others.) How did the Johansen family show *cooperation* in "Number the Stars"? (They worked together to convince the soldiers that Ellen was Lise Johansen.) Have students determine the definition of the word. (*Cooperation* means "working together.")

2 Demonstrate Have students answer questions to demonstrate understanding. How must the people working on the Coast Guard helicopter use *cooperation* to help others?

3 Apply Have students demonstrate their understanding. In "Number the Stars," why was the *cooperation* of each family member so important?

See p. OV•2 to teach *maneuver.*

Routines Flip Chart

Apply Amazing Words

Help students establish a purpose for reading as they read "Civil War Drummers" on p. 207. Have them think about why *cooperation* and proper *maneuvers* were important to the drummers in the Civil War.

Connect to reading

Explain that today students will read about soldiers who take risks to help others during war. As students begin to read the selection, have them think about how the Question of the Week and the Amazing Words *cooperation* and *maneuver* apply to taking risks to help others.

Connect to Social Studies

Coast Guard members work together to help others. One division does surveys used to update nautical charts, the "road maps" of the seas. Another division supplies them with updated instruments to make the charts as accurate as possible. A third division uses the survey information to create new charts. It even takes three crew members to read the nautical charts on Coast Guard ships. The crew member at the radar screen shouts out numbers as other crew members work together to plot their position, or figure out exactly where the ship is located and where it is heading. And it takes many more crew members to maneuver a Coast Guard ship through the seas.

ELL Reinforce Vocabulary
Use the Day 2 instruction on ELL Poster 7 to teach lesson vocabulary and the lesson concept.

ELL Poster 7

Word Analysis
French Word Origins

Teach French word origins

Tell students that some English words come from older French words. These words contain French roots, or word parts. Have students look for common roots to match French words with English words in the chart below.

Model the skill

Think Aloud The Old French word *confederacie* looks and sounds like the English word *confederacy.* All letters are the same, except the French word ends in *-ie,* and the English word ends in *-y.* The French word *confederacie* means "an agreement between people or groups to work together." During the Civil War, southern states formed a confederacy and agreed to work together.

French Words	English Words
confederacie (an agreement)	stallion
cantine (a container with edges)	quarrel
glorie (fame, honor, and praise)	union
rebellio (renewed war)	glory
querele (a complaint or dispute)	confederacy
estalon (a male horse)	rebellion
unio (oneness)	canteen

Guide practice

Have students look and listen for French roots in the English words. Have them use the French roots to determine the meanings of the English words.

On their own

Have students meet with a partner to explain how they paired each word with its root. Then have them check each word's origin in a dictionary. Follow the Strategy for Meaningful Word Parts to teach the word *canteen.*

ROUTINE Strategy for Meaningful Word Parts

1. **Introduce the strategy** We're going to use word parts, or roots, to help us read words. Write *canteen.* Circle *cant.*

2. **Introduce the word parts** The Latin root *cant* is related to the French word *cantine.*

3. **Connect to meaning** The Latin root *cant* means "corner, angle or edge." *Canteen* means "a metal container for drinks."

4. **Read the word** Blend the roots together as you read *canteen.* A canteen is a metal container for drinks that has corners and edges.

Continue the Routine with *glorie/glory* and *rebellio/rebellion.*

Literary Terms
Foreshadowing

Teach foreshadowing

Tell students that hints or clues about future events in a story that advance the story are called foreshadowing. Foreshadowing creates curiosity or suspense.

Model foreshadowing

 Think Aloud Turn to p. 203b. Let's think about the Read Aloud, *Number the Stars.* When Annemarie and Ellen woke up, they were *trembling.* Then an officer *barked* at them. How do these words foreshadow what will happen next? (The girls were trembling because they were afraid that the Nazi officers would hurt Ellen. The officer's harsh tone foreshadows several of the story's events, including his suspicion and him grabbing Ellen's hair.)

Guide practice

In *Number the Stars,* Mama speaks in a *strong* voice. Papa moves to the bookcase *swiftly.* Discuss how words such as *strong* and *swiftly* foreshadow what will happen. (These words show that Papa and Mama are calm and smart and that they will hide Ellen's true identify by being confident.)

On their own

Have students discuss foreshadowing in other selections.

Story Structure
Climax

Teach climax

In a story, incidents advance the story, giving rise to future events. The climax of the story is the high point, the place where these incidents all come to a head.

Model the strategy

 Think Aloud What is the climax, or high point, of *Number the Stars?* (The climax is when the officer looks at Lise's baby picture. He sees that she has dark hair, just like Ellen does.) What events give rise to this climax? (The officer asks about Ellen's hair, and Papa rips the photographs out of the album.)

Guide practice

Have students preview *Hold the Flag High* by looking at the illustrations on pp. 208–219. Direct their attention to the climax on p. 216, when Carney carries the flag. Ask students to predict what events led up to the climax using the illustrations.

On their own

Have students predict how the picture on p. 212 of *Hold the Flag High* will lead to the climax on p. 216.

Academic Vocabulary

foreshadowing hints and clues that indicate future events in a story

literary nonfiction tells the story of a true event or a real person

Objectives
◎ Use a dictionary or glossary to determine the meanings of unknown words.
• Read aloud with fluency and comprehension.

Vocabulary Strategy for
 Unknown Words

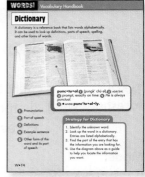

Student Edition W•14

Teach unknown words

Envision It!

Tell students that when they encounter an unknown word, they should use the strategy of checking a dictionary or glossary to look up the meaning. Explain how a dictionary or glossary can help students understand the meanings of unknown words. Refer students to *Words!* on p. W•14 in the Student Edition for additional practice.

Model the strategy

Think Aloud

Write on the board: *My sister Janice gets all the glory for the things we do together.* I can't figure out the meaning of *glory* by using context clues, so I will use a dictionary or glossary for help. When I look up *glory* in a dictionary or glossary, I see that it means "praise or honor." Now I understand that Janice gets the praise when the sisters do things together.

Guide practice

Write this sentence on the board: *When Janice and I quarrel, I get all the blame.* Have students determine the meaning of *quarrel* using context clues such as *blame*. Ask students: Are the sisters doing something bad or good? (something bad because it involves blame) If students need further clarification on the word *quarrel,* have them find the meaning of the word in a dictionary or glossary. Have students identify the syllabication, pronunciation, and part of speech of *quarrel* as well.

For additional support, use Envision It! Pictured Vocabulary Cards or Tested Vocabulary Cards.

On their own

Read "Civil War Drummers" on p. 207. Have students use a dictionary or glossary to list the meanings, syllabications, pronunciations, and parts of speech of the lesson vocabulary words. Go around the room and have students share their findings. For additional practice, use *Reader's and Writer's Notebook* p. 122.

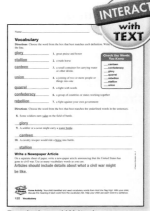

Reader's and Writer's Notebook p. 122

Objectives
- Use a dictionary, a glossary, or a thesaurus to locate information about words.

Envision It! Words to Know

canteen

glory

stallion

confederacy
quarrel
rebellion
union

**READING STREET ONLINE
VOCABULARY ACTIVITIES**
www.ReadingStreet.com

Vocabulary Strategy for

🎯 Unknown Words

Dictionary/Glossary When you read, you may come across a word you do not know. You can use a glossary or dictionary to find out the meaning of the word. A glossary lists and defines important words in a book. A dictionary lists all words, in alphabetical order, and gives their meanings, pronunciations, and other information.

Choose one of the *Words to Know* and follow these steps.

1. Check your book for a glossary. If there is no glossary, use a printed or electronic dictionary and find the entry for the word.
2. Read the pronunciation to yourself. Saying the word may help you recognize it.
3. Read all the meanings given for the word.
4. Choose the meaning that makes sense in your sentence.

As you read "Civil War Drummers," use the glossary or a dictionary to look up the meanings of this week's *Words to Know*.

Words to Write Reread "Civil War Drummers." Imagine you are a war drummer. Write a paragraph describing your experience. Use words from the *Words to Know* list.

Civil War DRUMMERS

In the Civil War, both the Union army and the army of the Confederacy relied on their drummers. The drummers were an essential part of their battles.

The Civil War was much more than a quarrel between the North and the South. It was a war, with fierce battles fought on the ground. For this reason, drummers were needed, and not just to play marching beats. Drummers were needed on the battlefield to alert soldiers when to retreat to safety. An officer mounted on his stallion would lean down to tell his drummer to play a drum call for a charge or some other troop movement. Off the battlefield, the drummers' beats alerted officers to planning meetings.

War drummers had to be brave. They marched onto the battlefield unarmed, carrying just their water canteens and their drums. Perhaps the drummers didn't get the glory that the soldiers did, but they performed important work for both the North and the South, as they fought during the rebellion.

Your Turn!

⏸ **Need a Review?** For additional help with using a dictionary or glossary to find out the meanings of unknown words, see *Words!*

▶ **Ready to Try It?** Read *Hold the Flag High* on pp. 208–219.

206   207

Student Edition pp. 206–207

Reread for Fluency
Accuracy

Model fluent reading

Read the second paragraph of "Civil War Drummers" carefully and accurately. Tell students that you are reading the passage with accuracy, paying special attention to new vocabulary.

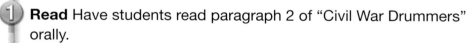
ROUTINE **Oral Rereading**

① **Read** Have students read paragraph 2 of "Civil War Drummers" orally.

② **Reread** To achieve optimal fluency and comprehension, students should reread the text three or four times.

③ **Corrective Feedback** Have students read aloud without you. Provide feedback about word accuracy and encourage students to adjust their reading to a rate at which they can read the words accurately. Listen for accuracy.

Routines Flip Chart

Lesson Vocabulary

canteen a container that holds drinks
confederacy a group of people, states, or countries that work together
glory praise, honor
quarrel a fight
rebellion a conflict that leads to war
stallion a male horse
union states that are united as one country

Academic Vocabulary

dictionary a book that explains words in a language
glossary a list in the back of a book or textbook that gives definitions for difficult words

Differentiated Instruction

SI Strategic Intervention

Dictionary Point out that sometimes a dictionary gives more than one definition. Help students find the definitions for *glory* and pick out the one that makes sense in the sentence.

 **ELL**

English Language Learners
Build Academic Vocabulary
Use the lesson vocabulary pictured on p. 206 to teach the meanings of *canteen, glory,* and *stallion.* Call on pairs to write the words on sticky notes and use them to label images of the words on the ELL Poster.

Objectives

- Understand the elements of literary nonfiction.
- Use text features to preview and predict.
- Set a purpose for reading.

Student Edition pp. 208–209

Build Background

Discuss Civil War soldiers

Team Talk Have students turn to a partner and discuss the Question of the Week and these questions about African American soldiers in the Civil War. Encourage students to consider each other's suggestions and identify points of agreement and disagreement.

- What did African American soldiers do during the Civil War?
- Where and when did they fight?
- What risks did African American soldiers take?

Connect to selection

Have students discuss their answers with the class. Possible responses: African Americans fought during the Civil War. An early, famous battle was at Fort Wagner, in which many of the Union soldiers were African American. Many of those African American soldiers died on the battlefield. They took risks by charging the fort and risking their lives to take it. For additional opportunities to build background, use the Background Building Audio.

Prereading Strategies

Genre
Remind students that **literary nonfiction** tells the story of a true event. It sometimes uses elements that are usually used in fiction, such as dialogue, illustrations, descriptions, and character thoughts.

Preview and predict
Have students preview the title, headings, and illustrations to gain an overview of the text. Ask them to locate the photo of William Carney. (p. 218) Have them predict the major events and themes in the story.

Set purpose
Prior to reading, have students set their own purposes for reading this selection. To help students set a purpose, ask them to think about the risks the African American soldiers took in order to fight for freedom.

Strategy Response Log

 INTERACT with TEXT

Have students read p. 13 in the *Reader's and Writer's Notebook* to identify the characteristics of literary nonfiction.

Small Group Time

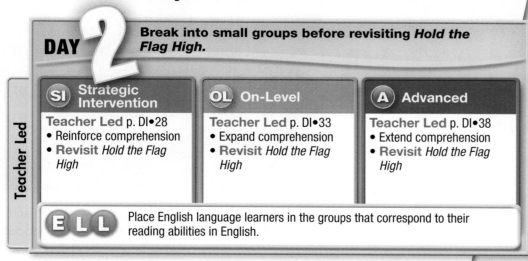

DAY 2 Break into small groups before revisiting *Hold the Flag High.*

Teacher Led

SI Strategic Intervention
Teacher Led p. DI•28
• Reinforce comprehension
• **Revisit** *Hold the Flag High*

OL On-Level
Teacher Led p. DI•33
• Expand comprehension
• **Revisit** *Hold the Flag High*

A Advanced
Teacher Led p. DI•38
• Extend comprehension
• **Revisit** *Hold the Flag High*

ELL Place English language learners in the groups that correspond to their reading abilities in English.

Practice Stations
• Words to Know
• Get Fluent
• Word Wise

Independent Activities
• Background Building Audio
• *Reader's and Writer's Notebook*
• Research and Inquiry

A Advanced
Compare and contrast Ask students to compare and contrast literary nonfiction and expository texts they've read.

 **Multidraft Reading**

For **Whole Group** instruction, choose one of the reading options below. For each reading, have students set the purpose indicated.

Option 1
Day 2 Read the selection. Use Guide Comprehension to monitor and clarify understanding.
Day 3 Reread the selection. Use Extend Thinking to develop higher-order thinking skills.

Option 2
Day 2 Read the first half of the selection, using both Guide Comprehension and Extend Thinking instruction.
Day 3 Read the second half of the selection, using both Guide Comprehension and Extend Thinking instruction.

ELL

English Language Learners
Build background To build background, review the selection summary in English (*ELL Handbook* p. 67). Use the Retelling Cards to provide visual support for the summary.

OPTION 1 Guide Comprehension Skills and Strategies

Teach Sequence

◎ **Sequence** Read the first sentence on p. 210. Ask which happened first, quarreling between the North and the South or the Civil War. (quarreling) Have students find clues. *(when, had been, for decades)*

Corrective Feedback

If... students are unable to determine the sequence,

then... model by asking students questions about sequence.

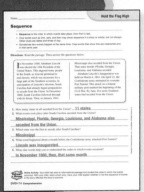

Let's Practice It!
TR DVD•74

Model the Skill

Think Aloud To understand the sequence of events, I will look for clue words. I see the time word *when* and the verb *had been quarreling.* So I know the quarreling had been going on for some time.

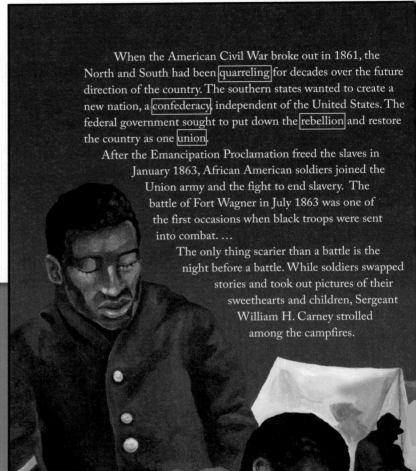

When the American Civil War broke out in 1861, the North and South had been quarreling for decades over the future direction of the country. The southern states wanted to create a new nation, a confederacy, independent of the United States. The federal government sought to put down the rebellion and restore the country as one union.

After the Emancipation Proclamation freed the slaves in January 1863, African American soldiers joined the Union army and the fight to end slavery. The battle of Fort Wagner in July 1863 was one of the first occasions when black troops were sent into combat. ....

The only thing scarier than a battle is the night before a battle. While soldiers swapped stories and took out pictures of their sweethearts and children, Sergeant William H. Carney strolled among the campfires.

210

Student Edition pp. 210–211

OPTION 2 Extend Thinking Think Critically

Higher-Order Thinking Skills

◎ **Sequence • Analysis** Reread the last half of page 211 and list troop events in the order they happened. Be sure to maintain the meaning of the story as you summarize. Use the words *first, next, then,* and *finally.* **Possible response:** First, troops paraded through the streets of Boston. Next, they set sail to South Carolina. Then, they set up camp. Finally, they waited for the battle.

Foreshadowing • Synthesis How do pages 210 and 211 give the reader hints or clues about events that will happen later in the story? Use textual evidence to support your answer. **Possible response:** The soldiers are nervous but excited for the battle. I can tell because they tell each other that the only thing scarier than a battle is the night before a battle. They also say that tomorrow will be a big day, the day they have all been waiting for, and that Ned will drum them to glory. I think these clues show that the battle will be big and important and that the soldiers will give everything to win.

How long did the North and South quarrel? **(for decades)** Were they still quarreling when Civil War broke out? **(yes)** So, the sequence is: First, they quarreled. Next, the Civil War broke out.

A homesick private played his harmonica sweet and low. Carney draped a blanket around the shoulders of Company C's drummer boy, a young slave who had run off from his master to join the fight. Carney assured him, "Tomorrow's gonna be a big day for us, Ned. You'll be drumming us to glory."

Carney was one of the few black officers in the Massachusetts Fifty-fourth, a new African American regiment formed in the spring of 1863.

Carney's men took pride in the shiny brass buttons on their uniforms and new rifles on their shoulders. Just a few weeks before, they had paraded through the streets of Boston. Ladies had waved handkerchiefs, and all had shouted hurrahs and farewells. Then the Fifty-fourth Regiment had set sail to fight in far-off South Carolina.

Once they arrived, the soldiers set up camp south of Charleston Bay. Their first battle would come tomorrow.

This was the day they had all been waiting for, the soldiers told themselves as they headed off to sleep.

211

On Their Own

Have students reread paragraph 2 on p. 210 and paraphrase the sequence of events using the words *first, next,* and *then.* (First, the Emancipation Proclamation freed the slaves. Next, African American soldiers joined the Union army. Then, the battle of Fort Wagner was fought.) For additional practice with sequence, use *Let's Practice It!* p. 74 on the *Teacher Resources DVD-ROM.*

E L L

English Language Learners
Activate prior knowledge To help students understand the setting, have them examine the pictures to tell where the soldiers are, and when it takes place.

Professional development: What ELL experts say about sheltering instruction "English language learners benefit when teachers shelter, or make comprehensible, their literacy instruction. One way to do this is to use consistent, simplified, clearly enunciated, and slower-paced oral language to explain literacy concepts or activities." —Dr. Georgia Earnest García

Inferring • Synthesis How would this story have been different if it had been an expository text? Use your background knowledge about expository text to make an inference. Possible response: Expository text usually gives an overview instead of a minute-to-minute literary story with dialogue and characters. If this story were an example of expository text, it probably would not have focused as much on characters like Carney and Ned. We would not have literary details like the homesick private playing his harmonica, and the story would not include dialogue between Carney and Ned. Instead, an expository text would probably focus on the entire regiment and tell what they did.

Objectives
• Compare and contrast to aid understanding.

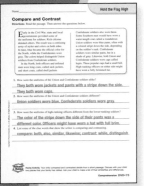

OPTION 1 — Skills and Strategies, continued

Teach Compare and Contrast

Review **Compare and Contrast**
What do Sergeant Carney and Ned, the drummer boy, have in common? How are they different? (Both are heading into battle. Carney has a higher rank and is more confident.)

Corrective Feedback

If... students are unable to compare and contrast,
then... model comparing and contrasting.

Model the Skill

Think Aloud Let's look at page 211 for information about Carney and Ned. Who has a higher rank? (Carney; he is a sergeant and one of the few black officers in the Massachusetts

Let's Practice It!
TR DVD•75

Fifty-Fourth. Ned is the drummer boy.) Now reread their conversation on page 212. How are their feelings toward the upcoming battle different? (Ned feels scared and doesn't know what the battle will be like.

> Carney kicked out the fire. An owl hooted in the distance. Ned, the drummer boy, wondered if it was really an owl. Maybe it was the signal of a Confederate spy.
>
> "Sarge, I don't know what it'll be like when the Rebs start shootin'. I'm feeling scared—and—and—" he stuttered, "and what if I get lost?"
>
> "Son, you just play that drum, and remember what we're fighting for: Old Glory will lead the way."
>
> "Old Glory?" Ned asked.
>
> "Sure, son, keep your eyes on the flag," said Carney. "Like hundreds before us and thousands after, just follow those Stars and Stripes, and you can't go wrong."
>
> "I can't go wrong," Ned murmured as Carney tucked him into his bedroll.

212

Student Edition pp. 212–213

OPTION 2 — Think Critically, continued

Higher-Order Thinking Skills

Review **Compare and Contrast** • **Synthesis** Compare and contrast Colonel Robert Gould Shaw with Carney and Ned. Use the text to support your understanding. Possible response: Colonel Shaw rides a horse and wears a sash, so we can infer that he is an important leader who has a higher rank than Carney or Ned. The text also mentions his pale face, which is almost a white as his stallion, so we can draw the conclusion that Shaw is white, not black. However, Ned sees fear in Shaw's face, something that all of the men may have in common. They are all fighting the same battle.

Draw Conclusions • **Evaluation** Read the last paragraph on page 213. Do you think Shaw gave an inspiring speech? Draw conclusions from the information presented by the author. Possible response: Yes. According to the text, the speech fired up the men and made them ready for battle. Their chests were swollen with pride and the soldiers could hardly wait to prove themselves. The soldiers were afraid before, so Shaw's speech must have inspired them.

Carney is confident. He tells Ned to just play his drum and keep his eyes on the flag.) From this, infer who has more experience in battle. (Carney) How are they similar? (Both are black soldiers, both are in the Fifty-Fourth Regiment, and both will be heading into battle tomorrow.)

On Their Own

Have students predict how Carney and Ned will act in battle. For additional practice, use *Let's Practice It!* p. 75 on the *Teacher Resources DVD-ROM*.

Differentiated Instruction

SI Strategic Intervention

Simile Focus students on the simile near the bottom of p. 213: *His pale face was nearly as white as his stallion.* Ask students what this simile tells about Shaw. Ask whether Shaw is African American (no). Ask whether Shaw is afraid (yes).

A Advanced

Compare and Contrast Have students find information about the ranks of officers in the armed forces. Ask them to list the ranks from top to bottom, making sure to include the ranks of sergeant and colonel.

Then the sergeant said a little prayer, hoping it would be true.

Long before the sun rose, the men of the Fifty-fourth awoke to prepare for the battle. They checked and rechecked their rifles, making sure the flints were dry and the bayonets sharp and shined. Ned worked hard, filling canteens with water.

After a breakfast of hardtack and coffee, each soldier had his name pinned onto the back of his uniform. This way soldiers who did not survive the battle could be identified. Soldiers who could write helped those who couldn't.

Carney tipped his hat at the color-bearer. He was the soldier who carried the regiment's flag into battle on a short flagpole, called a staff. "We're all counting on you, brother."

The wind whipped the banner, held aloft on its staff: back and forth; then again, back and forth.

Soldiers bristled with anticipation.

Ned could see their commanding officer, Robert Gould Shaw, approaching on horseback. As he galloped up, spurs gleaming on his heels and a fringed silk sash across his chest, the colonel seemed to own the day.

But when Shaw dismounted, Ned noticed that his pale face was nearly as white as his stallion. Ned wondered, *Could he be scared, too?*

Maybe Shaw *was* a bit afraid; he had already been wounded in battle once. But his speech to his troops betrayed no fears. Shaw fired up his men for battle. The Fifty-fourth had been picked to lead the charge against Fort Wagner—the Confederate outpost guarding Charleston. Chests swollen with pride, these soldiers could hardly wait. They would gladly follow Shaw to the ends of the Earth, eager to prove their courage under fire.

213

Cause and Effect • Analysis Do you think the officers expect that some soldiers will die? Explain how the selection shows you this cause-and-effect relationship. Possible response: Each soldier has his name pinned onto the back of his uniform, so if he doesn't survive he can be identified. In paragraph 3 on p. 213, the text tells the effect and then the cause, or why it happens.

Background Knowledge • Evaluation • Text to Self Have you ever witnessed an inspiring speech? Discuss what you think Shaw talked about with his soldiers. Possible response: My

sports coach gives good speeches. He talks about how important the game is and tells us he knows we can do well. I think Shaw told the soldiers how important the battle was. He told the soldiers they were fighting for freedom, and he told them that he knew they could win.

Check Predictions Have students look back at the predictions they made earlier and discuss whether they were accurate. Then have students preview the rest of the selection and either adjust their predictions accordingly or make new predictions.

ELL

English Language Learners

Vocabulary Write the word *sergeant* under the word *colonel*. Say each word and have students repeat after you. Point to the word *colonel* and explain that officers have different ranks, and colonels have more power and responsibility than sergeants.

If you want to teach this selection in two sessions, stop here.

Objectives
- Consult primary and secondary sources to conduct research.
- Recognize and correctly use possessive nouns.
- Spell words with irregular plurals.

Research and Inquiry
Navigate/Search

Teach

Remind students that they will research the famous incident they have chosen in which people took risks to help others. Have students search both electronic and print resources using their inquiry questions to guide them. Have students use a word processor to take notes as they read. Recording data this way will be particularly useful when they need to organize their information to create a table of contents.

Explain that they will need to consult both primary and secondary sources. A primary source is one that includes the exact words of the people involved or eyewitnesses. Secondary sources are written by people who have researched the incident or interviewed the people involved. Give students a few examples of primary and secondary sources and ask them to differentiate between the two.

Model

Think Aloud I'll start by looking at the encyclopedia entry about Harriet Tubman. This is a secondary source, but it gives background information about her life and also gives me ideas for keywords. I find out that Harriet Tubman took risks throughout her life. She escaped slavery and was a conductor on the Underground Railroad. I also found the years in which she lived, so I will search for newspaper articles from that time. I hope to find some quotes from Harriet Tubman herself. These will be good primary sources.

Guide practice

Have students continue their research. Students should carefully evaluate the relevance, validity, and reliability of the sources they consult.

On their own

Have students write down bibliographic information, including titles, authors, dates, and page numbers, for all the sources they use.

Conventions
Possessive Nouns

Teach

Write the phrases *the eyes of my father* and *my father's eyes* on the board. Point out that the possessive noun reduces wordiness so that the writing flows more smoothly.

Guide practice

Say these phrases. Have students eliminate the prepositional phrase by writing and saying a singular or plural possessive noun.

the anthem of our country	**a favorite book of the children**
a sweater of my sister	**a promise of the friends**

Daily Fix-It

Use Daily Fix-It numbers 3 and 4 in the right margin.

Connect to oral language

Have students look for and read aloud possessive nouns in *Hold the Flag High*. (*Company C's,* p. 203; *Carney's,* p. 203; *regiment's,* p. 205; *Fort Wagner's, sergeant's,* p. 208)

On their own

For additional practice, use the *Reader's and Writer's Notebook* p. 123.

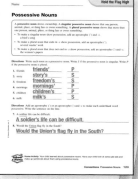

Reader's and Writer's Notebook p. 123

Spelling
Irregular Plurals

Teach

Remind students that some nouns have irregular plurals. They do not follow the usual rules for forming plural nouns. Write *chief* and *thief.* To make *chief* plural, we add an -*s.* Write *chiefs.* However, to make *thief* plural, we change the *f* to *v* and add -*es.* Write *thieves.* Irregular plurals often need to be memorized.

Guide practice

Write the remaining spelling words on the board. Have students write them and underline the letters that make the word plural.

On their own

For additional practice, use the *Reader's and Writer's Notebook* p. 124.

Reader's and Writer's Notebook p. 124

3. The many travelers belongings were left behine. *(travelers'; behind)*

4. Thay could not save theirself. *(They; themselves)*

E L L

English Language Learners
Conventions To provide students with practice on possessive nouns, use the modified grammar lessons in the *ELL Handbook* and Grammar Jammer online at: www.ReadingStreet.com

Language transfer: Possessive nouns In many languages, speakers show possession in phrases (such as *anthem of our country*) rather than noun endings (*our country's anthem*). If students have trouble with the English possessive forms, write these phrases on the board and have students insert apostrophes where they belong:

- a teachers desk
- the libraries books
- the womens soccer team

Writing—Informal Letter
Writer's Craft: Characterization

Introduce the prompt

Review the key features of an informal letter. Remind students that they should think about these features as they plan their writing. Then explain that they will begin the writing process for an informal letter today. Read aloud the writing prompt.

Writing Prompt

Think of a time when you or someone you know had to act with bravery. Write a letter to a friend or family member describing the event.

Select a topic

 Think Aloud The first step in the writing process is to select a topic. I know I will write a letter about a time someone acted with bravery, but I need to choose exactly who and what I will write about. I will make a chart to list my ideas. Display a T-chart, and model how to list ideas. In the first column, I will write the name of a person who has acted bravely. In the second column, I will describe his or her act of bravery. Call on students to name people they know who have acted bravely and fill in the columns with their examples. Encourage students to include times when they themselves have acted with bravery. Point out that once you have finished listing ideas, you will select only one act of bravery to write about.

Name of Person	Act of Bravery
• Me	• Outsmarted neighborhood bullies
• Cousin Dwayne	• Saved the guide during a rafting trip
• Great-grandpa B.T.	• Immigrated to the United States
• My friend Tina	• Helped fellow leukemia-sufferers cope with their illness

Corrective feedback

Circulate around the classroom as students use the T-chart to select a topic. Gather small groups of students who are having trouble listing ideas. Ask them to think about the bravest person they know and describe that person to the group. Alternatively, have students share a time when they overcame a fear in order to help someone. Guide students to gather ideas for their letters based on their conversations.

MINI-LESSON

Developing a Story Sequence Chart

■ Remind students that their letters will tell about an act of bravery. I'm going to write about the time my cousin Dwayne saved the guide on a family river-rafting trip. A story sequence chart will help me organize the events of my story.

■ In the *Beginning* box I will include details about how Dwayne felt about our trip. I will write *Dwayne was nervous about rafting.*

■ In the *Middle* box I will describe what happened on the trip. I will write *As we paddled through the rapids, our raft hit a rock and the guide fell off the raft's edge. We saw another set of rapids.*

■ In the *End* box, I will describe how Dwayne acted bravely. I will write *Dwayne helped us through the rapids. He then directed us toward the guide and pulled him back into the raft.*

Have students begin their own story sequence charts using the form on p. 125 of their *Reader's and Writer's Notebook.*

A Advanced

Sequence of events Challenge students to think of ways they could begin their story at a more dramatic point in the action, such as in the middle or at the end.

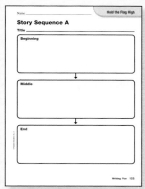

Reader's and Writer's Notebook p. 125

Teacher Tip

Do a periodic check of students' Quick Writes to make sure they are on task and communicating effectively with their partners.

ROUTINE

Quick Write for Fluency **Team Talk**

1. **Talk** Have pairs discuss how they used their story sequence charts.
2. **Write** Direct students to add one or two sentences to each box.
3. **Share** Partners read aloud each other's charts before sharing them with other groups.

Routines Flip Chart

Wrap Up Your Day

✔ **Build Concepts** What did you learn about being courageous despite the risks?

✔ **Sequence** How did it help you to summarize the events of the story in sequence?

✔ **Inferring** What inferences did you make?

Preview DAY 3

Tell students that tomorrow they will read about what happened at the battle at Fort Wagner.

Objectives
- Expand the weekly concept.
- Develop oral vocabulary.

Today at a Glance

Oral Vocabulary
nation, trembling

Comprehension Check/Retelling
Discuss Questions

Reading
Hold the Flag High

Think Critically
Retelling

Fluency
Accuracy

Research and Study Skills
Parts of a book

Research and Inquiry
Analyze

Spelling
Irregular plurals

Conventions
Possessive nouns

Writing
Informal letter

Concept Talk

Question of the Week
What are the risks in helping others?

Expand the concept

Remind students of the Question of the Week. Discuss how the question relates to Civil War soldiers. Tell students that today they will read about how the battle ends and what happens to William Carney. Encourage students to think about how they might feel if they were one of the soldiers. Have students think about the *sacrifices* soldiers make for their *nation*.

Anchored Talk

Develop oral vocabulary

Use text features—title and illustrations—to review pp. 208–213 of *Hold the Flag High.* Discuss the Amazing Words *cooperation* and *maneuver.* Add these and other concept-related words to the concept map. Use the following questions to develop students' understanding of the concept.

- Why is it a good *maneuver* to have a flag leading soldiers into battle? (It helps the soldiers to remain *unwavering* as they head into battle.)

- How is *cooperation* important when preparing for battle? (It helps ensure that the soldiers have what they need.)

Oral Vocabulary
Amazing Words

Amazing Words

poses	nation
officers	trembling
unwavering	sacrifice
cooperation	audacity
maneuver	brazen

Teach Amazing Words

 Amazing Words **Oral Vocabulary Routine**

1. **Introduce** Write the word *nation* on the board. Have students say it with you. During the Civil War, Union soldiers fought to keep their *nation* together. Have students determine a definition for *nation* using the context from your sentence. (*Nation* means "a group of people who live in the same country.")

2. **Demonstrate** Have students answer questions to demonstrate understanding. What might the people of a *nation* have in common? (similar history, descent, beliefs, language, or culture)

3. **Apply** Have students apply their understanding. What *nation* is to our north? (Canada) What *nation* is to our south? (Mexico) What other *nations* can you name?

See p. OV•2 to teach *trembling*.

Routines Flip Chart

Apply Amazing Words

Help students establish a purpose for reading as they read pages 214–219 of *Hold the Flag High*. Have them think about why the Union soldiers are fighting to keep their *nation* together. Have students think about why soldiers might be *trembling* as they head into battle.

Connect to reading

Explain that today students will read about the battle at Fort Wagner and the risks the soldiers took in helping others gain freedom. As students finish the main selection, have them think about how the Question of the Week and the Amazing Words *nation* and *trembling* relate to the risks in helping others.

ELL Expand Vocabulary Use the Day 3 instruction on ELL Poster 7 to help students expand vocabulary.

ELL Poster 7

Objectives

◎ Understand sequence to aid comprehension.

◎ Use the inferring strategy to aid comprehension.

◎ Use context clues to determine the meanings of unknown words.

Comprehension Check

Have students discuss each question with a partner. Ask several pairs to share their responses.

☑ Genre • Evaluation

Why do you think the author chose to inform readers about this historic event through literary nonfiction? How else might she have told the story? **Possible response: She could have told it as expository text, but she probably thought that telling it as a story would be most interesting and memorable.**

☑ Sequence • Analysis

In what order did the men prepare for battle on the day of the battle at Fort Wagner? **Possible response: First, they checked their rifles. Next, they ate breakfast. Then each soldier had his name pinned onto the back of his uniform. Finally, Robert Shaw appeared to fire up the men for battle.**

☑ Inferring • Synthesis

Infer why the soldiers are proud to fight in this battle. What evidence from the text supports this inference? **Possible response: They joined so they could fight to end slavery. It was one of their first chances to go into combat.**

☑ Unknown words • Synthesis

Use what you learned about the Union soldiers to determine a definition for the word *regiment*. Check your definition in a printed or electronic dictionary or glossary. **Possible response: A *regiment* must have to do with a group of soldiers because this word is used to refer to the soldiers in the story. The dictionary defines *regiment* as "a unit of soldiers."**

☑ Connect text to self

Tell how you would feel if you were one of the men preparing for battle. What qualities would you need most? **Possible response: I would be scared, so the qualities I would need most are courage and bravery.**

Strategy Response Log

Have students revisit p. 13 in the *Reader's and Writer's Notebook* to add additional information about literary nonfiction.

Check Retelling

Have students retell the first part of *Hold the Flag High*, summarizing the text in a logical order. Encourage students to use the text features in their retellings.

Corrective feedback

If... students leave out important details,
then... have students look back through the illustrations.

Small Group Time

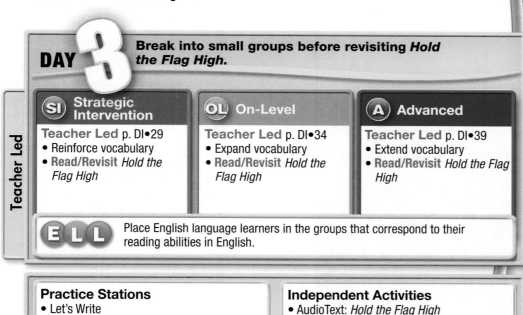

DAY 3 Break into small groups before revisiting *Hold the Flag High.*

Teacher Led

SI **Strategic Intervention**
Teacher Led p. DI•29
• Reinforce vocabulary
• **Read/Revisit** *Hold the Flag High*

OL **On-Level**
Teacher Led p. DI•34
• Expand vocabulary
• **Read/Revisit** *Hold the Flag High*

A **Advanced**
Teacher Led p. DI•39
• Extend vocabulary
• **Read/Revisit** *Hold the Flag High*

ELL Place English language learners in the groups that correspond to their reading abilities in English.

Practice Stations
• Let's Write
• Get Fluent
• Word Work

Independent Activities
• AudioText: *Hold the Flag High*
• *Reader's and Writer's Notebook*
• Research and Inquiry

ELL

English Language Learners
Check retelling To support retelling, review the multilingual summary for *Hold the Flag High* with the appropriate Retelling Cards to scaffold understanding.

Objectives
◎ Use a dictionary or glossary to determine the meanings of unknown words.

OPTION 1 Skills and Strategies, continued

Teach Unknown Words

👁 **Unknown Words** Have students use a dictionary to determine the meaning, pronunciation, and syllabication of the word *artillery* at the top of p. 214. Ask students to use context clues to clarify which meaning is correct in the sentence. ("the part of an army that uses large guns")

Corrective Feedback

If… students are unable to determine the meaning of *artillery,*

then… model using a dictionary to determine the meaning.

Reader's and Writer's Notebook p. 126

Multidraft Reading

If you chose…

Option 1 Return to Extend Thinking instruction starting on p. 210–211.
Option 2 Read pp. 214–219.
Use the Guide Comprehension and Extend Thinking instruction.

Student Edition pp. 214–215

OPTION 2 Think Critically, continued

Higher-Order Thinking Skills

👁 **Unknown Words • Synthesis** Use a dictionary or glossary to tell the meaning and part of speech of the word *helter-skelter,* which is found in paragraph 4 on page 214. Possible response: I can tell from the sentence that the word *helter-skelter* describes how the bullets were falling. When I look up *helter-skelter* in a dictionary or glossary, I find out that it is an adverb that means "with confusion and haste" or "in a haphazard manner."

Model the Skill

 Think Aloud When I look up the word *artillery* in a dictionary, it tells me that it is pronounced *är til' lər ē.* How many syllables do you hear? (four)

The artillery shelled all day, but finally the generals were ready to send in the infantry. "Forward, march!" the order rang out.

An endless line of men in blue snaked along the sand. They headed for the fortress towering on the horizon.

Ned solemnly drummed on the beat—footfalls and drumsticks in syncopation. He glanced at the flag snapping in the stiff breeze. The gulls gently swooped, as waves lapped the shore. …

In a split second, everything tilted. Cannonballs pounded the ground. Bullets pelted helter-skelter. A greenish-yellow glow of smoke rose at the same time bodies began to fall. Streams of blood flowed into the foam, washing out to sea. The metallic taste in Carney's mouth mixed with the fear rising in his throat.

Ned could barely hear the drum over the roar. Then a shell exploded behind him, and he fell to his knees. His heartbeat pounded in his ears as he tried to get his bearings. Uninjured but dazed, Ned scanned the horizon.

Far above, he could see Colonel Shaw lit by the firelight from exploding shells. He was mounting a rampart, saber in hand, shouting: "Forward, Fifty-fourth," as he disappeared into the breach. But where was the flag?

Carney felt a burning sensation as a bullet tore through his flesh. Just ahead, the soldier carrying Old Glory staggered to a halt, shot dead by a Confederate sharpshooter. As he sank toward the ground, Carney plunged forward to catch the falling flag. He lifted the banner above his head and two more shots slammed into him.

214

Draw Conclusions • Evaluation Reread paragraph 4 aloud. Do you think that many soldiers were shot and killed? How well does the author describe the scene? Summarize the supporting details the author presents that give you clues, maintaining meaning.
Possible response: Yes, many soldiers were shot and killed. The author is very descriptive, so I can picture the chaos. *Cannonballs pounded the ground. Bullets pelted helter-skelter. Bodies began to fall. Streams of blood flowed into the foam.* These details all indicate that soldiers were dying.

The dictionary says the word *artillery* can mean "a large gun" or "the part of an army that uses large guns." Which meaning works in the sentence? (Guns can't shell a fort by themselves. Here *artillery* means "the part of an army that uses large guns.") In the Civil War, the artillery used cannons.

On Their Own

Have students use a dictionary to figure out the meaning and pronunciation of the word *infantry.* ("soldiers on foot") For additional practice, use *Reader's and Writer's Notebook* p. 126.

Connect to Social Studies

Most people know that Harriet Tubman was a conductor on the Underground Railroad and helped slaves escape to freedom in the North. Few people, however, know that when the Civil War started, Tubman worked for the Union Army in many roles including a cook, laundress, scout, and spy. In fact, Harriet Tubman cooked for the men and watched the battle at Fort Wagner. Afterward, she nursed the injured and helped bury the dead.

215

Sequence • Analysis What sequence of events led to Carney carrying the flag? Paraphrase the last two paragraphs on page 214, maintaining meaning and logical order. Possible response: Ned looked for the flag. Carney was shot once. He watched as the flag bearer was shot. Carney caught the flag before it hit the ground. Then Carney lifted the banner above his head as he was shot two more times.

ELL

English Language Learners
Cognates Point out to Spanish-speaking students that the word *fortress* is *fortaleza* in Spanish. Have students say the word in both English and Spanish and compare the sounds. Refer students to the word *fortress* in paragraph 2 on p. 214. Suggest they use the Spanish cognate and context clues to figure out the meaning of *fortress* ("a military stronghold"). Help them look up the word in a dictionary and determine its meaning in the sentence.

Objectives
◎ Use inferring as a strategy to understand text.

OPTION 1 Skills and Strategies, continued

Teach Inferring

Inferring Ask students to use textual evidence to infer how Carney feels about his country and what his personality is like. (Carney is very brave and determined. He will fight for his soldiers and his country.)

Corrective Feedback

If... students have difficulty inferring that Carney was brave,

then... model using details and events to infer.

Student Edition pp. 216–217

Model the Strategy

Think Aloud We can infer what kind of person Carney is by paying attention to his actions in the text. What happened to Carney on page 216? (He was shot, but he still carried the flag to the end.)

> Fighting the pain, the sergeant triumphantly raised the Stars and Stripes over Fort Wagner's ramparts. The flag would show Ned and the others the way.
>
> Many hours later, when the Union bugler finally sounded retreat, the federal soldiers struggled away from the fort, defeated. Yet Carney carried the flag safely back behind Union lines before he collapsed. Ned and other members of the Fifty-fourth Regiment surrounded their wounded sergeant's cot. They congratulated him as Carney murmured,
>
> "The old flag never touched the ground."
>
> Those who survived the battle of Fort Wagner would never forget their brave Sergeant Carney, who showed the way by holding the flag high.

216

OPTION 2 Think Critically, continued

Higher-Order Thinking Skills

Cause and Effect • Analysis What event caused Carney to be the flag bearer? Carney grabbed the flag because a Confederate sharpshooter killed the soldier who was originally carrying Old Glory.

Sequence • Analysis We know that Carney took the flag and carried it when the flag bearer was shot and killed. What happened next? Carney continued to carry the flag until the federal soldiers retreated, and then he collapsed.

What kind of personality traits did Carney have to possess to do that? (He had to be determined and brave.) Why do you think Carney fought so hard? (He was proud of his flag and he wanted to help his men fight.)

217

On Their Own

Have students infer whether it was difficult for Carney to hold the flag. Encourage them to use textual evidence as they infer. (Yes; Carney was wounded and he collapsed.)

Unknown Words • Synthesis Use a dictionary to determine the meaning of the word *ramparts* in paragraph 1 on page 216. Why did Carney want to put the flag on the ramparts? According to the dictionary, *ramparts* are "wide banks of earth, often with a wall on top, built around a fortress to defend it." Carney knew everyone would be able to see the flag from the ramparts.

Inferring • Synthesis Why did Carney try so hard to carry the flag? Use textual evidence to infer. Carney wanted to show respect for the flag and inspire his men to fight bravely. He believed that the flag was very important. Back on p. 213, Carney told the soldier carrying the flag that the whole regiment was counting on him. Carney also told Ned to follow the flag if he felt afraid.

ELL

English Language Learners
Language Transfer Languages such as Cantonese, Hmong, and Vietnamese use words that are only one syllable. Students may need practice reading multisyllabic words, especially when endings are added. Say the word pairs and have students repeat after you, listening for syllables: *sound/sounded, defeat/defeated, congratulate/congratulated, murmur/murmured.* Also read and count syllables in the word pairs *struggle/struggled, collapse/collapsed,* and *touch/touched.*

DAY 3 Read and Comprehend

Objectives

◎ Use a dictionary or glossary to determine the meanings of unknown words.

OPTION 1 Skills and Strategies, continued

Teach Unknown Words

◉ **Unknown Words** Ask students to determine the meaning of *unveiling* in paragraph 2 of p. 219 by using an electronic dictionary to look up the prefix *(un-),* root word *(veil),* and affix *(-ing).* Then use an electronic dictionary to check the part of speech.

Corrective Feedback

If... students are unable to figure out the meaning of *unveiling,*

then... model finding prefixes and roots and then using a dictionary.

Model the Skill

Think Aloud When I see the word *unveiling,* I can identify some meaningful parts. I will look each part up in the dictionary. First, I see the prefix *un-,* which means "not" or "a lack of." The root word is *veil,* which means "to cover" or "a material that covers."

218

Student Edition pp. 218–219

OPTION 2 Think Critically, continued

Higher-Order Thinking Skills

◉ **Unknown Words • Analysis** Use an electronic dictionary to figure out the meanings of the words *preserve* and *tribute* in the last sentence of paragraph 2. Use context clues to identify the part of speech. *Preserve* is used as a verb that means "to keep safe or protect." *Tribute* is a noun that is "something done to show thanks or respect."

◉ **Sequence • Analysis** List these events in the correct sequence: The Shaw monument was dedicated; Carney was awarded the Congressional Medal of Honor; the battle at Fort Wagner took place. Explain how the organization of the text helped you understand. First, the battle at Fort Wagner took place. Next, the Shaw monument was dedicated. Then, Carney was awarded the Congressional Medal of Honor. I could tell because text is written in sequential order.

218–219 Doing the Right Thing • Unit 2 • Week 2

The affix *-ing* signals a verb or an adjective. When I look up *unveil,* I find that it can mean "to remove a veil" or "to announce publicly for the first time." In this context, I think the unveiling ceremony was when the government showed off the monument for the first time. *Unveiling* is an adjective.

On Their Own

Have students use an electronic dictionary to find the pronunciation and syllabication of *unveiling.* Encourage them to use audio if available.

EPILOGUE:

Confederate troops held their position and declared victory at Fort Wagner on July 19, 1863. However, the Massachusetts Fifty-fourth Regiment took great pride in their performance, tested in battle.

Long after the Civil War had ended, Sergeant Carney appeared in Boston in 1897 at an unveiling ceremony. A monument for Colonel Robert Gould Shaw, who lost his life at Fort Wagner, was being dedicated. Carney and other members of the Fifty-fourth had contributed funds to erect an impressive bronze memorial honoring their fallen leader. At this solemn occasion, Carney received a standing ovation. His courageous act to preserve the flag was a tribute to those who died to defend it.

William H. Carney was eventually awarded the Congressional Medal of Honor—the first African American to earn this tribute.

219

Differentiated Instruction

SI Strategic Intervention

Draw conclusions Have students study the photo of Sgt. Carney and tell what they see (an older soldier with a cane). Ask students what Carney did during the battle at Fort Wagner. Remind them of the gunshot wounds, if necessary. Ask how these might affect Carney in the future.

A Advanced

Have students reread the first paragraph on p. 219. Discuss why the battle at Fort Wagner was a kind of victory for the Fifty-Four Regiment even though the Confederacy triumphed.

ELL

English Language Learners
Leveled Support: Unknown words Have students practice finding the meanings of unknown words at their own language level.

Beginning Help students look up the words *pride, defend,* and *troops.* Use gestures, pictures, or motions to explain the words.

Intermediate Have students look up *performance, bronze,* and *ceremony.* Have them explain the words in short sentences.

Advanced Have students look up *dedicated, impressive,* and *contributed.* Ask them to name synonyms.

Advanced High Have students look up and read definitions for *erect, regiment,* and *memorial.* Ask them to apply the words to the story.

Comprehension Check

Spiral Review

Draw Conclusions • Synthesis Examine the photo of Carney on page 218. Using what you have learned about Carney, infer why Carney might have needed the cane. I know Carney was shot during the battle at Fort Wagner. I think he needed the cane because of the injuries he received during the Civil War.

Theme • Synthesis How do you think the outcome of the Civil War and the movement to free the slaves affected the theme of this piece of literature? Ask students to identify the outcome of the Civil War and the theme of the story before making a connection. The Union won the Civil War, and the theme of this story is about taking risks for others. If the Confederacy had won, the story may have focused on the Confederacy and the risks they took. The movement to free the slaves was also instrumental since this story is about the first black regiment.

Check Predictions Have students return to the predictions they made earlier and confirm whether they were accurate.

Objectives
◉ Use the strategy of inferring to support understanding.
◉ Maintain meaning by explaining sequence.

Check Retelling
SUCCESS PREDICTOR

Student Edition pp. 220–221

Retelling

Envision It!

Have students work in pairs to retell the selection, using the Envision It! Retelling Cards. Remind students that they should summarize the events and paraphrase important ideas using key vocabulary and maintaining meaning and logical order. Monitor students' retellings.

Plan to Assess Retelling

☑ **Week 1** Assess Strategic Intervention students.

☑ **This week assess Advanced students.**

☐ **Week 3** Assess Strategic Intervention students.

☐ **Week 4** Assess On-Level students.

☐ **Week 5** Assess any students you have not yet checked during this unit.

Scoring rubric

Top-Score Response A top-score response makes connections beyond the text, describes the events and important ideas using accurate information, evaluates facts and opinions, and draws conclusions from the text.

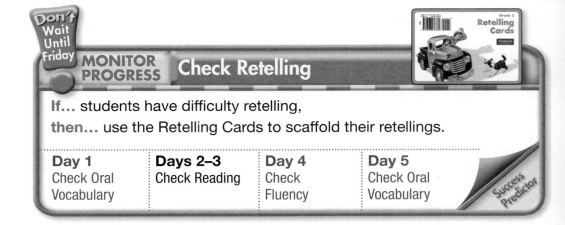

Don't Wait Until Friday

MONITOR PROGRESS **Check Retelling**

If... students have difficulty retelling,

then... use the Retelling Cards to scaffold their retellings.

Day 1	Days 2–3	Day 4	Day 5
Check Oral Vocabulary	Check Reading	Check Fluency	Check Oral Vocabulary

Success Predictor

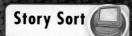
Think Critically

Text to world

1. Students' responses should include what students know about showing respect to the flag and how the American flag's stars and stripes are a symbol of the United States.

Think like an author

2. Sergeant Carney supports and encourages Ned. The author probably included Ned to give the reader someone they can relate to and to show that Sergeant Carney is a strong leader.

Sequence

3. Carney is shot; the flag bearer is shot dead; Carney grabs the flag before it hits the ground; Carney is shot twice again; Carney carries the flag until the end of the battle.

Inferring

4. The Confederate troops are positioned inside of Fort Wagner and have control of it. This is an important strategic advantage.

Writing on Demand

5. **Look Back and Write** To build writing fluency, assign a 10–15 minute time limit.

Suggest that students use a prewriting strategy, such as brainstorming or using a graphic organizer, to organize their ideas. Remind them to establish a topic sentence and support it with evidence from the text such as facts, details, or explanations. As students finish, encourage them to reread their responses, revise for organization and support, and proofread for errors in grammar and conventions.

Scoring rubric

> **Top-Score Response** A top-score response uses details to tell about the battle at Fort Wagner.
>
> **A top-score response should include:**
>
> • Who fought in this battle and why.
>
> • What happened during the battle.
>
> • How William H. Carney was recognized.

Differentiated Instruction

SI Strategic Intervention

Have students work in pairs to list the things Carney did to deserve the Congressional Medal of Honor.

Meet the Author

Have students read about Catherine Clinton on p. 221. Discuss with them why the battle of Fort Wagner probably attracted this author's interest.

Independent Reading

After students enter their independent reading information into their Reading Logs, have them paraphrase a portion of the text they have just read. Remind students that when we paraphrase we express the meaning of a passage, using other words and maintaining meaning and logical order.

English Language Learners

Retelling Number and display the Retelling Cards. Assign each student a number. Then have each student describe his/her card to a partner. Be sure partners do not have the same number.

Retelling

Success Predictor

Objectives
- Read grade-level text with accuracy.
- Reread for fluency.
- Identify parts of books.
- Use a table of contents.

Model Fluency
Accuracy

Model fluent reading

Have students turn to p. 216 of *Hold the Flag High.* Have students follow along as you read this page. Tell them to listen for accuracy as you read difficult and unfamiliar words. Read at a rate that allows you to pronounce each word correctly.

Guide practice

Have the students follow along as you read the page again. Then have them reread the page as a group without you until they read with accuracy. Continue in the same way on the next page.

Reread for Fluency

Corrective feedback

If... students are having difficulty reading with accuracy,
then... prompt:

- Did you read every word? Where do you see difficult words?
- How can you read with better accuracy?
- Read the sentence again. Make sure you read carefully and do not miss any words.

ROUTINE Oral Rereading

1. **Read** Have students read the Epilogue on p. 219 orally.
2. **Reread** To achieve optimal fluency, students should reread the text three or four times.
3. **Corrective Feedback** Have students read aloud without you. Provide feedback about their word accuracy and encourage them to adjust their reading to a rate at which they can read the words correctly. Listen for accuracy as students read.

Routines Flip Chart

Research and Study Skills
Parts of a Book

Teach

Ask students to name different parts of a book, such as the title page and the table of contents. Hold up a social studies or science textbook and define these features.

- A **title page** lists the title, author, and publisher. Sometimes, it lists the illustrator and the date and place of publication.

- A **copyright page** tells the year of publication, who holds the copyright (rights to the text or illustrations), and the publisher.

- A **table of contents** is a list of the chapters, articles, or stories in a book. It lists the page where each chapter or selection begins.

- A **chapter title** tells what the chapter is about. It appears in the table of contents and at the beginning of the chapter.

- A **glossary** is a list of words and definitions at the back of a book. A glossary only contains words that are used in the book.

- An **index** is an alphabetical listing of topics offered in a book. It lists the page numbers on which each topic can be found.

Ask students to turn to the table of contents in their Student Edition. Explain that this table uses text features such as headings, subheads, and page numbers, to give readers an overview of the contents of the book and to help readers locate specific information.

Guide practice

Discuss these questions:

Describe where we can find this week's selection, *Hold the Flag High*. (It is near the beginning of Unit 2, and it starts on p. 208.)

How many units does this book have? How do you know? (6; I know by looking at the big Unit headings and counting them.)

(About how many pages long is Unit 2? How can you figure this out? (Unit 2 starts around p. 170 and ends around p. 320. If I subtract, I find that this unit is roughly around 150 pages long.)

On their own

Then have volunteers pose similar questions that require classmates to use this table and its text features to find and interpret information. Have students complete pp. 127–128 of the *Reader's and Writer's Notebook*.

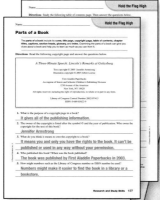

Reader's and Writer's Notebook
pp. 127–128

English Language Learners

Parts of a Book To help students understand the parts of a book, page through a textbook with students. Name the various book parts and have students repeat the names. Then name each book part and have students find it.

Objectives
- Analyze data for usefulness.
- Recognize and correctly use possessive nouns.
- Spell frequently misspelled words.

Research and Inquiry
Analyze

Teach

Tell students they will use their research to create a table of contents for an imaginary book about the incident they chose, telling how people took risks to help others.

Model

Think Aloud Some of the information I found on Harriet Tubman tells about her childhood and how she escaped from slavery. I also learned about risks she took as a conductor on the Underground Railroad during the Civil War. I ask myself, *What information should I use?* I will focus on risks Harriet Tubman took during the Civil War, since that is most relevant to my topic of taking risks to help others. My new inquiry question is *How did Harriet Tubman take risks to help others during the Civil War?*

Guide practice

Have students analyze their findings in a similar way. Have students work in groups if they have trouble narrowing their focus.

As students think about the information they will include in their table, have them examine an example of a table of contents and the factual or quantitative information it presents. For example, students should consider how long a chapter should be, how many chapters to include, and how to organize the facts they found into a table format.

On their own

Have students meet in groups to discuss the most important ideas about their incidents. Students might want to list the various people involved in the event or the risks they took and consider what chapters to include in a book about it.

 **Grammar Jammer**

Conventions
Possessive Nouns

Review

Remind students that this week they learned about possessive nouns.

- Add an apostrophe and -*s* to form a singular possessive noun.
- Add an apostrophe to a plural noun ending in -*s* to form the possessive. If the plural does not end in -*s*, add *'s.*

Daily Fix-It

Use Daily Fix-It numbers 5 and 6 in the right margin.

Connect to oral language

Have students choose an owner or owners from the first list and an object from the second list. Have them say the possessive form of the owner(s) with the object (e.g., *Sergeant's flag*).

> **Owners: Sergeant, the men, Ned, the officers, the Union**
>
> **Objects: drum, breakfast, army, flag, uniforms, banner**

On their own

For additional practice, use *Let's Practice It!* p. 76 on the *Teacher Resources DVD-ROM.*

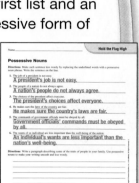

Let's Practice It!
TR DVD • 76

Spelling
Irregular Plurals

Frequently misspelled words

The words *no, know, new,* and *knew* are frequently misspelled. I'm going to read a sentence. Choose the correct word to complete the sentence and then write it correctly.

> **1. Terrence _____ most of the answers on the test.** (knew)
>
> **2. There were _____ cars in the empty parking lot.** (no)
>
> **3. The rising sun was a sign of the _____ day.** (new)
>
> **4. I _____ the music school has three pianos.** (know)

On their own

For additional practice, use the *Reader's and Writer's Notebook* p. 129.

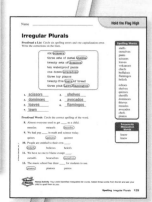

Reader's and Writer's
Notebook p. 129

Differentiated Instruction

SI Strategic Intervention

Possessive nouns Have students fill out a T-chart to record the rules for possessive nouns. Tell them to write the rule for singular possessive nouns on the left column of the chart. Have them place the rules for plural possessive nouns on the right. Once they have completed their charts, have partners work together to list examples for each column.

Daily Fix-It

5. Two mens' clothing stores had its windows broken. *(men's; their)*
6. Brave citizens hided refugees in several house. *(hid; houses)*

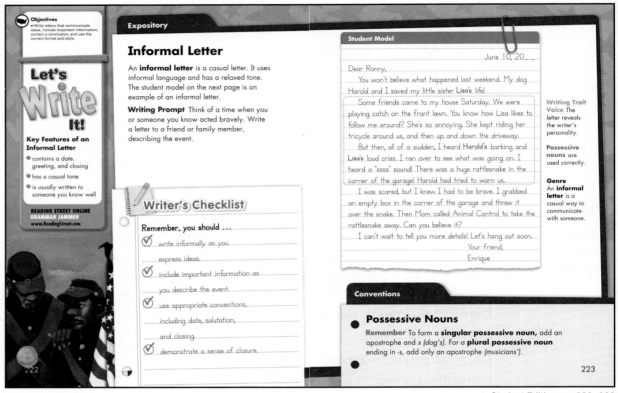

Student Edition pp. 222–223

Let's Write It!
Informal Letter

Teach

Use pp. 222–223 in the Student Edition. Direct students to read the key features of an informal letter, which appears on p. 222. Remind students that they can refer to the information in the Writer's Checklist as they write their own informal letters.

Read the student model on p. 223. Point out the date and greeting in the model, as well as the overall casual tone.

Connect to conventions

Remind students that a singular possessive noun is formed by adding an apostrophe and -s. For plural possessive nouns ending in s, add only an apostrophe. Point out the correct use of possessive nouns in the model. Have students write a sentence using a possessive noun.

Writing—Informal Letter
Writing Trait: Voice

Display rubric

Display Scoring Rubric 7 from the *Teacher Resources DVD* and go over the criteria for each trait under each score. Then, using the model in the Student Edition, choose students to explain why the model should score a 4 for one of the traits. If a student offers that the model should score below 4 for a particular trait, the student should offer support for that response. Remind students that this is the rubric that will be used to evaluate the informal letters they write.

Scoring Rubric: Informal Letter

	4	3	2	1
Focus/Ideas	Strong control of letter conventions such as date, greeting, and closing; well-developed body	Minor errors in letter conventions such as date, greeting, and closing; developed body	Many errors in letter conventions such as date, greeting, and closing; underdeveloped body	Numerous errors in letter conventions such as date, greeting, and closing; undeveloped body
Organization	Clearly organized sequence of events	Able to follow sequence of events	Sequence of events attempted but not clear	No organizational pattern evident
Voice	Writer is imaginative; achieves an animated voice and friendly, casual tone	Some evidence of animated voice and casual tone	Attempts an animated voice and casual tone	No attempt at an animated voice and casual tone
Word Choice	Strong use of vivid words	Adequate use of vivid words	Weak use of vivid words	No use of vivid words
Sentences	Clear sentences of various lengths and types	Sentences of a few lengths and types	Some incorrect sentences; little attempt at various lengths and types of sentences	Many incorrect sentences; no attempt at various lengths and types of sentences
Convention	Few, if any, errors; correct use of commas and possessive nouns	Several minor errors; mostly correct use of commas and possessive nouns	Many errors; inaccurate use of commas and possessive nouns	Numerous errors; no use of commas or possessive nouns

Story sequence chart

Have students get out the story sequence charts that they worked on yesterday. If their charts are not complete, allow students a few minutes of class time to build on their ideas and complete their charts.

Write

You will be using your story sequence charts to write the draft of your informal letter. When you are drafting, don't worry if your letter does not sound exactly as you want it. You will have a chance to revise it tomorrow. Try to get down the important information.

Objectives
- Write a first draft of an informal letter.
- Match tone to audience and purpose.

Writing, continued
Writing Trait: Voice

MINI-LESSON

Establishing the Tone

■ **Introduce** Explain to students that good writers choose their words carefully in order to establish their own voice in their writing. Tell students to consider the audience and purpose of their letters as they choose their words. Remind them that they are writing letters to tell about a time someone acted bravely. The audience will be a close friend or family member. Informal letters should have a casual and friendly tone. The reader should get a sense of your personality from the words you use. Include details and descriptive words to let your reader know what you think about your subject. Then display Writing Transparency 7A.

Writing Transparency 7A, TR DVD

Drafting Tips

✔ To get started, review your story sequence chart.
✔ Make sure to include the date and a friendly greeting before writing the main body of the letter. Include a closing at the end.
✔ Focus on getting your ideas down on paper. Don't worry about perfecting grammar and mechanics while drafting.

Think Aloud I'm going to write the first paragraph for the body of my letter. As I draft, I will refer to my story sequence chart to help me keep story events in chronological order. I will start my paragraph with a question to engage the reader in a friendly way. As I continue writing paragraphs, I will include descriptive words to let my reader know how I feel about my cousin Dwayne.

Direct students to use the drafting tips to guide them in writing their drafts. Remind them to include the date, a friendly salutation or greeting, and a closing and signature.

ROUTINE Quick Write for Fluency Team Talk

1. **Talk** Have pairs discuss the subjects of their letters.

2. **Write** Each student writes a paragraph describing how they feel about this person and how they expressed this attitude in their letters.

3. **Share** Have partners read each other's paragraphs and check for correct use of commas and possessive nouns.

Routines Flip Chart

Wrap Up Your Day

✔ **Build Concepts** Have students discuss Carney's courageous actions and why he took such risks.

✔ **Sequence** Why was the sequence of events important in *Hold the Flag High*?

✔ **Inferring** What can you infer about Carney's personality?

Differentiated Instruction

SI Strategic Intervention

Establishing the tone Have partners read aloud a sentence from their drafts. Each writer reads his or her sentence first in a friendly and informal tone and then again in a more serious manner. Partners determine whether the writing matches the informal tone.

Academic Vocabulary

Voice is a tool writers use to express themselves through the tone and style of their writing.

Preview DAY 4

Tell students that tomorrow they will read about how to fold the American flag.

Today at a Glance

Oral Vocabulary
sacrifice, audacity, brazen

21st Century Skills
Web site

Reading
"How to Fold the American Flag"

Let's Learn It!
Fluency: Accuracy
Vocabulary: Dictionary/Glossary
Listening/Speaking: Informational Speech

Research and Inquiry
Synthesize

Spelling
Irregular plurals

Conventions
Possessive nouns

Writing
Informal letter

Concept Talk

Question of the Week

What are the risks in helping others?

Expand the concept

Remind students that this week they have read about the risks people such as Sergeant Carney take in helping others. Tell students that today they will learn how to use Web sites on a computer to find more information about a topic related to the main selection: the American flag.

Anchored Talk

Develop oral vocabulary

Use the illustrations to review pp. 214–219 of *Hold the Flag High.* Discuss the Amazing Words *nation* and *trembling*. Add these and other concept-related words to the concept map. Use the following questions to develop students' understanding of the concept. Break into groups and have students elicit suggestions from other group members.

• What risks did Sergeant Carney take? (leading men into battle) Do you think Carney was *trembling* when he carried the flag? (Possible responses: Yes, because he had been shot several times. No, because he was brave.)

• In what ways do you think Sergeant Carney helped our *nation*? (He fought for freedom for African Americans; he helped his soldiers persevere through the battle.)

Strategy Response Log

Have students review the characteristics of literary nonfiction on p. 13 of the *Reader's and Writer's Notebook.* Then have them compare *Hold the Flag High* to another example of literary nonfiction they have read.

INTERACT with TEXT

Go Digital!

Concept Talk Video

Oral Vocabulary
Amazing Words

Amazing Words

poses	nation
officers	trembling
unwavering	sacrifice
cooperation	audacity
maneuver	brazen

Teach Amazing Words

Amazing Words Oral Vocabulary Routine

1 Introduce Write the concept word *sacrifice.* Have students say it aloud with you. Carney made a *sacrifice* when he carried the flag through great pain to encourage his soldiers. Have students use context clues such as *through great pain* and *encourage* to determine the meaning of the word *sacrifice.* ("giving up something for the greater good")

2 Demonstrate Have students answer questions to demonstrate understanding. What did Carney *sacrifice* during the battle at Fort Wagner? (his health; he also risked his life)

3 Apply Have students apply their understanding. Have you ever made a *sacrifice* so things could be better? What was it?

See p. OV•2 to teach *audacity* and *brazen.*

Routines Flip Chart

Apply Amazing Words

Help students establish a purpose for reading as they read "How to Fold the American Flag" on pp. 224–227. Have them think about what the flag stands for and what *sacrifices* others made for freedom. Discuss how people have acted with *audacity* or been *brazen* in order to defend the flag.

Connect to reading

As students read today's selection, have them think about how the Question of the Week and the Amazing Words *sacrifice, audacity,* and *brazen* relate to the Web sites in today's selection.

ELL Produce Oral Language Use the Day 4 instruction on ELL Poster 7 to extend and enrich language.

ELL Poster 7

21st Century Skills
Web sites

Introduce Web sites

Explain to students that technology is all around us. Tell them that Web sites are only one type of technology we use today. Ask students to share what they already know about Web sites and how they have used them.

Discuss the skill

Discuss with students how Web sites have changed the way we do research. For example, ask: If you wanted more information about the battle at Fort Wagner, where would you look? (Possible responses: Web site, library, books or journals, history center, teacher) Explain: Before computers, people weren't able to do research at a Web site because the technology did not exist. So, they did research using books, magazines, and papers. Let's take a closer look at the similarities and differences between Web sites and books.

On the board, draw a Venn diagram like the one below. Label the circles *Web site* and *Book*. Ask the following questions:

- How would you use a Web site on the Civil War to find information about the battle at Fort Wagner? Possible response: Look for a link about the battle at Fort Wagner and click on it to get information.

- How would you use a Civil War book to get the same information? Possible response: Use the table of contents or index.

- How are these ways alike? How are they different? Possible responses: Both are ways to get information on the battle at Fort Wagner. One is done online using Web sites, and the other is done at a library using books or journals.

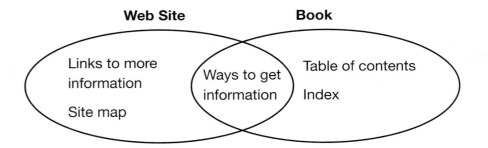

Guide practice

Have students work in pairs to list in a T-chart the benefits of using a Web site and the benefits of using a book. Ask them to share their lists with the class. Remind students that many Web sites are informal and are not appropriate for some purposes, such as research papers. Challenge students to give examples of formal and informal Web sites.

Connect to reading

Tell students that they will now read an article that shows how to use a Web site to find information on how to fold the American flag. Have the class think about times when using a Web site might be helpful.

Small Group Time

DAY 4

Break into small groups before reading or revisiting "How to Fold the American Flag."

Teacher Led

(SI) Strategic Intervention

Teacher Led p. DI•30
• Practice retelling
• Genre focus
• **Read/Revisit** "How to Fold the American Flag"

(OL) On-Level

Teacher Led p. DI•35
• Practice retelling
• Genre focus
• **Read/Revisit** "How to Fold the American Flag"

(A) Advanced

Teacher Led p. DI•40
• Genre focus
• **Read/Revisit** "How to Fold the American Flag"

ELL Place English language learners in the groups that correspond to their reading abilities in English.

Practice Stations
• Read for Meaning
• Get Fluent
• Words to Know

Independent Activities
• AudioText: "How to Fold the American Flag"
• *Reader's and Writer's Notebook*
• Research and Inquiry

ELL

English Language Learners

Language Transfer Students with literary skills in Spanish may pronounce *site* with an initial *e,* as an initial *s* in Spanish is pronounced *es.* Do not correct students, but pronounce the word correctly when using it.

Objectives
• Use a Web site to find information.

Student Edition pp. 224–225

Guide Comprehension
Skills and Strategies

Teach Web sites

21st Century Skills: Web site Have students preview "How to Fold the American Flag" on pp. 224–227. Have them look at the structure of the Web site and discuss the various parts. Then ask: Why are the links labeled with phrases such as "History of the American flag"?

Corrective feedback

If... students are unable to explain why the links are labeled with descriptive phrases,

then... use the model to guide students in understanding links.

Model the skill

Think Aloud I know that clicking on a link will take me to a different page on the Web site. Before I click on a link, I need to know what information will be covered on that page. That way I know which link to click. By using a phrase to label the link, the author of the Web page tells me where I can find the information for which I am looking.

On their own

Have students pick a subject and make a list of names for links to other pages that they would put on the front page of a Web site for their subject. Then have students interpret the step-by-step details from the Web site to complete the task of folding a flag themselves. If a flag is not available, students can fold a piece of paper.

Extend Thinking
Think Critically

Higher-order thinking skills

Text Structure • Evaluate How does a Web site present information in a way that is different from another kind of media, such as a book? Which is easier to use? **Possible response:** A Web site contains lots of different bits of information linked to each other, while a book contains pages of information that usually stand alone. For example, a Web site page might provide you with a link to take you right away to another Web site on a related topic, while a book can at best only recommend a related book, and then you have to track that book down and search through it yourself to find the information. That makes a Web site easier to use than a book.

 Inferring • Analysis Make an inference about why the author of this Web page might have included links to the subjects of the history of the American flag and the symbolism of the American flag. What evidence from the text supports this inference? **Possible response:** The introductory paragraph at the top of this Web page mentions that the flag is a symbol of our country. When people read that, they will probably want to know more specific information about what kind of symbol it is. Also, I know that people who are interested in one part of a subject are often interested in learning more about other parts of it as well. For those reasons, I think the author of this page wanted to link the reader to pages where the reader can find more about the related subjects of the flag's history and symbolism.

Differentiated Instruction

 Strategic Intervention

Formal and informal language Work with students to determine the difference between formal and informal language. Talk about Web site topics that could be written about using more informal language and Web site topics that should be presented using more formal language. Have students make a T-chart to organize their ideas.

A **Advanced**

Author's purpose Ask students to use evidence from the text to identify the author's feelings about the topic of folding the American flag. Then have them discuss what the author's purpose for creating this Web site might be.

English Language Learners
Formal and informal language Remind students that we use different language in formal and informal situations. Ask: Would you talk to your parents with formal or informal language? (*informal*) Would you talk to a salesperson with formal or informal language? (*formal*) Invite volunteers to model greeting a parent and requesting help from a salesperson. Then ask students what kind of language they would expect to find in each of the following. Discuss whether any of these could contain both.

- a note from a friend
- a Web site about pet care
- a magazine article

Objectives

• Analyze information and graphics found on a Web site.

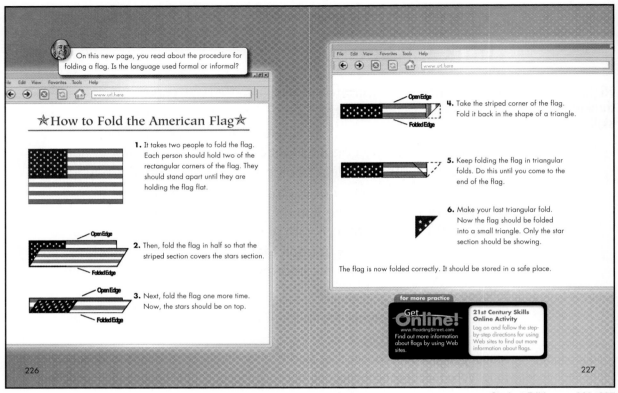

Student Edition pp. 226–227

Guide Comprehension
Skills and Strategies

Teach Web sites

21st Century Skills: Web site Explain that Web sites often contain both text and graphics that give information about a topic. Then ask: What kind of graphic sources does this Web site contain and why might the author have included these particular graphic sources?

Corrective feedback

If... students are unable to analyze the graphics for this Web site, **then...** use the model to guide students in analyzing Web site graphics.

Model the skill

 Think Aloud I know that the purpose of any graphic source is to provide information beyond what the text alone can tell you. It looks like this author has included diagrams that show how to fold the flag during each step. I think that the author included these diagrams so that the reader knows exactly what the flag is supposed to look like during each step of folding.

On their own

Have students analyze the level of formality and informality of graphic sources from other Web sites.

Extend Thinking
Think Critically

Higher-order thinking skills

Graphic Sources • Analysis Review the pictures in Steps 2–5 on pages 226–227. Estimate how many folds it takes to properly fold the American flag. Answers will vary but should match what is shown in the diagram.

Sequence • Evaluation Why does the author use a numbered list to explain the sequence of steps someone must follow to fold the American flag? Possible response: If a person trying to fold the flag correctly performed the wrong action first, the flag would not be folded properly and with respect. A numbered list helps the author organize this information in a clear way.

21st Century Skills
Web site

For more practice

Show students how to locate the Web site by clicking on the appropriate links. Be sure that they follow the step-by-step instructions for using a Web site to find out more information about flags. Discuss with students how some Web sites may be written using formal language, while others present information using more informal language.

Connect to Social Studies

When properly folded, the American flag takes the shape of a triangle. According to the Sons of the American Revolution, this is in remembrance of the three-cornered hats worn by the soldiers of the American colonies who fought for freedom from Great Britain during the American Revolution.

ELL

English Language Learners
Graphic organizer Provide support to students when creating a T-chart. Help them choose two heads for their T-charts, and then work together to add details in each column.

Objectives

- Read aloud stories with fluency and comprehension.
- ⊚ Use a dictionary to determine meanings of unknown words.
- Give an informational speech.

Check Fluency WCPM
SUCCESS PREDICTOR

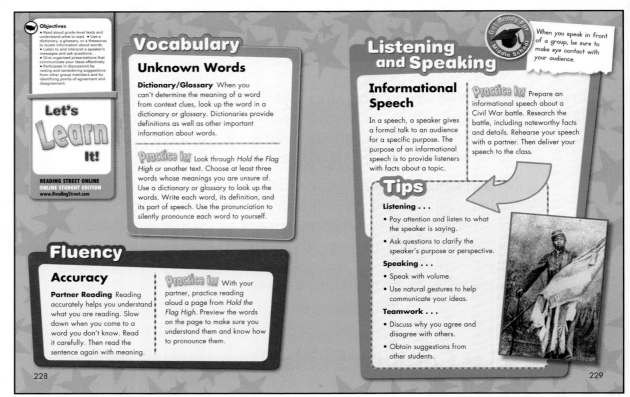

Student Edition pp. 228–229

Fluency
Accuracy

Guide Practice

Use the Student Edition activity as an assessment tool. Make sure the reading passage is at least 200 words in length. As students read aloud with partners, walk around to make sure they are reading words with accuracy.

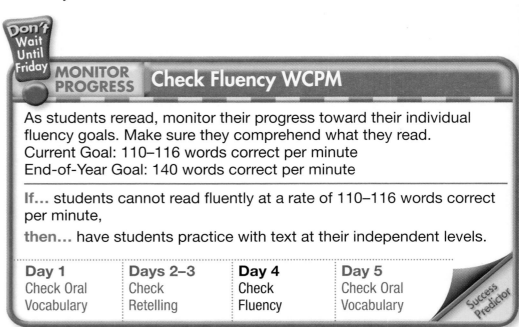

Don't Wait Until Friday

MONITOR PROGRESS   Check Fluency WCPM

As students reread, monitor their progress toward their individual fluency goals. Make sure they comprehend what they read.
Current Goal: 110–116 words correct per minute
End-of-Year Goal: 140 words correct per minute

If... students cannot read fluently at a rate of 110–116 words correct per minute,

then... have students practice with text at their independent levels.

Day 1	Days 2–3	Day 4	Day 5
Check Oral Vocabulary	Check Retelling	Check Fluency	Check Oral Vocabulary

Success Predictor

Vocabulary
 Unknown Words

Teach unknown words

Dictionary/Glossary Write these words on the board:

civil	courage	decade	eager

Have students read each word with you. Remind them that a dictionary or glossary can also help them pronounce the word.

Guide practice

Have students use a dictionary or glossary to determine the meaning of each word. Then have them practice saying the word chorally, emphasizing the pronunciation and syllabication they found in the dictionary.

On their own

Walk around the room as students work with partners to make sure the definitions and parts of speech they have written are correct. Check to make sure students can pronounce the words correctly. If students are using an electronic dictionary or glossary, make sure they know how to use each part of the entry.

Listening and Speaking
Informational Speech

Teach

Tell students that to give a good presentation, they must be organized. Remind students this begins with organized research and depends on a good delivery.

Guide practice

Have partners practice giving their presentations in pairs. Remind students to employ eye contact, speaking rate, volume, enunciation, natural gestures, and conventions of language to communicate ideas effectively. Check that students have researched properly and completely, and clear up any areas of confusion.

On their own

Have students give their presentations to the class. As students listen, remind them to interpret the speaker's messages, both verbal and nonverbal. If necessary, have students in the audience ask questions to clarify the speaker's purpose or perspective.

Informational Speech

As students speak, ask the audience to note their nonverbal communication elements. Watch for good confident posture, eye contact, a clear, slow speaking voice, expressive variations in volume, and appropriate facial expressions and gestures. Encourage the audience to use other successful students as models for their own speech.

ELL

English Language Learners
Practice pronunciation Assist pairs of students by modeling the correct pronunciation of the words from the glossary, then having students repeat after you.

Fluency

Success Predictor

Objectives
- Use a table to present information.
- Review possessive nouns.
- Spell words with irregular plurals correctly.

Research and Inquiry
Synthesize

Teach

Have students synthesize their research. Encourage students to use a word web to brainstorm about aspects of their famous person or event. For the Harriet Tubman example, different chapters may describe different times she helped others during the Civil War or different people she helped.

Remind students that their table of contents should include factual information from their research as well as a page number and chapter number for each chapter. The title of each chapter should be based on research findings.

Guide practice

Have students begin to create their table of contents. Remind them that this table will be used in their presentation on Day 5. Check to see that students included all of the necessary parts, such as page numbers. Work with students who need help dividing their topic into chapters. Suggest that they focus on a different event or aspect for each chapter.

On their own

Have students reread their table of contents on the word processor, and encourage them to copy and paste text until the chapters appear in a logical order. This will help to clarify the relationships between ideas. Then have students prepare for their presentations by practicing orally in groups.

Conventions
Possessive Nouns

Test practice

Remind students that grammar skills, such as correctly forming possessive nouns, are often assessed on important tests. Remind students that possessive nouns show ownership.

- Add an apostrophe and -s to form a singular possessive noun.

- Add an apostrophe to a plural noun ending in -s to form the possessive. If the plural does not end in -s, add an apostrophe and -s.

Daily Fix-It

Use Daily Fix-It numbers 7 and 8 in the right margin.

On their own

For additional practice, use the *Reader's and Writer's Notebook* p. 130.

Reader's and Writer's Notebook p. 130

Daily Fix-It

7. The boy had no belt for he pantz. *(his pants)*

8. If she had a pare of scisors, Mama would fix them. *(pair; scissors)*

Spelling
Irregular Plurals

Practice spelling strategy

Have pairs of students write each word from the spelling list on a note card and group them according to how the plural was formed. Have students compare and explain their reasons for grouping. Have partners take turns asking each other to name and spell a word that is an additional example for each grouping rule. Students should check their spelling using a print or online dictionary.

On their own

For additional practice, use *Let's Practice It!* p. 77 on the *Teacher Resources DVD-ROM.*

Let's Practice It!
TR DVD•77

Objectives
- Revise draft of an informal letter.
- Apply revising strategy of subtracting.

Writing—Informal Letter
Revising Strategy

MINI-LESSON

Revising Strategy: Subtracting

◼ Yesterday you wrote informal letters about a time when you or someone you know acted bravely. Today we will revise our drafts. The goal is to make your writing clearer and more organized and interesting.

◼ Display Writing Transparency 7B. Remind students that revising does not include corrections of grammar and mechanics. Tell them that this will be done later. Then introduce the revising strategy of subtracting.

◼ During revisions, ask yourself *Did I include irrelevant details that stray from the purpose of my letter?* Subtracting is the strategy in which unnecessary details are removed in order to leave a more tightly-structured and focused story. Notice the following sentence in our letter: *It reminded me of last summer when we went to the beach.* This detail goes off the topic of the rafting trip. I will take out this sentence because it doesn't relate to the immediate story.

Writing Transparency 7B, TR DVD

Tell students that they should also make sure they pay attention to the tone of their letter, and give readers a sense of closure towards the end.

Revising Tips

✔ Subtract irrelevant details that take away from the story.

✔ Make sure your tone is friendly and engaging.

✔ Review your writing for varied sentence lengths and types.

Peer conferencing

Peer Revision Have pairs of students exchange letters for peer revision. After partners have read and made notes on each other's writings, have students gather in groups of four. Tell students to switch papers with another person in their group until everyone has read and made notes on every letter. Students can then debrief, one at a time, on each other's writings. Alternatively, writers can collect the group notes about their letter to review on their own without commentary.

Have students revise their letters using the group notes they received during Peer Revision as well as the key features of an informal letter to guide them. Be sure that students are using the revising strategy subtracting.

Corrective feedback

Circulate around the room to monitor students and have conferences with them as they revise. Remind students correcting errors that they will have time to edit tomorrow. They should be working on content and organization today.

Write Guy
Jeff Anderson

Life in a Fishbowl

When a teacher can't confer with every student, a "fishbowl conference" with one willing student can allow other students to observe, listen, and explore how to appropriately respond to others writing. Reflect on what the student is doing well and how a draft might be revised and improved.

ROUTINE | **Quick Write for Fluency** | **Team Talk**

1. **Talk** Have pairs compare and contrast the subject of their letters with Sergeant Carney in *Hold the Flag High*.

2. **Write** Each student writes a few sentences summarizing their comparisons.

3. **Share** Partners read aloud their sentences, then check one other's writing for details that can be subtracted.

Routines Flip Chart

English Language Learners

Support revising Help students recognize details that do not belong. Write a list of familiar words on the board, such as *red, blue, circle, and yellow.* Call on students to identify the odd detail and use the appropriate revision mark to eliminate the word from the list.

Differentiated instruction
If students have extensive difficulty with their writing, such as sentence fragments, encourage them to rewrite a fresh first draft so that they have a clean copy to work from.

Wrap Up Your Day

✔ **Build Concepts** What did you learn about the American flag?

✔ **Oral Vocabulary** Monitor students' use of oral vocabulary as they respond to this question: *Why is it necessary to treat the flag with respect?*

✔ **Text Features** Discuss how the numbered list on pp. 226–227 helped students understand the text.

Preview DAY 5

Remind students to think about why people take risks for the American flag and for the country.

Objectives
- Review the weekly concept.
- Review oral vocabulary.

Today at a Glance

Oral Vocabulary

Comprehension
⊙ Sequence

Lesson Vocabulary
⊙ Unknown words

Word Analysis
French word origin

Literary Terms
Foreshadowing

Assessment
Fluency
Comprehension

Research and Inquiry
Communicate

Spelling
Irregular plurals

Conventions
Possessive nouns

Writing
Informal letter

Check Oral Vocabulary
SUCCESS PREDICTOR

Concept Wrap Up

Question of the Week
What are the risks in helping others?

Review the concept

Have students look back at the reading selections to find examples that demonstrate the risks of helping others.

Review Amazing Words

Display and review this week's concept map. Remind students that this week they have learned ten Amazing Words related to the risks in helping others. Have students use the Amazing Words and the concept map to answer the Question of the Week, *What are the risks in helping others?*

Risks in helping others
- Motivation
  - nation
  - officers
  - accomplishment
  - ideals
- Qualities
  - audacity
  - brazen
  - unwavering
  - trained
- Ways to help
  - cooperation
  - sacrifice

ELL **Check Concepts and Language** Use the Day 5 instruction on ELL Poster 7 to monitor students' understanding of the lesson concept.

ELL Poster 7

Amazing Ideas

Connect to the Big Question

Have pairs of students discuss how the Question of the Week connects to the Big Question: *What makes people want to do the right thing?* Tell students to use the concept map and what they have learned from this week's Anchored Talks and reading selections to form an Amazing Idea—a realization or "big idea" about Doing the Right Thing. Then ask each pair to share their Amazing Idea with the class. Have students consider each other's suggestions and identify points of agreement and disagreement.

Amazing Ideas might include these key concepts:

- Soldiers risk their lives in war, but their bravery can help others be free.

- Sometimes, a sacrifice is required to make things right. Sacrifices can be small, like a child being embarrassed as he or she sticks up for a friend, or large, like a soldier dying in battle.

- Many people take risks to save others or ensure that their lives will be better.

Write about it

Have students write a few sentences about their Amazing Idea, beginning with "This week I learned…"

It's Friday

MONITOR PROGRESS | Check Oral Vocabulary

Have individuals use this week's Amazing Words to describe the risks in helping others. Monitor students' abilities to use the Amazing Words and note which words you need to reteach.

If... students have difficulty using the Amazing Words,

then... reteach using the Oral Vocabulary Routine, pp. 203a, 206b, 214b, 224b, OV•2.

Day 1	Days 2–3	Day 4	Day 5
Check Oral Vocabulary	Check Retelling	Check Fluency	Check Oral Vocabulary

Success Predictor

Amazing Words

poses	nation
officers	trembling
unwavering	sacrifice
maneuver	audacity
cooperation	brazen

E L L

English Language Learners

Concept map Work with students to add new words to the concept map.

Oral Vocabulary

Success Predictor

Comprehension **Review**
↻ Sequence

Teach sequence

Review the definition of sequence on p. 204. Remind students that sequence is the order of events in a story. For additional support, have students review p. EI•13 on sequence.

Envision It!

Guide practice

On the board, write these events from *Hold the Flag High: The Fifty-fourth Regiment is picked to lead a charge against Fort Wagner. Sergeant Carney tells Ned to follow the flag if he feels afraid. The soldier carrying the flag is shot. Carney takes the flag and raises it over the ramparts, even as he suffers from bullet wounds.* Have students describe how earlier events foreshadow or give rise to later events.

On their own

For additional practice with sequence, use *Let's Practice It!* p. 78 on the *Teacher Resources DVD-ROM.*

Student Edition p. EI•13

Let's Practice It!
TR DVD•78

Vocabulary **Review**
↻ Unknown Words

Teach unknown words
Guide practice

Remind students to use a printed or electronic dictionary or glossary to help them understand the meanings of unknown words.

Ask students to look up the word *glory* in a dictionary or glossary. Explain that there may be more than one definition for the word. Review with students how to find the correct meaning of *glory,* as well as its prounciation, syllabication, and part of speech. Then have students use context clues to determine the correct definition for *glory* in this sentence: *The commander's actions at the battle earned him fame and glory.* Have students make up their own sentences for the other definitions of *glory.*

On their own

Have students work with partners to write sentences using this week's lesson vocabulary words. Ask partners to trade sentences and identify the context clues that help them determine each word's meaning.

Word Analysis Review
French Word Origins

Teach French word origin

Review words with French origins with students. Tell them the Old French word for *stallion* is *estalon,* which means "a horse kept in a stall" or "a male horse." Determine the meaning of *stallion.*

Guided practice

Display the following words: *union, glory, rebellion, quarrel.* Use the Strategy for Meaningful Word Parts to teach *union.*

> **ROUTINE** **Strategy for Meaningful Word Parts**
>
> 1. **Introduce the strategy** We can use French roots to help us read English words. Write *union.* Circle *unio.*
> 2. **Introduce the word parts** The root *unio* comes from the Old French word *unio.* When a final *n* is added, it makes the English word *union.*
> 3. **Connect to meaning** If I know that *unio* in Old French means "oneness or being united," then I can infer that *union* means "something that is united or made into one."
> 4. **Read the word** Run your hand under the word parts as you read *union.* Then have students read the word.
>
> Routines Flip Chart

On their own

Have students work in pairs to write and circle the French roots in *rebellio/rebellion* and *glorie/glory.* Have them use the roots to determine the meaning of each English word.

Literary Terms Review
Foreshadowing

Teach foreshadowing

Have students reread the first half of *Hold the Flag High* on pp. 210–213. Remind students that foreshadowing gives clues that indicate future events in a story.

Guide practice

Focus students on the last paragraph on p. 210. Discuss how this paragraph provides hints and clues that create suspense about future events.

On their own

With students, use a T-chart labeled *Clues* and *Events* to list and explain more examples of foreshadowing on pp. 210–213.

Lesson Vocabulary

canteen a container that holds drinks

confederacy a group of people, states, or countries that work together

glory praise, honor

quarrel a fight

rebellion a conflict that leads to war

stallion a male horse

union states that are united as one country

ELL

English Language Learners
French word origin Ask students to think of words from their home languages that are similar to English words. Discuss how noticing similarities is helpful when learning English. Then supply students with cards of the French words and the English words derived from the French words. Ask students to match the words by looking for similar word parts.

Objectives
- Read aloud grade-level text with fluency.

Plan to Assess Fluency

☑ **Week 1** Assess Advanced students.

☑ **This week assess Strategic Intervention students.**

☐ **Week 3** Assess On-Level students.

☐ **Week 4** Assess Strategic Intervention students.

☐ **Week 5** Assess any students you have not yet checked during this unit.

Set individual goals for students to enable them to reach the year-end goal.

- Current Goal: 110–116 WCPM
- Year-End Goal: 140 WCPM

Assessment

Check words correct per minute

Fluency Make two copies of the fluency passage on p. 229k. As the student reads the text aloud, mark mistakes on your copy. Also mark where the student is at the end of one minute. To figure words correct per minute (WCPM), subtract the number of mistakes from the total number of words read in one minute. Make sure students comprehend what they read.

Corrective feedback

If... students cannot read fluently at a rate of 110–116 WCPM,
then... make sure they practice with text at their independent reading levels. Provide additional fluency practice by pairing nonfluent readers with fluent readers.

If... students already read at 140 WCPM,
then... have them read a book of their choice independently.

Small Group Time

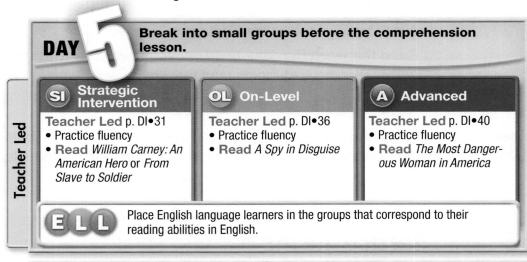

DAY 5 Break into small groups before the comprehension lesson.

Teacher Led

SI Strategic Intervention
Teacher Led p. DI•31
- Practice fluency
- Read *William Carney: An American Hero* or *From Slave to Soldier*

OL On-Level
Teacher Led p. DI•36
- Practice fluency
- Read *A Spy in Disguise*

A Advanced
Teacher Led p. DI•40
- Practice fluency
- Read *The Most Dangerous Woman in America*

ELL Place English language learners in the groups that correspond to their reading abilities in English.

Practice Stations
- Words to Know
- Get Fluent
- Read for Meaning

Independent Activities
- Grammar Jammer
- Concept Talk Video
- Vocabulary Activities

Runaway Car!

My grandfather frequently talks about an event that occurred when he   11

was a teenager. He wasn't old enough to legally drive, but he was aware of   26

how cars operated.   29

Grandfather was strolling down a slight hill. At the bottom of the hill   42

stood a cluster of youngsters chatting. As Grandfather approached them,   52

something made him glance back. He saw an old sedan coming down the   65

hill. He was surprised that he hadn't heard the car's engine. Then he saw   79

there wasn't a driver in the car! It was rolling down the hill on its own! It   96

appeared to be rapidly picking up speed.   103

Grandfather instantly thought of the kids down the hill. They couldn't hear   115

the car either. And it would roll faster and faster and probably hit them!   129

Just then, the car rolled past him. Grandfather chased it and in a few   143

strides, he caught up. When he put his hand on the driver's door handle, the   158

car nearly yanked him down. But Grandfather kept his balance and opened   170

the car door. He jumped into the seat and pushed the brake pedal hard.   184

The brakes squealed! The youngsters heard that and scattered. Grandfather   194

stopped the car. The kids were safe.   201

A woman ran up to Grandfather. "Young man," she shouted. "You're   212

driving too fast!"   215

The woman had not seen Grandfather's whole adventure. She had just   226

seen the end. But Grandfather didn't mind. He knew he had just saved the   240

lives of several youngsters.   244

MONITOR PROGRESS   • Check Fluency

Objectives
• Read grade-level text with comprehension.

Assessment

Check sequence

🎯 **Sequence** Use "The Battle Begins" on p. 229m to check students' understanding of sequence.

1. Why is this battle important, and what made it difficult to prepare for? Summarize the text, maintaining meaning and order. (The battle is important because if the Allies lost, they could lose their freedom. The preparation for the battle was difficult because it involved thousands of ships and risked hundreds of lives, and weather was bad and unpredictable.)

2. Put these three events in the correct order: Eisenhower waited for better weather; Eisenhower sent the men into battle; Eisenhower supervised plans for the battle. (Eisenhower supervised plans for the battle. Eisenhower waited for better weather. Eisenhower sent the men into battle.)

3. In paragraph 6, two events happened at the same time. What phrase tells the reader they happened at the same time? (While Eisenhower waits for better weather, he walks around and talks to the soldiers. The phrase *in those waiting days* tells the reader these two events happened at the same time.)

Corrective feedback

If… students are unable to answer the comprehension questions, **then…** use the Reteach lesson in the *First Stop* book.

Name _____

The Battle Begins

In January 1944, World War II had been raging for more than five years. So much depended on who won. If the United States and its allies did, freedom would win too. If Nazi Germany and its partners did, freedom would die. No war had meant more.

American General Dwight Eisenhower understood that well. Starting that January, he led the preparation for a great battle. It would involve thousands of ships and airplanes. It would risk hundreds of thousands of lives. These forces would have to cross the English Channel. That was the unpredictable sea between Great Britain and France.

The goal was to attack the German army that hid on the cliffs and beaches of the French coast. This attack would begin a long series of battles that Eisenhower hoped would completely defeat Germany.

Over the first months of 1944, Eisenhower supervised the planning for the battle, training of troops, and assembling of ships and airplanes. In late May, he and his forces were ready. But the weather was not. Storms postponed the attack, day after day.

During the wait for better weather, Eisenhower had time to think. He knew that many soldiers who landed on the French beaches wouldn't live to see who won. Later, many more soldiers would die in other battles. There was no way to change that. In those waiting days, Eisenhower talked to the men about their homes. He knew that many men would never see those homes again. He hoped their sacrifices would be worth it.

Finally on June 5, Eisenhower got a promising weather forecast. Tomorrow morning the storms would briefly let up. On the morning of June 6, the English Channel was filled with 6,000 ships. Some were great battleships. Some were small landing craft carrying brave soldiers from the United States, Great Britain, and Canada. As the crafts neared the coast, soldiers peered out at the beaches and cliffs ahead. The great battle was about to begin.

MONITOR PROGRESS

• Sequence

Objectives
- Communicate inquiry results.
- Take spelling test.
- Review possessive nouns.

Research and Inquiry
Communicate

Teach

Have students share their inquiry results by presenting their tables of contents and giving a brief talk on their research. Have them give organized presentations. Have students display or pass out copies of the table of contents they made on Day 4. As they explain their findings, have them interpret the factual or quantitative information included in their tables for the class. Encourage them to give organized presentations employing eye contact, speaking rate, volume, enunciation, natural gestures, and conventions of language to communicate ideas effectively.

Listening and speaking

Remind students how to be good speakers and how to communicate effectively with their audience.

- Keep eye contact with audience members.
- Speak clearly, loudly, and at an appropriate rate (not too fast or too slow).
- Use standard grammar and language conventions appropriate for your audience.
- Respond to relevant questions with appropriate details.

Remind students to follow these tips for being a good listener.

- Wait until the speaker has finished before raising your hand to ask a relevant question.
- Be polite, even if you disagree.

Point out that they should listen to and interpret all of a speaker's messages, both verbal and nonverbal. As they listen, they will focus on determining the main ideas and supporting ideas in the speaker's message.

Spelling Test
Irregular Plurals

Spelling test To administer the spelling test, refer to the directions, words, and sentences on p. 205c.

Conventions
Extra Practice

Teach Remind students that possessive nouns show ownership. Add an apostrophe and -s to form a singular possessive noun. To form plural possessive nouns, add an apostrophe to plural nouns ending in -s. Add an apostrophe and -s for plural nouns that do not.

Guide practice Have students replace the following phrases with the correct form of a possessive noun.

> **the pets of the children** (the children's pets)
>
> **the honesty of the man** (the man's honesty)
>
> **the eyes of the people** (the people's eyes)
>
> **the necks of the giraffes** (the giraffes' necks)
>
> **the voices of the women** (the women's voices)

Daily Fix-It Use Daily Fix-It numbers 9 and 10 in the right margin.

On their own Write these sentences. Have students look back in *Hold the Flag High* to find the correct possessive noun to fill in the blanks.

1. _____men took pride in the shiny brass buttons on their uniforms and new rifles on their shoulders. (Carney's)

2. He was the soldier who carried the _____ flag into battle on a short flagpole, called a staff. (regiment's)

3. Fighting the pain, the sergeant triumphantly raised the Stars and Stripes over _____ ramparts. (Fort Wagner's)

4. Ned and other members of the Fifty-fourth Regiment surrounded their wounded _____ cot. (sergeant's)

Students should complete *Let's Practice It!* p. 79 on the *Teacher Resources DVD-ROM*.

Let's Practice it!
TR DVD•79

Objectives

- Proofread revised drafts for correct use of possessive nouns.
- Proofread revised drafts for correct use of commas.
- Create and present final draft.

Writing—Informal Letter

Review
Revising

Remind students that yesterday they revised their informal letters, paying particular attention to removing unnecessary details to make the writing more focused and engaging. Today they will proofread their letters.

MINI-LESSON

Proofread for Possessive Nouns

Teach The proofreading stage gives us a chance to look closely at our work, searching for errors in mechanics such as spelling, capitalization, punctuation, and grammar. Today we will focus on making sure that possessive nouns are used correctly.

Model Let's take a look at a paragraph from the letter we began yesterday. Display Writing Transparency 7C. Explain that you will look for errors in the use of possessive nouns. I see a problem in the first sentence. The possessive noun here is supposed to refer to just one family and not several *families.* To make a singular possessive noun, I add an apostrophe and *-s* to the word. Change *families'* to *family's.* Then explain to students that they should reread their letters several times, each time looking for different types of errors: spelling, punctuation, capitalization, and grammar. Remind them that with letters, they should pay particular attention to the correct use of commas in the address, date, greeting, and closing.

Writing Transparency 7C,
TR DVD

Proofread

Display the Proofreading Tips. Ask students to proofread their compositions, using the Proofreading Tips and paying particular attention to possessive nouns and correct use of commas. Circulate around the room answering students' questions. When students have finished editing their own work, have pairs proofread each other's letters.

Proofreading Tips

✓ Check for correct use of commas in the date, greeting, and closing of the letter.

✓ Be sure that possessive nouns are used correctly.

✓ Check for correct spelling, punctuation, capitalization, and grammar.

Have students incorporate revisions and proofreading edits into their letters to create a final draft.

Present

Provide students with options for presenting their letters: a dramatic oral reading or a poster. Encourage students sharing orally to read aloud their letters with appropriate phrasing and attention to drama. Have students practice reading their letters expressively before making final presentations. Students creating posters should include a visual aspect to accompany their writing, such as hand-drawn illustrations, photographs from magazines, or other graphics. When students have finished, have each complete a Writing Self-Evaluation Guide.

ROUTINE Quick Write for Fluency Team Talk

1. **Talk** Have pairs discuss what they learned about informal letters this week.

2. **Write** Each student writes a paragraph summarizing what they learned.

3. **Share** Partners read their summaries to one another.

Routines Flip Chart

Teacher Note

Writing Self-Evaluation Guide Make copies of the Writing Self-Evaluation Guide on p. 39 of the *Reader's and Writer's Notebook* and hand out to students.

ELL

English Language Learners

Support presenting Help students present their letters orally by modeling eye contact. Speak while looking down or away from the audience. Then model the same speech while making direct eye contact. Discuss with students how the second presentation is more effective.

Poster preview Prepare students for next week by using Week 3, ELL Poster 8. Read the Poster Talk-Through to introduce the concept and vocabulary. Ask students to identify and describe objects and actions in the art.

Selection summary Send home the summary of *The Ch'i-lin Purse* in English and students' home languages, if available. They can read the summary with family members.

Preview NEXT WEEK

What are the rewards in helping others? Tell students that next week they will read about a woman who received a reward for helping someone in need.

Weekly Assessment

Use pp. 47–52 of *Weekly Tests* to check:

✔ **Word Analysis** French Word Origins

✔  **Comprehension Skill** Sequence

✔ Review **Comprehension Skill**
Compare and Contrast

✔ **Lesson Vocabulary**

canteen	rebellion
confederacy	stallion
glory	union
quarrel	

Weekly Tests

Advanced

On-Level

Strategic Intervention

Differentiated Assessment

Use pp. 37–42 of *Fresh Reads for Fluency and Comprehension* to check:

✔  **Comprehension Skill** Sequence

✔ Review **Comprehension Skill** Compare and Contrast

✔ **Fluency** Words Correct Per Minute

Fresh Reads for Fluency and Comprehension

Managing Assessment

Use *Assessment Handbook* for:

✔ **Weekly Assessment Blackline Masters for Monitoring Progress**

✔ **Observation Checklists**

✔ **Record-Keeping Forms**

✔ **Portfolio Assessment**

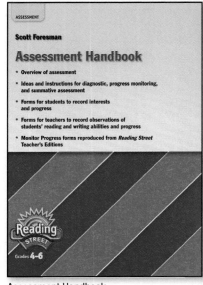
Assessment Handbook

"Number the Stars"

Continued from p. 203b

was written the date. And the real Lise Johansen had been born twenty-one years earlier.

"Kirsten Elisabeth," the officer read, looking at Kirsti's baby picture. He let the photograph fall to the floor.

"Annemarie," he read next, glanced at her, and dropped the second photograph.

"Lise Margrete," he read finally, and stared at Ellen for a long, unwavering moment. In her mind, Annemarie pictured the photograph that he held: the baby, wide-eyed, propped against a pillow, her tiny hand holding a silver teething ring, her bare feet visible below the hem of an embroidered dress. The wispy curls. Dark.

The officer tore the photograph in half and dropped the pieces on the floor. Then he turned, the heels of his shiny boots grinding into the pictures, and left the apartment. Without a word, the other two officers followed. Papa stepped forward and closed the door behind him.

Small Group Time

DAY 1

Build Background

- **Reinforce the Concept** Discuss the weekly question *What are the risks in helping others?* Some people have jobs where they take risks for other people as part of their work. This is true of soldiers in the military, police officers, firefighters, and rescue workers. What are some reasons that people are willing to take these risks? *(Possible answers: they want to help people; they have family members in these jobs; they like dangerous jobs; they feel like heroes helping others.)* Discuss the words on the concept map on pp. 202–203 in the Teacher Edition.

- **Connect to Reading** Have students recall a story they have read or heard about where someone risked his or her life to help others, either in the news or in their own town. Then ask students when they might have put themselves at risk to help someone. Even ordinary people can do amazing things. For example, someone might run into a burning building to rescue a child. This week you will read about one person in particular who risked his life to encourage his fellow soldiers.

5-Day Plan

DAY 1	• Reinforce the concept • Read Leveled Readers Concept Literacy Below Level
DAY 2	• Sequence • Inferring • Revisit Student Edition pp. 208–213
DAY 3	• Unknown Words • Revisit Student Edition pp. 214–219
DAY 4	• Practice Retelling • Read/Revisit Student Edition pp. 224–227
DAY 5	• Reread for fluency • Reread Leveled Readers

3- or 4-Day Plan

DAY 1	• Reinforce the concept • Read Leveled Readers
DAY 2	• Sequence • Inferring • Revisit Student Edition pp. 208–213
DAY 3	• Unknown Words • Revisit Student Edition pp. 214–219
DAY 4	• Practice Retelling • Read/Revisit Student Edition pp. 224–227 • Reread for fluency • Reread Leveled Readers

3-Day Plan: Eliminate the shaded box

Objectives
• Interpret a speaker's messages (both verbal and nonverbal).

For a complete literacy instructional plan and additional practice with this week's target skills and strategies, see the **Leveled Reader Teaching Guide.**

Concept Literacy Reader

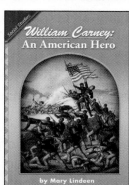

- **Read** *William Carney: An American Hero*

- **Before Reading** Preview the text with students, focusing on key concepts and vocabulary. Then have them set a purpose for reading.

- **During Reading** Read the first two pages of the text aloud while students track the print. If students are able, have them finish reading the text with a partner.

- **After Reading** After students finish reading the text, connect it to the weekly question *What are the risks in helping others?*

Below-Level Reader

- **Read** *From Slave to Soldier*

- **Before Reading** Have students preview the text, using the illustrations. Then have students set a purpose for reading.

- **During Reading** Do a choral reading of the first four pages. If students are able, have them read and discuss the remainder of the book with a partner. Have partners discuss the following questions:

  - How did Caleb know how to read and write? *(His master taught him.)*

  - What effect did the Emancipation Proclamation have on his life? *(He was finally free to do what he wanted.)*

  - Why did he want to join the 54th regiment instead of helping people at home? *(He wanted to fight to show that African Americans could be soldiers.)*

- **After Reading** Have students look at and discuss the concept map. Connect the Below-Level Reader to the weekly question *What are the risks in helping others?*

MONITOR PROGRESS

If... students have difficulty reading the selection with a partner,

then... have them follow along as they listen to the Leveled Readers DVD-ROM.

If... students have trouble understanding the effect of the Emancipation Proclamation,

then... reread the relevant pages and discuss how this legislation changed the Civil War.

Objectives
- Interpret a speaker's messages (both verbal and nonverbal).

Student Edition p. EI•13

More Reading

Use additional Leveled Readers or other texts at students' instructional levels to reinforce this week's skills and strategies. For text suggestions, see the Leveled Reader Database or the Leveled Readers Skills Chart on pp. CL 24–CL 29.

SI *Strategic Intervention*

DAY 2

Reinforce Comprehension

Skill Sequence Review with students *Envision It!* EI•13 on sequence. Then use p. 204 to review the definition of sequence. The sequence is the order in which events take place, from first to last. Clue words, such as *first, next, then,* and *finally* can help you follow the order. Other clues are dates and the time of day.

Strategy Inferring Review the definition of inferring. Remind students that sometimes the order of events is not stated directly in the text. Students can use context clues to guess, or infer, the order. For additional support, refer students to *Envision It!* p. EI•18.

Revisit *Hold the Flag High* on pp. 208–213. Have students begin reading the selection aloud with a partner. As they read, have them apply the comprehension skill and strategy to the selection. Have students read paragraph two of the text.

• What is the correct sequence of the following events?

  • Battle of Fort Wagner takes place *(third)*

  • Emancipation Proclamation frees slaves *(first)*

  • African Americans join the Union army *(second)*

• What clue word is used in the first sentence to show sequence? *(after)*

• What other details in the paragraph provide clues to the order of events? *(the dates January 1863 and July 1863)*

Use the During Reading Differentiated Instruction for additional support for struggling readers.

MONITOR PROGRESS

If... students have difficulty reading along with the group,

then... have them follow along as they listen to the AudioText.

Objectives
• Make inferences about text.
• Identify sequence of events.

 **SI** Strategic Intervention

DAY **3**

Reinforce Vocabulary

Unknown Words/Dictionary/Glossary Read the following sentence from the text: "After a breakfast of hardtack and coffee, each soldier had his name pinned to the back of his uniform."

- What do the context clues "breakfast" and "coffee" tell you about the word *hardtack*? *(It is something to eat.)*

- Do the clues tell you exactly what *hardtack* is? *(no)*

When I can't figure out the meaning of a word from context clues, I need to look it up in a dictionary or glossary. The dictionary entry for *hardtack* gives the pronunciation, part of speech, and explains that the word means "a kind of hard biscuit or cracker."

Read another sentence from *Hold the Flag High:* "He was mounting a rampart, saber in hand, shouting: 'Forward, Fifty-fourth,' as he disappeared into the breach." Which words in this sentence might you want to look up in the dictionary? *(rampart, saber, breach)*

Revisit *Hold the Flag High* on pp. 214–219. Review *Words!* on p. W•14. As students finish reading the selection, encourage them to use a dictionary or glossary to figure out the meaning of any unfamiliar words when context clues are not enough to help them.

Use the During Reading Differentiated Instruction for additional support for struggling readers.

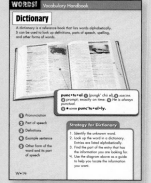

Student Edition p. W•14

More Reading

Use additional Leveled Readers or other texts at students' instructional levels to reinforce this week's skills and strategies. For text suggestions, see the Leveled Reader Database or the Leveled Readers Skills Chart on pp. CL 24–CL 29.

MONITOR PROGRESS

If... students need more practice with the lesson vocabulary, **then...** use *Envision It! Pictured Vocabulary Cards.*

Objectives
- Use a dictionary or glossary (printed or electronic) to determine meanings of words.

SI Strategic Intervention — DAY 4

Practice Retelling

- **Retell** Have students work in pairs and use the Retelling Cards to retell *Hold the Flag High*. Monitor retelling and prompt students as needed. If students struggle, model a fluent retelling.

Genre Focus

- **Before Reading or Revisiting** "How to Fold the American Flag" on pp. 224–227, read aloud the genre information about Web sites on p. 224. Explain to students that Web sites contain information about a topic and give links to other Web sites.

  Then have students preview "How to Fold the American Flag."

  - How do you get to the main page of this Web site? *(by typing the URL for the site into the Web browser)*

  - What three Web links appear on the main page? *(History of the American Flag, Symbolism of the American Flag, How to Fold the American Flag)*

  Have students set a purpose for reading based on their preview.

- **During Reading or Revisiting** Have students read along with you while tracking the print or do a choral reading of the Web site. Stop to discuss any unfamiliar words, such as *symbol* and *triangular.*

- **After Reading or Revisiting** Have students share their reactions to the Web site. Then guide them through the Get Online! activity.

MONITOR PROGRESS

If... students have difficulty retelling the selection,

then... have them review the story using the illustrations.

Objectives
- Analyze various digital media venues for levels of formality.

 Go Digital!

eSelection

eReaders

Differentiated Instruction

SI *Strategic Intervention*

SI *Strategic Intervention*

DAY **5**

For a complete literacy instructional plan and additional practice with this week's target skills and strategies, see the **Leveled Reader Teaching Guide.**

Concept Literacy Reader

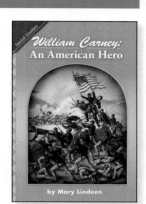

- **Model** Model the fluency skill of accuracy for students. Ask students to listen as you read aloud the following sentence: "When William Carney was 23, he joined the Union, or Northern, army." If I read too quickly, I might reverse the numerals, reading 32 for 23, or leave out the little word *or*, reading "Union Northern army."

- **Fluency Routine**

  1. Have students reread sentences from *William Carney: An American Hero* with a partner.

  2. For optimal fluency, students should reread each sentence three or four times.

  3. As students read, monitor accuracy and provide corrective feedback. If students are skipping words, mispronouncing words, or reading the wrong words, have them read at a slower pace.

  See *Routines Flip Chart* for more help with fluency.

- **Retell** Have students retell *William Carney: An American Hero*. Prompt as necessary.

Below-Level Reader

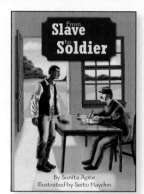

- **Model** Ask students to listen carefully as you read aloud the first two pages of *From Slave to Soldier*, emphasizing accurate reading.

- **Fluency Routine**

  1. Have students reread passages from *From Slave to Soldier* with a partner or individually.

  2. For optimal fluency, students should reread each sentence three or four times.

  3. As students read, monitor accuracy and provide corrective feedback. If students are skipping words or reading the wrong words, have them read at a slower pace.

  See *Routines Flip Chart* for more help with fluency.

- **Retell** For additional practice, have students retell *From Slave to Soldier* page-by-page, using the illustrations. Prompt as necessary.

  • Where and when does the story take place?

  • What happens to Caleb that changes his life?

MONITOR PROGRESS

If... students have difficulty reading fluently,

then... provide additional fluency practice by pairing nonfluent readers with fluent ones.

Objectives
• Read aloud grade-level stories with fluency.

Small Group Time

Pacing Small Group Instruction

⏱ 15–20 mins.

5-Day Plan

DAY 1	• Expand the concept • Read On-Level Reader
DAY 2	• ⊙ Sequence • ⊙ Inferring • Revisit Student Edition pp. 208–213
DAY 3	• ⊙ Unknown Words • Revisit Student Edition pp. 214–219
DAY 4	• Practice Retelling • Read/Revisit Student Edition pp. 224–227
DAY 5	• Reread for fluency • Reread On-Level Reader

3- or 4-Day Plan

DAY 1	• Expand the concept • On-Level Reader
DAY 2	• ⊙ Sequence • ⊙ Inferring • Revisit Student Edition pp. 208–213
DAY 3	• ⊙ Unknown Words • Revisit Student Edition pp. 214–219
DAY 4	• Practice Retelling • Read/Revisit Student Edition pp. 224–227 • Reread for fluency • Reread On-Level Reader

3-Day Plan: Eliminate the shaded box.

OL On-Level **DAY 1**

Build Background

■ **Expand the Concept** Connect the weekly question and expand the concept. In some ways, spies in wartime take bigger risks than soldiers do. If spies are captured, they will not be treated like ordinary soldiers but will probably be killed right away. Discuss the meaning of the words on the concept map on pp. 202–203 in the Teacher Edition.

On-Level Reader

For a complete literacy instructional plan and additional practice with this week's target skills and strategies, see the **Leveled Reader Teaching Guide.**

■ **Before Reading** *A Spy in Disguise,* have students preview the reader by looking at the title, cover, and pictures in the book.

• What is the topic of this book? *(an African American woman serves as a spy during the Civil War)*

• What is unusual about how she did her work? *(She used different disguises, including fooling people into believing she was a man.)*

Have students create web diagrams with *Adventures of Sarah Emma Edmonds* in the center. This book is about the adventures of a Union spy during the Civil War. Use your web to organize Edmonds's different adventures as a spy.

■ **During Reading** Read aloud the first three pages of the book as students follow along. Then have them finish reading the book on their own. Remind students to add different adventures to their webs as they read.

■ **After Reading** Have partners compare their web diagrams.

• What kinds of risks did Edmonds take as a spy?

• How does the topic relate to the weekly question *What are the risks in helping others?*

Objectives
• Interpret a speaker's messages (both verbal and nonverbal).

OL On-Level

DAY 2

Expand Comprehension

◉ **Skill Sequence** Use p. 204 to review the definition of sequence. For additional review, see p. EI•13 in *Envision It!* Remind students that clue words, such as *first, next, then,* and *finally,* show sequence. Other clues are dates and the time of day.

◉ **Strategy Inferring** Review the definition of inferring. Point out to students that when they infer they combine their own knowledge with evidence in the text. They can use this strategy to help them understand the sequence of events. What can you infer from the fact that Colonel Shaw reached the rampart of Fort Wagner before the 54th's colorbearer? *(Colonel Shaw was leading the charge of the 54th Massachusetts.)* For additional support, refer students to *Envision It!* p. EI•18.

Revisit *Hold the Flag High* on pp. 208–213. As students read, have them apply the comprehension skill and strategy to the text.

• What clue words in the text tell you when the selection begins? *(the phrase "the night before a battle")*

• What clue tells you that the next day has arrived? *(the phrase "long before the sun rose")*

Have students create a sequence chart for the major historical events mentioned in *Hold the Flag High.* Have them use clue words in each box to indicate the sequence. *(Possible chart: First, Civil War broke out. Next, the Emancipation Proclamation was passed. Then, the battle of Fort Wagner was fought. Long after, the Robert Gould Shaw Memorial was unveiled. Finally, William Carney was awarded the Congressional Medal of Honor.)*

Student Edition p. EI•13

More Reading

Use additional Leveled Readers or other texts at students' instructional levels to reinforce this week's skills and strategies. For text suggestions, see the Leveled Reader Database or the Leveled Readers Skills Chart on pp. CL 24–CL 29.

Objectives
• Make inferences about text.
• Identify sequence of events.

On-Level

DAY 3

Expand Vocabulary

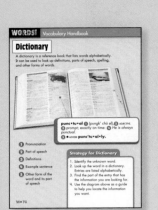

Student Edition p. W•14

More Reading

Use additional Leveled Readers or other texts at students' instructional levels to reinforce this week's skills and strategies. For text suggestions, see the Leveled Reader Database or the Leveled Readers Skills Chart on pp. CL 24–CL 29.

Unknown Words/Dictionary/Glossary Read the first sentence of the text: "When the American Civil War broke out in 1861, the North and South had been quarreling for decades over the future direction of the country." The context does not provide sufficient clues to figure out the meaning of *decades*. When I can't determine the meaning of the word from context, I need to look it up in a dictionary or glossary.

Write the sentences below on the board. Have students look up the meanings of the underlined words in a dictionary and then rewrite the sentences, substituting the dictionary meanings for the unfamiliar words.

- Soldiers <u>bristled</u> with <u>anticipation</u>. *(Soldiers rose up with eagerness to fight.)*

- The <u>artillery</u> shelled all day, but finally the generals were ready to send in the <u>infantry</u>. *(The cannon shelled all day, but finally the generals were ready to send in the foot soldiers.)*

- Ned <u>solemnly</u> drummed on the beat—footfalls and drumbeats in <u>syncopation</u>. *(Ned seriously drummed on the beat—footfalls and drumbeats in offbeat rhythm.)*

Revisit *Hold the Flag High* on pp. 214–219. Review *Words!* on p. W•14. As students finish reading, encourage them to use dictionaries and glossaries to figure out the meaning of any unfamiliar words.

Have students recall what has happened in the selection so far. Ask: Why is Shaw's speech so important? *(It shows no fear, and it inspires the soldiers to follow Shaw confidently into battle.)*

Objectives
- Use a dictionary or glossary (printed or electronic) to determine meanings of words.

 **OL** On-Level

DAY 4

Practice Retelling

■ **Retell** To assess students' comprehension, use the Retelling Cards. Monitor retelling and prompt students as needed.

Genre Focus

■ **Before Reading or Revisiting** "How to Fold the American Flag" on pp. 224–227, read aloud the information about Web sites on p. 224. *What kinds of information and links might appear on a museum Web site? (the museum's address, phone number, and hours of operation; links to maps and directions, museum history, current and future exhibitions, the gift shop, membership, and volunteer and employment opportunities)*

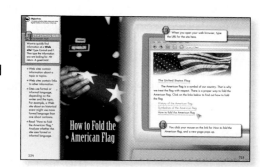

Have students preview "How to Fold the American Flag" and set a purpose for reading.

- *What can you tell from looking at the text? (It is a Web site about folding the flag; the text is a numbered list of steps.)*

- *How do the illustrations make the text more effective? (They show step-by-step folds in the flag in an easy-to-follow visual way.)*

■ **During Reading or Revisiting** Have students read along with you while tracking the print.

- *How many people are needed to properly fold an American flag? (two)*

- *Where are they standing when they begin to fold the flag? (at either end of the flag, far enough apart so that the flag is held flat between them)*

- *What section of the flag is showing when it has been completely folded? (the star section)*

■ **After Reading or Revisiting** Have students share their reaction to the Web site. Then have them write a paragraph describing a favorite Web site and which of its features are most effective.

Objectives
• Analyze various digital media venues for levels of formality.

Small Group Time

On-Level Reader

■ **Model** Model the fluency skill of accuracy for students. Stress the importance of previewing any difficult words or ideas on the page so they can practice them. Read aloud a sentence from *A Spy in Disguise.*

■ **Fluency Routine**

1. Have students reread sentences from *A Spy in Disguise* with a partner.

2. For optimal fluency, students should reread each sentence three to four times.

3. As students read, monitor accuracy and provide corrective feedback. If students are skipping words or reading the wrong words, have them read at a slower pace.

See *Routines Flip Chart* for more help with fluency.

■ **Retell** For additional practice, have students use headings and photographs as a guide to retell *A Spy in Disguise.* Prompt as necessary.

- Where does Emma's story begin? *(as a farmer's daughter in Canada)*

- What form does the writer use to tell the story? *(a sequence of dates)*

- What event changes her life? *(She joins the Union army.)*

- What results from this change? *(She becomes a successful spy.)*

Objectives
• Read aloud grade-level stories with fluency.

A *Advanced*   **DAY** 1

Build Background

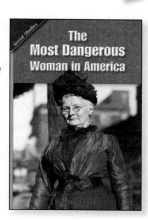
The Most Dangerous Woman in America

■ **Extend the Concept** Discuss the weekly question *What are the risks in helping others?*

• Why are military personnel given medals for heroism? *(Medals show gratitude for the risks such people take in serving others.)*

• Who else is affected by the risks taken by military personnel? *(their families, friends, and communities)*

Advanced Reader

For a complete literacy instructional plan and additional practice with this week's target skills and strategies, see the **Leveled Reader Teaching Guide.**

■ **Before Reading** *The Most Dangerous Woman in America,* tell students to recall the Read Aloud "Number the Stars."

• What danger threatens Ellen Rosen? *(a Nazi death camp)*

• What risk is the Johansen family taking? *(They may be sent to a camp themselves if they are caught hiding Ellen.)*

Today you will read about a woman who risked her life working to improve the lives of those who had little power to help themselves.

Have students look at the illustrations in the book and use them to predict what will be explained in the text. Then have students set a purpose for reading.

■ **During Reading** Have students read the Advanced Reader independently. Encourage them to think critically. For example, ask:

• Why would someone like Mother Jones want to risk her life for others?

• What do you think made her such a "dangerous" woman?

■ **After Reading** Have students review the concept map and explain how *The Most Dangerous Woman in America* helps students answer the weekly question *What are the risks in helping others?* Prompt as necessary.

■ **Now Try This** Assign "Now Try This" at the end of the Advanced Reader.

Objectives
• Interpret a speaker's messages (both verbal and nonverbal).

Pacing Small Group Instruction
15–20 mins.

5-Day Plan

DAY 1	• Extend the concept • Read Advanced Reader
DAY 2	• Sequence • Inferring • Revisit Student Edition pp. 208–213
DAY 3	• Unknown Words • Revisit Student Edition pp. 214–219
DAY 4	• Web site • Read/Revisit Student Edition pp. 224–227
DAY 5	• Reread for fluency • Reread Advanced Reader

3- or 4-Day Plan

DAY 1	• Extend the concept • Advanced Reader
DAY 2	• Sequence • Inferring • Revisit Student Edition pp. 208–213
DAY 3	• Unknown Words • Revisit Student Edition pp. 214–219
DAY 4	• Web site • Read/Revisit Student Edition pp. 224–227 • Reread for fluency • Reread Advanced Reader

3-Day Plan: Eliminate the shaded box.

More Reading

Use additional Leveled Readers or other texts at students' instructional levels to reinforce this week's skills and strategies. For text suggestions, see the Leveled Reader Database or the Leveled Readers Skills Chart on pp. CL 24–CL 29.

A Advanced   **DAY 2**

Extend Comprehension

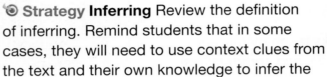

◉ **Skill** **Sequence** Use p. EI•13 to review the definition of sequence. Remind students that signal words can help them understand the order in which events occur.

◉ **Strategy** **Inferring** Review the definition of inferring. Remind students that in some cases, they will need to use context clues from the text and their own knowledge to infer the sequence. For additional support, refer students to *Envision It!* p. EI•18.

■ **Revisit** *Hold the Flag High* on pp. 208–213. Have students apply the comprehension skill and strategy as they read.

Write the following events on the board. Have students put them into correct order and identify the clue words in the text that indicate their sequence.

- battle of Fort Wagner *(fourth; "tomorrow")*
- parade through Boston *(first; "a few weeks before")*
- camping south of Charleston Bay *(third; "once they arrived")*
- sailing to South Carolina *(second; "then")*

■ **Critical Thinking** Encourage students to think critically as they read the selection.

- How would the men have felt if Captain Shaw had not led the charge? *(They may have felt that he didn't trust them or that he wasn't brave enough to lead.)*

- What if the flag had touched the ground? How might this have affected the troops? *(Having the flag touch the ground was like surrendering. The troops may have felt that the battle was lost.)*

- Why do you think it was important that the 54th regiment were the first soldiers into the battle? *(They had a lot to prove to others about whether African American soldiers could fight. It takes a lot of courage to be the first to face enemy fire.)*

Objectives
- Make inferences about text.
- Identify sequence of events.

DAY 3

Extend Vocabulary

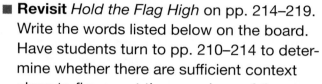

Unknown Words/Dictionary/Glossary
Remind students that when they cannot determine the meaning of an unfamiliar word from context clues, they should look it up in a dictionary or glossary.

■ **Revisit** *Hold the Flag High* on pp. 214–219. Write the words listed below on the board. Have students turn to pp. 210–214 to determine whether there are sufficient context clues to figure out the meanings of these words. If so, have them write a definition for the word. If not, have them look the word up in a dictionary and write down the meaning.

- decade *(insufficient context; period of ten years)*

- regiment *(sufficient context; army unit)*

- emancipation *(sufficient context; act of freeing)*

- bristled *(insufficient context; rose up, stood stiffly)*

- anticipation *(insufficient context; eagerness about the future)*

- infantry *(sufficient context; foot soldiers)*

- syncopation *(insufficient context; offbeat rhythm)*

■ **Critical Thinking** Have students recall what has happened in the selection so far. Encourage critical thinking.

- Why was it important to form an all-black regiment at this time in the Civil War?

- What do you think made Captain Shaw willing to risk his career to lead such a regiment?

More Reading

Use additional Leveled Readers or other texts at students' instructional levels to reinforce this week's skills and strategies. For text suggestions, see the Leveled Reader Database or the Leveled Readers Skills Chart on pp. CL 24–CL 29.

Objectives
• Use a dictionary or glossary (printed or electronic) to determine meanings of words.

A Advanced

Genre Focus

- **Before Reading or Revisiting** "How to Fold the American Flag" on pp. 224–227, read the sidebar information on Web sites. Ask students use the text features to set a purpose for reading and then have them read the selection on their own.

- **During Reading or Revisiting** Remind students that a Web site often contains links to other information.

  - What other Web links might be appropriate for a Web site on the American flag? *(possible answers: the Flag Code; lists of holidays on which to display the flag; texts of patriotic songs, such as "The Star-Spangled Banner," "The Stars and Stripes Forever," "You're A Grand Old Flag")*

- **After Reading or Revisiting** Have students do the Get Online! activity independently.

Objectives
- Analyze various digital media venues for levels of formality.

A Advanced

- **Reread For Fluency** Have students silently reread passages from *The Most Dangerous Woman in America*. Then have them reread aloud with a partner or individually. As students read, monitor accuracy and provide corrective feedback. If students read accurately on the first reading, they do not need to reread three to four times. Assess the accuracy of students in this group using p. 229j.

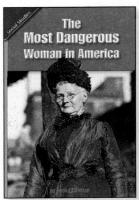

- **Retell** Have students summarize the main idea and key details from the Advanced Reader, *The Most Dangerous Woman in America*.

- **Now Try This** Have students complete their projects. You may wish to review their work before they share it with classmates.

Objectives
- Read aloud grade-level stories with fluency.

Support for English Language Learners

The ELL lessons are organized by strands. Use them to scaffold the weekly curriculum of lessons or during small group time instruction.

Academic Language

Students will hear or read the following academic language in this week's core instruction. As students encounter the vocabulary, provide a simple definition or concrete example. Then ask students to suggest an example or synonym of the word and identify available cognates.

Skill Words	sequence	possessive (posesivo)
	accuracy	inflected endings
	characterization	
Concept Words	risk	brave
	courage	honor (honor)

*Spanish cognates in parentheses

Concept Development

 What are the risks in helping others?

■ **Preteach Concept**

- **Prior Knowledge** Have students turn to pp. 202–203 in the Student Edition. Call attention to the picture of the man helping the woman across the water and have students use their prior experiences to understand the meaning of *risk*. Have you ever helped someone do something that might be dangerous?

- **Discuss Concept** Elicit students' knowledge and experience of taking risks to help others. Do you think people should take risks to help others? The soldiers in the picture took risks to save other people's lives. Do you think that was a good thing to do? Why? Supply background information.

- **Poster Talk-Through** Read the Poster Talk-Through on ELL Poster 7 aloud and work through the Day 1 activities.

■ **Daily Concept and Vocabulary Development** Use the daily activities on ELL Poster 7 to build concept and vocabulary knowledge.

Objectives
- Use prior knowledge and experiences to understand meanings in English.
- Use accessible language and learn new and essential language in the process.
- Speak using grade-level content area vocabulary in context to internalize new English words and build academic language proficiency.

Content Objectives
- Use concept vocabulary related to risks involved in helping others.

Language Objectives
- Express ideas in response to art and discussion.
- Use prior experience to understand meaning.

Daily Planner

DAY 1	• **Frontload Concept** • **Preteach** Comprehension Skill, Vocabulary, Phonics/Spelling, Conventions • **Writing**
DAY 2	• **Review** Concept, Vocabulary, Comprehension Skill • **Frontload Main Selection** • **Practice** Phonics/Spelling, Conventions/Writing
DAY 3	• **Review** Concept, Comprehension Skill, Vocabulary, Conventions/Writing • **Reread Main Selection** • **Practice** Phonics/Spelling
DAY 4	• **Review Concept** • **Read ELL/ELD Readers** • **Practice** Phonics/Spelling, Conventions/Writing
DAY 5	• **Review** Concept, Vocabulary, Comprehension Skill, Phonics/Spelling, Conventions • **Reread ELL/ELD Readers** • **Writing**

*See the ELL Handbook for ELL Workshops with targeted instruction.

Concept Talk Video

Use the Concept Talk Video Routine (*ELL Handbook,* p. 477) to build background knowledge about the risks in helping others. For more listening practice, see *Use Classroom Resources* (*ELL Handbook,* pp. 406–407).

Support for English Language Learners

Language Objectives

- Understand and use basic vocabulary
- Learn meanings of grade-level vocabulary
- Review to learn basic vocabulary.

Language Opportunity: Speaking

To help them internalize new English words, have students speak using grade-level social studies content area vocabulary, such as *war, guns, soldiers, army, conflict* and so on. Students can tell a partner about the Civil War or another war. Create sentence frames for Beginning students (_____ and _____ fought a war.) Give Intermediate and Advanced students key content area vocabulary to include when they speak. Advanced High students can also prepare questions to ask their partners.

Language Opportunity: Writing

Have students write using content-based lesson vocabulary. Have them write about a topic in Social Studies or a short article that could appear in a newspaper.

Basic Vocabulary

■ **High-Frequency Words** Use different learning strategies to acquire basic vocabulary. Model for students how to use a memorization strategy to learn basic vocabulary. Students can create flash cards with one high-frequency word written on each card—*come, these, know, see, use, get, like, then, first,* and *any.* Pair students and have one student offer clues while the other student tries to guess the word. Provide support and guidance as necessary.

Lesson Vocabulary

■ **Preteach** Use the following routine to preteach the Lesson Vocabulary:

1. Write the lesson vocabulary words on note cards or use this week's Word Cards (*ELL Handbook*, p. 65)—*stallion, quarrel, union, Confederacy, rebellion, glory,* and *canteen.*

2. Display each word and say it for students. Then ask students to repeat the word.

3. If students have difficulty with a word, model how a word's meaning can be expressed with other similar words. For example, say, The cowboy rode a *stallion*, or male horse.

4. **Write** Randomly distribute the word cards to students. Have them say and write a sentence using the word on the card. Then have students switch cards and say and write more sentences.

Beginning Give students a sentence frame to assist them in speaking and then writing a sentence.

Intermediate Have students say and write one sentence using the lesson vocabulary word.

Advanced Have students say and write two sentences using the same lesson vocabulary word.

Advanced High Have students say and write two sentences using more than one lesson vocabulary word.

Objectives
- Use strategic learning techniques such as concept mapping, drawing, memorizing, comparing, contrasting, and reviewing to acquire basic and grade-level vocabulary.
- Use accessible language and learn new and essential language in the process.

 ELL English Language Learners

■ **Reteach** Distribute a copy of the Word Cards and eight blank cards to pairs of students. Have partners write a clue or simple picture on a blank card for each word. Have students mix the Word Cards and clue cards together and spread them out, facedown, on a table. Students take turns choosing two cards and trying to match a word with its clue. When students make a match, have them read the word aloud and use it in a sentence.

■ **Writing** Have pairs of students select a Word Card. Ask each pair to draw a picture illustrating the selected word. Circulate among students, helping each pair write a caption that includes the selected word and describes the picture. Have each pair share their picture and sentence with the class. Before students begin, model the activity by drawing a picture of a horse. Write the following sentence under the picture and say it aloud: The stallion stands in a field.

 Leveled Support

Beginning Write the sentence for the students. Have the pair copy the sentence and practice speaking it correctly.

Intermediate Have students write the sentence. Review their work and offer suggestions before each pair presents their picture to the class.

Advanced/Advanced High Have students select two Word Cards and draw a picture using both words. Have students write two sentences using both words.

MINI-LESSON

Represent Words

It is helpful for English learners to learn new words by grouping together words that are related to a specific theme, quality, or activity. Because many of this week's vocabulary words relate to taking risks, use a concept web to show the connection between words such as rebellion, quarrel, union, and glory. Have students brainstorm other related word and explain the relationships.

Language Objective

- Produce drawings, phrases, and short sentences to show understanding of Lesson Vocabulary

- Use a concept web as a strategy to understand words.

Objectives

- Use strategic learning techniques such as concept mapping, drawing, memorizing, comparing, contrasting, and reviewing to acquire basic and grade-level vocabulary.
- Expand and internalize initial English vocabulary by learning and using high-frequency English words necessary for identifying and describing people, places, and objects by retelling simple stories and basic information represented or supported by pictures and by learning and using routine language needed for classroom communication.

Content Objectives

- Monitor and adjust oral comprehension.

Language Objectives

- Discuss oral passages.
- Use a graphic organizer as visual support to aid comprehension.

ELL Teacher Tip

Remind students that words like *first, next, then,* and *last* can help them order the events in a story.

ELL English Language Learners

Listening Comprehension

The Photograph

It is September 29, 1943, in Denmark. Nazi soldiers from Germany are sending Jewish people to death camps. A Jewish girl named Ellen Rosen is staying with her best friend, Annemarie Johansen.

Three Nazi officers come into the apartment. The officers ask the girls what their names are. Annemarie says her name is Annemarie Johansen. Ellen pretends to be her sister, Lise Johansen.

The officer looks at Ellen and grabs her hair. He says that the other children in the family have blond hair. But Ellen has dark hair. He asks, "Where did you get her?"

Papa shows the officer three pictures. Papa says that they are pictures of his three daughters. The pictures show three girls as babies. Mama had written the name of each baby on each photograph. The real Lise Johansen was now 21 years old.

The officer looks at each photograph. He looks at the one that says "Lise Margrete." The baby in the picture has dark hair just like Ellen. The officer tears up the photograph and leaves the apartment. The other two officers follow. Papa closes the door.

Prepare for the Read Aloud The modified Read Aloud above prepares students for listening to the oral reading "Number the Stars" on p. 203b.

- **First Listening: Listen to Understand** Write the title of the Read Aloud on the board. This story takes place during World War II. It is about a Jewish girl in Denmark who must hide from German soldiers. What does she do? Afterward, ask the question again and have students share their answers.

- **Second Listening: Listen to Check Understanding** Using Story Map A (*ELL Handbook,* p. 483) work with students to list what happened in the story. Now listen again to check that the details are in the right order. Help students adjust the details.

Objectives

- Demonstrate English comprehension and expand reading skills by employing basic reading skills such as demonstrating understanding of supporting ideas and details in text and graphic sources, summarizing text and distinguishing main ideas from details commensurate with the content area.

ELL English Language Learners

Phonics and Spelling

■ **Irregular Plurals** Use Sound-Spelling Cards 139–142 to teach the sounds, pronunciations, and spellings of irregular plurals.

Display card 141. For many words in English, you add -s to the end to make it plural. *Dog* becomes *dogs.* Write the word on the board and circle the -s.

Display card 139. If a word in English ends in s, x, ch, or sh, you add -es to the end to make it plural. Write the word and circle the -es.

Display card 142. If a word in English ends in a consonant plus y, change the y to i and add -es to make it plural. Write the word and circle the -ies.

Display card 140. If a noun ends with -fe, you change the f to v and add -s to make it plural. *Wolf* becomes *wolves.* Write the word and circle the -ves.

Word Analysis: Inflected Endings -ed, -ing

■ **Teach/Model** The inflected endings *-ed* and *-ing* are added to verbs to change the tense, or time (past, present, future) that the action of the verb shows. Write the words *quarreling, drumming* and *moving* on the board. Write sentences on the board and have students explain how the inflected ending changes meaning.

■ **Practice** Display the following spelling rules: To make the *-ed* and *-ing* forms of a verb, add *-ed* and *-ing* to most verbs. Drop the silent e before adding *-ed* or *-ing*.

Write these verbs on the board: *jump, hike, fish, drink.* Have students follow spelling rules as they add inflected endings to each of these words.

 Leveled Support

Beginning/Intermediate Have students add the ending *-ing* to each of the verbs. Then have them use each word aloud in a sentence.

Advanced/Advanced High Have students add *-ed* and *-ing* to the verbs. Challenge them to write a sentence using two or more of the verbs.

Content Objectives
• Identify words with inflected endings *-ed, -ing.*
• Identify words with irregular plurals.

Language Objectives
• Apply phonics and decoding skills to vocabulary.
• Spell words with inflected endings with increasing accuracy.
• Use contexted support to develop vocabulary.

 Transfer Skills

Irregular Plurals English learners may add -s to irregular nouns in sentences for which English uses the singular form for a quantity: *sheeps, womens, clothings.*

Content Objectives

- Describe the sequence of a text.
- Identify sequence to aid comprehension.

Language Objectives

- Employ and expand the skill of determining sequence to comprehend text.
- Retell the sequence in a reading.
- Write a sequence.

ELL English Language Learners

Comprehension
Sequence

■ **Preteach** Explain the basic reading skill of determining sequence. A sequence is the order in which things happen. First I opened the book. Then I started to read. Have students turn to Envision It! on p. El•13 in the Student Edition. Read the text aloud together. Have students employ the skill as they tell the sequence that they see in the pictures. Discuss how this skill helps them understand what they read.

■ **Reteach** Distribute copies of the Picture It! (*ELL Handbook*, p. 66). Have students look at the images. Have the students reread the passage, thinking about the order of events. Have them explain to a partner the process for donations. Then, as a class use the passage to place the steps in the correct order. As you write the steps on the board, have the students find the sentence in the text and number it to verify the order. Discuss how the text follows a logical sequence. (1. Donate on line 2. Money is sent to the center. 3. Volunteers buy supplies.)

 Beginning/Intermediate Read the passage to the students. Then write a 3-column chart on the board, labeled first, second, and third. Guide the students in sequencing the three events for supporting the cause.

Advanced/Advanced High Have students reread the passage. Ask the students to think about the sequence of events in the passage to explain what happens once you donate. Then, discuss as a class how they put the events into a logical sequence.

MINI-LESSON

Social Language

Tell students that people often use sequence when they are describing things that happened to them in the past. For example: First, I waited in line. Then I got my ticket. And then I went into the movie theater. Write these topics on the board: *Yesterday, Last Summer, This Morning.* Have students choose one of the topics to talk about. Provide these sentence frames: First I ____. Then I ____.

Objectives

- Monitor oral and written language production and employ self-corrective techniques or other resources.
- Understand the general meaning, main points, and important details of spoken language ranging from situations in which topics, language, and contexts are familiar to unfamiliar.

English Language Learners

Reading Comprehension
Hold the Flag High

■ **Frontloading** Have students look through *Hold the Flag High,* pp. 200–213 in the Student Edition. Distribute copies of the English summary of *Hold the Flag High* (*ELL Handbook,* p. 67). Have students read the summary aloud with you. Encourage them to ask questions about any ideas or unfamiliar words. For prereading support, have students preview the pictures. Use the pictures to build background and enhance comprehension of language.

Student Edition pp. 208–209

Sheltered Reading Ask questions such as the following to guide students' comprehension. As students are able, have them read silently for increasing periods of time. Check comprehension.

• p. 210: When did the American Civil War start? (1861)

• p. 211: Who were in the Massachusetts Fifty-Fourth? (African American soldiers) When was it formed? (spring of 1863)

• p. 211: Who were the Massachusetts Fifty-Fourth fighting against? (Fort Wagner, a Confederate outpost)

• pp. 212–213: Why did Sergeant Carney hold the American flag high up? (to show Ned and the other soldiers the way to go)

• p. 213: What award did Sergeant Carney receive for his bravery in the Civil War? (the Congressional Medal of Honor)

■ **Fluency: Read with Accuracy** Read the first paragraph on p. 210. Model accurate reading. Have pairs of students choose a paragraph on p. 212. Have students read to the passage to their partners for feedback.

After Reading Have students use peer support to comprehend the text. They can use the Retelling Cards to summarize and discuss the text.

Objectives
• Use visual and contextual support and support from peers and teachers to read grade-appropriate content area text, enhance and confirm understanding, and develop vocabulary, grasp of language structures, and background knowledge needed to comprehend increasingly challenging language.
• Read silently with increasing ease and comprehension for longer periods.

Content Objectives
• Monitor and adjust comprehension.

• Make and adjust predictions.

Language Objectives
• Understand important details of spoken language.

• Use peer support to increase comprehension.

• Use prereading support to build comprehension.

• Use media for language attainment.

• Read silently

Audio Support

Students can prepare for reading *Hold the Flag High* by using the eSelection or the AudioText CD. Have students use the audio for language attainment. They can talk about the events on the audio and read aloud with the audio to grasp language structures.

Language Opportunity: Listening

Students may find the language of this piece challenging. Read aloud for students, asking them to listen for details. Set the stage for the selection by reading pp. 210–211 of the Student Edition. As you read, ask questions to elicit understanding of the important details.

Support for English Language Learners

ELL Reader   ELD Reader

For additional leveled instruction, see the **ELL/ELD Reader Teaching Guide.**

Comprehension: *Making a Difference in Denmark*

■ **Before Reading** Distribute copies of the ELL and ELD Readers, *Making a Difference in Denmark,* to students at their reading level.

• **Preview** Read the title aloud with students. This is a nonfiction text about people in Denmark who helped Jewish people hide from the Germans during World War II.

• **Set a Purpose for Reading** Let's read to figure out how people in Denmark helped the Jews.

■ **During Reading** Follow the Reading Routine for both reading groups.

1. Read the entire Reader aloud slowly.

2. Reread pp. 2–5, pausing to build background knowledge or model comprehension. Use the questions in the chart to check students' comprehension.

3. Have students reread pp. 2–5 in pairs, taking turns reading alternate pages.

4. Repeat the steps for pp. 6–8.

■ **After Reading** Use the exercises on the inside back cover of each Reader and invite students to share their writing. In a whole-group discussion, ask students, How did some people in Denmark make a difference to the Jews? Record their answers on the board and invite them to point to pictures in the book to support their answers.

ELD Reader Beginning/Intermediate

■ **p. 5** Why did the Germans plan to take Danish Jews on the Jewish New Year? (because most Jews would be home with their families)

■ **p. 7** How did the Jewish people get to Sweden? (by boat)

Writing Where did some of the Jews go when the Danes after the Danes helped them? Find the sentence in the book that tells where they went. Copy the sentence. Then read it aloud to your partner.

ELL Reader Advanced/Advanced High

■ **p. 5** Why was it dangerous for Jews in Denmark in 1940? (because Germany was now in control of Denmark)

■ **pp. 6–8** How did the Danes help the Jews during World War II? (They hid them and helped them escape to Sweden.)

Study Guide Distribute copies of the ELL Reader Study Guide (*ELL Handbook,* p. 70). Help students look back through the Reader in order to fill in the graphic organizer with the correct question for each answer. (See *ELL Handbook,* pp. 209–212.)

Objectives

• Express opinions, ideas, and feelings ranging from communicating single words and short phrases to participating in extended discussions on a variety of social and grade-appropriate academic topics.

Conventions
Possessive Nouns

■ **Preteach** Remind students that nouns name a person, place, thing, or idea. Explain that nouns can be possessive. A possessive noun shows that someone owns, or possesses, something. Point out the grammatical structure of possessive nouns: the possessive comes before the object that is owned. In the phrase *child's toy*, the child owns the toy.

Write these sentences:

Mrs. Diaz's class is fun!
Juan's backpack is missing.

■ **Practice** Help students generate sentences using possessive nouns.

 Beginning/Intermediate Work with students to generate additional sentences containing words with *'s*. Have volunteers identify and underline the possessive nouns.

Advanced/Advanced High Have students work in pairs to create two new sentences using possessive nouns. Tell pairs to circle the possessive nouns.

■ **Reteach** Display these sentences. Ask volunteers to identify and underline the possessive nouns.

Pizza was Bob's favorite food.
The dog's bone was buried in the yard.

■ **Practice** Have students create original sentences with possessive nouns. They should first speak using the grammatical structure and then write. Have them create sentences based on the content of the reader.

 Beginning/Intermediate Have students work in pairs to create sentences with possessive nouns. Have one student say a sentence aloud and the other identify the possessive noun in that sentence.

Advanced/Advanced High Have students independently create one or two sentences with possessive nouns. Tell students to circle the possessive nouns in their sentences.

Content Objectives
• Decode and use possessive nouns.

Language Objectives
• Speak using the grammatical structure of possessive nouns.

• Write phrases and sentences with possessive nouns.

 Transfer Skills
Possessive Nouns In Spanish, an apostrophe is not used to show possession. Possession is shown by using special words (e.g., Esa pluma es *de* Juan. That pen is *Juan's*.)

Grammar Jammer
For more practice with nouns, use the Grammar Jammer for this target skill. See the Grammar Jammer Routine (*ELL Handbook,* p. 478) for suggestions on using this learning tool.

Objectives
• Speak using a variety of grammatical structures, sentence lengths, sentence types, and connecting words with increasing accuracy and ease as more English is acquired.

Support for English Language Learners

Content Objectives

- Identify characterization in text.

Language Objectives

- Distinguish between formal and informal English.
- Adapt spoken language for informal purposes.
- Write paragraphs that include characterization.
- Edit for pronoun agreement.

ELL English Language Learners

Characterization

■ **Introduce** Display the paragraph model and read it aloud. Explain that writers often give readers clues about a character by describing the ways that a character looks, speaks, and acts. What does the paragraph tell you about Laura? (that she is shy, scared, nervous) We learned what Laura is like from the description of how she looked and acted.

Writing Model

Laura sat alone in her chair. Her head was bent down, and her hair hid most of her face. She twisted her hands in her lap and did not say a word.

■ **Practice** Write the following incomplete character sketch on the board. Work with students to fill in more details about the person.

John was furious. He slammed his _____ on his _____. His feet _____ down the hallway. His eyes were _____, and his mouth was _____.

■ **Write** Have students write a character sketch about a friend or family member. Have students edit for agreement between pronouns and antecedents.

Beginning Have students write the name of the person and draw a picture of the person. They can dictate sentences.

Intermediate Supply students with a list of character details from which they can choose to describe their friend or family member.

Advanced/Advanced High Have students develop their character sketch independently. Then have pairs exchange papers for feedback.

MINI-LESSON

Formal and Informal English

Tell students that characterization often uses dialogue. While writing a characterization requires formal language, dialogue may be informal language. Have students list other places in which they would use both formal and informal English. Then have students adapt their language for the informal purpose of speaking with a friend. Then they could speak with a friend about the same character.

Objectives

- Write using a variety of grade-appropriate sentence lengths, patterns, and connecting words to combine phrases, clauses, and sentences in increasingly accurate ways as more English is acquired.
- Narrate, describe, and explain with increasing specificity and detail to fulfill content area writing needs as more English is acquired.

This Week's ELL Overview

ELL Handbook

- Maximize Literacy and Cognitive Engagement
- Research Into Practice
- Full Weekly Support for Every Selection

The Chî-lin Purse
- Multi-Lingual Summaries in Five Languages
- Selection-Specific Vocabulary Word Cards
- Frontloading/Reteaching for Comprehension Skill Lessons
- ELD and ELL Reader Study Guides

- Transfer Activities
- Professional Development

Daily Leveled ELL Notes

ELL notes appear throughout this week's instruction and ELL Support is on the DI pages of your Teacher's Edition. The following is a sample of an ELL note from this week.

English Language Learners

Beginning Write three simple sentences on the board. Help students identify the action or linking verb in each.

Intermediate Have students copy the sentences. Then have them circle the action or linking verb and orally complete this sentence: _____ is (a/an) (action/linking) verb.

Advanced Display images from online or print resources that convey emotions or actions. Have students work in pairs to make up sentences that contain action and linking verbs.

Advanced High Have students write a message to someone at home. Have them explain how they found something they had lost and how they felt. Then have read the messages aloud. Allow others to identify the action and linking verbs.

ELL by Strand

The ELL lessons on this week's Support for English Language Learners pages are organized by strand. They offer additional scaffolding for the core curriculum. Leveled support notes on these pages address the different proficiency levels in your class. See pages DI•66–DI•75.

ELL Guy
Dr. Jim Cummins

The Three Pillars of ELL Instruction

ELL Strands	Activate Prior Knowledge	Access Content	Extend Language
Vocabulary pp. DI•67–DI•68	Preteach	Reteach	Leveled Writing Activities
Reading Comprehension pp. DI•72–DI•73	Frontloading	Sheltered Reading	After Reading
Phonics, Spelling, and Word Analysis p. DI•70	Preteach	Model	Leveled Practice Activities
Listening Comprehension p. DI•69	Prepare for the Read Aloud	First Listening	Second Listening
Conventions and Writing pp. DI•74–DI•75	Preteach	Leveled Practice Activities	Leveled Writing Activities
Concept Development p. DI•66	Activate Prior Knowledge	Discuss Concept	Daily Concept and Vocabulary Development

This Week's Practice Stations Overview

Six Weekly Practice Stations with Leveled Activities can be found at the beginning of each week of instruction. For this week's Practice Stations, see pp. 230h–230i.

Small Group Teacher-led

Classroom Management Handbook for Differentiated Instruction Practice Stations

Practice Stations

Daily Leveled Center Activities

⬤ Below   ⬛ Advanced

△ On-Level   **ⒺⓁⓁ**

Practice Stations Flip Charts

	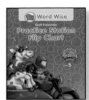 **Word Wise**	**Word Work**	 **Words to Know**	 **Let's Write**	 **Read for Meaning**	**Get Fluent**
Objectives	• Spell words with irregular plurals.	• Identify and write words with irregular plural forms.	• Identify the meaning of unknown words.	• Write a friendly letter.	• Identify the sequence of events.	• Read aloud with accuracy.
Materials	• *Word Wise* Flip Chart Activity 8 • Teacher-made word cards • paper • pencils	• *Word Work* Flip Chart Activity 8 • Teacher-made word cards • paper • pencils	• *Words to Know* Flip Chart Activity 8 • magazines • dictionary • paper • pencils	• *Let's Write* Flip Chart Activity 8 • paper • pencils	• *Read for Meaning* Flip Chart Activity 8 • Leveled Readers • paper • pencils	• *Get Fluent* Flip Chart Activity 8 • Leveled Readers

This Week on Reading Street!

Doing the Right Thing

Question of the Week

What are the rewards in helping others?

Daily Plan

Don't Wait Until Friday

Whole Group
- ⊙ Compare and Contrast
- ⊙ Greek and Latin Roots
- • Fluency/Expression
- • Research and Inquiry

MONITOR PROGRESS	Success Predictor		
Day 1 Check Oral Vocabulary	Days 2–3 Check Retelling	Day 4 Check Fluency	Day 5 Check Oral Vocabulary

Small Group

Teacher-Led
- • Reading Support
- • Skill Support
- • Fluency Practice

Practice Stations

Independent Activities

Customize Literacy More support for a balanced literacy approach, see pp. CL•1–CL•47

Customize Writing More support for a customized writing approach, see pp. CW•1–CW•10

Whole Group
- • Writing: Poem
- • Conventions: Action and Linking Verbs
- • Spelling: Vowel sounds with *r*

Assessment
- • Weekly Tests
- • Day 5 Assessment
- • Fresh Reads

You Are Here! Unit 2 Week 3

This Week's Reading Selections

Main Selection Genre: **Folk Tale**

Paired Selection Genre: **Origin Myth**

Leveled Readers

ELL and ELD Readers

Resources on Reading Street!

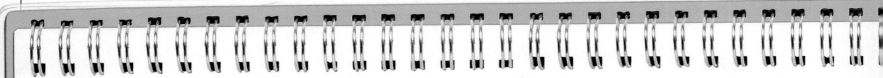

	Build Concepts	**Comprehension**
Whole Group	 Let's Talk About pp. 230–231	  Envision It! Skills/ Strategies Comprehension Skills Lesson pp. 232–233
Go Digital	• Concept Talk Video	• Envision It! Animations • eSelections
Small Group and Independent Practice	 The Ch'i–lin Purse ELL and Leveled pp. 236–237 ELD Readers Readers	  The Ch'i–lin Purse ELL and Leveled Envision pp. 236–237 ELD Readers Readers It! Skills/ Strategies Reader's Practice and Writer's Station Notebook Flip Chart
Go Digital	• eReaders • eSelections	• Envision It! Animations • eSelections • eReaders
Customize Literacy	• Leveled Readers	• Envision It! Skills and Strategies Handbook • Leveled Readers
Go Digital	• Concept Talk Video • Big Question Video • eReaders	• Envision It! Animations • eReaders

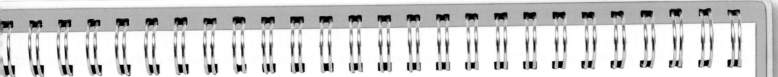

Vocabulary

Envision It!
Vocabulary
Cards

Vocabulary Skill Lesson
pp. 234–235

- Envision It! Vocabulary Cards
- Vocabulary Activities

Envision It!
Vocabulary
Cards

The Ch'i–lin Purse
pp. 236–237

Practice
Station
Flip Chart

Words!

Reader's
and Writer's
Notebook

- Envision It! Vocabulary Cards
- Vocabulary Activities
- eSelections

- Envision It! Vocabulary Cards

- Vocabulary Activities

Fluency

Let's Learn It!
pp. 256–257

- eSelections
- eReaders

The Ch'i–lin Purse
pp. 236–237

Practice
Station
Flip Chart

Leveled
Readers

ELL and ELD
Readers

- eSelections
- eReaders

- Leveled Readers

- eReaders

Let's Write It! pp. 252–253

- Grammar Jammer

Reader's
and Writer's
Notebook

The Ch'i–lin
Purse
pp. 236–237

Practice
Station
Flip Chart

- Grammar Jammer

- Reader's and Writer's Notebook

- Grammar Jammer

You Are
Here!
Unit 2
Week 3

My 5-Day Planner for Reading Street!

MONITOR PROGRESS — Don't Wait Until Friday

	Check Oral Vocabulary **Day 1** pages 230j–233f	**Check Retelling** **Day 2** pages 234a–243e

Get Ready to Read	**Concept Talk,** 230j
	Oral Vocabulary, 231a
	  stranded, favor, panic, distress
	Listening Comprehension, "The Call of the Sea", 231b
		Concept Talk, 234a
		Oral Vocabulary, 234b
		  praise, nurture
		Word Analysis, 234c
		  Suffixes *-tion, -ion*
		Literary Terms, 234d
		  Symbolism
		Story Structure, 234d
		  Resolution

Read and Comprehend	**Comprehension Skill,**
	  ◉ Compare and Contrast, 231c
	Comprehension Strategy,
	  ◉ Story Structure, 231c
	READ **Comprehension,** "Ah Tcha's Leaves," 232–233
	Model Fluency, Expression, 232–233
	Introduce Lesson Vocabulary, 233a
	  astonished, behavior, benefactor, distribution, gratitude, procession, recommend, sacred, traditions
		Vocabulary Skill, ◉ Greek and Latin Roots, 234e
		Vocabulary Strategy, Word Structure, 234e
		Lesson Vocabulary, 234–235
		  astonished, behavior, benefactor, distribution, gratitude, procession, recommend, sacred, traditions
		READ **Vocabulary,** 234–235
		Model Fluency, Expression, 234–235
		READ **Main Selection,** *The Ch'i-lin Purse,* 236–243e

Language Arts	**Research and Inquiry,** Identify Questions, 233b **Spelling,** Vowel Sounds with *r*, 233c **Conventions,** Action and Linking Verbs, 233d **Handwriting,** Cursive *t* and *T*, 233d **Writing,** Poem, 233e–233f	**Research and Inquiry,** Navigate/Search, 243b **Conventions,** Action and Linking Verbs, 243c **Spelling,** Vowel Sounds with *r*, 243c **Writing,** Poem, Organization, 243d–243e

You Are Here! Unit 2 Week 3

Question of the Week
What are the rewards in helping others?

Check Retelling	Check Fluency	Check Oral Vocabulary
Day 3 pages 244a–253c	**Day 4** pages 254a–257e	**Day 5** pages 257f–257q

Concept Talk, 244a
Oral Vocabulary, 244b
  aid, selflessness
Comprehension Check, 244c
Check Retelling, 244d
	Concept Talk, 254a
	Oral Vocabulary, 254b
	  social worker, victim
	Genre,
	  Origin Myth, 254c
		Concept Wrap Up, 257f
		Check Oral Vocabulary, 257g
		  stranded, favor, panic, distress,
		  praise, nurture, aid, selflessness,
		  social worker, victim
		Amazing Ideas, 257g
		  Review ◉ Compare and Contrast,
		  257h
		  Review ◉ Greek and Latin Roots,
		  257h
		  Review Word Analysis, 257i
		  Review Literary Terms, 257i

READ Main Selection, *The Ch'i-lin
  Purse,* 244–249a
Retelling, 250–251
Think Critically, 251a
Model Fluency, Expression, 251b
Research and Study Skills, Textbook/
Trade book, 251c
	READ Paired Selection,
	  "The Story of Phan Ku,"
	  254–255
	Let's Learn It! 256–257a
	  Fluency: Expression
	  Vocabulary: Greek and
	  Latin Roots
	  Listening and Speaking:
	  Readers' Theater
		Fluency Assessment,
		  WCPM, 257j–257k
		Comprehension Assessment,
		  ◉ Compare and Contrast,
		  257l–257m

Research and Inquiry, Analyze, 251d
Conventions, Action and Linking
  Verbs, 251e
Spelling, Vowel Sounds with *r*, 251e
Let's Write It! Poem, 252–253
Writing, Poem, Poetic Style,
  253a–253c
	Research and Inquiry,
	  Synthesize, 257b
	Conventions, Action and Linking
	  Verbs, 257c
	Spelling, Vowel Sounds with *r*,
	  257c
	Writing, Poem, Revising,
	  257d–257e
		Research and Inquiry, Communicate,
		  257n
		Conventions, Action and Linking
		  Verbs, 257o
		Spelling Test, Vowel Sounds with *r*,
		  257o
		Writing, Poem, Action and Linking
		  Verbs, 257p–257q
		Quick Write for Fluency, 257q

Week 3

Grouping Options for Differentiated Instruction
Turn the page for the small group time lesson plan.

Planning Small Group Time on Reading Street!

SMALL GROUP TIME RESOURCES

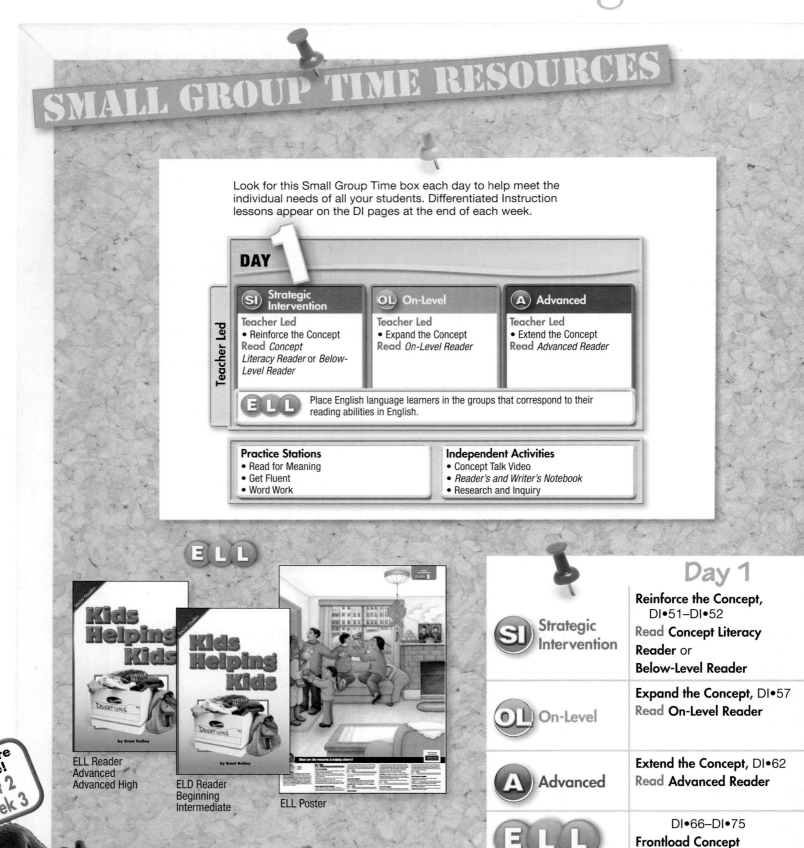

Look for this Small Group Time box each day to help meet the individual needs of all your students. Differentiated Instruction lessons appear on the DI pages at the end of each week.

DAY 1

Teacher Led

SI Strategic Intervention

Teacher Led
• Reinforce the Concept
Read *Concept Literacy Reader* or *Below-Level Reader*

OL On-Level

Teacher Led
• Expand the Concept
Read *On-Level Reader*

A Advanced

Teacher Led
• Extend the Concept
Read *Advanced Reader*

ELL Place English language learners in the groups that correspond to their reading abilities in English.

Practice Stations
• Read for Meaning
• Get Fluent
• Word Work

Independent Activities
• Concept Talk Video
• *Reader's and Writer's Notebook*
• Research and Inquiry

ELL

ELL Reader
Advanced
Advanced High

ELD Reader
Beginning
Intermediate

ELL Poster

You Are Here!
Unit 2
Week 3

Day 1

SI Strategic Intervention	**Reinforce the Concept,** DI•51–DI•52 **Read Concept Literacy Reader** or **Below-Level Reader**
OL On-Level	**Expand the Concept,** DI•57 **Read On-Level Reader**
A Advanced	**Extend the Concept,** DI•62 **Read Advanced Reader**
ELL English Language Learners	DI•66–DI•75 **Frontload Concept Preteach Skills Writing**

Reading Street Response
to Intervention Kit

Reading Street
Practice Stations Kit

SI Strategic Intervention

Below-Level
Reader

Concept Literacy Reader

The Ch'i-lin Purse pp. 236–237

OL On-Level

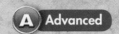

On-Level Reader

A Advanced

Advanced
Reader

The Story of Phan Ku pp. 254–255

Small Group Weekly Plan

Day 2	Day 3	Day 4	Day 5
Reinforce Comprehension, DI•53 Revisit **Main Selection**	**Reinforce Vocabulary,** DI•54 Read/Revisit **Main Selection**	**Reinforce Comprehension,** Practice Retelling DI•55 Genre Focus Read/Revisit **Paired Selection**	**Practice Fluency,** DI•56 Reread **Concept Literacy Reader** or **Below-Level Reader**
Expand Comprehension, DI•58 Revisit **Main Selection**	**Expand Vocabulary,** DI•59 Read/Revisit **Main Selection**	**Expand Comprehension,** Practice Retelling DI•60 Genre Focus Read/Revisit **Paired Selection**	**Practice Fluency,** DI•61 Reread **On-Level Reader**
Extend Comprehension, DI•63 Revisit **Main Selection**	**Extend Vocabulary,** DI•64 Read/Revisit **Main Selection**	**Extend Comprehension,** Genre Focus DI•65 Read/Revisit **Paired Selection**	**Practice Fluency,** DI•65 Reread **Advanced Reader**
DI•66–DI•75 **Review Concept/Skills** **Frontload Main Selection** **Practice**	DI•66–DI•75 **Review Concept/Skills** Reread **Main Selection** **Practice**	DI•66–DI•75 **Review Concept** Read **ELL/ELD Readers** **Practice**	DI•66–DI•75 **Review Concept/Skills** Reread **ELL/ELD Readers** **Writing**

Week 3

Practice Stations for Everyone on Reading Street!

Word Wise
Irregular plurals

Objectives
• Spell words with irregular plurals.

Materials
• *Word Wise* Flip Chart Activity 8
• Teacher-made word cards
• paper • pencils

Differentiated Activities

🔵 Choose five word cards. Write your words in a list. Write sentences using each of the words. Next to each irregular plural word, write its singular form.

🔺 Choose seven word cards, and write your words in a list. Write sentences using each of the words. Next to each irregular plural, write its singular form.

🟥 Choose ten word cards. Write your words in a list. Write sentences using each of the words. Next to each irregular plural, write its singular form.

Technology
• Online Dictionary

Word Work
Irregular plurals

Objectives
• Identify and write words with irregular plural forms.

Materials
• *Word Work* Flip Chart Activity 8
• Teacher-made word cards
• paper • pencils

Differentiated Activities

🔵 Choose six word cards. Write your words in a list. Quietly say each word. Think of other words that have an irregular plural form. Add the words to your list.

🔺 Choose eight word cards, and write your words in a list. Quietly each word. Add other words with irregular plural forms to your list. Use some of your words in a funny, four-line poem.

🟥 Choose ten word cards, and write your words in a list. Quietly each word. Add other words with irregular plural forms to your list. Write a funny, eight-line poem using some of the words.

Technology
• Modeled Pronunciation Audio CD

Words to Know
Unknown words

Objectives
• Identify the meaning of unknown words.

Materials
• *Words to Know* Flip Chart Activity 8
• magazines • dictionary
• paper • pencils

Differentiated Activities

🔵 Use a magazine to find four unknown words. Use the dictionary to find each word's meaning and part of speech. Write sentences using each of your words.

🔺 Use a magazine to find six unknown words. Use the dictionary to find each word's meaning and part of speech. Write sentences using each of your words.

🟥 Use a magazine to find eight unknown words. Find each word's meaning and part of speech in the dictionary. Write sentences using your words.

Technology
• Online Dictionary

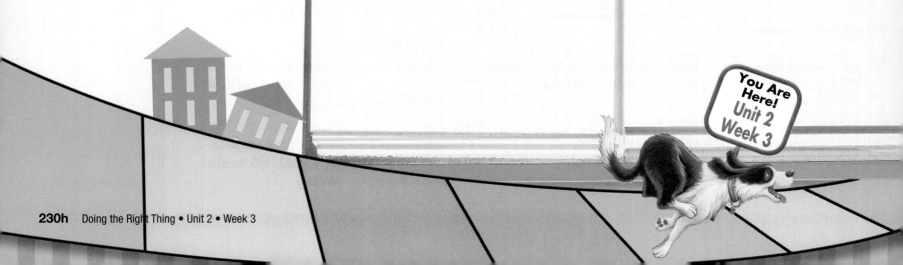

You Are Here!
Unit 2
Week 3

Use this week's materials from the Reading Street Leveled Practice Stations Kit to organize this week's stations.

Key
● Below-Level Activities
▲ On-Level Activities
■ Advanced Activities

Practice Station Flip Chart

Let's Write!
Friendly letter

Objectives
• Write a friendly letter.

Materials
• *Let's Write!* Flip Chart Activity 8
• paper • pencils

Differentiated Activities

● Think of a time when something surprising happened. Write a letter to a friend describing the event. Write your letter in a voice that expresses your personality.

▲ Write a friendly letter to someone describing a surprising event. Use a writing voice that expresses your personality. Include the date, an opening greeting, and a closing in your letter.

■ Write a friendly letter to someone describing a surprising event. Include the date, an opening salutation, and a closing in your letter. Use a writing voice that expresses your personality.

Technology
• Online Graphic Organizers

Read for Meaning
Sequence of events

Objectives
• Identify the sequence of events.

Materials
• *Read for Meaning* Flip Chart Activity 8
• Leveled Readers
• paper • pencils

Differentiated Activities

● Choose a book from those your teacher provided. Think about the order of events in the selection. Write three sentences that tell what happened *first, next,* and *finally*.

▲ Choose a book from those your teacher provided. Think about the selection's sequence of events. Write four sentences that tell the selection's sequence of events in the order they happened.

■ Choose a book from those your teacher provided. As you read, think about the sequence of events. Write a short paragraph that tells the selection's important events in the order they occurred.

Technology
• Leveled Reader Database

Get Fluent
Practice fluent reading.

Objectives
• Read aloud with accuracy.

Materials
• *Get Fluent* Flip Chart Activity 8
• Leveled Readers

Differentiated Activities

● Work with a partner. Choose a Concept Literacy Reader or Below-Level Reader. Take turns reading a page from the book. Use the reader to practice accuracy. Provide feedback as needed.

▲ Work with a partner. Choose an On-Level Reader. Take turns reading a page from the book. Use the reader to practice accuracy. Provide feedback as needed.

■ Work with a partner. Choose an Advanced Reader. Take turns reading a page from the book. Use the reader to practice accuracy. Provide feedback as needed.

Technology
• Leveled Reader Database
• Reading Street Readers CD-ROM

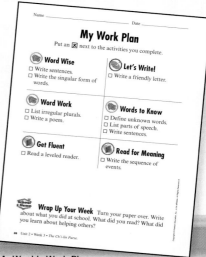

My Weekly Work Plan

Week 3

The Ch'i-lin Purse **230i**

Objectives
- Introduce the weekly concept.
- Develop oral vocabulary.

Today at a Glance

Oral Vocabulary
stranded, favor, panic, distress

Comprehension
◉ Compare and contrast
◉ Story structure

Reading
"Ah Tcha's Leaves"

Fluency
Expression

Lesson Vocabulary
Tested vocabulary

Research and Inquiry
Identify questions

Spelling
Vowel sounds with *r*

Conventions
Action and linking verbs

Handwriting
Cursive letters *t* and *T*

Writing
Poem

Concept Talk

Question of the Week

What are the rewards in helping others?

Introduce the concept

To further explore the unit concept of Doing the Right Thing, this week students will read, write, and talk about the rewards in helping others. Write the Question of the Week on the board.

ROUTINE — Activate Prior Knowledge — Team Talk

1. **Think** Have students think about how someone might be rewarded for helping others.

2. **Pair** Have groups of students discuss the Question of the Week. Have them elicit and consider suggestions from other group members.

3. **Share** Call on a few students to share their ideas and comments with the class. Guide the discussion and encourage elaboration with prompts such as:

   - What kinds of good deeds for others might people do?

   - What did you discuss about possible rewards people can attain from helping others?

Routines Flip Chart

Anchored Talk

Develop oral vocabulary

Have students turn to pp. 230–231 in their Student Editions. Look at each of the photos. Then use the prompts below to guide discussion and create *The rewards in helping others* concept map.

- How is this teacher helping the boy? (She is helping him understand a concept.) What other jobs let you help people? (police officers, firefighters, librarian, etc.) Let's add *Helpers* to the concept map.

- How do you think the child felt before the man helped the cat? (worried, afraid) How does the child show thanks? (by the look on his face) Let's add *Ways to show thanks* to the concept map.

stranded	nurture
favor	aid
panic	selflessness
distress	social worker
praise	victim

Writing on Demand

Writing Fluency

Ask students to respond to the photos on pp. 230–231 by writing as well as they can and as much as they can about the rewards in helping others.

• How does the social worker help the child? (by talking to him and playing a game) A social worker helps people. People who help others often have good character and are kind and generous. Let's add *Character traits* to the concept map.

Connect to reading

Tell students that this week they will be reading about the rewards we receive for helping others. Throughout this week, encourage students to add concept-related words to this week's concept map.

ELL Preteach Concepts Use the Day 1 instruction on ELL Poster 8 to assess and build background knowledge, develop concepts, and build oral vocabulary.

ELL

English Language Learners

ELL support Additional ELL support and modified instruction is provided in the *ELL Handbook* and in the ELL Support lessons on pp. DI•66–DI•75.

Listening comprehension English learners will benefit from additional visual support to understand the key terms in the concept map. Use the pictures on pp. 230–231 to scaffold understanding.

Frontload for Read Aloud Use the modified Read Aloud on p. DI•69 in the ELL Support lessons to prepare students to listen to "The Call of the Sea" (p. 231b).

ELL Poster 8

The Ch'i-lin Purse **230–231**

Objectives
• Develop listening comprehension.
• Build oral vocabulary.

Check Oral Vocabulary
SUCCESS PREDICTOR

Oral Vocabulary
Amazing Words

Introduce Amazing Words

In "The Call of the Sea" on p. 231b, a man does a favor for a mermaid and she helps him in return. Tell students to listen for this week's Amazing Words—*stranded*, *favor*, *panic*, and *distress*—as you read.

Model fluency

As you read "The Call of the Sea," model appropriate expression by adjusting your voice to demonstrate a lively, fluent reader.

Amazing Words Oral Vocabulary Routine

> stranded
> favor
> panic
> distress

Teach Amazing Words

① **Introduce** Write the word *stranded* on the board. Have students say the word aloud with you. I can use context to help me determine and clarify the meaning of *stranded*. In "The Call of the Sea" a mermaid is *stranded* on land. Is she stuck, or can she leave? (She is stuck.) Supply a student-friendly definition. *Stranded* means "stuck or in trouble."

② **Demonstrate** Break students into groups. Have students answer questions and elicit suggestions from group members to demonstrate understanding in a student-led group discussion. How is being *stranded* dangerous for a mermaid? How did the sailors become *stranded*?

③ **Apply** Have students discuss people or animals that were *stranded*. See p. OV•3 to teach *favor*, *panic*, and *distress*.

Routines Flip Chart

Apply Amazing Words

To build oral language, lead the class in a discussion about the meanings of the Amazing Words.

MONITOR PROGRESS **Check Oral Vocabulary**

During discussion, listen for students' use of the Amazing Words.

If... students are unable to use the Amazing Words to discuss the concept,

then... use Oral Vocabulary Routine in the Routines flip chart to demonstrate words in different contexts.

Day 1	Days 2–3	Day 4	Day 5
Check Oral Vocabulary	Check Retelling	Check Fluency	Check Oral Vocabulary

The Call of the Sea

by Geraldine McCaughrean

This is a legend from the Channel Islands about a man who helped a stranded mermaid get back out to seas. She returns the favor when he calls her with a special comb.

When the tide goes out in Bonuit Bay, it leaves rock pools studded with limpets and starry with sea urchins. Joseph Rolande, after a day's fishing, would often stroll along the beach... watching the sunset tinge the red sea. One evening he found more than peace and tranquility. A woman lay up to her waist in one of the tide pools...crying bitterly into hands of her long salt-spangled hair. She called out in panic: "Please! Don't go! Help me! I stayed too long! The tide went out and left me stranded here. Carry me down to the sea or I shall die!" As she reached out toward him, he glimpsed the ripple of scales and a huge tail fin.

"Oh, no! Oh, no!" said Joseph, backing away. "You're a mermaid, and I've heard what you mermaids do! I've heard how you'll lure a man down into your own world and drown him there!"

"I'll die if I dry!" she sobbed.

Joseph was a good man. So lifting her in his arms...he carried her past the third wave, where she spilled out of his arms like a shining salmon.

Something sharp pricked his palm. She had slid the amber comb from her hair and was pressing it into his hand—a gift, a thank-you present. "If you ever need my help, pass this three times through the water and I will come." With a thrash of a gleaming tail, she was gone.

One night, the rain beat on Joseph's roof like a thousand galloping hooves. A storm worse than anyone could remember rived the sea to a frenzy of leaping waves. It drove a ship onto the Bonuit rocks, and the Bonuit distress rockets went up.

Every soul who lived in the bay ran to the shore and peered through the downpour. All but one of the little boats lying along the shore was overturned and smashed. The screams of the sailors clinging to the wreckage on the rocks were all but washed away. "It's hopeless. No one can get to them," said one of the men watching.

"Help me launch my boat!" shouted...Joseph Rolande.

He and his boat disappeared beyond the mountainous waves into...Bonuit Bay. Only when the lightning flashed could those onshore glimpse the little rowing boat and the pounded wreck with its sad clutch of crew.

(Continued on page 257s)

Oral Vocabulary

Success Predictor

Objectives
◎ Compare and contrast to aid comprehension.
◎ Analyze the story structure to aid comprehension.
• Read grade-level text with expression.

Skills Trace

◉ **Compare and contrast**
Introduce U2W1D1; U2W3D1; U6W3D1
Practice U2W1D2; U2W1D3; U2W3D2; U2W3D3; U6W3D2; U6W3D3
Reteach/Review U2W1D5; U2W3D5; U2W4D2; U2W4D3; U6W3D5
Assess/Test
Weekly Tests U2W1; U2W3; U6W3
Benchmark Tests U2

KEY:
U=Unit   W=Week   D=Day

Skill ↔ Strategy
⟳ Compare and Contrast
⟳ Story Structure

Introduce compare and contrast

Envision It!

When you compare and contrast things, you tell how they are alike and different. How can we compare the sun and the moon? (They are both round and in the sky.) How can we contrast the sun and moon? (We see the sun in the daytime and the moon at night.) Have students turn to p. EI•6 in the Student Edition to review compare and contrast. Then read "Ah Tcha's Leaves" with students.

Student Edition p. EI•6

Model the skill

Think Aloud
Today we're going to read a folk tale about the origin of tea. Have students follow along as you read the first paragraph of "Ah Tcha's Leaves." We can compare the workers in this paragraph because they all grumble about the hard work. We can contrast Nu Wu with them because she complains the most.

Guide practice

Have students finish reading "Ah Tcha's Leaves" on their own. After they read, have them use a graphic organizer like the one on p. 232 and compare and contrast elements in the passage.

Strategy check

Story Structure Tell students that understanding a story's structure helps them understand how and why things happen in a story. Model identifying the elements of story structure to better understand the story.

Model the strategy

Envision It!

Think Aloud
One of Ah Tcha's unhappy workers creates the conflict in the story. When Ah Tcha angers Nu Wu, she makes him sleep too much. In the rising action, Ah Tcha sleeps so much that he becomes poor. When Nu Wu comes to him for food, he prepares the only thing he has—a drink made with leaves. The climax is when Nu Wu charms the leaves so that Ah Tcha can stay awake. In the resolution, he becomes wealthy again. Each event gives rise to another event. Have students review story structure on p. EI•22 of the Student Edition.

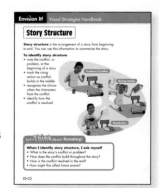
Student Edition p. EI•22

On their own

Use p. 131 in the *Reader's and Writer's Notebook* for additional practice with compare and contrast.

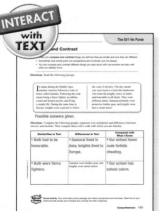
Reader's and Writer's Notebook, p. 131

Objectives
• Describe specific events in the story or novel that result in or hint at future events.

Envision It! | Skill Strategy

Skill

Envision It! Visual Skills Handbook
Compare and Contrast

Draw Conclusions

Strategy

Envision It! Visual Strategies Handbook
Story Structure

READING STREET ONLINE
ENVISION IT! ANIMATIONS
www.ReadingStreet.com

Comprehension Skill

Compare and Contrast

• When you compare and contrast things, you tell how they are alike or different.

• Sometimes clue words point out comparisons and contrasts, but not always.

• You can compare and contrast things within a story, or one story with another.

• Use a graphic organizer like the one below to help you write a folk tale. Include ideas that are similar to and different from "Ah Tcha's Leaves."

Similarities in Text	Differences in Text	Compare with What I Know

Comprehension Strategy

Story Structure

Active readers pay attention to story structure. Generally, authors identify the problem of the main character at the start. They work through the problem as the action rises in the middle, and then solve it with the climax and outcome. Authors also use story incidents to foreshadow or give rise to future events.

Ah Tcha's Leaves

Ah Tcha was a wealthy man. He owned seven farms and seven rice mills in China. He paid his workers in gold, but some grumbled about the hard work. An old woman, Nu Wu, complained the most.

One night, Ah Tcha found mice eating his rice. A cat slept nearby. Ah Tcha threw a giant sack at the cat to wake her. Poof! The cat changed into Nu Wu. She was angry with Ah Tcha. She cried, "You will sleep eleven hours out of every twelve!"

Ah Tcha slept nearly every day and night. He lost everything and became poor. One night, Nu Wu pounded on Ah Tcha's door, waking him. She wanted food. Ah Tcha had only leaves from a bush by his house, so he tossed them into hot water. Nu Wu grumbled, but drank her cup and left.

Ah Tcha drank a cup. He did not fall asleep! He smiled. "Nu Wu thanked me by charming the leaves to banish my sleepiness."

Ah Tcha sold the leaves. He planted extra bushes and became rich. Throughout China, people asked for the "drink of Ah Tcha" or "Tcha." In time, *Tcha* became *Tay*, and finally *tea*.

Skill How is Ah Tcha's current situation different from his situation at the beginning of the story?

Skill Find two times Nu Wu changed Ah Tcha's life. How were those times alike? How were they different?

Strategy How do the events in the story give rise to the ending?

Your Turn!

Need a Review? See the *Envision It! Handbook* for help with comparing, contrasting, and story structure.

Ready to Try It? As you read *The Ch'i-lin Purse*, look for story incidents that foreshadow or give rise to future events.

232

233

Student Edition pp. 232–233

Skill At the beginning of the story, Ah Tcha owned many farms and rice mills. At the end of the story, he became rich by selling tea leaves. At both the beginning and the end of the story, Ah Tcha was rich.

Skill Near the beginning, Nu Wu cursed Ah Tcha by making him sleepy. Toward the end, Nu Wu helped Ah Tcha with tea leaves that would wake him up. Both instances change Ah Tcha's sleeping habits, but they change him in opposite ways.

Strategy The events in the story lead to the problem that Ah Tcha is too sleepy. It is solved when he drinks and sells tea that keeps him awake.

Model Fluency
Expression

Model fluent reading

Have students listen as you read paragraph 2 of "Ah Tcha's Leaves" with appropriate expression. Explain that you will adjust your voice level to stress important words and phrases.

ROUTINE Oral Rereading

1. **Read** Have students read paragraph 2 of "Ah Tcha's Leaves" orally.

2. **Reread** To achieve optimal fluency, students should reread the text three or four times.

3. **Corrective Feedback** Have students read aloud without you. Provide feedback about their expression and encourage them to adjust their voice level to stress important words, such as *Poof!* and Nu Wu's words. Listen for use of appropriate expression.

Routines Flip Chart

ELL

English Language Learners
Compare and contrast Have students complete sentence frames to compare and contrast two familiar objects. For example, *Both notebooks are _____. One is _____ but the other is_____.*

Objectives
- Activate prior knowledge of words.
- Identify questions for research.

Vocabulary
Tested Vocabulary

Lesson vocabulary

Use the following question-and-answer activity to help students acquire word knowledge. Note that some of these words have Greek or Latin roots that can help students determine meaning and analyze word structure.

Activate prior knowledge

Display the lesson vocabulary words. Have students tell what they already know about these words. Then ask questions like those below. Students should respond *yes* or *no* and give reasons for their choice.

- When you are *astonished*, are you shocked?
- Does your *behavior* include what you say and do?
- Is someone who helps a student pay for college a *benefactor*?
- Can the cafeteria line be called a *distribution* line?
- Should you show your *gratitude* by being rude?
- If you are in a *procession,* are you alone?
- Would you *recommend* a book that you did not like?
- When something is *sacred*, do you throw it away?
- Would attending your mother's school be a family *tradition?*

Synonyms

Use the word *astonished* to point out that synonyms can help us understand new words. Tell students that a synonym for *astonished* is *shocked*. Ask students how knowing the synonym for a new word helps them remember its meaning.

By the end of the week, students should use lesson words to write *yes* and *no* questions for classmates to answer.

Preteach Academic Vocabulary

 Academic Vocabulary Write the following words on the board:

word structure	**linking verbs**
folk tale	**alliteration**
symbolism	**onomatopoeia**

Have students share what they know about this week's Academic Vocabulary. Use the students' responses to assess their prior knowledge. Preteach the Academic Vocabulary by providing a student-friendly description, explanation, or example that clarifies the meaning of each term. Then ask students to restate the meaning of the Academic Vocabulary term in their own words.

Research and Inquiry
Identify Questions

Teach

Discuss the Question of the Week: *What are the rewards in helping others?* Tell students they will research and summarize folk tales. They will create a summary of good deeds in folk tales and present their findings to the class on Day 5.

Model

Think Aloud I am interested in learning about folk tales in which good deeds are rewarded, so an inquiry question might be: *What are some folk tales in which a character does a good deed and is rewarded for it? What good deeds are characters rewarded for?*

Guide practice

After students have brainstormed ideas and created open-ended inquiry questions, explain that tomorrow they will conduct research using their questions. Help students identify stories in their textbook or in trade books that will guide their research. Review how to take notes on a word processor and how to summarize.

On their own

Have students work individually, in pairs, or in small groups to write an inquiry question. Encourage them to consult with others.

INTERNET GUY
Don Leu

21st Century Skills

Weekly Inquiry Project

Day 1 Identify Questions

Day 2 Navigate/Search

Day 3 Analyze

Day 4 Synthesize

Day 5 Communicate

Academic Vocabulary

word structure a strategy for determining meaning by looking for common roots

Small Group Time

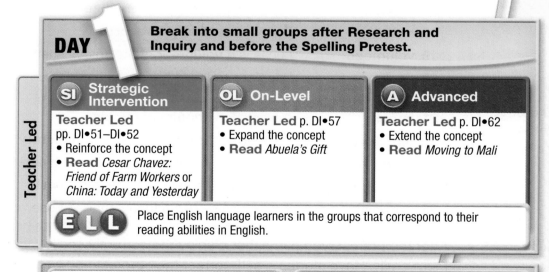

DAY 1 Break into small groups after Research and Inquiry and before the Spelling Pretest.

Teacher Led

SI Strategic Intervention	**OL** On-Level	**A** Advanced
Teacher Led pp. DI•51–DI•52 • Reinforce the concept • **Read** *Cesar Chavez: Friend of Farm Workers* or *China: Today and Yesterday*	**Teacher Led** p. DI•57 • Expand the concept • **Read** *Abuela's Gift*	**Teacher Led** p. DI•62 • Extend the concept • **Read** *Moving to Mali*

ELL Place English language learners in the groups that correspond to their reading abilities in English.

Practice Stations
• Read for Meaning
• Get Fluent
• Word Work

Independent Activities
• Concept Talk Video
• *Reader's and Writer's Notebook*
• Vocabulary Activities

 **ELL**

English Language Learners
Multilingual vocabulary
Students can apply knowledge of their home languages to acquire new English vocabulary by using Multilingual Vocabulary Lists (*ELL Handbook*, pp. 431).

Objectives
- Spell words with vowel sounds with *r*.
- Use action and linking verbs.
- Write cursive lowercase *t* and capital *T* with correct letter spacing.

Spelling Pretest
Vowel Sounds with *r*

Introduce   Tell students to think of words with r-controlled vowels, where the *r* affects the sound of the vowel *(report, smear, spare).* This week we will use spelling rules and patterns to spell words with r-controlled vowel sounds.

Pretest   Use these sentences to administer the spelling pretest. Say each word, read the sentence, and repeat the word.

1. snore	Do I **snore** when I sleep?
2. tornado	The **tornado** carried the barn away.
3. spare	I have a **spare** pencil for the test.
4. appear	You **appear** to be upset with me.
5. career	Gabby would like a **career** as a musician.
6. square	The **square** has four even sides.
7. report	Rafael wrote a **report** about eagles.
8. prepare	Please **prepare** the table for dinner.
9. pioneer	She is a **pioneer** in the field of science.
10. chair	Adji sat in the most comfortable **chair**.
11. beware	**Beware** of the attack dog!
12. smear	I like to **smear** peanut butter on bread.
13. repair	Kai needs to **repair** his bicycle.
14. sword	My dad has a **sword** from the civil war.
15. ignore	I will **ignore** my cell phone while I study.
16. order	Do you want to **order** pizza for dinner?
17. engineer	Shayla is a mechanical **engineer**.
18. resort	Can we vacation at a **resort**?
19. volunteer	Lucas is a **volunteer** at the animal shelter.
20. declare	I **declare** today to be Best Friend Day.

Challenge words

21. impair	A mask can **impair** your vision.
22. directory	Look up her name in the school **directory**.
23. hardware	Satellite television uses a lot of **hardware**.
24. clearance	The **clearance** sale has cheap clothes!
25. porpoise	The **porpoise** has a funny-shaped nose.

Self correct   After the pretest, you can either display the correctly spelled words or spell them orally. Have students self-correct their pretests by writing misspelled words correctly.

On their own   For additional practice, use *Let's Practice It!* p. 80 on the *Teacher Resources DVD-ROM.*

Let's Practice It!
TR DVD•80

Conventions
Action and Linking Verbs

Teach
Display Grammar Transparency 8, and read aloud the explanation and examples in the box. Point out the action verb *flooded* and the linking verb *were*.

Model
Model underlining the verbs and then identifying whether they are action or linking to complete numbers 1 and 2. Explain to students that you looked for the presence of actions to determine the type of verb.

Grammar Transparency 8, TR DVD

Guide practice
Guide students to complete items 3–10. Remind them to underline the verbs in the sentences and look for actions. Record the correct responses on the transparency.

Daily Fix-It
Use Daily Fix-It numbers 1 and 2 in the right margin.

Connect to oral language
Have students read sentences 11 to 15 on the transparency and write the verbs in either the *action* or *linking* columns.

Handwriting
Cursive Letter *t* and *T*

Model letter formation
Display the cursive capital *T* and lowercase *t*. Follow the stroke instruction pictured to model letter formation.

Model letter spacing
Explain that writing legibly means letters have proper spacing between them. The spaces are not too large or too small. Model writing this sentence with correct letter spacing: *The tall tree has many branches.* Make sure the letters aren't too light, dark, or jagged.

Guide practice
Have students write these sentences: *Terese talks to her aunt twice a week. Thomas taught me about time lines.* Circulate around the room, guiding students.

Academic Vocabulary
Linking verbs are verbs that join the subject of a sentence to a word or words in the predicate.

Daily Fix-It
1. Six years ago, she gives away her weding gift. *(gave; wedding.)*
2. Were that girl mean or just spoiled. *(Was; spoiled?)*

English Language Learners
Action and linking verbs
Review the definitions of linking verbs. Then provide practice for students at their own proficiency levels.

Beginning Write three simple sentences on the board. Help students identify the action or linking verb in each.

Intermediate Have students copy the sentences. Then have them circle the action or linking verb and orally complete this sentence: _____ is (a/an) (action/linking) verb.

Advanced/Advanced High Display images from online or print resources that convey emotions or actions. Have students work in pairs to make up sentences that contain action and linking verbs.

Handwriting: Letter spacing
To further model cursive capital and lowercase *t* and *T* and to reinforce legibility through letter spacing, write the sample sentence with spacing that is too wide and too narrow. Go over sentences with students, pointing to the incorrect spacing.

DAY 1 Language Arts

Writing—Poem
Introduce

MINI-LESSON

5 Day Planner
Guide to Mini-Lessons

DAY 1	Read Like a Writer
DAY 2	Organizational Web
DAY 3	Stylizing a Poem
DAY 4	Revising Strategy: Adding
DAY 5	Proofread for Action and Linking Verbs

MINI-LESSON

Read Like a Writer

■ **Introduce** This week you will write a poem. A poem uses special structures and techniques. Poems are a form of literary expression.

Prompt	Write a poem about an important event in your life, or the life of someone you know.
Trait	Organization/Poetic Structure
Mode	Narrative

Reader's and Writer's Notebook, p. 132

■ **Examine Model Text** Let's read an example of a poem that describes an important event in the writer's life. Have students read "The Day I Learned to Fish" on p. 132 of their *Reader's and Writer's Notebook.*

■ **Key Features** Poems often use verse, rhyme, and rhythm. Read the poem aloud. Guide students to realize that the first two lines and the last two lines of each stanza rhyme. Have students circle the rhymes.

Poems use **poetic techniques,** such as onomatopoeia, assonance, and alliteration. Onomatopoeia is when words imitate sounds. Have students underline the words that imitate sounds in the poem. Assonance is the repetition of vowel sounds, such as *sweep* and *feet.* Have students give an example of assonance from the poem. Alliteration is when the same beginning letter sound is repeated in a line of poetry. Point out the sounds in "made me" and "bags of bait."

Poems may also include **sensory language.** Have students reread the second stanza and explain what images the words create.

Review
key features

Review the key features of a poem with students. You may want to post the key features with additional examples in the classroom for students to refer to as they work on their poems.

Key Features of a Poem

- uses verse to communicate ideas
- may use poetic techniques, rhyme, or sound patterns
- often includes sensory details or vivid language

ROUTINE — Quick Write for Fluency — Team Talk

1. **Talk** Have pairs discuss the three forms of poetic techniques.
2. **Write** Each student writes the definition of one technique and one poetry line that uses the technique.
3. **Share** Partners read their definitions and poetry lines to one another.

Routines Flip Chart

Wrap Up Your Day

✔ **Build Concepts** What did you learn about helping others?

✔ **Oral Vocabulary** Have students use the Amazing Words they learned in context sentences.

✔ **Homework** Send home this week's Family Times newsletter in *Let's Practice It!* pp. 81–82 on the *DVD-ROM.*

Let's Practice It!
TR DVD•81–82

Write Guy
Jeff Anderson

What Do You Notice?

When students are examining the model text, ask, "What do you notice?" By giving students the responsibility of commenting on what they find effective in the text, they build self-confidence and often begin to notice features of the writing they might not have otherwise. Eventually they will start trying them in their writing. Relish students' movement toward correctness and beauty.

ELL

English Language Learners

Read like a writer Read the writing model aloud and help students understand it. Remind students that poems express feelings and emotions through the special use of words. This model tells about the day the poet learned to fish. Ask students about outdoor and indoor sports they enjoy, and what makes the sports fun or interesting.

Preview DAY 2

Tell students that tomorrow they will read a folk tale with a message about helping others.

Objectives

- Expand the weekly concept.
- Develop oral vocabulary.

Today at a Glance

Oral Vocabulary
praise, nurture

Word Analysis
Suffixes *-tion, -ion*

Literary Terms
Symbolism

Story Structure
Resolution

Lesson Vocabulary
Greek and Latin roots

Reading
"The Meaning of Tales"
The Ch'i-lin Purse

Fluency
Expression

Research and Inquiry
Navigate/Search

Spelling
Vowel sounds with *r*

Conventions
Action and linking verbs

Writing
Poem

Concept Talk

Question of the Week

What are the rewards in helping others?

Expand the concept

Remind students of the weekly concept question. Tell students that today they will begin reading *The Ch'i-lin Purse.* As they read, encourage students to think about the rewards in helping others.

Anchored Talk

Develop oral vocabulary

Use the photos on pp. 230–231 and the Read Aloud, "The Call of the Sea," to talk about the Amazing Words: *stranded, favor, panic,* and *distress.* Add the concept-related words to the concept map to develop students' knowledge of the topic. Break students into groups. Have them discuss the following questions, considering suggestions from other group members.

- How can being *stranded* cause a person great *distress*? (A stranded person would be lost or stuck, without a way to escape, so the person would probably feel panic.)
- Describe a time when you did a *favor* for someone. (Possible response: I helped my parents with their chores.)
- Why is it important not to *panic* in a difficult situation? (If you panic, you may stop thinking clearly.)

Oral Vocabulary
Amazing Words

Amazing Words

stranded	nurture
favor	aid
panic	selflessness
distress	social worker
praise	victim

Teach Amazing Words

Amazing Words — Oral Vocabulary Routine

1 Introduce Write the Amazing Word *praise* on the board. Have students say it aloud with you. Relate *praise* to the photographs on pp. 230–231 and "The Call of the Sea." Joseph deserves *praise* for saving the mermaid, and the mermaid deserves *praise* for saving the sailors. Have students use context clues to determine the definition of the word. If you *praise* someone, you express warm approval or admiration.

2 Demonstrate Have students answer questions to demonstrate understanding. How does an audience *praise* musicians for a good show? How can we *praise* a puppy that has learned a new trick?

3 Apply Have students apply their understanding. Name a time that you *praised* someone.

See p. OV•3 to teach *nurture*.

Routines Flip Chart

Apply Amazing Words

Before students read "The Meaning of Tales" on p. 235, help them to establish a purpose for reading. Have them think about how a fairy godmother might *nurture* someone and why a gallant hero might do something that deserves *praise*.

Connect to reading

Explain that today students will read *The Ch'i-lin Purse.* As they read, they should think about how the Question of the Week and the Amazing Words *praise* and *nurture* apply to the characters in *The Ch'i-lin Purse.*

ELL Reinforce Vocabulary Use the Day 2 instruction on ELL Poster 8 to teach lesson vocabulary and the lesson concept.

ELL Poster 8

Word Analysis
Suffixes *-tion, -ion*

Teach suffixes *-tion, -ion*

Remind students that suffixes are letters added to the end of a word that change the part of speech of a word. The Latin suffixes *-tion* and *-ion* change a verb into a noun that means "the state or result of." Write the following words on the board: *fascination, distribution, procession, prevention, companion,* and *reaction.* Have students identify the base word and suffix in each word.

Model

Think Aloud The word *fascination* has the suffix *-tion*. The base word is *fascinate. Fascinate* is a verb that means "to interest intensely." Adding the suffix *-tion* changes the verb *fascinate* into the noun *fascination,* which means "the state of being intensely interested."

Guide practice

After students name each base word and suffix, have them tell how the suffix changes the meaning and part of speech of the word.

On their own

Have students use a dictionary to verify or revise the words' definitions and parts of speech. Follow the Strategy for Meaningful Word Parts to teach the word *invention.*

ROUTINE **Strategy for Meaningful Word Parts**

1. **Introduce the strategy** Let's use suffixes and base words to help us understand words with *-tion*. Write the word *invention* on the board.

2. **Introduce the word parts** Base words often have suffixes at the end. Here, I see the base word *invent* and the suffix *-tion*. Point out that adding a prefix sometimes involves dropping a letter of the base word. In this case, adding *-tion* requires us to drop the *t* in *invent.*

3. **Connect to meaning** Adding a suffix can change a word's meaning and part of speech. *Invent* is a verb that means "to create." When the suffix *-tion* is added, the word becomes a noun that means "the result of creating" or "a creation."

4. **Read the word** Blend the word parts together as you run your hand beneath them. First I read the base word, *invent*. Then I read the suffix, *-tion*. I blend the parts together to read the word: *invent tion, invention.*

Continue the Routine with the words *distribution* and *procession.*

Routines Flip Chart

Literary Terms
Symbolism

Teach symbolism

Explain that a symbol is a person, place, or thing that represents an abstract idea. For example, one common symbol is a dove. It is a bird, but it also stands for peace.

Model symbolism

Think Aloud Let's look at "Ah Tcha's Leaves" on page 233. In folk tales, characters often symbolize, or stand for, certain types of people in real life. Ah Tcha is very wealthy at the beginning and end of the story. I think he symbolizes wealthy, powerful people.

Guide practice

Ask students what the laborer, Nu Wu, might symbolize. (laborers or people who complain) Have students find clues in the text that help them understand the symbols.

On their own

Have students study the illustrations in *The Ch'i-lin Purse*. Have them predict what might be a symbol in this story and why. (The purse might be a symbol because it shows up repeatedly.)

Story Structure
Resolution

Teach resolution

Remind students that authors structure their stories with plot elements such as conflict, rising action, climax, and resolution. In the **resolution,** the conflict is resolved, the action winds down, and the story ends. Tell students that the resolution happens when a story's problem or conflict is solved.

Model the strategy

Think Aloud When I look at "Ah Tcha's Leaves," I see that the resolution is when Nu Wu charms the leaves and Ah Tcha is able to stay awake. The action winds down and the story ends as we learn that Ah Tcha becomes wealthy again. I can see how other events in the story lead up to this resolution. The resolution solves the problem of Ah Tcha falling asleep. I remember Nu Wu appeared earlier, so it makes sense that she is part of the resolution.

Guide practice

Discuss with students how the resolution in "Ah Tcha's Leaves" is related to other events in the story.

On their own

Have students recall the story "The Call of the Sea," found on p. 231b. Ask them to identify the story's resolution. Discuss how the story's earlier events foreshadow and give rise to the resolution.

DAY 2 Read and Comprehend
40–45 mins.

Objectives
◎ Use word structure to determine the meanings of words with Greek and Latin roots.
• Read grade-level text with expression.

Vocabulary Strategy for
🎯 Greek and Latin Roots

Student Edition W•9

Teach Greek and Latin roots

Envision It!

Read and discuss the first paragraph on p. 234. Tell students that Greek and Latin roots make up the basic parts of many English words. Knowing the meaning of a root can help students use the strategy of word structure to determine the meanings of new words with that root. Refer students to *Words!* on p. W•9 in the Student Edition for additional practice.

Model the strategy

On the board, write this sentence: *I took a photograph of the mountain.*

Think Aloud In Greek, *photo* means "light" and *graph* means "write." The exact translation of the combined roots is "to write with light." This makes sense in the sentence because I know I need light to take a picture with a camera and the light "writes" the image. Knowing this word will help me understand other words with the roots *photo* and *graph,* such as *photographic, biography,* and *telegraph.*

Guide practice

Have students determine the meanings of *photographic, biography,* and *telegraph.* Then write this sentence on the board: *The family's benefactor helped them build a new home.* Tell students that the Latin root *bene* means "well" or "good." Have students use word structure to determine the meaning of *benefactor.* Then have them find the words in a dictionary and revise or confirm their definitions. For additional support, use *Envision It! Pictured Vocabulary Cards* or *Tested Vocabulary Cards.*

On their own

Read "The Meaning of Tales" on p. 235. Have students use Latin roots to find the meanings of the lesson vocabulary words. Encourage them to use a printed or electronic dictionary to check the meanings of English words and their Greek or Latin roots. For additional practice, use *Reader's and Writer's Notebook* p. 133.

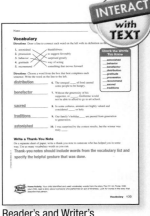

Reader's and Writer's Notebook, p. 133

Student Edition pp. 234–235

Objectives
• Determine the meaning of English words with roots from Greek, Latin, and other languages.

Envision It! Words to Know

astonished

gratitude

procession

behavior
benefactor
distribution
recommend
sacred
traditions

READING STREET ONLINE
VOCABULARY ACTIVITIES
www.ReadingStreet.com

234

Vocabulary Strategy for
Greek and Latin Roots

Word Structure When you come to an unknown word, particularly an academic vocabulary word, look for a root within the word. For example, the Latin root *bene-* means "well" or "good," as in *benefit* and *benefactor*. The Greek root *myth-* means "fable" or "legend," as in *myth* and *mythology*. You can use roots to figure out the meaning of an unknown word.

1. Find a root in the word. Think about other words you know that also have this root.

2. Do the words you know give you clues about the meaning of the unknown word?

3. Check to see if the meaning makes sense in the sentence.

Read "The Meaning of Tales" on page 235. Look for roots to help you figure out the meanings of this week's *Words to Know* or words such as *mysterious, triumph,* or *celebrate.*

Words to Write Reread "The Meaning of Tales." Write a myth or tale of your own that explains something or teaches a lesson about life. Use words from the *Words to Know* list.

The Meaning of Tales

Myths, fairy tales, and folk tales are time-honored traditions in many countries. Before people could write, they told stories to make each other laugh, cry, or shake with fear. These stories do more than just entertain. They preserve the earliest ideas and history of a people. A myth may explain why something happens in nature. It may tell what causes the seasons, for example. A tale may show us the rewards for our behavior and teach us a lesson. Often, both myths and tales are tied to what people in earlier times found sacred and mysterious.

Fairy tales reach into the world of fancy. A poor girl finds a benefactor, such as a fairy godmother. A handsome prince discovers the girl and is astonished by her beauty. They fall in love. Someone evil tears them apart, and they suffer great misery. A magic being helps them defeat the evil. They feel a joyful gratitude. They celebrate their triumph in a grand procession through the kingdom.

The distribution of these stories all over the world shows how important they are to all people. Do you want to understand the nature of people? I recommend that you study tales.

Your Turn!

📖 **Need a Review?** For additional help with Greek and Latin roots, see *Words!*

▶ **Ready to Try It?** Read *The Ch'i-lin Purse* on pp. 236–249.

235

Reread for Fluency
Expression

Model fluent reading

Read paragraph 1 of "The Meaning of Tales" aloud, using changes in pitch for emphasis and expression. Tell students that you change the pitch of your voice to emphasize key details.

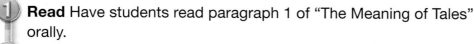
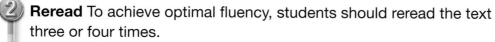

ROUTINE **Oral Reading**

1. **Read** Have students read paragraph 1 of "The Meaning of Tales" orally.

2. **Reread** To achieve optimal fluency, students should reread the text three or four times.

3. **Corrective Feedback** Have students read aloud without you. Provide feedback about their expression and encourage them to adjust their voice level to stress important words and phrases. Listen for use of appropriate expression.

Routines Flip Chart

Lesson Vocabulary

astonished surprised; amazed

behavior a way of acting

benefactor a person who has given money or help

distribution sharing something among a number of people

gratitude feeling thankful; showing appreciation

procession a number of people or vehicles moving forward in an orderly way

recommend to speak in favor of; to suggest

sacred worthy of reverence

traditions customs or beliefs handed down from generation to generation

 ELL

English Language Learners
Visual learning Use pantomimes, pictures, and synonyms to teach the lesson vocabulary words. For example, tell students that *behavior* means "actions" or "manners." Have a few students walk in a line and call it a *procession*. Then have students teach the words to each other.

Build Academic Vocabulary
Use the lesson vocabulary pictured on p. 234 to teach the meanings of *astonished, gratitude,* and *procession*. Call on pairs to write the words on sticky notes and use them to label images of the words on the ELL Poster.

Objectives

- Understand the elements of folk tales.
- Use illustrations to preview and predict.
- Set a purpose for reading.

The Ch'i-lin Purse

retold by Linda Fang
illustrated by Ed Young

Question of the Week
What are the rewards in helping others?

Genre **Folk tales** are stories or legends that are told over and over from one generation to the next. As you read, imagine that someone is sitting next to you telling you the story.

236

237

Student Edition pp. 236–237

Build Background

Discuss good deeds

Team Talk Have students turn to a partner and discuss the Question of the Week and these questions about good deeds. Ask students to elicit suggestions from their partner and consider those suggestions.

- What might make us want to do a good deed?
- What kinds of good deeds have you or others you know done?
- What reward did you receive for doing that deed?
- How long might it take to be rewarded for a good deed?

Connect to selection

Have students discuss their answers with the class. Possible responses: We might do a good deed to help someone. Some good deeds include returning lost items, sharing, and helping with difficult tasks. People are rewarded with gifts and friendship. Sometimes favors are returned. Good deeds might be rewarded right away or years later. For additional opportunities to build background, use the Background Building Audio.

Prereading Strategies

Genre
Tell students that a **folk tale** is a story that has been passed down through oral tradition over many generations. Folk tales often reflect the customs and beliefs of a particular culture. The characters are often stereotypes, and they fulfill one particular function. The conflicts are usually resolved by good being rewarded and evil being punished.

Preview and predict
Have students preview the selection by looking at the illustrations. Then have them predict what will happen to the main character, Hsiang-ling.

Set purpose
Prior to reading, have students establish their own purposes for reading. To help them, ask them to think about how good deeds can come back to help people later.

Strategy Response Log

 INTERACT with TEXT

Have students use p. 14 in the *Reader's and Writer's Notebook* to identify the characteristics of folk tales.

Small Group Time

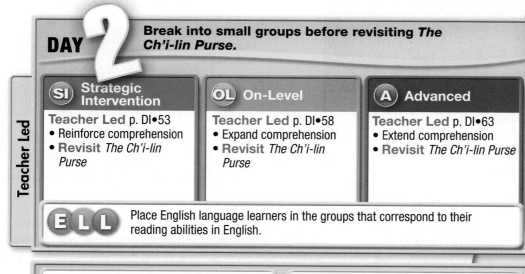

DAY 2
Break into small groups before revisiting *The Ch'i-lin Purse*.

Teacher Led

(SI) Strategic Intervention
Teacher Led p. DI•53
• Reinforce comprehension
• **Revisit** *The Ch'i-lin Purse*

(OL) On-Level
Teacher Led p. DI•58
• Expand comprehension
• **Revisit** *The Ch'i-lin Purse*

(A) Advanced
Teacher Led p. DI•63
• Extend comprehension
• **Revisit** *The Ch'i-lin Purse*

ELL Place English language learners in the groups that correspond to their reading abilities in English.

Practice Stations
• Words to Know
• Get Fluent
• Word Wise

Independent Activities
• Background Building Audio
• *Reader's and Writer's Notebook*
• Research and Inquiry

Differentiated Instruction

 (A) Advanced
Compare and contrast Have students find out about a Chinese tradition and compare and contrast it to a modern tradition in the United States.

Double Day Reads  **Multidraft Reading**

For **Whole Group** instruction, choose one of the reading options below. For each reading, have students set the purpose indicated.

Option 1
Day 2 Read the selection. Use Guide Comprehension to monitor and clarify understanding.
Day 3 Reread the selection. Use Extend Thinking to develop higher-order thinking skills.

Option 2
Day 2 Read the first half of the selection, using both Guide Comprehension and Extend Thinking instruction.
Day 3 Read the second half of the selection, using both Guide Comprehension and Extend Thinking instruction.

ELL

English Language Learners
Build background To build background, review the selection summary in English (*ELL Handbook* p. 73). Use the Retelling Cards to provide visual support for the summary.

Objectives

◉ Compare and contrast story elements to improve comprehension.

Student Edition pp. 238–239

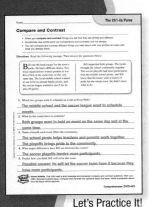

Let's Practice It!
TR DVD•83

OPTION 1 Guide Comprehension Skills and Strategies

Teach Compare and Contrast

◉ **Compare and Contrast** Read paragraphs 1–3 on p. 238. Compare and contrast Hsiang-ling's life with the life of a modern-day girl her age in the United States. (Some girls in the United States are also beautiful, intelligent, and spoiled. But Hsiang-ling lived in China many years ago. She is getting married at 16 to a man found by a matchmaker, and she will have a dowry.)

Corrective Feedback

If… students have difficulty comparing and contrasting,

then… model how to compare and contrast.

Model the Skill

Think Aloud What words describe Hsiang-ling? *(beautiful, intelligent, spoiled)* Can girls in the United States be beautiful, intelligent, or spoiled? **(yes)** So this is a similarity.

It is said that many years ago in China, in a small town called Teng-chou, there lived a wealthy widow, Mrs. Hsüeh. She had only one daughter, Hsüeh Hsiang-ling. Hsiang-ling was beautiful and intelligent, and her mother loved her dearly. But since everything Hsiang-ling wanted was given to her, she became rather spoiled.

When Hsiang-ling was sixteen years old, her mother decided that it was time for her to marry. Through a matchmaker, Hsiang-ling was engaged to a young man from a wealthy family in a neighboring town.

Mrs. Hsüeh wanted to prepare a dowry for Hsiang-ling that no girl in town could match. But Hsiang-ling was hard to please. Almost everything her mother bought for her was returned or exchanged at least two or three times.

When the dowry was finally complete, Mrs. Hsüeh decided to add one more item to it. It was the Ch'i-lin Purse, a red satin bag embroidered on both sides with a *ch'i-lin*, a legendary animal from ancient times. The *ch'i-lin* had scales all over its body and a single horn on its head. In the old Chinese tradition, the *ch'i-lin* is the symbol of a promising male offspring. Mrs. Hsüeh wanted to give Hsiang-ling the purse because she hoped that her daughter would give birth to a talented son.

When the purse Mrs. Hsüeh had ordered was ready, a family servant brought it home. But Hsiang-ling was not satisfied at all. "I don't like the pattern, take it back!" she said.

238

OPTION 2 Extend Thinking Think Critically

Higher-Order Thinking Skills

◉ **Compare and Contrast • Analysis** Compare and contrast Hsiang-ling and the servant. Explain what the reader learns about both characters from their conflict. Then describe the relationship between Hsiang-ling and her servant. Possible response: Hsiang-ling is hard to please, but the servant is not. However, neither person is mean-spirited. Hsiang-ling has very high expectations for her servant, but she tries not to be unreasonable since he has been with her family for more than 40 years.

Genre • Synthesis Recall what you know about folk tales. What do you think will happen to someone as spoiled as Hsiang-ling? Possible response: Folk tales teach a lesson. Usually, good is rewarded and bad is punished. I think Hsiang-ling might be punished for being so spoiled.

Now let's look for differences. What is the setting? (many years ago in China) Explain what is going to happen to Hsiang-ling at the age of 16. (She is getting married with help from a matchmaker, and her mother is going to prepare a dowry.) Are these differences? (yes)

The servant returned to the store and ordered another. But when it was brought home, Hsiang-ling merely glanced at it and said, "The colors of the *ch'i-lin* are too dark, take it back!"

The servant went to place another order, but the new purse still did not please her. This time the servant broke down in tears.

"I won't go back again, young mistress. The people in the store laugh at me. They say I am hard to please. This is not true. You are the one who is hard to please. If you don't want this purse, I am going to leave you and work for someone else."

Although Hsiang-ling was spoiled, she was not a mean-spirited person. She somehow began to feel sorry for the old man, who had been with her family for more than forty years. So she looked at the purse and said, "All right, I will have this one. You may go and pay for it." The servant went back to the store, paid for the purse, and gave it to Mrs. Hsüeh.

Hsiang-ling's wedding fell on the eighteenth day of the sixth month according to the lunar calendar. It was the day Hsiang-ling had longed for since her engagement. She was very excited and yet a bit sad, because she knew she was leaving her mother and the home she had lived in for sixteen years.

Hsiang-ling wore a red silk dress and a red silk veil over her head. As she sat in her *hua-chiao*, a sedan chair draped with red satin, and waited to be carried to her new home, her mother came to present her with the Ch'i-lin Purse.

"My dear child," she said as she lifted up the satin curtain in front, "this is your *ta-hsi-jih-tzu*, your big, happy day. I am delighted to see you get married even though I will miss you terribly. Here is the Ch'i-lin Purse. I have put some wonderful things in it. But don't open it now. Wait until you are in your new home, and you will feel that I am with you."

239

On Their Own

Have students reread paragraph 4 on p. 238. Have them compare and contrast the *ch'i-lin* with an eagle. For additional practice, use *Let's Practice It!* p. 83 on the *Teacher Resources DVD-ROM*.

Author's Purpose • Analysis Reread paragraph 4 on page 239. Why do you think the author mentions that Hsiang-ling is not mean-spirited? How might this foreshadow future events in the story? **Possible response:** The author wants the reader to know that though Hsiang-ling is spoiled, she is not all bad. I think that later on in the story, we might learn that Hsiang-ling is not as selfish as she seems.

Summarize • Synthesis Summarize what we have read so far, maintaining meaning and logical order. **Possible response:** Hsiang-ling is a spoiled young girl. Her mother used a matchmaker to find a husband for her at 16. Hsiang-ling was very picky about the things in her dowry, especially the Ch'i-lin Purse. Hsiang-ling's mother filled the purse with gifts and gave it to Hsiang-ling for her wedding day.

Differentiated Instruction

 Strategic Intervention

Summarize Divide the text into three sections. Have students work with partners to give a short summary of each section.

(A) Advanced

Vocabulary Help students pronounce the Chinese words in the story, particularly Hsiang-ling's name, which is pronounced *Sheeang-leen* and means "cute and smells good." Practice pronouncing the word *ch'i-lin*: *sCHEE-leen*.

Connect to Social Studies

In many cultures, the bride's family prepares a dowry, which consists of daily necessities, ornaments for the home, or valuable jewels and money. The bride's family uses a dowry to express their love for their daughter and to display their wealth to the community and to the groom's family.

ELL

English Language Learners
Activate prior knowledge Help students use context clues to determine the meaning of the word *spoiled* on p. 238, paragraph 1. Ask students to describe how a spoiled person might act by having them complete the following sentences: *Hsiang-ling acts spoiled by ____.* (rejecting her purse) *Spoiled people might ____.* (expect to get anything they ask for)

Objectives

◎ Use Greek and Latin roots to determine the meanings of words.

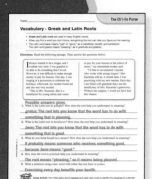

Reader's and Writer's Notebook p. 137

OPTION 1 Skills and Strategies, continued

Teach Greek and Latin Roots

👁 **Greek and Latin Roots** Tell students that the Latin root *cess* means "go" or "yield." Ask students to determine the meaning of the vocabulary word *procession*. (Knowing the meaning of *cess* tells us that *procession* has something to do with either going or yielding.)

Corrective Feedback

If... students have difficulty answering the question,

then... model how to use the Latin root *cess* to understand the word *procession*.

Model the Skill

Think Aloud The Latin root *cess* is part of many words, such as the word *procession*.

Hsiang-ling was hardly listening. She was thinking about the wedding and wondering about her husband-to-be, whom she had never met. She took the purse and laid it on her lap. A few minutes later, four footmen came. Picking up the *hua-chiao*, they placed it on their shoulders, and the wedding procession began.

As the procession reached the road, it started to rain. Soon it was pouring so heavily that the footmen could not see well enough to continue. The wedding procession came to a halt, and the *hua-chiao* was carried into a pavilion that stood alongside the road.

There was another *hua-chiao* in the pavilion. It was shabby, with holes in the drapes. Hsiang-ling could hear a girl sobbing inside. This annoyed her, because she believed that a person crying on her wedding day could bring bad luck. So she told her maid to go and find out what was wrong.

240

Student Edition pp. 240–241

OPTION 2 Think Critically, continued

Higher-Order Thinking Skills

👁 **Greek and Latin Roots • Analysis** The bride in the other *hua-chiao* had been through a trauma. The Greek root *traum* means "wound." Let's use the root to determine the meaning of *trauma*. Then use a dictionary to check. Possible response: Since the other bride is crying, we can tell she has been through a difficult experience: getting married with no money. It seems that she has an emotional "wound." According to the dictionary, *trauma* means "a distressing or disturbing experience."

Inferring • Synthesis Why do you think Hsiang-ling instructs her maid not to mention her name? What does this tell the reader about Hsiang-ling's character? Possible response: Hsiang-ling does not want credit for her good deed. This shows that Hsiang-ling can be generous. She may not want the other bride to feel that she owes Hsiang-ling anything in return for the purse.

By knowing that *cess* means either "go" or "yield," I know that a procession is something that either moves forward or slows down. The story says that *the procession continued on its way,* so I can guess that a *procession* is a group that is moving forward.

"The bride is very sad," the maid said when she returned. "She is poor and has nothing to take to her new home."

Hsiang-ling couldn't help feeling sorry for the girl. Then her eyes fell on the Ch'i-lin Purse in her lap. She realized that she was lucky to have so many things, while this girl had nothing. Since she wasn't carrying any money with her, she handed the Ch'i-lin Purse to her maid. "Give this to the girl, but don't mention my name."

So the maid went over and gave the purse to the other bride. The girl stopped crying at once. Hsiang-ling had given away her mother's wedding gift without ever finding out what was inside.

241

On Their Own

Tell students that the Latin root *cess* also appears in the words *process* and *access.* Have them suggest meanings for these words and then look up the words in a dictionary to clarify or revise their definitions. For more practice, use *Reader's and Writer's Notebook* p. 137.

 Greek and Latin Roots • Analysis

Hsiang-ling's actions show that she has an active *conscience.* The Greek root *sci* means "know." What does that tell us about the word *conscience*? Possible response: Since *sci* means "know," I think the word *conscience* has to do with what Hsiang-ling knows. She has done something kind, so she knows how to do what is right. The dictionary says a *conscience* means "an inner feeling or voice that tells what is right and wrong."

Literary Elements: Plot • Evaluation

Consider whether what Hsiang-ling has done with the purse is the right or wrong thing to do. Predict how this incident might give rise to other events in the story. Possible response: Hsiang-ling has done the right thing by giving her purse to the poor bride. I think this will cause something important to happen. I also think that the brides may meet again and that we will learn more about the purse.

Differentiated Instruction

SI Strategic Intervention

Greek and Latin roots Work with students in a small group to review Greek and Latin roots. Guide students to see the relationship between words with the same roots. Use examples such as *process* and *procession* (both have to do with going forward), *benefactor* and *benefit* (both have good connotations and have to do with helping), and *gratitude* and *grateful* (both have to do with being thankful).

Connect to Social Studies

In China, a man was traditionally head of the household. Because the family was based on the male lineage, boys were usually treated better than girls, who would be married one day and become part of another family. Therefore, it became very important for women to bear sons.

ELL

English Language Learners
Monitor and clarify Have students work with partners to ask and answer each other's questions about what is happening on these pages. Encourage them to reread sections to clarify any misunderstandings.

Objectives

◎ Analyze the story structure to aid comprehension.

OPTION 1 — Skills and Strategies, continued

Teach Story Structure

Story Structure Tell students that authors give their stories a plot structure that includes a conflict, rising action, a climax, and a resolution. Ask students to identify the conflict (the flood) and rising action (Hsiang-ling gets a job) so far in this story. Tell students that identifying important events can help them anticipate what will happen next.

Corrective Feedback

If... students have difficulty answering the question,
then... model how to identify the conflict and rising action.

Model the Strategy

 Think Aloud I can look back at page 242 to find the conflict. The flood took Hsiang-ling's home and then she lost her family, too. This left her alone, homeless, and hungry.

> A few minutes later, the rain stopped, the footmen picked up Hsiang-ling's *hua-chiao,* and the procession continued on its way. In an hour, Hsiang-ling arrived at her new home. She was happily married that evening, and to her delight she found her husband to be a wonderful and handsome young man. In a year's time, when she became the mother of a little boy, she felt she was the happiest woman in the world.
>
> But six years later, there came a terrible flood. Hsiang-ling and her family lost their home and everything they owned. When they were fleeing their town, Hsiang-ling became separated from her husband and young son in the crowds of other townspeople. After searching for them in vain, Hsiang-ling followed a group of people to another town called Lai-chou. She had given up hope that she would ever see her husband and child again.

Student Edition pp. 242–243

242

OPTION 2 — Think Critically, continued

Higher-Order Thinking Skills

Story Structure • Analysis Explain how the conflict foreshadows what will happen later in the story. Possible response: I know that Hsiang-ling needs a home, food, and her family. The rest of the story will probably be about her solving her problems by finding what she has lost.

Greek and Latin Roots • Analysis Look at the word *gratefully* at the bottom of page 243. It includes the Latin root *grat,* which means "pleasing or thankful." How does knowing the meaning of *grat* help us understand how Hsiang-ling accepted the butler's offer? Possible response: By knowing that *grat* means "pleasing or thankful," we can tell that Hsiang-ling accepted the offer in a nice, thankful way.

On page 243 the rising action begins. Hsiang-ling finds a food distribution shack. She gives her food to another woman and the butler recommends her for a job. I can predict that this new job will help Hsiang-ling solve her problems.

As Hsiang-ling sat, exhausted and alone, at the side of the road leading to Lai-chou, a woman came up to her and said, "You must be hungry. Don't you know that a *li* (one-third of a mile) down the road there is a food-distribution shack? Yüan-wai Lu has opened it to help the flood victims. Talk to his butler. I am sure you can get something to eat there."

Hsiang-ling thanked the woman, followed her directions, and found the place. A long line of people with bowls in their hands was waiting to get a ration of porridge. Hsiang-ling had never done such a thing in her life. As she stood in line holding a bowl and waiting her turn, she felt distraught enough to cry, but she forced herself to hold back the tears.

Finally, when it was her turn, Yüan-wai Lu's butler scooped the last portion of porridge into her bowl and said to the rest of the people in line, "Sorry, no more porridge left. Come back early tomorrow."

The person behind Hsiang-ling began to sob. Hsiang-ling turned around and saw a woman who reminded her of her mother, except that she was much older. Without a word, she emptied her porridge into the woman's bowl and walked away.

The butler was surprised at what Hsiang-ling had done. Just as she had made her way back to the road, he caught up with her and said, "Young lady, I don't understand. Why did you give away your porridge—are you not hungry?"

"I am hungry," said Hsiang-ling, "but I am young and I can stand hunger a bit longer."

"You are very unselfish," said the man. "I would like to help you. My master, Yüan-wai Lu, is looking for someone to take care of his little boy. If you are interested, I would be happy to recommend you."

Hsiang-ling gratefully accepted his offer and was brought to the house where Yüan-wai Lu and his wife lived.

243

On Their Own

Have students explain how the conflict (the flood) gave rise to Hsiang-ling being recommended for a job. (The flood left Hsiang-ling homeless and hungry, so she had to go find work to be able to buy food.)

Monitor and Clarify • Evaluation • Text to World How does the flood seem to change Hsiang-ling's attitude? Why does this happen? Explain what background knowledge led you to this. Possible response: Hsiang-ling seems more giving and selfless after the flood. This may be because she has been through a hardship for the first time in her life. I know that hardships often let people realize how lucky they are.

Check Predictions Have students look back at the predictions they made earlier and discuss whether they were accurate. Then have students preview the rest of the selection and either adjust their predictions accordingly or make new predictions.

Differentiated Instruction

 Strategic Intervention
Genre Remind students that in a folk tale, goodness is rewarded and evil is punished. So far Hsiang-ling has been punished and rewarded. Ask students if they think her life will continue to improve. Ask them to explain their reasoning.

(A) Advanced
Latin roots Have students look up the words *accessible*, *attribute*, and *gratify* in a dictionary. Have them check the Latin roots and explain how the roots relate to the English meanings.

ELL

English Language Learners
Latin root cognates *Grat* is the root of Spanish words such as *gratificar* ("to reward"), *gratis* ("free"), and *gratitude* ("gratitude"). The sound of the Spanish word *gracias* ("thanks") may also help some students to remember the meaning of *grateful* and the Latin root *grat*.

 If you want to teach this selection in two sessions, stop here.

Objectives
- Find pertinent information from print and electronic sources.
- Recognize and correctly use action and linking verbs.
- Practice correctly spelling words with vowel sounds with *r*.

Research and Inquiry
Navigate/Search

Teach

Tell students they will read a variety of folk tales and use a computer to take notes about good deeds they find. They can research folk tales online or read through collections of folk tales in the library or resource center. They also may find folk tales in literature textbooks or in trade books.

Model

Think Aloud When I use a search engine to look for information about folk tales, I find hundreds of folk tales from around the world. There are many different topics and lessons, so it is difficult to know where to start reading. I will use keywords to see if I can locate a certain kind of folk tale—the kind in which good deeds are rewarded. My keywords can include *folk tales good deeds or folk tales rewards.* When I find folk tales about characters who do good deeds, I will read them and make notes about my inquiry topic. I'll make my notes on a computer and record exactly where I'm finding my information.

Guide practice

Have students identify useful folk tales from Web sites, textbooks, or trade books. For each print source, have students write the title, author, publisher, and publication date at the top of the file. Remind them to take notes on any useful information they find. They should always cite the page number.

For each online source, students will need to record the Web address, author, title, and date. Notes for each source should be in a separate file. As they take notes, they may want to group relevant information together to help them see the relationships between ideas.

On their own

Have students continue to summarize the good deeds they find in folk tales. Tell them that they should focus on the main ideas. They can practice summarizing as they take notes.

Conventions
Action and Linking Verbs

Teach

Write these sentences on the board: *Jana ate the sandwich. Pedro is happy today.* Point out that *ate* is an action verb because it describes the action of eating. Then point out that *is* is a linking verb because it links *Pedro* with being *happy* without using an action.

Guide practice

Say these phrases. Have students tell you whether the verbs are action or linking.

Rita writes	**The wind blew**
Mom and Dad are	**The grey cat purrs**

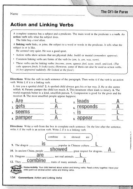

Reader's and Writer's Notebook p. 134

Daily Fix-It

Use Daily Fix-It numbers 3 and 4 in the right margin.

Connect to oral language

Have students look for and read aloud action and linking verbs in *The Ch'i-lin Purse.* (*loved,* p. 238; *returned,* p. 239; *was,* p. 240; *is,* p. 241; *become,* p. 249)

On their own

For additional practice use the *Reader's and Writer's Notebook,* p. 134.

Spelling
Vowel Sounds with *r*

Teach

Remind students of the rule that when vowels and vowel digraphs are followed by *r*, the vowel sound is changed. Write *repair, repaint.* Underline the *air* in *repair* and *ain* in *repaint*. Listen for the vowel sound as I say each word. Repair, repaint.

Guide practice

Write the remaining spelling words on the board. Have students write them and underline the vowel or vowel digraph pattern that is followed by *r*.

Reader's and Writer's Notebook p. 135

On their own

For additional practice use the *Reader's and Writer's Notebook,* p. 135.

Daily Fix-It

3. Today families spends years planning a childs wedding. *(spend; child's)*

4. Ever detail should be prefect. *(Every; perfect)*

 ELL

English Language Learners

Conventions To provide students with practice on regular and irregular plural nouns, use the modified grammar lessons in the *ELL Handbook* and the Grammar Jammer online at: www.ReadingStreet.com

Practice pronunciation Remind students that *r* can change the way a vowel sounds. Provide support based on students' proficiency levels.

Beginning Write the following words on the board: *dollar, singer, nurse.* Have students orally repeat /ar/ and then the word after you.

Intermediate Have students copy the sample words. Then have them underline the vowels that are affected by *r* and say the words aloud.

Advanced/Advanced High Have students work in pairs to create lists of words that have vowels affected by *r.* Encourage them to use a dictionary if needed.

Objectives
• Organize ideas to prepare for writing.

Writing—Poem
Writing Trait: Organization

Introduce the prompt

Review the key features of a poem with students. Remind them that they should think about these features as they plan their writing. Then explain that today they will begin writing their own poem. Read aloud the writing prompt.

> **Writing Prompt**
>
> Write a poem about an important event in your life, or the life of someone you know.

Select a topic

Think Aloud To help choose a topic, or controlling idea for the poem, let's make a list of important events in our lives and the lives of people we know. **Display a T-Chart.** In *The Ch'i-lin Purse*, we learned about a flood that affected the main character. Yesterday, we read "The Day I Learned to Fish," about when the poet first learned how to fish. **Add the information to the T-Chart. Ask students to name important events from their own lives, and fill in the chart as they give examples.**

Gather information

Remind students that they can conduct interviews to help them find more information about important events in their life or in the life of someone they know to use in their poems. Remember to keep this chart as the students will refer back to it tomorrow as they draft.

Important Events in Other's Lives	Important Events in My Life
the day Grandma won the car	when I won the spelling bee
the day Ryan hit a homerun	when I went horseback riding
the day Roen's little brother was born	the day I moved to the United States

Corrective feedback

Circulate around the room as students use the chart to choose an important event to write about. Have brief discussions with students who are having problems making a choice. Ask them guiding questions, such as *When was a time when you felt really happy?*

MINI-LESSON

Organizational Web

■ I'll write a poem about when I won the spelling bee. Instead of figuring out of the words in advance, I'll make an organizational web. I'll write my topic in the center. Write *When I Won the Spelling Bee* in the center.

■ In the other circles, I'll write elements I need in my poem: organization and poetic structure. Poems have stanzas with a set amount of lines. In one circle, I'll write *Use four-line stanzas*. I also need poetic techniques. In the other circles, write *alliteration*, *onomatopoeia*, and *assonance*.

Have students create their own organizational webs using the form on p. 136 of the *Reader's and Writer's Notebook*.

ROUTINE — Quick Write for Fluency — Team Talk

1 **Talk** Have pairs discuss important events in their charts.

2 **Write** Students write sentences about what makes events important.

3 **Share** Each partner reads his or her writing to the other.

Routines Flip Chart

Wrap Up Your Day

✔ **Build Concepts** Have students discuss why it is important to help others.

✔ **Compare and Contrast** How did it help you to compare and contrast Hsiang-ling's life with the life of a modern-day girl?

✔ **Story Structure** Identify conflict and rising action in this story.

Differentiated Instruction

 Advanced

Find relevant connections Challenge students to think of relevant rhyming word pairs they would like to use in their poems. Have them create a list to keep with their organizational web.

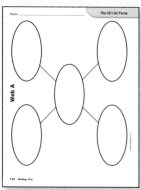

Reader's and Writer's Notebook, p. 136

Teacher Tip

Write examples on the board of how poem lines can rhyme, such as *abab* or *aabb*. Then help students understand rhythm by clapping along to the beat of "The Day I Learned to Fish" from the *Reader's and Writer's Notebook* p. 132.

Preview DAY 3

Tell students that tomorrow they will read about what happened to Hsiang-ling.

Objectives
- Expand the weekly concept.
- Develop oral vocabulary.

Today at a Glance

Oral Vocabulary
aid, selflessness

Comprehension Check/Retelling
Discuss questions

Reading
The Ch'i-lin Purse

Think Critically
Retelling

Fluency
Expression

Research and Study Skills
Textbook/trade book

Research and Inquiry
Analyze

Spelling
Vowel sounds with *r*

Conventions
Action and linking verbs

Writing
Poem

Concept Talk

Question of the Week

What are the rewards in helping others?

Expand the concept

Remind students of the weekly concept question. Discuss how the question relates to the events in Hsiang-ling's life. Tell students that today they will read about what happens when Hsiang-ling goes to the Lus' home for a job. Encourage students to think about whose actions are worthy of praise.

Anchored Talk

Develop oral vocabulary

Use illustrations to review pp. 236–243 of *The Ch'i-lin Purse*. Discuss the Amazing Words *praise* and *nurture*. Add these and other concept-related words to the concept map. Use the following questions to develop students' understanding of the concept. If possible, break students into groups and have them identify points of agreement and disagreement in their discussions.

- Do you think Hsiang-ling deserves *praise* for giving away her purse? Why or why not? (Hsiang-ling never really liked her purse, so it was not hard for her to give it away. However, she acted out of sympathy, so it was a generous act.)

- Do you think Hsiang-ling's mother *nurtured* her daughter properly? Explain your answer. (Hsiang-ling's mother gave Hsiang-ling everything she could ever want. But as a result, Hsiang-ling became rather spoiled.)

Oral Vocabulary
Amazing Words

Amazing Words

stranded	nurture
favor	aid
panic	selflessness
distress	social worker
praise	victim

Teach Amazing Words

Amazing Words — Oral Vocabulary Routine

1. **Introduce** Write the word *selflessness* on the board. Have students say it with you. Yesterday we read about Hsiang-ling's *selflessness* in the food line. Have students use context clues to determine a definition of *selflessness*. (*Selflessness* is the concern for other people's needs before your own.)

2. **Demonstrate** Have students answer questions to demonstrate understanding. If your friend forgets her lunch, how can you show *selflessness* to her? (I can share my lunch with her.)

3. **Apply** Have students apply their understanding. Name some other ways people can show *selflessness*.

See p. OV•3 to teach *aid*.

Routines Flip Chart

Apply Amazing Words

Before students read pp. 244–249 of *The Ch'i-lin Purse*, help them establish a purpose for reading. Have them consider how the Amazing Words *selflessness* and *aid* relate to the lives of Hsiang-ling and those around her.

Connect to reading

Explain that today students will read what happens to Hsiang-ling now that she has lost her home and family. As they read, students should think about how the Question of the Week and the Amazing Words *aid* and *selflessness* relate to the events in Hsiang-ling's life.

ELL Expand Vocabulary Use the Day 3 instruction on ELL Poster 8 to help students expand vocabulary.

ELL Poster 8

Objectives

◎ Compare and contrast story elements to aid comprehension.

◎ Use story structure to aid comprehension.

◎ Use Greek and Latin roots to determine the meanings of words.

Comprehension Check

Have students discuss each question with a partner. Ask several pairs to share their responses.

☑ **Genre • Analysis**

Why does the author choose not to develop her characters with more distinctive traits? Possible response: Character development is not what is important in this kind of story because it could distract the reader from the main purpose, which is to teach a lesson.

☑ **Compare and contrast • Analysis**

Compare and contrast Hsiang-ling's behavior toward the servant with her behavior toward the poor bride. Possible response: At first she is impatient with the servant and annoyed with the bride, but then she feels sorry for both of them and shows that she can be kindhearted.

☑ **Story structure • Evaluation**

The author reveals certain incidents of Hsiang-ling's life in more detail than others. Why does the author do this? How does this help drive the plot? Possible response: Explaining every detail of Hsiang-ling's life would distract from the importance of events involving the Ch'i-lin Purse. Mrs. Hsüeh's gift gave rise to Hsiang-ling's gift to the poor bride, which will probably give rise to another important event later in the story.

☑ **Greek and Latin roots • Synthesis**

Therm is a Greek root word meaning "heat," and *bene* is a Latin root meaning "well" or "good." Use the roots to determine the meanings of the words *thermos* and *benefit* as they appear in these sentences: *The hikers carried hot soup in a thermos. Regular exercise will benefit your heart.* Possible response: If *therm* means "heat," then a thermos must be a container that keeps things hot. *Bene* means "good or well," so *benefit* in this context means "do something good for."

☑ **Connect text to text**

Compare and contrast the hardships endured by the main characters in *The Ch'i-lin Purse* and *Hold the Flag High.* Possible response: Hsiang-ling loses family and Carney loses troops. Hsiang-ling keeps strong by finding a job and Carney keeps strong by carrying the flag.

Strategy Response Log

Have students revisit p. 14 in the *Reader's and Writer's Notebook* to add additional information about folk tales.

INTERACT with TEXT

Check Retelling

Have students retell the first half of *The Ch'i-lin Purse.*
Encourage students to paraphrase the selection in their
retellings, maintaining meaning and logical order.

Corrective feedback

If... students leave out important details,

then... have students look back through the illustrations in the
selection.

Small Group Time

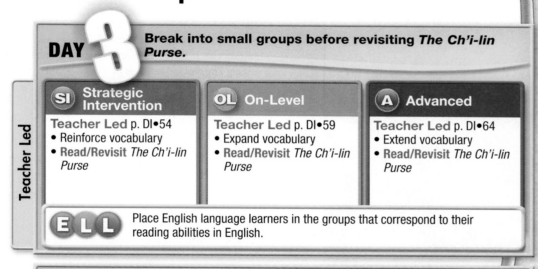

DAY 3 Break into small groups before revisiting *The Ch'i-lin Purse.*

Teacher Led

SI Strategic Intervention	**OL** On-Level	**A** Advanced
Teacher Led p. DI•54	Teacher Led p. DI•59	Teacher Led p. DI•64
• Reinforce vocabulary	• Expand vocabulary	• Extend vocabulary
• **Read/Revisit** *The Ch'i-lin Purse*	• **Read/Revisit** *The Ch'i-lin Purse*	• **Read/Revisit** *The Ch'i-lin Purse*

ELL Place English language learners in the groups that correspond to their
reading abilities in English.

Practice Stations	**Independent Activities**
• Let's Write	• AudioText of *The Ch'i-lin Purse*
• Get Fluent	• *Reader's and Writer's Notebook*
• Word Work	• Research and Inquiry

English Language Learners
Check retelling To support
retelling, review the multilingual
summary for *The Ch'i-lin Purse*
with the appropriate Retelling
Cards to scaffold understanding.

Objectives
• Identify sequence to aid comprehension.

OPTION 1

Skills and Strategies, continued

Teach Sequence

Review **Sequence** Have students paraphrase the events on pp. 244–245 in sequence. (First, Hsiang-ling becomes a governess. Next, the little boy loses his ball. Then, Hsiang-ling goes into Pearl Hall to find the ball and sees a Ch'i-lin Purse. She starts to cry. Finally, Mrs. Lu finds Hsiang-ling in the hall.) Ask them which event caused the other events.

Corrective Feedback

If… students have difficulty paraphrasing the events in order,

then… model how to sequence events.

Let's Practice It!
TR DVD•84

Double Day Read **Multidraft Reading**

If you chose…

Option 1 Return to Extend Thinking instruction starting on p. 238–239.
Option 2 Read pp. 244–249.
Use the Guide Comprehension and Extend Thinking instruction.

Student Edition pp. 244–245

OPTION 2

Think Critically, continued

Higher-Order Thinking Skills

Review **Sequence • Analysis** Look for the words *suddenly* and *finally* in the second half of page 246. What do these words tell you about how soon the events happen? Possible response: *Suddenly* means that the ball disappeared quickly. *Finally* means that Hsiang-ling took some time to decide whether to enter the Pearl Hall.

Model the Skill

Think Aloud I will scan for important events. First, Hsiang-ling becomes a governess. What happens next? (The boy loses his ball.) What happens to Hsiang-ling when she chases after the ball?

Yüan-wai Lu, a man in his early thirties, was impressed by Hsiang-ling's graceful bearing, and he agreed to hire her. "My wife's health is very delicate and she seldom leaves her room. Your job is to take care of our son. You may play with him anywhere in the garden, but there is one place you must never go. That is the Pearl Hall, the house that stands by itself on the east side of the garden. It is a sacred place, and if you ever go in there, you will be dismissed immediately."

So Hsiang-ling began her life as a governess. The little boy in her care was very spoiled. Whenever he wanted anything, he wanted it right away, and if he didn't get it, he would cry and cry until he got it. Hsiang-ling was saddened by his behavior; it reminded her of how spoiled she had been as a child.

One day, Hsiang-ling and the little boy were in the garden. Suddenly, the ball they were playing with disappeared through the window of the Pearl Hall. The boy began to wail, "I want my ball, I want my ball! Go and get my ball."

"Young Master, I cannot go into the Pearl Hall," said Hsiang-ling. "Your father doesn't allow it. I will be dismissed if I do."

But the little boy only cried louder, and finally Hsiang-ling decided that she had no choice. She walked over to the east side of the garden and looked around. No one was in sight. She quickly walked up the steps that led to the Pearl Hall and again made sure that no one was watching. Then she opened the door and stepped in.

244

◉ **Greek and Latin Roots • Synthesis** The events in this story are told in chronological order. *Chron* is a Greek root meaning "time." How does the root *chron* help us understand the meaning of *chronological*? Possible response: Knowing the root *chron* helps us to understand that the word *chronological* has to do with time. This story is told in time order.

((She ends up in Pearl Hall and sees the purse. Then Mrs. Lu finds her.) Which event caused the other events? (The boy's lost ball caused Hsiang-ling to find the purse.)

On Their Own

Have students reread p. 244 and identify which event happened first, Hsiang-ling remembers being a spoiled child or the boy cries for his ball. (Hsiang-ling remembers being a spoiled child.) For more practice, use *Let's Practice It!* p. 84 on the *Teacher Resources DVD-ROM*.

Differentiated Instruction

SI Strategic Intervention
Compare and contrast Have students identify the contrast Hsiang-ling makes in the first paragraph on page 245. (She used to have everything, and now she has nothing. She was once happy, but now she is sad.)

A Advanced
Have students explain why the author has Hsiang-ling compare herself as a child to the little boy. What does the author want to show about Hsiang-ling's character? (This shows that Hsiang-ling has matured into a less selfish person.)

She found herself standing in front of an altar, where two candles and some incense sticks were burning. But in the place where people usually put the wooden name-tablets of their ancestors was a Ch'i-lin Purse! Instantly she recalled the events of her wedding day and how happy she had been. She thought of her wonderful husband and her own son and how much she missed them. She had everything then, and now she had nothing! Hsiang-ling burst into tears.

Suddenly, she felt a hand on her shoulder. When she turned around she found herself face-to-face with Mrs. Lu, her mistress, and a young maid.

"What are you doing here?" Mrs. Lu asked angrily.

"Young Master told me to come here and pick up his ball," Hsiang-ling replied.

245

ELL

English Language Learners
Leveled Support: Sequence
Beginning Use numbers to explain the concept of sequence. Sequence the events for students and have them repeat after you.

Intermediate Give students sentence stems such as: *First, Hsiang-ling _____. Next, the little boy _____.*

Advanced Have students answer sequence questions in short but complete sentences. For example, ask: *What happened first? What happened after that?*

Advanced High Guide students to describe the sequence of events using complete sentences with proper word order, intonation, and phrasing.

Compare and Contrast • Analysis In paragraph 2 on page 244, how does Hsiang-ling compare herself to the little boy? What does this show about Hsiang-ling's relationship with the boy? Possible response: She recognizes that she was spoiled as a child, just as he is. This shows that although Hsiang-ling doesn't like the boy's behavior, she understands why he acts that way.

Inferring • Synthesis How do the Lus feel about the Ch'i-lin Purse? How does the reader know this? Use textual evidence and

background knowledge to support your answer. Possible response: The purse is sacred to the Lu family. They keep it in a place of honor—in a special building, on an altar with candles and incense. In paragraph 1 on p. 245, it says: *In the place where people usually put the wooden name-tablets of their ancestors was a Ch'i-lin Purse!* I know that ancestors are important in Chinese culture, so the Ch'i-lin Purse must be very important for the Lu family.

OPTION 1 Skills and Strategies, continued

Teach Compare and Contrast

◉ **Compare and Contrast** Tell students that illustrations can emphasize important ideas in a text. Have them compare and contrast the illustrations of Hsiang-ling on p. 238 and on p. 247. What do you notice? (In the second illustration she is no longer rich and she doesn't have a servant. Instead, she is poor and is a servant herself.)

Corrective Feedback

If... students have difficulty answering the question,
then... model how to compare and contrast.

Model the Skill

 Think Aloud On page 238, Hsiang-ling looks wealthy and fancy. She is holding a mirror. What does this mean?

246

Student Edition pp. 246–247

OPTION 2 Think Critically, continued

Higher-Order Thinking Skills

◉ **Compare and Contrast • Analysis** Compare and contrast the lives of Hsiang-ling and Mrs. Lu up to this point in the story. Possible response: Hsiang-ling started out wealthy but has become poor. Mrs. Lu started out poor but has become wealthy. In the illustration, Mrs. Lu appears kind, just as Hsiang-ling has become. They also both have sons.

◉ **Greek and Latin Roots • Synthesis** *Trib* is a Latin root that means "give." Some words I know with this root are *tribute, distribute,* and *contribute.* What is similar about the meaning of each of these words? They all have to do with giving. How does this help us understand the meaning of the vocabulary word *distribution*? *Distribution* also has to do with giving. Let's check the meaning in a dictionary. *Distribution* means "sharing something among a number of people." If you distribute something, you give it to people, so the definition fits the meaning of the Latin root *trib.*

(She cares about her appearance, and she seems to think a lot of herself.) What is different on page 247? (Hsiang-ling seems humble. She is dressed simply.)

247

Literary Elements: Character and Plot • Evaluation Hsiang-ling takes a risk by entering the Pearl Hall. Tell how the changes in Hsiang-ling's life have given rise to her taking more risks. Possible response: The challenges Hsiang-ling has been through, such as being through a flood and losing her family, have made her brave.

On Their Own

Have students compare and contrast Hsiang-ling's attitude on p. 238 with that of Mrs. Lu on p. 247. What does this tell the reader about the characters and their relationships? (Mrs. Lu is kind and generous to her servants, but Hsiang-ling was too demanding.)

Predicting • Analysis Mrs. Lu puts her hand on Hsiang-ling's shoulder. What does this suggest about how she will treat Hsiang-ling now that she has broken a rule and entered the Pearl Hall? Possible response: Mr. and Mrs. Lu seem to be kind, generous people. I think Mrs. Lu will listen to Hsiang-ling's reason for entering the Pearl Hall and will forgive her.

Differentiated Instruction

SI Strategic Intervention
Latin roots Show students the word *tribute.* Ask a student to circle the root word *trib.* Have another student use a dictionary to find the meaning, "give." Show students the tribute the Lu family has made for their ancestors on p. 246. Then discuss how the meaning of the root *trib* is similar to the meaning of the whole word *tribute.*

ELL English Language Learners
Professional Development: What experts say about think alouds "Think alouds can be particularly informative when used with second-language students. Through this type of dialogue, the teacher can discover not only the types of challenges that students encounter with the text, but also how they deal with such challenges." —Dr. Georgia Earnest García

Objectives
◎ Analyze story structure to aid comprehension.

OPTION 1 Skills and Strategies, continued

Teach Story Structure

Story Structure Have students identify the climax and resolution in *The Ch'i-lin Purse.* (The climax is Mrs. Lu's revelation that Hsiang-ling gave her the purse. The resolution is that Mrs. Lu found Hsiang-ling's family, and the families became close friends.)

Corrective Feedback

If... students have difficulty with the task,

then... model identifying the climax and resolution.

Student Edition pp. 248–249

OPTION 2 Think Critically, continued

Higher-Order Thinking Skills

Story Structure • Analysis Explain how Hsiang-ling's two acts of kindness led to the resolution of this story. How did the author foreshadow Hsiang-ling's kindness? Possible response: First, Hsiang-ling gave her purse to a young bride who turns out to be Mrs. Lu, so Mrs. Lu rewards her. Later, Hsiang-ling gave her porridge to another woman. The butler sees this and recommends Hsiang-ling for a job with the Lu family. The author foreshadowed Hsiang-ling's kindness by showing that she was nice to her servant.

Model the Strategy

Think Aloud The climax is usually near the end of the story, so I'm going to look for it on pages 248 and 249. What is the climax, the most exciting event?

"Then why are you weeping at the altar?"

"Because I saw the purse which once belonged to me."

Mrs. Lu looked startled. "Where are you from?" she asked, as she took the purse from the altar and sat down on a chair that leaned against a long table. There was a tremble in her voice.

"I am from Teng-chou."

"Bring her a stool," said Mrs. Lu, motioning to her maid. Not wanting to wait on another servant, the maid grudgingly brought a stool and put it to Mrs. Lu's right. "You may sit down," said Mrs. Lu. Somewhat confused, Hsiang-ling sat down.

"What was your maiden name?"

"Hsüeh Hsiang-ling."

"When were you married?"

"On the eighteenth day of the sixth moon, six years ago."

"Bring her a chair and put it to my left," Mrs. Lu ordered the maid. Hsiang-ling was told to move to the chair. She was surprised to see herself treated as a guest of honor.

"Tell me how you lost the purse," said Mrs. Lu.

"It was a gift from my mother. My wedding procession was stopped on the road because of a storm, and my *hua-chiao* was carried into a pavilion. There was another *hua-chiao* in it, and the bride was crying."

"Move her chair to the middle and move mine to the right side," ordered Mrs. Lu. The chairs were switched, and once again Hsiang-ling was told to sit down. She was astonished to find herself sitting in the middle seat—the place of the highest honor.

"Please continue," said Mrs. Lu.

"I gave the bride my purse. I never saw it again, and I have no idea how it got here."

Mrs. Lu dropped to her knees in front of Hsiang-ling and cried, "You are my benefactor! All these years I have been praying here for your well-being. When I got to my new home, I opened the purse and found it full of valuables, including this." She opened the purse and

248

Monitor and Clarify • Analysis Why does Mrs. Lu move Hsiang-ling from one place to another on page 248? Use your background knowledge and think about places of honor in American culture. Possible response: Mrs. Lu moves Hsiang-ling to the middle chair—the place of honor because she is her benefactor. In the United States, the head of the table is a similar position of honor.

(Mrs. Lu finds out that Hsiang-ling gave her the purse and explains that she and her husband used the valuables in the purse to gain wealth.) What events follow as a resolution? (Mr. and Mrs. Lu share their wealth with Hsiang-ling and help her find her husband and son, and they all become friends.)

took out a piece of jade. "My husband and I were able to pawn it for a large sum of money. Using the money, we started a business and have now become very wealthy. So I reclaimed the jade and have kept it here in the purse since. We also built the Pearl Hall to house the purse and to honor you.

"I knew that you lived in the Teng-chou area, so when I heard about the flood I prayed day and night in that direction, begging Buddha to protect you from harm. I was hoping that one day I would find you and show you my gratitude. And here you are, taking care of my son! I know what we must do. We shall divide our property and give you half of it. That will make us all very happy."

Hsiang-ling was speechless as Mrs. Lu placed the purse in her hands. That same day, Yüan-wai Lu sent out servants in all directions to look for Hsiang-ling's husband and son. Soon they were found, in a village not far from Teng-chou.

A great friendship developed between the two families. Later, whenever Hsiang-ling told people about her purse, she would always end the tale by saying, "If you have a chance to do something good, be sure to do it. Happiness will come back to you."

249

On Their Own

Have students write a summary of the story that includes these elements of the story's structure: conflict, rising action, climax, and resolution. Make sure students maintain meaning as they summarize.

Differentiated Instruction

SI Strategic Intervention

Story structure Review the meaning of the terms *story structure, conflict, rising action, climax,* and *resolution.* Have students work in pairs to identify each element in *The Ch'i-lin Purse.*

A Advanced

Discuss how this story could have been told differently. What if the author had followed the *ch'i-lin* purse after Hsiang-ling gave it away instead of following Hsiang-ling? What if this story had been told in first person or as a letter?

Connect to Social Studies

Jade is a green, shiny stone that people use to make tools, weapons, utensils, and decorative items. In ancient China, only wealthy aristocrats were allowed to own jade items. It was and continues to be honored as a royal gemstone in Chinese culture.

ELL

English Language Learners

Monitor comprehension After reading, have students ask questions about what they read. Make sure students use question words such as *when, where, why, how,* and *what.* Encourage students to answer each other's questions.

Comprehension Check

Spiral Review

Literary Elements: Theme • Synthesis What lesson can you learn from reading this folk tale? It reminds me that if I have a chance to do a good deed, I should do it, and happiness might come back to me. Make a thematic connection between *The Ch'i-lin Purse* and the Read Aloud, "The Call of the Sea." Both of these stories are about someone who does a good deed and gets rewarded for it.

Cause and Effect • Evaluation Name the effects of Mrs. Lu learning Hsiang-ling's identity. Which effect was most important to Hsiang-ling's future? Why? Possible response: Mrs. Lu gives Hsiang-ling half of her wealth, finds her family, and becomes her friend. Finding her family was most important because together they could rebuild their lives.

Check Predictions Have students return to the predictions they made earlier and confirm whether they were accurate.

Objectives

- ☉ Compare and contrast story elements to aid comprehension.
- ☉ Analyze the story structure to aid comprehension.

— Check Retelling
SUCCESS PREDICTOR

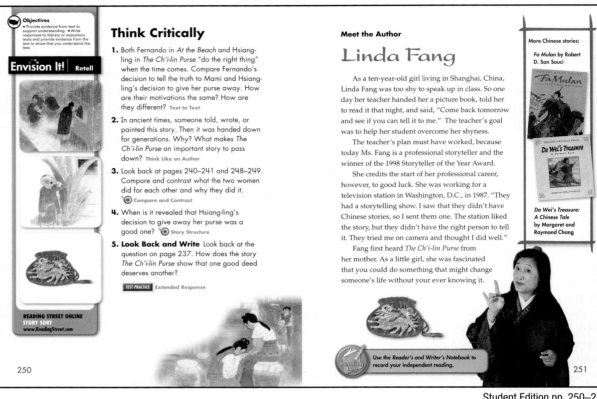

Student Edition pp. 250–251

Retelling

Envision It!

Have students work in pairs to retell the selection, using the Envision It! Retelling Cards as prompts. Remind students that they should accurately summarize the plot and paraphrase important ideas using key vocabulary as they retell. Monitor students' retellings.

Scoring rubric

Top-Score Response A top-score response makes connections beyond the text, describes the plot and important ideas using accurate information, and draws conclusions from the text.

Plan to Assess Retelling

☑ **Week 1** Assess Strategic Intervention students.

☑ **Week 2** Assess Advanced students.

☑ **This Week assess Strategic Intervention students.**

☐ **Week 4** Assess On-Level students.

☐ **Week 5** Assess any students you have not yet checked during this unit.

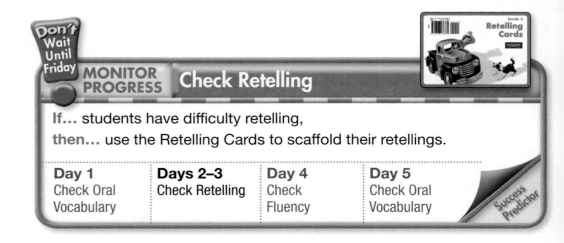

MONITOR PROGRESS Check Retelling

If... students have difficulty retelling,

then... use the Retelling Cards to scaffold their retellings.

Day 1 Check Oral Vocabulary	**Days 2–3** Check Retelling	**Day 4** Check Fluency	**Day 5** Check Oral Vocabulary

Think Critically

Text to text

1. Fernando tells the truth because he feels guilty for lying and because he feels sorry for his cousins. Hsiang-ling gives away her purse because she feels sorry for the poor bride. Unlike Fernando, she has done nothing wrong and does not feel guilty.

Think like an author

2. This story has continued to be shared because the main character's actions and their results teach the audience a moral lesson about the benefits of doing good things for others.

Compare and contrast

3. Hsiang-ling gives her purse to Mrs. Lu but unknowingly gives away her valuables. Mrs. Lu intentionally gives Hsiang-ling half her property as a reward.

Story structure

4. The climax of the story, when Mrs. Lu understands who Hsiang-ling really is, reveals that Hsiang-ling made a good choice when she gave her purse away.

 Writing on Demand

5. **Look Back and Write** To build writing fluency, assign a 10–15 minute time limit.

Suggest that students use a prewriting strategy, such as brainstorming or using a graphic organizer, to organize their ideas. Remind them to establish a topic sentence and support it with facts, details, or explanations to demonstrate understanding. As students finish, encourage them to reread their responses, revise for organization and support, and proofread for errors in grammar and conventions.

Scoring rubric

Top-Score Response A top-score response uses details to show that Hsiang-ling's good deeds were rewarded and that the rewards were well deserved.

A top-score response should include:

- Hsiang-ling gave her purse to a poor bride.
- Hsiang-ling gave her porridge to a hungry woman.
- Hsiang-ling was given a job and later, half of the Lus' fortune. Then her family was found.
- An explanation of how important events give rise to and foreshadow future events.

Differentiated Instruction

SI **Strategic Intervention**
Model prewriting for students by having them help you write an outline beginning with a topic sentence that explains the main idea of the paragraph, followed by a list of Hsiang-ling's good deeds and their results. Encourage students to add a concluding idea.

Meet the Author

Have students read about Linda Fang on p. 251. Ask them how *The Ch'i-lin Purse* shows that we can do things that can change other people's lives without our ever knowing it.

Independent Reading

After students enter their independent reading information into their Reading Logs or a journal, have them summarize what they have read, maintaining meaning and logical order. Remind students that a summary should be no more than a few sentences about the main idea of a text.

ELL

English Language Learners
Retelling Use the Retelling Cards to summarize the selection with students. Then have partners describe each scene or setting shown on the cards.

Retelling

Success Predictor

DAY 3 Read and Comprehend

Objectives
- Read grade-level text with expression.
- Reread for fluency.
- Distinguish between textbooks and trade books.

Model Fluency
Expression

Model fluent reading

Have students turn to p. 241 of *The Ch'i-lin Purse.* Have students follow along as you read paragraphs 1–2 on this page. Tell them to listen to how the expression in your voice changes as you read the dialogue between Hsiang-ling and her servant. Adjust your voice to stress important words and phrases and express the emotions of the characters.

Guide practice

Have students follow along as you read the passage again. Then have them reread the passage as a group without you until they read with the right expression and with no mistakes. Continue the same way as you read paragraph 3.

Reread for Fluency

Corrective feedback

If... students are having difficulty reading with the right expression, **then...** prompt:

- Which word is a problem? Let's read it together.
- Read the sentence again to be sure you understand it.
- Tell me the sentence. Now read it as if you are speaking to me.

ROUTINE Oral Reading

1. **Read** Have students read p. 241 of *The Ch'i-lin Purse* orally.

2. **Reread** To achieve optimal fluency, students should reread the text three or four times.

3. **Corrective Feedback** Have students read aloud without you. Provide feedback about their expression and encourage them to adjust their voice level to stress important words and phrases. Listen for use of appropriate expression.

Routines Flip Chart

Research and Study Skills
Textbook/Trade Book

Teach

Ask students where they would look to find a collection of folk tales, in a textbook or a trade book. (trade book) Show students examples of textbooks and trade books and explain their features.

- A **textbook** is a book used to teach a certain subject. It is written to be used in a classroom or home school, and is often accompanied by additional materials such as tests and workbooks.

- A **trade book** is any book that is not a textbook, magazine, or reference book, such as a collection of short stories or a nonfiction book about Franklin D. Roosevelt. Trade books can be read for pleasure or to seek information.

- Both textbooks and trade books may have the same parts: title and copyright page, table of contents, divisions such as chapters or units, graphic sources such as maps and photos, a glossary, and an index.

- Previewing a textbook or trade book before reading will help the reader understand the material contained in it and its purpose.

Provide groups with examples of either of type of book. Have each group show its book to the class, tell what type it is, and its purpose.

Guide practice

Discuss these questions:

Which type of book is a novel? (a trade book) Which is a math book? (a textbook) How can you tell? (A math book teaches math and is used in class.)

On their own

Have students complete pp. 138–139 of the *Reader's and Writer's Notebook*.

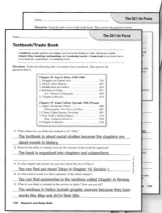

Reader's and Writer's
Notebook, pp. 138–139

ELL

English Language Learners
Leveled support: Textbook/Trade Book Teach the differences between the books using several classroom examples with which the students are already familiar. Then have students answer questions according to their ability level.

Beginning Have students gesture, point, or answer *yes* or *no* to questions such as *Show me a trade book. Does a textbook help teach us?*

Intermediate Ask students questions that include answer choices such as, *Do we use a textbook to learn or to read for fun? What does this textbook teach, math or reading?*

Advanced/Advanced High Ask students to compare and contrast textbooks and trade books. Guide students to use complex and compound sentences with key compare and contrast words such as *and, but,* or *though.*

Objectives
- Analyze data for usefulness.
- Recognize and use action and linking verbs.
- Spell frequently misspelled words.

Research and Inquiry
Analyze

Teach

Tell students they will analyze the information they found about folk tales. They may need to refine the research question once they ask themselves about what they have found.

Model

Think Aloud Originally, I thought I would write about the different kinds of good deeds that are done in folk tales. But I found so many folk tales when I searched. I asked myself, *What do all of these folk tales have in common?* I realized that I don't have time to read all of the folk tales I found. So I decided to refine my inquiry question to name only one or two folk tales. That way I can focus on those good deeds. Now my inquiry question is *How are good deeds rewarded in "The Lion and the Mouse" and "We Are All One"?*

Guide practice

Have students analyze their findings. Help them narrow their focus to a manageable number of folk tales by refining their research question.

As students continue to research, walk around the room to make sure they are taking notes in an organized way. Help them identify information they will need for their Works Cited page.

On their own

Have students discuss their research question and their findings with a partner. Encourage them to explain whether they have changed their research question and why.

Conventions
Action and Linking Verbs

Review

Remind students that this week they learned about action and linking verbs.

- An action verb tells what the subject does. It can express physical or mental action.
- A linking verb links, or joins, the subject to a word or words in the predicate.

Daily Fix-It Use Daily Fix-It numbers 5 and 6 in the right margin.

Connect to oral language Have students identify whether the underlined verbs listed below are action or linking verbs.

She <u>flies</u> the plane.	Birds <u>peck</u> at the birdfood.
They <u>are</u> not hungry.	I <u>feel</u> sad today.

On their own For additional support, use *Let's Practice It!* p. 85 on the *Teacher Resources DVD-ROM.*

Let's Practice It
TR DVD•85

Spelling
Vowel Sounds with *r*

Frequently misspelled words

The words *caught* and *there's* are words that students often misspell. I'm going to read a sentence. Choose the right word to complete the sentence and then write it. Use an electronic or print dictionary to check your spellings.

1. _____ a letter for you on the table. (There's)

2. I _____ a foul ball. (caught)

3. She _____ the fly in the jar. (caught)

4. I see that _____ a red cardinal in the tree. (there's)

On their own For additional practice, use the *Reader's and Writer's Notebook* p. 140.

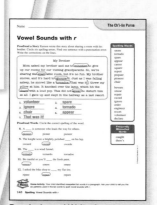

Reader's and Writer's
Notebook p. 140

Differentiated Instruction

SI Strategic Intervention

Action and linking verb support Create note cards for students that contain the bulleted information from Grammar Transparency 8. Encourage students to use the note cards to help them determine whether a verb is action or linking.

Daily Fix-It

5. A purse are a bag for mony. (*is; money*)

6. Today most women carried a purse for small ojects. (*carry; objects*)

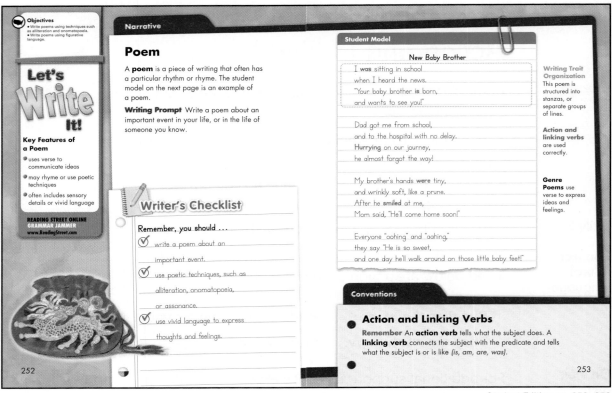

Student Edition pp. 252–253

Let's Write It!
Poem

Teach

Use pp. 252–253 in the Student Edition. Direct students to read the key features of a poem, which appear on p. 252. Remind students that they can refer to the information in the Writer's Checklist as they write their own poems.

Read the student model on p. 253. Point out the four-line stanzas and the *abab* rhyme in the model. Help students analyze how sound effects like alliteration, internal rhyme, onomatopoeia, and rhyme scheme reinforce meaning in the poem.

Connect to conventions

Remind students that verbs can be action or linking. Point out the correct use of action and linking verbs in the model.

Writing—Poem
Writer's Craft: Poetic Style

Display rubric

Display Scoring Rubric 8 from the *Teacher Resources DVD* and go over the criteria for each trait under each score. Then, using the model in the Student Edition, choose students to explain why the model should score a 4 for one of the traits. If a student offers that the model should score below 4 for a particular trait, the student should offer support for that response. Remind students that this is the rubric that will be used to evaluate the poems they write.

Scoring Rubric: Poem

	④	③	②	①
Focus/Ideas	Vivid poem with well-chosen details	Fairly vivid poem with some details	Few details and/or lack of focus in poem	Lacks clarity and development of ideas
Organization	Uses lines and stanzas with clear organization	Uses some lines and stanzas; can follow organization	Very few lines or stanzas; organization not clear	No lines, stanzas, or organization
Sentences	Sentences show strong rhythm	Sentences show some rhythm	Little rhythm in sentences	Sentences lack rhythm
Word Choice	Vivid style created by use of exact nouns, strong verbs, and exciting adjectives	Some style created by strong and precise words	Little style created by strong, precise words; some lack of clarity	Word choice vague or incorrect
Voice	Clear use of alliteration, onomatopoeia, or assonance creates strong voice	Mostly clear use of alliteration, onomatopoeia, or assonance	Not always clear or correct use of alliteration, onomatopoeia, or assonance	No use of alliteration, onomatopoeia, or assonance
Conventions	Excellent control and accuracy; action and linking verbs used correctly	Good control, few errors; action and linking verbs used correctly	Weak control; action and linking verbs used incorrectly	Serious errors that obscure meaning

Web

Have students get out the organizational webs they worked on yesterday. If their webs are not complete, have them use the Internet and print resources to gather information, take notes, and complete their webs.

Write

You will be using your organizational web as you write the draft of your poem. When you are drafting, don't worry if the poem does not sound exactly as you want it. You will have a chance to revise it tomorrow.

Objectives
- Write a first draft of a poem.
- Use poetic organization and structure.

Writing, continued
Writer's Craft: Poetic Style

MINI-LESSON

Stylizing a Poem

■ **Introduce** Explain to students that poems use specific styles or organizations to show creativity. Display the Drafting Tips for students. Remind them that the focus of drafting is to get their ideas down in an organized way. Then display Writing Transparency 8A.

Spelling Superstar

I am a spelling superstar!
I never thought I'd get this far!
I used to not know how to spell.
The judges always touched the bell.

I studied the dictionary morning and night.
I would not choose to quit without a fight.
I learned to spell without a cough
And even with the lights turned off.

I was the words for all my friends.
We were them all over agin.
On the day of the big spelling be,
guess who won. That's right—me!

Unit 2 The Ch'i-lin Purse   Writing: Model 8A

Writing Transparency 8A, TR DVD

Drafting Tips

✔ Make sure to write in stanzas and use the same number of lines for each stanza.

✔ Choose words for rhyme, sound, and meaning.

✔ Make an X over the parts of your organizational web that you have already included in your poem, so you can see what you are still missing.

 Think Aloud I'm going to write a poem about when I won the spelling bee called *Spelling Superstar*. When I draft, I develop my ideas. I don't worry about revising or proofreading because those tasks will come later. I will refer to my organizational web to make sure I include all of the elements I need in my poem.

Direct students to use the drafting tips to guide them in writing their drafts. Instruct them to develop their drafts by building on their ideas from yesterday to create focused, organized, and coherent poems. Remind them to make sure that they are using graphic elements, such as line lengths and capital letters, as well the poetic techniques of alliteration, onomatopoeia, and assonance. Remind students to include figurative language in their poems to add meaning to their writing.

ROUTINE **Quick Write for Fluency** **Team Talk**

1 **Talk** Pairs talk about which topic they chose for their poems.

2 **Write** Each student writes a brief paragraph about the information or special words they want to use in their poems.

3 **Share** Partners read one another's writing and then check each other's paragraphs for correct use of action and linking verbs.

Routines Flip Chart

Differentiated Instruction

 Advanced

Restructuring Challenge students to add one extra line to each of their stanzas, either building on or changing their rhyming and rhythm schemes.

Wrap Up Your Day

✔ **Build Concepts** Have students discuss the rewards Hsiang-ling received when she helped someone in need.

✔ **Compare and Contrast** How are Hsiang-ling and Mrs. Lu alike? How are they different?

✔ **Story Structure** Ask students to identify the climax and the resolution in this story.

Preview DAY 4

Tell students that tomorrow they will read an origin myth about how the mountains and valleys on Earth were created.

Objectives
• Expand the weekly concept.
• Develop oral vocabulary.

Today at a Glance

Oral Vocabulary
social worker, victim

Genre
Origin myth

Reading
"The Story of Phan Ku"

Let's Learn It!
Fluency: Expression
Vocabulary: Word structure
Listening/Speaking: Readers' Theater

Research and Inquiry
Synthesize

Spelling
Vowel sounds with *r*

Conventions
Action and linking verbs

Writing
Poem

Concept Talk

Question of the Week
What are the rewards in helping others?

Expand the concept

Remind students that this week they have read stories in which the characters were rewarded for helping others. Tell students that today they will read a Chinese origin myth about how the earth was created.

Anchored Talk

Develop oral vocabulary

Use illustrations to review pp. 244–249 of *The Ch'i-lin Purse*. Discuss the Amazing Words *selflessness* and *aid*. Add concept-related words to the concept map. Use the following questions to develop students' understanding of the concept. Break students into groups and have them identify points of agreement in their discussions.

• People can show their *selflessness* by providing *aid* to those in need. How can someone show *selflessness*? (by donating time, money, or supplies to people or organizations that help others)

• In what ways can you provide *aid* to others in your community? (Answers will vary, but suggestions should be specific and local.)

Strategy Response Log

INTERACT with TEXT

Have students review the characteristics of folk tales on p. 14 of the *Reader's and Writer's Notebook.* Then have them compare *The Ch'i-lin Purse* to another folk tale that they have read or know about.

Oral Vocabulary
Amazing Words

Amazing Words

stranded	nurture
favor	aid
panic	selflessness
distress	social worker
praise	victim

Teach Amazing Words

Amazing Words — Oral Vocabulary Routine

1 Introduce Write the word *victim* on the board. Have students say it aloud with you. On pages 242 and 243 we read that Yüan-wai Lu supplied food for the hungry flood *victims* and that Hsiang-ling became a flood *victim* when she lost her home, family, and belongings. What context clues help you understand the word *victims*? (Context clues include *lost* and *hungry*. *Victims* mean "people who have been harmed because of an event, accident, or other disaster.")

2 Demonstrate Have students answer questions to demonstrate understanding. What kinds of situations produce *victims*? (natural disasters such as floods, tornados, or hurricanes)

3 Apply Have students apply their understanding. Is a *victim* the person who has been hurt or the person who is helping? (the person who has been hurt)

See p. OV•3 to teach *social worker*.

Routines Flip Chart

Differentiated Instruction

SI Strategic Intervention

Amazing Words Have students write a list of ways to help people who are victims of a natural disaster such as a fire or flood. Make sure they use the Amazing Words.

Apply Amazing Words

Have students read "The Story of Phan Ku" on pp. 254–255. Encourage them to think about how the Amazing Words *social worker* and *victim* relate to the Question of the Week. Ask students to think about how Phan Ku helped others by making the world a better place.

Connect to reading

As students read today's selection, have them think about how the Question of the Week and the Amazing Words relate to the origin myth.

ELL Produce Oral Language Use the Day 4 instruction on ELL Poster 8 to extend and enrich language.

ELL Poster 8

The Ch'i-lin Purse **254b**

Let's Think About Genre
Origin Myth: Culture

Introduce the genre

Explain to students that what we read is structured according to the author's reasons for writing and what kind of information he or she wishes to convey. Different types of texts are called genres. Tell them that an origin myth is one type of genre.

Discuss the genre

Discuss with students where we get folk tales. Explain that origin myths grew out of the beliefs of a particular culture. They are passed down orally from one generation to the next. As a result, myths are embedded in a culture's history and its customs. Most myths are hundreds or thousands of years old. Myths include supernatural events involving gods, humans, and forces of nature. The origin myth, in particular, explains the beginnings of different natural phenomena.

On the board, draw a Venn diagram like the one below. Label the sides *The Ch'i-lin Purse* and "The Eagle and the Bat." Ask the following questions:

- Which story is a folk tale and which is a legend? **Possible response:** *The Ch'i-lin Purse* is a folk tale and "The Eagle and the Bat" is a legend.

- What is similar about *The Ch'i-lin Purse* and "The Eagle and the Bat"? How are their themes similar to and differ from the theme of an origin myth? **Possible response:** Both stories teach a lesson. An origin myth explains how something in nature came to be.

- What is different about these two stories? **Possible responses:** *The Ch'i-lin Purse* is a realistic tale about a Chinese girl, and teaches the idea that good things will happen to you if you do good first. "The Eagle and the Bat" is an imaginary tale that has animal characters who learn that honesty is the best policy.

The Ch'i-lin Purse   **"The Eagle and the Bat"**

Folk tale, Realistic, one good deed deserves another | Fiction, Teaches lesson | Legend, Not realistic, honesty is the best policy

Guide practice

Have students work in pairs to brainstorm the customs, traditions, and stories of their own cultures. Have them elicit and consider suggestions from each other in their discussion. Ask them to share their ideas with the class.

Connect to reading

Tell students they will read a Chinese origin myth about the formation of the world. Have the class think about how origin myths have shaped our own and other cultures.

Small Group Time

DAY 4 Break into small groups before reading or revisiting "The Story of Phan Ku."

Teacher Led

SI Strategic Intervention	**OL** On-Level	**A** Advanced
Teacher Led p. DI•55	**Teacher Led** p. DI•60	**Teacher Led** p. DI•65
• Practice retelling	• Practice retelling	• Genre focus
• Genre focus	• Genre focus	• Read/Revisit "The Story of Phan Ku"
• Read/Revisit "The Story of Phan Ku"	• Read/Revisit "The Story of Phan Ku"	

ELL Place English Language learners in the groups that correspond to their reading abilities in English.

Practice Stations
• Read for Meaning
• Get Fluent
• Words to Know

Independent Activities
• AudioText of "The Story of Phan Ku"
• *Readers and Writer's Notebook*
• Research and Inquiry

Academic Vocabulary

folk tale a story that has been passed down through oral tradition

ELL

English Language Learners
Cognates The words *origin* and *myth* both have cognates in Spanish: *origen* and *mito*.

Objectives

◎ Compare and contrast the elements of and lessons learned from myths.

◎ Analyze the story structure to aid comprehension.

Student Edition pp. 254–255

Guide Comprehension
Skills and Strategies

Teach the genre

Origin Myth: Culture Have students preview "The Story of Phan Ku" on pp. 254–255. Explain that the characters in a myth have few qualities and there may be little or no dialogue. Add that the plot often has one or only a few incidents, the setting is general, and the theme is broad. Then ask: What kind of character do you think Phan Ku will be?

Corrective feedback

If... students have difficulty making predictions about Phan Ku, **then...** model thinking about the elements of an origin myth.

Model the genre

Think Aloud I know that mythological characters might be humans, gods, animals, or forces of nature, so Phan Ku could be any of those. I see the words *giant, horns,* and *tusks* in the first two paragraphs, so I'm going to guess that Phan Ku is a magical creature. Since the characters in myths have very few qualities, I don't think we will learn about Phan Ku's personality. However, I think he will play an important role in a big event.

On their own

Have students work in pairs to list the elements of myths from various cultures. Have them make predictions about what they will learn in the selection.

Extend Thinking
Think Critically

Higher-order thinking skills

 Compare and Contrast • Analysis Explain how and why Phan Ku's behavior changed in the middle of page 255. Possible response: For thousands of years he had worked hard and was very tired. He must have felt so bad that it made him cry. The storytellers also needed a way for Phan Ku to fill the rivers and lakes and then disappear.

Story Structure • Evaluation How is this selection organized? Is this the most effective way to organize an origin myth? Why or why not? Possible response: It is told in chronological order. This is the best way to tell the story because the reader does not need extra details to understand the theme. Instead, the reader reads the events in the order in which they happened.

Let's Think About...

Phan Ku used a chisel to carve rivers and pushed dirt and rocks into piles to make mountains.

Reading Across Texts

Have students complete a Venn diagram to organize their thoughts and compare and contrast the sacrifices made by Phan Ku and Hsiang-Ling. Encourage students to make connections between the texts and provide textual evidence.

Writing Across Texts

Have students use their Venn diagrams to help them describe the lessons they learned from the sacrifices made by Phan Ku and Hsiang-Ling. Instruct them to compare and contrast the moral lessons from each story as the main idea of their paragraph and use the information on their Venn diagrams as supporting details.

Differentiated Instruction

 Strategic Intervention
Story structure Have pairs of students create a time line that includes each incident from the selection. Then ask them to write one sentence that explains why the events are told in chronological order.

A **Advanced**
Origin myth Have groups of students create their own origin myths. Tell one student in each group to write a short paragraph describing the origin of something in nature. Then have the student read the paragraph to another student who will rewrite it by memory and then elaborate. Continue the process until each group member has had a chance to participate. Have groups compare their first and final versions.

 **English Language Learners**
Leveled support: Story structure
Beginning Have students illustrate the tale and label their illustrations with words from the text.

Intermediate Give students a pattern for summarizing the selection: At first ____. Then Phan Ku ____. Finally ____.

Advanced/Advanced High Guide students to retell the events in the order they occurred in the selection, using complete sentences with proper word order, intonation, and phrasing.

Objectives

- Read with fluency and comprehension.
- ⊚ Determine the meanings of English words derived from Greek and Latin roots.
- Perform in a Readers' Theater.

Check Fluency WCPM

SUCCESS PREDICTOR

Objectives
• Read aloud grade-level texts and understand what is read. • Determine the meaning of English words with roots from Greek, Latin, and other languages. • Listen to and interpret a speaker's messages and ask questions. • Participate in discussions by raising and considering suggestions from other group members and by identifying points of agreement and disagreement.

Vocabulary

Greek and Latin Roots

Word Structure Many English words contain Greek or Latin roots and affixes. You can use these roots to help you find the meanings of English words.

Practice It! The Latin root *bene* means "good" or "well," and *sacr* means "holy." The Greek root *derm* means "skin." The Greek prefix *anti-* means "against." Look through stories you've read this year, and list and define as many words as you can that are formed using these roots and affixes.

Let's Learn It!

READING STREET ONLINE
ONLINE STUDENT EDITION
www.ReadingStreet.com

Fluency

Expression

Partner Reading When you read with expression, you bring the characters in a story to life. Change your tone of voice as you read to reflect each character's feelings or personality.

Practice It! With a partner, practice reading aloud a page from *The Ch'i-Lin Purse.* Adjust your tone of voice to represent the emotions of the characters.

Listening and Speaking

Get Ready For Middle School
When you participate in a performance, make eye contact with others.

Readers' Theater

In Readers' Theater, actors read from a script to present a story as a drama without a stage or costumes.

Practice It! With a group, choose a scene from *The Ch'i-lin Purse.* Use the scene to create a script. Assign roles, and use details from the story to find clues about how to speak each character's dialogue. Then perform for the class.

Tips

Listening . . .
- Listen carefully to each speaker.
- Interpret what each speaker says.

Speaking . . .
- Use volume to make sure your listeners can hear you.
- Speak clearly and vary your speaking rate.

Teamwork . . .
- Identify points of agreement and disagreement.
- Consider suggestions from other group members.

256 257

Student Edition pp. 256–257

Fluency
Expression

Guide practice

Use the Student Edition activity as an assessment tool. Make sure the reading passage is at least 200 words. As students read aloud with partners, walk around to make sure their expression is appropriate and that their pitch changes to enhance the meaning of what they are reading.

Don't Wait Until Friday

MONITOR PROGRESS   Check Fluency WCPM

As students reread, monitor their progress toward their individual fluency goals. Make sure they comprehend what they read.

Current Goal: 110–116 words correct per minute

End-of-Year Goal: 140 words correct per minute

If... students cannot read fluently at a rate of 110–116 words correct per minute,

then... have students practice with text at their independent levels.

Day 1	Days 2–3	Day 4	Day 5
Check Oral Vocabulary	Check Retelling	Check Fluency	Check Oral Vocabulary

Success Predictor

Vocabulary
Greek and Latin Roots

Teach Greek and Latin roots

Word Structure Write the words *asteroid* and *inspect* on the board. Remind students that many English words come from a Greek or Latin root. Remind students that using word structure is using what they know about a word's parts to determine the meaning of the whole word.

Guide practice

Tell students that the Greek root *ast* means "star," and the Latin root *spec* means "see." Instruct students to use word structure to determine the meaning of the words *asteroid* and *inspect*. Have students use a dictionary to revise or confirm their definitions and to find more words with the roots *ast* and *spec*.

On their own

As students look through the selections for words with Greek and Latin roots, help them use the roots to find the meaning of the English words. If they have trouble, model the process.

Listening and Speaking
Readers' Theater

Teach

Tell students that in order for a play to be successful, everyone must work together. Tell students to elicit and consider ideas from other students about where the actors will stand, how they will move, and how their faces, voices, and bodies can express the story.

Guide practice

Make sure each group member has a chance to share his or her ideas. Encourage students to bring their characters to life with body language, tone of voice, gestures, and facial expressions. Remind them to pay attention to eye contact and good grammar and to maintain appropriate rate, volume, and enunciation when speaking.

On their own

As students perform, have the audience listen to and interpret the speakers' verbal and nonverbal messages. After students perform their scenes for the class, help students analyze the similarities and differences between the original text and its dramatic adaptation. Ask questions such as: Was the dialogue the same? Did you get more information about the characters' thoughts in the book or in the performance? Did the actors show you something new about the story? Make sure students give evidence for their answers.

Readers' Theater
Remind students that volume and tone of voice are important when speaking. They should also use eye contact with other actors and with their audience to make their message strong and to communicate their ideas effectively.

English Language Learners
Practice pronunciation Model performing two or three lines of dialogue while students read along. Have students repeat the lines after you. Provide feedback on their pronunciation.

Fluency
Success Predictor

30–35 mins.

Objectives

- Synthesize research into a written presentation.
- Use action and linking verbs.
- Correctly spell words with vowel sounds with *r*.

Research and Inquiry
Synthesize

Teach Tell students they will synthesize their research into a written or oral presentation that summarizes findings and uses evidence to support its conclusions. They should write a summary of what they learned about good deeds in the folk tales they researched. Review how to choose relevant information from a number of sources and organize it logically.

Guide practice Monitor students as they use a word processing program to prepare their summaries for presentation on Day 5. Make sure students are summarizing information and excluding unnecessary details. They should also have proper citation information for each source.

On their own Have students write a brief summary of their research findings. Then have them organize and combine information for their presentation.

Conventions
Action and Linking Verbs

Test practice

Remind students that grammar skills, such as the correct use of action and linking verbs, are often assessed on important tests. Remind students that:

- An action verb tells what the subject does. It can express physical or mental action.

- A linking verb links, or joins, the subject to a word or words in the predicate.

Reader's and Writer's Notebook p. 141

Daily Fix-It

Use Daily Fix-It numbers 7 and 8 in the right margin.

On their own

For additional practice, use the *Reader's and Writer's Notebook,* p. 141.

Spelling
Vowel Sounds with *r*

Practice spelling strategy

Remind students to use the spelling patterns and rules they've learned to help them complete this activity. Have students work in pairs to create a crossword puzzle featuring at least five spelling words. Students should first design the puzzle by writing the words on grid paper so that they intersect. Then have them number each word near its first letter, and write clues. Finally have them copy the shape of the puzzle, the numbers, and the clues onto clean grid paper. Students can exchange puzzles with other pairs and solve each other's puzzles. They can use a print or online dictionary to check their spellings.

Let's Practice It! TR DVD•86

On their own

For additional practice, use *Let's Practice It!* p. 86 on the *Teacher Resources DVD-ROM.*

Daily Fix-It

7. Purses is often made of manufactured materiels or fabric. *(are; materials)*

8. A plastic handbag may appeer to be made of lether. *(appear; leather)*

E L L

English Language Learners

Leveled support: Vowel sounds with *r* Creating a word search puzzle may be too difficult for English Language Learners. Provide instruction for students based on their proficiency levels.

Beginning Have students write all the spelling words that begin with *s*. Then have them echo: /or/ snore; /air/ spare, square; /ear/ smear; /or/ sword.

Intermediate Have students locate and write all the spelling words that have the vowel sound /or/. Have them echo /or/ along with the words.

Advanced Have students write the spelling words two at a time in a word search puzzle format focusing on the *r,* such as connecting snore and tornado by the *r.* Then have them read the pairs aloud.

Objectives
- Revise draft of a poem.
- Apply revising strategy of Adding.
- Include figurative language and poetic techniques.

Writing—Poem
Revising Strategy

MINI-LESSON

Revising Strategy: Adding

■ Yesterday we wrote poems about important events in our lives or the lives of others. Today we will revise our drafts.

■ Display Writing Transparency 8B. Remind students that revising does not include corrections of grammar and mechanics. Then introduce the revising strategy Adding.

Writing Transparency 8B, TR DVD

■ When you revise, ask yourself *What poetic techniques are missing?* The revising strategy **Adding** is the strategy in which you add in new words to make sure you are covering the key features of a poem. Let's look at the fourth line of my poem. *Touched* does not describe the sound of the bell that was used to signal misspellings. I will change *touched* to *rang*. Write in *rang* and repeat the poetry line aloud. *Morning* can change to *day* for alliteration. *Quit* can change to *lose* for assonance. Reread your composition for places where you can add sound effects, such as alliteration, onomatopoeia, and assonance.

Tell students that as they revise, they should also check for the use of sensory language to bring their poems to life. Have them focus on revising their drafts to clarify meaning and enhance style after questions of purpose and genre have been addressed.

Revising Tips

✔ Make sure the poem tells about an important event in a way that makes sense.

✔ Review writing to make sure you have included poetic techniques.

✔ Make sure your poem has rhyming words and sensory language.

Peer conferencing

Peer Revision Have pairs of students exchange papers for peer revision. Have them read each other's poems aloud, tapping on the table to mark rhythm. Partners should put an X near words in the poem that do not work rhythmically. Refer to the *Reader's and Writer's Notebook* for more information about peer conferencing.

Have students revise their poems using the advice their partners gave during Peer Revision as well as the features of a poem to guide them.

Corrective feedback

Circulate around the room to monitor students and have conferences with partners as they incorporate each other's suggestions into their poems.

Write Guy
Jeff Anderson

Adding Without Leaving Readers Hanging

A student might add worthwhile information to his or her writing, but they often write sentence fragments. I like to encourage the writer by welcoming the idea and, at the same time, helping students form solid sentences or add dependent parts in order to communicate.

ROUTINE **Quick Write for Fluency** **Team Talk**

1 **Talk** Pairs discuss how they used poetic techniques in their poems.

2 **Write** Each student writes one line of poetry using that technique.

3 **Share** Partners read their writing to one another and check each other's lines for the correct use of the technique.

Routines Flip Chart

Wrap Up Your Day

✔ **Build Concepts** Have students discuss Phan Ku and his actions.

✔ **Oral Vocabulary** Monitor students' use of oral vocabulary as they respond: Think about this week's selections. Who was in distress? Did anyone nurture or give aid to someone less fortunate?

✔ **Text Features** Ask students how the illustrations in The *Ch'i-lin Purse* helped them understand the selection.

ELL

English Language Learners
Recognizing onomatopoeia
Have pairs work together to generate lists of words that imitate sounds. Encourage them to look at graphic novels, comics, or picture books to gather ideas. Then have students read the list aloud to one another.

Preview DAY 5

Remind students to think about the rewards in helping others.

Objectives
- Review the weekly concept.
- Review oral vocabulary.

Today at a Glance

Oral Vocabulary

Comprehension
◉ Compare and contrast

Lesson Vocabulary
◉ Greek and Latin roots

Word Analysis
Suffixes *-tion, -ion*

Literary Terms
Symbolism

Assessment
Fluency
Comprehension

Research and Inquiry
Communicate

Spelling
Vowel sounds with *r*

Conventions
Action and linking verbs

Writing
Poem

Check Oral Vocabulary
SUCCESS PREDICTOR

Concept Wrap Up

Question of the Week

What are the rewards in helping others?

Review the concept

Have students look back at the reading selections to find examples that best demonstrate the rewards in helping others.

Review Amazing Words

Display and review this week's concept map. Remind students that this week they have learned ten Amazing Words related to the rewards in helping others. Have students use the Amazing Words and the concept map to answer the question *What are the rewards in helping others?*

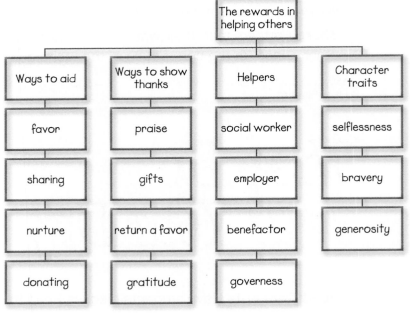

The rewards in helping others

Ways to aid	Ways to show thanks	Helpers	Character traits
favor	praise	social worker	selflessness
sharing	gifts	employer	bravery
nurture	return a favor	benefactor	generosity
donating	gratitude	governess	

ELL **Check Concepts and Language** Use the Day 5 instruction on ELL Poster 8 to monitor students' understanding of the lesson concept.

ELL Poster 8

Concept Talk Video

Amazing Ideas

Connect to the Big Question

Have pairs of students discuss how the Question of the Week connects to the Big Question: *What makes people want to do the right thing?* Tell students to use the concept map and what they have learned from this week's Anchored Talks and reading selections to form an Amazing Idea—a realization or "big idea" about Doing the Right Thing. Encourage students to elicit suggestions from other group members. Then ask each pair to share their Amazing Idea with the class.

Amazing Ideas might include these key concepts:

• We should help others when we can. One day, we may need help, too.

• We all have the ability to help others in some way, whether we are young, old, rich, or poor.

• It may not be easy and it may take a strong character to help others, but it is worthwhile.

Write about it

Have students write a few sentences about their Amazing Idea, beginning with "This week I learned…."

 It's Friday

MONITOR PROGRESS **Check Oral Vocabulary**

Have individuals use this week's Amazing Words to describe the rewards in helping others. Monitor students' abilities to use the Amazing Words and note which words you need to reteach.

If… students have difficulty using the Amazing Words,

then… reteach using the Oral Vocabulary Routine, pp. 231a, 234b, 244b, 254b, OV•3.

Day 1	**Days 2–3**	**Day 4**	**Day 5**
Check Oral Vocabulary	Check Retelling	Check Fluency	Check Oral Vocabulary

Success Predictor

Amazing Words

stranded	nurture
favor	aid
panic	selflessness
distress	social worker
praise	victim

ELL

English Language Learners

Concept map Work with students to add new words to the concept map.

257g

Oral Vocabulary

Success Predictor

Objectives
◎ Review compare and contrast.
◎ Review Greek and Latin roots.
• Review suffixes -tion, -ion.
• Review symbolism.

Comprehension Review
Compare and Contrast

Teach compare and contrast

Envision It!

Review the definitions of compare and contrast on p. 232. Remind students that they can compare and contrast ideas between two stories. They can also compare and contrast characters, events, and ideas in a story. For additional support, have students review p. EI•6 on compare and contrast.

Student Edition EI•6

Guide practice

Have pairs of students make two comparisons and contrasts. First, have the pairs compare and contrast two characters in *The Ch'i-lin Purse*. Then have the pairs compare the theme in *The Ch'i-lin Purse* and the theme in "Ah Tcha's Leaves." (Both have the theme "What goes around, comes around," but the stories illustrate the theme in different ways.) Have the pairs share their character comparisons and thematic links for the class to discuss.

On their own

For additional practice with compare and contrast, use *Let's Practice It!* p. 87 on the *Teacher Resources DVD-ROM.*

Let's Practice It!
TR DVD•87

Vocabulary Review
Greek and Latin Roots

Teach Greek and Latin roots
Guide practice

Remind students that knowing the meaning of common Greek and Latin roots can help them understand the meaning of new words.

Tell students that the Latin root *cess* means "go" or "yield." Remind students that if they do not know the meaning of a word or its root, they can look in a dictionary. Explain that *cess* is the root for English words such as *process, procession,* and *access.* Have students determine the meaning of each of these words using the Latin root *cess.* Point out that all of these words have to do with moving forward.

On their own

Write the Latin roots *dis* ("apart"), *tribuere* ("assign"), and *grat* ("pleasing, thankful") on the board. Have students use the roots to determine the meanings of *distribution* and *gratitude.* Then have students use the Greek root *therm* ("heat") to determine the meaning of *thermal.* Have them use a dictionary to check the meanings of the words.

Word Analysis `Review`
Suffixes *-tion, -ion*

Teach suffixes *-tion, -ion*

Review the Latin suffixes *-tion* and *-ion* with students. Display *expression* and *construction*. Point out each suffix and base word. Explain how the suffix changes the part of speech of each word.

Guide practice

Display the following words: *confusion, vacation, decoration, education,* and *graduation*. Use the strategy for Meaningful Word Parts to teach the word *confusion*.

`ROUTINE` Strategy for Meaningful Word Parts

1. **Introduce the strategy** We are going to use word parts to help us read words. Write the word *confusion* on the board.

2. **Introduce the word parts** The base word is the verb *confuse*. The suffix is *-ion*. There is a spelling change.

3. **Connect to meaning** *Confuse* is a verb that means "to make unclear or uncertain." The suffix *-ion* makes it a noun that means "the state of being confused."

4. **Read the word** Blend the word parts as you run your hand beneath them: *confuse ion, confusion*.

Routines Flip Chart

On their own

Have students use the Routine to analyze the remaining words. Discuss how adding each suffix affects each word's meaning.

Literary Terms `Review`
Symbolism

Teach symbolism

Remind students that a symbol is an object that represents an important idea or concept.

Guide practice

Discuss the symbol of the *ch'i-lin,* which is an imaginary animal whose appearance coincides with imminent life or death in Chinese folklore.

On their own

Have students draw an idea web with the word *ch'i-lin* in the center. Have students tell how the *ch'i-lin* might symbolize life, death, or rebirth at different parts of the story.

Lesson Vocabulary

astonished surprised; amazed

behavior a way of acting

benefactor a person who has given money or help

distribution sharing something among a number of people

gratitude feeling thankful; showing appreciation

procession a number of people or vehicles moving forward in an orderly way

recommend to speak in favor of; to suggest

sacred worthy of reverence

traditions customs or beliefs handed down from generation to generation

Differentiated Instruction

 Advanced

Suffixes *-tion, -ion* Have students use their knowledge of suffixes to determine the meaning of the following words: *revolution, appreciation, conservation, inscription, hesitation, realization, opposition,* and *contemplation*. Then have them use some of the words in sentences. Challenge them to use these *-tion* and *-ion* words to talk about this week's concept, the rewards in helping others.

ⒺⓁⓁ

English Language Learners
Cognates Point out to Spanish speakers that the word for *symbol* in Spanish is *símbolo*. The Spanish word for *symbolism* is *simbolismo*.

Objectives
• Read grade-level text with fluency.

Plan to Assess Fluency

☑ **Week 1** Assess Advanced students.

☑ **Week 2** Assess Strategic Intervention students.

☑ **This week assess On-Level students.**

☐ **Week 4** assess Strategic Intervention students.

☐ **Week 5** Assess any students you have not yet checked during this unit.

Set individual goals for students to enable them to reach the year-end goal.

• Current Goal: 110–116 WCPM

• Year-End Goal: 140 WCPM

Assessment

Check words correct per minute

Fluency Make two copies of the fluency passage on p. 257k. As the student reads the text aloud, mark mistakes on your copy. Also mark where the student is at the end of one minute. To figure words correct per minute (WCPM), subtract the number of mistakes from the total number of words read in one minute. Make sure students comprehend what they read by having them retell what was read.

Corrective feedback

If... students cannot read fluently at a rate of 110–116 WCPM,
then... make sure they practice with text at their independent reading level. Provide additional fluency practice by pairing nonfluent readers with fluent readers.

If... students already read at 140 WCPM,
then... have them read a book of their choice independently.

Small Group Time

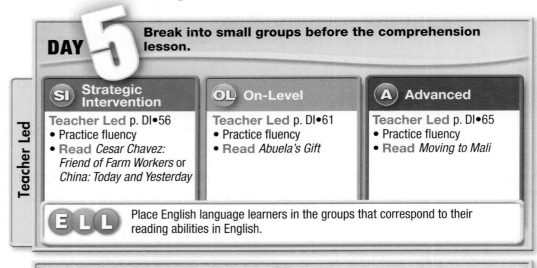

DAY 5 Break into small groups before the comprehension lesson.

Teacher Led

SI Strategic Intervention
Teacher Led p. DI•56
• Practice fluency
• Read *Cesar Chavez: Friend of Farm Workers* or *China: Today and Yesterday*

OL On-Level
Teacher Led p. DI•61
• Practice fluency
• Read *Abuela's Gift*

A Advanced
Teacher Led p. DI•65
• Practice fluency
• Read *Moving to Mali*

ELL Place English language learners in the groups that correspond to their reading abilities in English.

Practice Stations
• Words to Know
• Get Fluent
• Read for Meaning

Independent Activities
• Grammar Jammer
• Concept Talk Video
• Vocabulary Activities

Name _____

A Happy Tune

Lars was the best musician in all the land. When he played his flute, no 15

one could resist the beautiful notes. If he played a happy tune, everyone who 29

heard the music smiled, and some even danced. If he played a sad tune, 43

everyone who heard shook their heads sadly and many cried. Lars played his 56

flute at every happy wedding and every sad funeral. 65

But it was a poor time and if Lars was paid at all, it was only with a few 84

coins. One day as Lars rested on a tree stump near the riverbank, he began 99

to play a sad tune. He was feeling lonely and hungry. He felt that his life 115

might never improve. 118

To Lars's surprise, the river began to churn around and around until a 131

white column rose up in the middle. The figure of a young maiden dressed in 146

river moss appeared before Lars. The maiden was crying and her tears turned 159

to silver minnows as they hit the river. Lars was upset to see the maiden cry 175

and he began to cry, too. 181

Finally, when they had both cried their limit of tears, the maiden asked 194

him, "Why are you so sad?" Lars told her about how lonely and hungry he 209

was. He said that he couldn't play at even one more wedding. "I'll only play 224

sad tunes for funerals." 228

The maiden reached into the river and began to toss the silver minnows 241

at Lars. As each minnow hit the ground, it turned to real silver. Soon, Lars was 257

standing in the middle of thousands of minnows made of real silver. 269

Lars and the river maiden married in June, and Lars played a happy tune! 283

MONITOR PROGRESS

• Check Fluency

Objectives
• Read grade-level text with comprehension.

Assessment

Check compare and contrast

🔘 **Compare and Contrast** Use "How Tom Got Beautiful Feathers" on p. 257m to check students' understanding of compare and contrast.

1. How is the moral lesson in this selection similar to the lessons in *The Ch'i-lin Purse* and "Ah Tcha's Leaves"? **Possible response: All three stories show how people can be rewarded for kindness to others but can be punished for being vain or unfriendly.**

2. Compare and contrast Tom and Mia. Include their changes from the beginning to the end of the selection. **Possible response: At the beginning, Tom has brown feathers and Mia's are colorful. Tom is in love, but Mia has no time for Tom. After helping Mia, Tom grows beautiful feathers and Mia's feathers remain brown.**

3. Compare and contrast the characters Mia from "How Tom Got Beautiful Feathers" and Ah Tcha from "Ah Tcha's Leaves." **Possible response: Mia and Ah Tcha both had good lives at first. But they were not kind. As a result, Mia loses her beauty and Ah Tcha becomes poor. In the end, Ah Tcha regains his wealth after showing kindness, but Mia doesn't regain her colorful feathers.**

Corrective feedback

If... students are unable to answer the comprehension questions, **then...** use the Reteach lesson in the *First Stop* book.

Name _____

How Tom Got Beautiful Feathers

In a long ago time, there lived a bird that had the most beautiful blue and green feathers. Her name was Mia and every day she would walk down to the edge of the river so that she could look at herself. High up in a tree, a peacock named Tom watched her. Every day, Tom was astonished at Mia's great beauty and vowed that one day he would marry her. But Mia was in love only with her shimmering blue and green reflection and had no time for Tom and his short, dull, brown feathers.

One day Mia stepped closer to the river bank so she could get a better look at herself. She tripped on an old tree root and fell into the river. She began to sputter and flap. Tom flew down to help her. He reached out to Mia but something in the river was pulling at her!

"Help me!" she screamed. Tom pulled hard but something in the river pulled even harder! Finally, with one great effort, Tom pulled Mia out of the river, where she fell to the ground. In the river, an old turtle with blue and green feathers in his mouth dove under the water, sorry that he had missed his chance to catch the bird.

Once the river was still, Mia looked at her reflection. She couldn't believe what she saw! Her blue and green feathers were gone, leaving behind short, dull, brown feathers. "I'm not beautiful!" Mia cried. "I'm as ugly as...." But before she could finish, Tom said, "You're beautiful and you always have been."

At that moment, blue and green feathers began to sprout on Tom. Mia spent the rest of her life in short, dull, brown feathers. They lived happily ever after.

MONITOR PROGRESS

• **Compare and Contrast**

Objectives
- Communicate inquiry results.
- Take a spelling test.
- Review action and linking verbs.

Research and Inquiry
Communicate

Present ideas   Have students share their summaries of folk tales by presenting their information and giving a brief organized presentation about their research. Have students display the summaries they created on Day 4 and read parts of them aloud to the class.

Listening and speaking   Remind students how to be good speakers and how to communicate effectively with their audience.

- Respond to questions with additional details from your research.
- Speak clearly and loudly, with a slow enough rate so that everyone can understand you.
- Use gestures to help tell the story.
- Use good grammar and use language appropriate for your audience.
- Maintain eye contact with audience members.

Remind students of these tips for being a good listener.

- Wait until the speaker has finished before raising your hand to ask a question.
- Be polite, even if you disagree.
- Make sure you listen to and understand all of the speaker's ideas. Gestures, expression and other nonverbal cues may give you hints about what is important.

Spelling Test
Vowel Sounds with *r*

Spelling test

To administer the spelling test, refer to the directions, words, and sentences on page 233c.

Conventions
Extra Practice

Teach

Remind students that action verbs tell what the subject of a sentence does and linking verbs join the subject of a sentence to the word or words in the predicate.

Guide practice

Have students work with a partner to identify the verbs in these sentences. Then have them identify whether the verbs are action or linking.

> **The bus <u>stops</u> at the corner.** (action)
> **The bread <u>tastes</u> salty.** (linking)

Daily Fix-It

Use Daily Fix-It numbers 9 and 10 in the right margin.

On their own

Write these sentences. Have students look back in *The Ch'i-lin Purse* to find the correct action and linking verbs to fill in the blanks. Remind students to look for actions to help determine which type of verb they need.

1. **Hsiang-ling _____ beautiful and intelligent, and her mother _____ her dearly.** (was, loved)

2. **But Hsiang-ling _____ not satisfied at all.** (was)

3. **The servant _____ to the store and _____ another.** (returned, ordered)

4. **Hsiang-ling could _____ a girl sobbing inside.** (hear)

5. **I _____ sure you can get something to eat there.** (am)

Students should complete *Let's Practice It!* p. 88 on the *Teacher Resources DVD-ROM.*

Daily Fix-It

9. Yesterday the bride sitted on a sedan chare. (*sat; chair*)

10. Everyone celebrated at the Grand feast? (*grand; feast.*)

Let's Practice It!
TR DVD•88

Objectives
- Proofread revised drafts of poems, including correct use of action and linking verbs.
- Create and present final draft.
- Participate in a poetry reading.

Writing—Poem
Action and Linking Verbs

Review **revising**

Remind students that yesterday they revised their poems, paying particular attention to poetic techniques and poetic structure. Today they will proofread their poems.

MINI-LESSON

Proofread for Action and Linking Verbs

■ **Teach** When we proofread, we look closely at our work, searching for errors in mechanics. Today we will focus on action and linking verbs.

■ **Model** Let's look at the last stanza from the poem we started yesterday. Display Writing Transparency 8C. Explain that you will look for errors in action and linking verbs. I see a problem in the first line. There is a linking verb *was* instead of an action verb. I will change *was* to *spelled*. In the second sentence, I used a linking verb again. I will use the action word *practiced* instead. Explain to students that they should reread their poems a number of times while proofreading. Each time, look for spelling, punctuation, capitalization, and grammar errors.

Writing Transparency 8C, TR DVD

Proofreading Tips

✔ Be sure your usage of linking and action verbs is correct.

✔ If you use a computer, print out a copy of your poem. It is sometimes easier to spot errors on paper than on a computer screen.

✔ Use a consistent capitalization style for the beginnings of your lines.

Proofread   Display the Proofreading Tips. Ask students to proofread their poems, using the Proofreading Tips and paying particular attention to action and linking verbs. Circulate around the room answering students' questions. When students have finished editing their own work, have pairs proofread one another's poems.

Present   Have students incorporate revisions and proofreading edits into their poems, including the feedback from Peer Revision yesterday, to create a final draft.

Have students create poster-sized versions of their poems. Help students use a computer to enlarge their fonts or help them draw ruler lines on the poster to write on. Have students find or create art or other graphics to accompany their writing. Display the poems around the room, and then have students participate in a poetry reading. Encourage students to change their intonation or expression while reading their poems, including any words that involve onomatopoeia to match the sounds of the words. Have the classroom clap after each reading. When students are finished, have each complete a Writing Self-Evaluation Guide.

ROUTINE — Quick Write for Fluency — Team Talk

1. **Talk** Pairs discuss what they learned about important events in people's lives this week.

2. **Write** Each student writes a short paragraph about one important event they learned about.

3. **Share** Partners read their paragraphs to one another.

Routines Flip Chart

Teacher Note

Writing Self-Evaluation Guide
Make copies of the Writing Self-Evaluation Guide on p. 39 of the *Reader's and Writer's Notebook* and hand out to students.

ELL

English Language Learners
Support for linking verb be
English learners may have difficulty choosing the correct form and tense of the linking verb *be*. Provide support by displaying samples of sentences that include the present and past tense forms of *be*.

Poster preview Prepare students for next week by using Week 4, ELL Poster 9. Read the Poster Talk-Through to introduce the concept and vocabulary. Ask students to identify and describe objects and actions in the art.

Selection summary Send home the summary of *A Summer's Trade*, in English and the students' home language, if available. They can read the summary with family members.

Preview NEXT WEEK

Why do people make sacrifices for others? Tell students that next week they will read about the sacrifices people make for their family members.

Weekly Assessment

Use pp. 53–58 of *Weekly Tests* to check:

✔ **Word Analysis** Suffixes *-tion, -ion*

✔  **Comprehension Skill** Compare and Contrast

✔ Review **Comprehension Skill** Sequence

✔ **Lesson Vocabulary**

astonished	procession
behavior	recommend
benefactor	sacred
distribution	traditions
gratitude	

Weekly Tests

A
Advanced

OL
On-Level

SI
Strategic
Intervention

Differentiated Assessment

Use pp. 43–48 of *Fresh Reads for Fluency and Comprehension* to check:

✔  **Comprehension Skill** Compare and Contrast

✔ Review **Comprehension Skill** Sequence

✔ **Fluency** Words Correct Per Minute

Fresh Reads for Fluency and Comprehension

Managing Assessment

Use *Assessment Handbook* for:

✔ **Weekly Assessment Blackline Masters for Monitoring Progress**

✔ **Observation Checklists**

✔ **Record-Keeping Forms**

✔ **Portfolio Assessment**

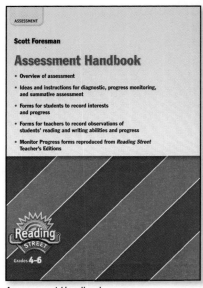

Assessment Handbook

"The Call of the Sea"
Continued from p. 231b

The lightning burst and faded...but surely they could not all have been mistaken? There was someone else besides Joseph out there...a gigantic fish? A drowning woman? "You called me with the comb and I came, Joseph. At last you called me!"

"Help me save these men!" he shouted back, his mouth full of rain.

And she did. She caught up each sailor washed off the wreck, and swam with them to Joseph's boat.

Small Group Time

SI *Strategic Intervention*

DAY 1

Build Background

■ **Reinforce the Concept** Discuss the weekly question *What are the rewards in helping others?* Ask students how people have helped them, for example, with homework, with something they wanted to learn, when they were sick or hurt, or when they needed to build or make something. Helping others involves doing things for other people. These acts can be as small as loaning a friend a pencil or as large as changing a person's life. Discuss the words on the concept map on pp. 230–231 in the Teacher Edition.

■ **Connect to Reading** Have students recall the Read Aloud "The Call of the Sea." Why do you think Joseph helped the mermaid when he knew mermaids sometimes lured people to their deaths? *(He had a kind heart and couldn't bear to see the mermaid die.)* What reward did he receive? *(A magic comb he used to save others.)* Sometimes helping someone is just a one-time action that has big effects. This week you will read about people helping others in ways that change both people's lives.

5-Day Plan

DAY 1	• Reinforce the concept • Read Leveled Readers Concept Literacy Below Level
DAY 2	• ◉ Compare and Contrast • ◉ Story Structure • Revisit Student Edition pp. 236–243
DAY 3	• ◉ Greek and Latin Roots • Revisit Student Edition pp. 244–249
DAY 4	• Practice Retelling • Read/Revisit Student Edition pp. 254–255
DAY 5	• Reread for fluency • Reread Leveled Readers

3- or 4-Day Plan

DAY 1	• Reinforce the concept • Read Leveled Readers
DAY 2	• ◉ Compare and Contrast • ◉ Story Structure • Revisit Student Edition pp. 236–243
DAY 3	• ◉ Greek and Latin Roots • Revisit Student Edition pp. 244–249
DAY 4	• Practice Retelling • Read/Revisit Student Edition pp. 254–255 • Reread for fluency • Reread Leveled Readers

3-Day Plan: Eliminate the shaded box

Objectives
• Interpret a speaker's messages (both verbal and nonverbal)

Go Digital! **eReaders**

Differentiated Instruction

SI Strategic Intervention

DAY 1

For a complete literacy instructional plan and additional practice with this week's target skills and strategies, see the **Leveled Reader Teaching Guide.**

Concept Literacy Reader

- **Read** *Cesar Chavez: Friend of Farm Workers*

- **Before Reading** Preview the selection with students, focusing on key concepts and vocabulary. Then have them set a purpose for reading.

- **During Reading** Read the first two pages of the selection aloud while students track the print. Then have students finish reading the selection with a partner.

- **After Reading** After students finish reading the selection, connect it to the weekly question *What are the rewards in helping others?*

Below-Level Reader

- **Read** *China: Today and Yesterday*

- **Before Reading** Have students preview the book, using the pictures. Then have students set a purpose for reading.

- **During Reading** Do a choral reading of the first few pages. If students are able, have them read and discuss the remainder of the book with a partner. Have partners discuss the following questions:

  - From the pictures, what can you tell about the lives of the leaders of China long ago?

  - How are they different from the lives of the common workers? *(The leaders seem to have many comforts; the workers had a harder life.)*

- **After Reading** Have students look at and discuss the concept map. Connect the Below-Level Reader to the weekly question *What are the rewards in helping others?* How might the leaders of China long ago have helped the common workers to have a better life?

MONITOR PROGRESS

If... students have difficulty reading the selection with a partner,

then... have them follow along as they listen to the Leveled Readers DVD-ROM.

If... students have trouble visualizing the location of China,

then... reread p. 3 and discuss the map in relation to the continents and countries with which students are familiar.

Objectives
- Interpret a speaker's messages (both verbal and nonverbal).

Small Group Time

Reinforce Comprehension

⊚ **Skill Compare and Contrast** Review with students *Envision It!* p. EI•6, Compare and Contrast. Then use p. 232 to review the definitions of compare and contrast.

⊚ **Strategy Story Structure** Review the definition of story structure. Remind students to think about what is the main conflict or problem as they read the story. How is the conflict or problem resolved? For additional support, refer students to *Envision It!* p. EI•22.

Revisit *The Ch'i-lin Purse* on pp. 236–243. Have students begin reading aloud *The Ch'i-lin Purse* with a partner. As they read, have them apply the comprehension skill and strategy to the story.

- What difference did Hsiang-ling see between herself and the girl next to her on her wedding day? *(She was lucky to have so many things, while the other girl had nothing.)*

- What clue word in the text helped you figure out the previous question? *(while)*

- How are Mrs. Hsueh and the servant similar? *(They both try to please Hsiang-ling.)*

Use the During Reading Differentiated Instruction for additional support for struggling readers.

MONITOR PROGRESS

If... students have difficulty reading along with the group,

then... have them follow along as they listen to the AudioText.

Student Edition p. EI•6

More Reading

Use additional Leveled Readers or other texts at students' instructional levels to reinforce this week's skills and strategies. For text suggestions, see the Leveled Reader Database or the Leveled Readers Skills Chart on pp. CL 24–CL 29.

Objectives
- Compare and contrast ideas and information.
- Describe incidents that advance the story or novel, explaining how each incident gives rise to or foreshadows future events.

 SI Strategic Intervention

DAY 3

Reinforce Vocabulary

Greek and Latin Roots/Word Structure Say the word *biography* as you write it on the board. Circle the roots *bio* and *graph*.

When I circle the word roots, I see that the first one is *bio*. I know that *bio* is the Greek root meaning "life." I see that the second root is "graph," which is the Greek root for "write." When I put together those meanings, I see that the word has to do with writing and life. That helps me figure out that *biography* is a type of writing that tells the story of someone's life.

Revisit *The Ch'i-lin Purse* on pp. 244–249.
Review *Words!* on p. W•9. Then have students finish reading the selection. Encourage them to use Greek and Latin roots to figure out the meaning of any unfamiliar words.

- Point out the word lunar on the second page of the story. If the Latin root *lun* means "moon," what do you think a *lunar* calendar is? *(It is a calendar that uses the moon to keep track of time.)*

- Look at the word *gratitude* on the last page of the story. The Latin root *grat* means "thank." What do you think *gratitude* might mean? *(thankfulness)*

Use the During Reading Differentiated Instruction for additional support for struggling readers.

> **MONITOR PROGRESS**
>
> **If...** students need more practice with the lesson vocabulary,
> **then...** use *Envision It! Pictured Vocabulary Cards.*

Student Edition p. W•9

More Reading

Use additional Leveled Readers or other texts at students' instructional levels to reinforce this week's skills and strategies. For text suggestions, see the Leveled Reader Database or the Leveled Readers Skills Chart on pp. CL 24–CL 29.

Objectives
- Determine the meaning of grade-level academic English words sDerived from Latin roots.
- Use word structure to analyze and decode new words.

Small Group Time

Practice Retelling

■ **Retell** Have students work in pairs and use the Retelling Cards to retell *The Ch'i-lin Purse.* Monitor retelling and prompt students as needed. For example, ask:

- Where and when does the story take place?

- What is the main character in the story like?

- What is the author trying to teach us?

If students struggle, model a fluent retelling.

Genre Focus

■ **Before Reading or Revisiting** "The Story of Phan Ku" on pp. 254–255, read aloud the genre information about myths on p. 254. Some myths explain the natural world and how it came to be. These are called "origin myths." For example, an African origin myth tells how the sun, moon, stars, and animals came into being.

Have students preview "The Story of Phan Ku." Ask:

- What text features do you see? *(title, subtitle)*

- What do the illustrations show? *(different events in the myth)*

Then have students set a purpose for reading based on their preview.

■ **During Reading or Revisiting** Have students read along with you while tracking the print, or do a choral reading of the myth. Stop to discuss any unfamiliar words, such as *tusks* and *chisel.*

■ **After Reading or Revisiting** Have students share their reactions to the origin myth. Then guide them through the Reading Across Texts and Writing Across Texts activities.

> **MONITOR PROGRESS**
>
> **If...** students have difficulty retelling the selection,
> **then...** have them review the story using the illustrations.

Objectives
- Describe phenomena explained in origin myths from various cultures.

 SI Strategic Intervention

DAY 5

For a complete literacy instructional plan and additional practice with this week's target skills and strategies, see the **Leveled Reader Teaching Guide.**

Concept Literacy Reader

- **Model** Model the fluency skill of expression for students. Ask students to listen carefully as you read aloud the first two pages of *Cesar Chavez: Friend of Farm Workers*. Have students note how the tone of your voice changes to show the feelings of Cesar Chavez and the farm workers throughout their story.

- **Fluency Routine**

  1. Have students reread passages from *Cesar Chavez: Friend of Farm Workers* with a partner.

  2. For optimal fluency, students should reread three to four times.

  3. As students read, monitor fluency and provide corrective feedback. Have students note the expression and emotion in your voice.

  See *Routines Flip Chart* for more help with fluency.

- **Retell** Have students retell *Cesar Chavez: Friend of Farm Workers*. Prompt as necessary.

Below-Level Reader

- **Model** Ask students to listen carefully as you read aloud the first two pages of *China: Today and Yesterday,* emphasizing expression.

- **Fluency Routine**

  1. Have students reread passages from *China: Today and Yesterday* with a partner or individually.

  2. For optimal fluency, students should reread three to four times.

  3. As students read, monitor fluency and provide corrective feedback. Point out that students can make their voice louder when describing the emperors and softer when describing common people.

  See *Routines Flip Chart* for more help with fluency.

- **Retell** For additional practice, have students retell *China: Today and Yesterday* page-by-page, using the pictures. Prompt as necessary.

  • What does this section tell you about?

  • What information do you learn on this page?

MONITOR PROGRESS

If... students have difficulty reading fluently,

then... provide additional fluency practice by pairing nonfluent readers with fluent ones.

Objectives
• Read aloud grade-level stories with fluency.

Small Group Time

Pacing Small Group Instruction

⏱ 15–20 mins.

5-Day Plan

DAY 1	• Expand the concept • Read On-Level Reader
DAY 2	• ⊙ Compare and Contrast • ⊙ Story Structure • Revisit Student Edition pp. 236–243
DAY 3	• ⊙ Greek and Latin Roots • Revisit Student Edition pp. 244–249
DAY 4	• Practice Retelling • Read/Revisit Student Edition pp. 254–255
DAY 5	• Reread for fluency • Reread On-Level Reader

3- or 4-Day Plan

DAY 1	• Expand the concept • On-Level Reader
DAY 2	• ⊙ Compare and Contrast • ⊙ Story Structure • Revisit Student Edition pp. 236–243
DAY 3	• ⊙ Greek and Latin Roots • Revisit Student Edition pp. 244–249
DAY 4	• Practice Retelling • Read/Revisit Student Edition pp. 254–255 • Reread for fluency • Reread On-Level Reader

3-Day Plan: Eliminate the shaded box.

OL On-Level   **DAY 1**

Build Background

■ **Expand the Concept** Connect the weekly question *What are the rewards in helping others?* and expand the concept. One way to help others is to show them we care about them. When we are generous to others, it shows them that they are important to us. Discuss the meaning of the words on the concept map on pp. 230–231 in the Teacher Edition.

On-Level Reader

For a complete literacy instructional plan and additional practice with this week's target skills and strategies, see the **Leveled Reader Teaching Guide.**

■ **Before Reading** *Abuela's Gift,* have students preview the On-Level Reader by looking at the title, cover, and pictures in the book. Ask:

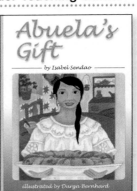

• Who are the main characters in the story? *(a girl and her grandmother)*

• When does the story take place? *(at Christmas)*

Have students create a three-column chart with the following heads: "Lupe and Abuela: Similarities"; "Lupe and Abuela: Differences"; and "Compared with My Life." Have students complete the chart as they read.

This book tells the story of a girl who spends Christmas with her grandmother. As you read, notice what is the same about the way the girl and the grandmother live and what is different. Also notice how the story compares with your life. Record the information on your chart.

■ **During Reading** Read aloud the first three pages of the book as students follow along. Then have them finish reading the book on their own. Remind students to add similarities and differences to their charts as they read.

■ **After Reading** Have partners compare their charts.

• How are Lupe and Abuela alike and different?

• How does the story relate to the weekly question *What are the rewards in helping others?*

Objectives
• Interpret a speaker's messages (both verbal and nonverbal).

 OL On-Level

DAY 2

Expand Comprehension

◉ **Skill** **Compare and Contrast** Use p. 232 to review the definitions of compare and contrast. For additional review, see p. E1•6 in *Envision It!*

Sometimes you can spot comparisons and contrasts by finding clue words. The clue words *like* or *as* show a comparison: *A baseball is round like a basketball.* The clue words *but* or *while* show a contrast: *A baseball is small, while a basketball is large.*

◉ **Strategy** **Story Structure** Review the definition of story structure. As students read, encourage them to think about the conflict in the story and how it is resolved. For additional support, refer students to the Extend Thinking questions or *Envision It!* p. E1•22.

Revisit *The Ch'i-lin Purse* on pp. 236–243. As students begin reading aloud, have them apply the comprehension skill and strategy to the story.

- How was Hsiang-ling different after she had a son from the way she was when she was younger? *(She was not as selfish.)*

- How did the Chinese culture treat men and women differently? *(When women married, they left their homes and families, but men did not.)*

Student Edition p. E1•6

More Reading

Use additional Leveled Readers or other texts at students' instructional levels to reinforce this week's skills and strategies. For text suggestions, see the Leveled Reader Database or the Leveled Readers Skills Chart on pp. CL 24–CL 29.

Objectives
- Compare and contrast ideas and information.
- Describe incidents that advance the story or novel, explaining how each incident gives rise to or foreshadows future events.

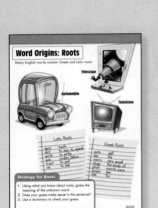

Student Edition p. W•9

More Reading

Use additional Leveled Readers or other texts at students' instructional levels to reinforce this week's skills and strategies. For text suggestions, see the Leveled Reader Database or the Leveled Readers Skills Chart on pp. CL 24–CL 29.

 On-Level

DAY  3

Expand Vocabulary

Greek and Latin Roots/Word Structure Write the word *benefactor* as you say it aloud. Help students to identify the Latin roots *bene* and *fact*. Then ask:

- What does the Latin root *bene* mean? *("good" or "well")*

- What does the Latin root *fact* mean? *("do" or "make")*

- What does the suffix *-or* mean? *("someone who")*

- What meaning do you get when you combine the meaning of both roots with the suffix? *("someone who does good")* A *benefactor* is someone who does good things for others by giving them money or other kinds of help.

Revisit *The Ch'i-lin Purse* on pp. 244–249. As students finish reading the selection, help them to apply the strategy as they read.

Recall what has happened in the selection so far. Ask:

- How has the Ch'i-lin Purse helped Mrs. Lu? *(She and her husband pawned a piece of jade and were able to start a successful business.)*

- How does Mrs. Lu repay Hsiang-ling? *(She divides her wealth with Hsiang-ling and sends servants to find her lost husband and son.)*

Objectives
- Determine the meaning of grade-level academic English words derived from Latin roots.
- Use word structure to analyze and decode new words.

 **OL** On-Level

DAY 4

Practice Retelling

■ **Retell** To assess students' comprehension, use the Retelling Cards. Monitor retelling and prompt students as needed.

Genre Focus

■ **Before Reading or Revisiting** "The Story of Phan Ku" on pp. 254–255, read aloud the genre information about origin myths on p. 254. Then have students preview the selection and set a purpose for reading. Ask:

- What does the subtitle of the story tell you about this myth? *(It is an origin myth from China.)*

- How does this selection differ from a nonfiction selection about the history of China? *(It is fictional, not factual.)*

■ **During Reading or Revisiting** Have students read along with you while tracking the print.

- According to this origin myth, what existed before the world was created? *(There was only a large egg.)*

- Why do you think the story contains no scientific information about what Earth materials are made of? *(This is an ancient story about the Earth's creation, which was made up long before any scientific information was available.)*

■ **After Reading or Revisiting** Have students share their reaction to the origin myth. Then have them write a short two-page myth of their own about how something in nature was created, such as a certain flower or animal.

Objectives
- Describe phenomena explained in origin myths from various cultures.

Small Group Time

On-Level Reader

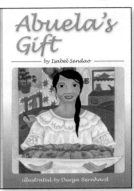

■ **Model** Read aloud the first page of the On-Level Reader *Abuela's Gift,* emphasizing expression through your tone of voice to make the dialogue more realistic. For example, you can make your voice sound more frail for the grandmother and more lively and energetic for the granddaughter. You can also vary the volume and rate to show how each person speaks differently.

■ **Fluency Routine**

1. Have students reread passages from *Abuela's Gift* with a partner.

2. For optimal fluency, students should reread passages three to four times.

3. As students read, monitor fluency and provide corrective feedback. Have students recall the different tones you used to convey emotions. Then have students practice changing their tone of voice to give each character a "voice" of their own.

See *Routines Flip Chart* for more help with fluency.

■ **Retell** For additional practice, have students use illustrations as a guide to retell *Abuela's Gift*. Prompt as necessary.

• Who are the characters in the story?

• What is the story mostly about?

Objectives
• Read aloud grade-level stories with fluency.

A Advanced

DAY 1

Build Background

■ **Extend the Concept** Discuss the weekly question *What are the rewards in helping others?* What are some ways that people can help newcomers? For example, if new neighbors arrived in your town, what might you do to help them feel at home? *(possible answers: show them around town, invite them over for a visit)* What reward might you get for your actions? *(possible answer: making new friends)*

Advanced Reader

For a complete literacy instructional plan and additional practice with this week's target skills and strategies, see the **Leveled Reader Teaching Guide.**

■ **Before Reading** *Moving to Mali,* tell students to recall the Read Aloud "The Call of the Sea." How did the mermaid repay Joseph for his help? *(She rescued the sailors.)* Today you will read about a woman who helps a family in Africa and how they repay her.

Have students look at the illustrations in the book and use them to predict what will happen in the text. Then have students set a purpose for reading.

■ **During Reading** Have students read the Advanced Reader independently. Encourage them to think critically. For example, ask:

• When has someone helped you?

• What is an unusual way to show gratitude without using words?

• How has someone shown you gratitude in an unusual way?

■ **After Reading** Have students review the concept map and explain how *Moving to Mali* helps them answer the weekly question *What are the rewards in helping others?* Prompt as necessary.

• What motivated Georgia to join the Peace Corps? *(She wants to learn about the world and help others.)*

• What surprised her about the people and culture of Mali? *(the fasting during Ramadan, the gift of the mud cloth)*

• What do you think Georgia gained from helping others?

■ **Now Try This** Suggest that students research stories about Peace Corps volunteers and what they learned while living in a foreign country.

Objectives
• Interpret a speaker's messages (both verbal and nonverbal).

Pacing Small Group Instruction
15–20 mins.

5-Day Plan

DAY 1	• Extend the concept • Read Advanced Reader
DAY 2	• ◉ Compare and Contrast • ◉ Story Structure • Revisit Student Edition pp. 236–243
DAY 3	• ◉ Greek and Latin Roots • Revisit Student Edition pp. 244–249
DAY 4	• Origin Myth • Read/Revisit Student Edition pp. 254–255
DAY 5	• Reread for fluency • Reread Advanced Reader

3- or 4-Day Plan

DAY 1	• Extend the concept • Advanced Reader
DAY 2	• ◉ Compare and Contrast • ◉ Story Structure • Revisit Student Edition pp. 236–243
DAY 3	• ◉ Greek and Latin Roots • Revisit Student Edition pp. 244–249
DAY 4	• Origin Myth • Read/Revisit Student Edition pp. 254–255 • Reread for fluency • Reread Advanced Reader

3-Day Plan: Eliminate the shaded box.

More Reading

Use additional Leveled Readers or other texts at students' instructional levels to reinforce this week's skills and strategies. For text suggestions, see the Leveled Reader Database or the Leveled Readers Skills Chart on pp. CL 24–CL 29.

A Advanced   DAY 2

Extend Comprehension

◉ **Skill** **Compare and Contrast** To broaden students' understanding of compare and contrast, encourage them to think about clue words and phrases they can look for, such as *while, but, yet, although,* and *so.*

◉ **Strategy** **Story Structure** Review the definition of the strategy. Remind students that the plot is driven by the main conflict. Ask them to think about how the different actions of the main character help to resolve the conflict. During reading, use the Extend Thinking questions and the During Reading Differentiated Instruction for additional support.

■ **Revisit** *The Ch'i-lin Purse* on pp. 236–243. Have students apply the comprehension skill and strategy as they read.

• What similarities and differences exist between Hsiang-ling and the woman in the food line? *(Both are hungry. The woman is much older than Hsiang-ling.)*

• How do these similarities and differences affect what Hsiang-ling does next? *(They motivate her to give away her food.)*

■ **Critical Thinking** Encourage students to think critically as they read *The Ch'i-lin Purse.*

• What makes someone look past his or her own concerns and see the suffering of others?

• How can small actions have large consequences for someone?

Objectives
• Compare and contrast ideas and information.
• Describe incidents that advance the story or novel, explaining how each incident gives rise to or foreshadows future events.

Extend Vocabulary

◉ Greek and Latin Roots/Word Structure
The following sentence contains a word with a Latin root: "It was The Ch'i-lin Purse, a red satin bag embroidered on both sides with a *ch'i-lin,* a *legendary* animal from ancient times…"

- The Latin root *leg* comes from the word *legere,* meaning "to read." What does this tell you about the meaning of *legendary*? *("something that was written down or read")*

- What smaller word, containing the root, can you find within the larger word *legendary*? *(legend)* What does this word mean? *("a story about past events that might not be true")*

Discuss how the root and word part can help define *legendary:* "a story told or read about the past that might not be true."

- **Revisit** *The Ch'i-lin Purse* on pp. 244–249. As students read, help them use Greek and Latin roots to figure out the meanings of unfamiliar words.

- **Critical Thinking** Have students recall what has happened in the selection so far. Encourage them to think critically. For example, ask:

- How can someone be both spoiled and helpful?

- How would the story change if Hsiang-ling were spoiled but not helpful?

More Reading
Use additional Leveled Readers or other texts at students' instructional levels to reinforce this week's skills and strategies. For text suggestions, see the Leveled Reader Database or the Leveled Readers Skills Chart on pp. CL 24–CL 29.

Objectives
- Determine the meaning of grade-level academic English words derived from Latin roots.
- Use word structure to analyze and decode new words.

Genre Focus

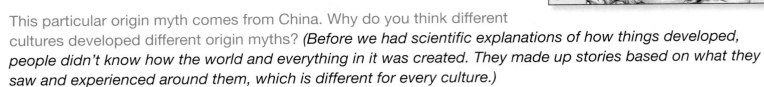

- **Before Reading or Revisiting** "The Story of Phan Ku" on pp. 254–255, read the panel information on origin myths. Ask students to preview the selection and use the illustrations to set a purpose for reading. Then have them read "The Story of Phan Ku" on their own.

- **During Reading or Revisiting** Ask students to think about the things in nature that are created in the story.

  This particular origin myth comes from China. Why do you think different cultures developed different origin myths? *(Before we had scientific explanations of how things developed, people didn't know how the world and everything in it was created. They made up stories based on what they saw and experienced around them, which is different for every culture.)*

- **After Reading or Revisiting** Have students discuss Reading Across Texts. Then have them do Writing Across Texts independently.

Objectives
- Describe phenomena explained in origin myths from various cultures.

- **Reread For Fluency** Have students silently reread passages from the Advanced Reader *Moving to Mali*. Then have them reread aloud with a partner or individually. As students read, monitor fluency and provide corrective feedback. If students read fluently on the first reading, they do not need to reread three to four times. Assess the fluency of students in this group using p. 257j.

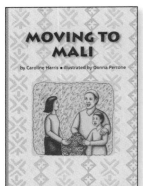

- **Retell** Have students summarize the main idea and key details from the Advanced Reader *Moving to Mali*.

- **Now Try This** Have students complete their research projects. You may wish to review their work to see if they need additional ideas. Have them share their finished work with classmates.

Objectives
- Read aloud grade-level stories with fluency.

The ELL lessons are organized by strands. Use them to scaffold the weekly curriculum of lessons or during small group time instruction.

Academic Language

Students will hear or read the following academic language in this week's core instruction. As students encounter the vocabulary, provide a simple definition or concrete example. Then have students use their background knowledge of English to give an example or synonym of the word.

Skill Words	expression *(expresión)* vowel sounds suffix *(sufijo)*	action and linking verbs compare and contrast
Concept Words	reward gift mermaid	poetic techniques

*Spanish congnates in parentheses

Concept Development

 What are the rewards in helping others?

■ **Preteach Concept**

• **Prior Knowledge** Have students turn to pp. 230–231 in the Student Edition. Call attention to the picture of the teacher with the students and tap into students' knowledge of teachers. What do teachers do? How do they help students? Why do you think teachers enjoy helping students?

• **Discuss Concept** Elicit students' knowledge and experience of the rewards in helping others. Look at the man who helped the boy get his kitten back. How do you think the boy feels? How do you think the man feels? Why do you think some people like to help others? Supply background information as needed.

• **Poster Talk-Through** Read aloud the Poster Talk-Through on ELL Poster 8 and work through the Day 1 activities.

■ **Daily Concept and Vocabulary Development** Use the daily activities on ELL Poster 8 to build concept and vocabulary knowledge.

Objectives
• Use prior knowledge and experiences to understand meanings in English.
• Use accessible language and learn new and essential language in the process.
• Speak using grade-level content area vocabulary in context to internalize new English words and build academic language proficiency.

Content Objectives
• Use concept vocabulary related to the rewards of helping others.

Language Objectives
• Express ideas in response to art and discussion.
• Use prior exeriences to understand meaning.
• Derive meaning of concept from media.

Daily Planner

DAY 1	• **Frontload Concept** • **Preteach** Comprehension Skill, Vocabulary, Phonics/ Spelling, Conventions • **Writing**
DAY 2	• **Review** Concept, Vocabulary, Comprehension Skill • **Frontload Main Selection** • **Practice** Phonics/Spelling, Conventions/Writing
DAY 3	• **Review** Concept, Comprehension Skill, Vocabulary, Conventions/ Writing • **Reread Main Selection** • **Practice** Phonics/Spelling
DAY 4	• **Review Concept** • **Read ELL/ELD Readers** • **Practice** Phonics/Spelling, Conventions/Writing
DAY 5	• **Review** Concept, Vocabulary, Comprehension Skill, Phonics/Spelling, Conventions • **Reread ELL/ELD Readers** • **Writing**

*See the ELL Handbook for ELL Workshops with targeted instruction.

Concept Talk Video

Use the Concept Talk Video Routine (*ELL Handbook*, p. 477) to build background knowledge about helping others. After reading, have students tell what they learned about the concept of the rewards in helping others.

Support for English Language Learners

Language Objectives

- Understand and use basic vocabulary.
- Learn meanings of grade-level vocabulary.
- Internalize basic language by using it in speaking acivities.
- Understand the general meaning of spoken language.
- Use high-frequency words.

Language Opportunity: Listening

Use text on Student Edition p. 235 as a listening exercise. Read the text aloud as students listen for the general meaning. After they restate the general meaning, write the lesson vocabulary on the board. Have students restate the general meaning using at least one of the words.

ELL English Language Learners

Basic Vocabulary

- **High-Frequency Words** Use the vocabulary routines and the High-Frequency Word list on p. 449 of the *ELL Handbook* to systematically teach newcomers the first 300 sight words in English. Students who began learning ten words per week at the beginning of the year are now learning words 71–80.

Lesson Vocabulary

- **Preteach** Use the following routine to introduce the Lesson Vocabulary:

  1. Distribute copies of this week's Word Cards (*ELL Handbook,* p. 71).
  2. Display ELL Poster 8 and reread the Poster Talk-Through.
  3. Using the poster illustrations, model how a word's meaning can be expressed with other similar words: One of the *traditions,* or customs, is to hang pictures of family members.
  4. Use these sentences to reveal the meaning of the other words.

     - His *behavior* that night was not good. (manner of acting)
     - My *benefactor* gave me money to buy supplies for school. (a helper or supporter)
     - I was *astonished* to see the fireworks. (amazed)
     - The woman accepted the gift with *gratitude*. (thanks)
     - The *procession* wound through the street. (line of people or things moving along)
     - The *distribution* of gifts to all the children lasted an hour. (act of handing out or delivering something)
     - I *recommend* you see the movie. (suggest, advise)
     - A temple is a *sacred* place of worship. (holy)

Objectives
- Internalize new basic academic language by using it and reusing it in meaningful ways in speaking and writing activities that build concept attainment.
- Use accessible language and learn new and essential language in the process.

 ELL English Language Learners

■ **Reteach** Distribute a copy of the Word Cards to pairs of students. Each student takes a turn picking a card, and, without the guesser seeing the word, provides clues about the word (phrases, sentences, gestures) but does not say the word itself. The guesser identifies the word.

Time the play and have students take turns so that every student has an opportunity to present and identify words.

■ **Writing** Place students into mixed proficiency groups. Put the Word Cards facedown and have each group draw one or two cards. In a jigsaw activity, assign students to create a Word Grid (*ELL Handbook*, p. 493) of the words they picked. Circulate to provide assistance as needed. Afterward, have groups share their grids. Before students begin, model using a graphic organizer: Word: *astonished;* Meaning: *amazed;* Picture: Draw a stick figure with a shocked expression. Example: *I was astonished to see my friend at the amusement park.* Non-example: *I was not astonished to see my friend at school.*

Beginning Have students draw pictures for the grids. Then have them copy the word.

Intermediate Ask students to write an example of the word.

Advanced Assign students to write a sentence that gives a non-example.

Advanced High Have students supply the word's meaning. Encourage them to look up the words in the glossary of the Student Edition.

Language Objectives

• Produce drawings, phrases, and short sentences to show an understanding of the Lesson Vocabulary.

ELL Teacher Tip

As you introduce new vocabulary to your students, be sure to create daily opportunities for them to listen to and use the language they are learning in the classroom. For this week's vocabulary, you might have pairs of students role-play the characters in the story, using the vocabulary words.

Graphic Organizer

Word Grid astonished	
Meaning:	Example:
Drawing:	Non-example:

ELL Workshop

As students speak using new vocabulary, they may need assistance knowing how to adapt spoken English for formal purposes. *Use Formal English (ELL Handbook, pp. 392–393) provides extra support.*

Objectives

• Expand and internalize initial English vocabulary by learning and using high-frequency English words necessary for identifying and describing people, places, and objects, by retelling simple stories and basic information represented or supported by pictures, and by learning and using routine language needed for classroom communication.

• Write using a variety of grade-appropriate sentence lengths, patterns, and connecting words to combine phrases, clauses, and sentences in increasingly accurate ways as more English is acquired.

Support for English Language Learners

Content Objectives

- Monitor and adjust oral comprehension.

Language Objectives

- Seek clarification of spoken language.
- Discuss oral passages.
- Use a graphic organizer to take notes.

ELL Teacher Tip

Students might benefit from a third listening to help them fill in any missed details.

Language Opportunity: Speaking

Have students tell what they know about China or another country in a presentation to the class. Encourage them to speak using grade-level content area vocabulary, such as *traditions, language,* and *culture,* in context to help them internalize new English words.

Help Beginning students by giving them questions with content area vocabulary, such as "What is the *language* there?" and "What *traditions* do people follow?" Give Intermediate and Advanced students key words to include in their presentation. Advanced High students can develop their own presentation and can compare two different countries.

ELL English Language Learners

Listening Comprehension

Read Aloud

Joseph and the Mermaid

Joseph Rolande went fishing every day. One day on the beach, he saw a woman in a tide pool. The woman was crying. "Please help me!" she said. "The tide went out and left me here. Carry me back to the sea or I will die!"

Joseph saw that she had scales and a tail fin. She was a mermaid! Joseph thought that mermaids took men under the sea and drowned them. The mermaid begged Joseph to help her, so he carried her out to sea. The mermaid gave Joseph a comb from her hair as a gift. She said, "If you ever need my help, pass this comb through the water three times and I will come."

One night there was a terrible storm. Only one boat was fine. The sailors on the smashed boats were screaming for help. Joseph Rolande shouted, "Help me launch my boat!" Then he and the little boat disappeared into the waves.

The people on the shore then saw a woman in the water with Joseph. She was the mermaid. Joseph had called her with the comb. Joseph shouted, "Help me save these men!" She caught each sailor who was struggling in the water. She swam with each one to Joseph and his boat.

Prepare for the Read Aloud The modified Read Aloud above prepares students for listening to the oral reading "The Call of the Sea" on p. 231b.

First Listening: Listen to Understand Write the title of the Read Aloud on the board. Listen to find out what happens to the mermaid. How does Joseph help her? Afterward, ask the question again and have students share their answers. Have students ask questions to clarify their understanding of spoken language.

Second Listening: Listen to Check Understanding Using a Venn diagram work with students to compare and contrast the characters of Joseph and the mermaid. Now listen again to make sure you included all the ways that the characters are alike and different.

Objectives

- Demonstrate listening comprehension of increasingly complex spoken English by following directions, retelling or summarizing spoken messages, responding to questions and requests, collaborating with peers, and taking notes commensurate with content and grade-level needs.

Phonics and Spelling

■ **Vowel Sounds with _r_** Use Sound-Spelling Cards 55 and 91 to teach the sounds, pronunciations, and spellings of _r_-controlled vowels.

• Display card 55 to teach _ar._ This is an artist. _Artist_ has the sound /ar/. Say it with me: /ar/. Point out the spelling pattern: the _r_ comes after the vowel. Repeat using card 91 for the sound /or/ in _orchestra._

• Have students distinguish between vowel sounds and sounds of _r_-contolled vowels. The sound of a vowel changes when it is followed by an _r._ These kinds of vowels are called _r_-controlled vowels. Write the following words on the board: _barn, ban, harp, jar, thorn, chop, chore, more, core, cot._ Point to each word and say it aloud.

• Provide and opportunity to have students demonstrate recognition of elements of the English sound system. I will say some words. Raise your hand if you hear an _r_-controlled vowel: _cart, chew, chore, far, store, feet, stand, more._ Have students say words aloud with _r_-controlled vowels to practice to pronounce words in a comprehensible manner. Then have them spell the words using the spelling words.

Word Analysis: Suffixes _-tion, -ion_

■ **Preteach and Model** Write the following words on the board: _perfection, decision, reaction, action._ Focus on the language structure. Tell students that each of these words is made up of a base word and a suffix. Circle the suffix _-tion_ in the first word. Ask volunteers to find the suffixes in the other three words. If you add one of these suffixes to a verb, the word then describes an action or a state of being. _Perfection_ means "the state of being perfect." Model creating a new word by adding the suffix _-tion_ or _-ion_ to other words.

■ **Practice** Have students create three-column charts with these headings: _root word, -tion, -ion._ Give students the root words _connect, transmit,_ and _demonstrate._ Help them write the words with the correct ending in the appropriate column. Have students use the words in sentences.

Objectives
• Learn relationships between sounds and letters of the English language and decode (sound out) words using a combination of skills such as recognizing sound-letter relationships and identifying cognates, affixes, roots and base words.
• Spell familiar English words with increasing accuracy, and employ English spelling patterns and rules with increasing accuracy as more English is acquired.

Content Objectives
• Identify words with suffixes _-tion_ and _-ion._
• Use English spelling patterns.

Language Objectives
• Distinguish sounds of English.
• Recognize the sound element of _r_-controlled vowels.
• Produce sounds in English.
• Use contextual support to understand language structures.
• Discuss meaning of words with suffixes _-tion_ and _-ion._

Transfer Skills

_r_-**Controlled Vowels** The /r/ sound is flapped or rolled in languages such as Spanish, so speakers of this language may have difficulty pronouncing words with _r_-controlled vowels. However, students may still be able to comprehend words with _r_-controlled vowels.

Suffixes The suffix _-tion_ has similar forms in other languages, including French (_-tion_), Spanish (_-cion, -sion_), and Portuguese (_-cao_). Students can look for cognates for _-tion_ words in other languages.

ELL Teaching Routine

To practice, use the Sound-by-Sound Blending Routine (_ELL Handbook,_ p. 472).

Support for English Language Learners

Content Objectives

- Identify the difference between *compare* and *contrast.*

Language Objectives

- Use academic language on a writing activity.
- Compare and contrast a character in a reading.
- Write comparisons and contrasts about a character in a reading.

Language Opportunity:

Have students write using academic language. They can use the words *compare, contrast, same,* and *different* as they write to compare *The Ch'i-lin Purse* with another story they know.

ELL English Language Learners

Comprehension
Compare and Contrast

- **Preteach** When writers compare two things, they show how they are alike. When writers contrast two things, they show how they are different. Have students turn to Envision It! on p. El•6 in the Student Edition. Read aloud the text together. Have students compare and contrast the two bicycles.

- **Reteach** Choose two objects in the classroom. Draw a T-chart with one column labeled *Alike* and the other labeled *Different.* Have students compare and contrast the two items. Then guide students in completing the chart.

  Distribute copies of the Picture It! (*ELL Handbook,* p. 72). Read the directions aloud. Then read aloud the "New Year Celebration" descriptions as students read along.

  Beginning/Intermediate Guide students as they look for similarities and differences in the text and pictures. Then help them fill in the graphic organizer. (*Similarities:* fireworks and parades; *Differences:* dragons, ball dropping in Times Square, date new year begins; *Compared With What I Know:* Answers will vary.)

  Advanced/Advanced High Have students reread the paragraphs, comparing the text and pictures as they read. Have them fill in the graphic organizer and share something special they do to celebrate the New Year.

MINI-LESSON

Social Language

Display the words *similarities* and *differences* and explain how they relate to the words *compare* and *contrast.* When we look for similarities, we are looking for things that are the same so we can compare them. When we look for differences, we are looking for things that are different so we can contrast them. Display two classroom books. Have students name similarities and differences between the books.

Objectives

- Monitor oral and written language production and employ self-corrective techniques or other resources.
- Learn new language structures, expressions, and basic and academic vocabulary heard during classroom instruction and interactions.
- Understand the general meaning, main points, and important details of spoken language ranging from situations in which topics, language, and contexts are familiar to unfamiliar.

ELL *English Language Learners*

Reading Comprehension
The Ch'i-lin Purse

Student Edition pp. 236–237

■ **Frontloading** Read the title aloud and explain what the Ch'i-lin Purse is. In the story, the Ch'i-lin Purse is a special red purse that is embroidered with the design of an animal from an ancient Chinese legend. I wonder why this purse is important to the story. Let's look through the selection to find clues. Guide students on a picture walk through *The Ch'i-lin Purse.* Ask students to predict why the Ch'i-lin Purse is important and how it could be a reward. During the reading, provide teacher support by helping students adjust their predictions and by explaining the meanings of difficult words and phrases. Provide students with a story sequence chart to fill out as they read the selection. Supply these headings: *What happened first? Next? Last?*

Sheltered Reading Ask questions such as the following to guide students' comprehension:

• p. 238: Who wanted to give a Ch'i-lin Purse to Hsiang-ling? (her mother)

• pp. 240–241: Why did Hsiang-ling give her Ch'i-lin Purse away to another girl? (because she felt sorry that the girl had nothing for her new home)

• pp. 242–243: Where did Hsiang-ling find the Ch'i-lin Purse? (Pearl Hall)

• p. 243: What lesson did Hsiang-ling learn about doing good things for other people? (If you do something good for someone, happiness will come back to you.)

■ **Fluency: Read with Expression** Remind students that reading with expression means to read like you are speaking to a friend. Point out that the pitch, or rise and fall of your voice, changes when you read dialogue. Read the first paragraph on p. 243, modeling the way your voice goes up at the end of the question. Point out that the question mark gives a clue how to read expressively. Have pairs choose a paragraph that includes dialogue on p. 239. Have students read expressively as their partners listen. Afterward, have students offer feedback on their partners' expressive reading. For more practice, use the Fluency: Oral Rereading Routine (*ELL Handbook,* p. 474).

Content Objectives

• Monitor and adjust comprehension.

• Make and adjust predictions.

Language Objectives

• Derive meaining from media to build language attainment.

• Use teacher support to read content-area text.

• Summarize text using visual support.

Graphic Organizer

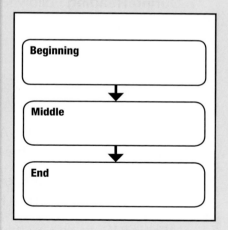

Audio Support

Students can prepare for reading *The Ch'i-lin Purse* by using the eSelection or the AudioText CD. After listening, have students retell the story to show language attainment. Have them reread aloud with the audio to attain language.

Objectives
• Use visual and contextual support and support from peers and teachers to read grade-appropriate content area text, enhance and confirm understanding, and develop vocabulary, grasp of language structures, and background knowledge needed to comprehend increasingly challenging language.

Support for English Language Learners

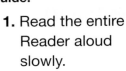

ELL Reader ELD Reader

For additional leveled instruction, see the **ELL/ELD Reader Teaching Guide.**

Comprehension
Kids Helping Kids

■ **Before Reading** Distribute copies of the ELL and ELD Readers, *Kids Helping Kids,* to students at their reading level.

• **Preview** Read the title aloud with students. This is a nonfiction text about kids who helped kids in New Orleans after a terrible storm destroyed their city. Have them predict how kids might have helped.

• **Set a Purpose for Reading** Let's read to figure out how some kids helped other kids.

■ **During Reading** Follow the Reading Routine for both reading groups.

1. Read the entire Reader aloud slowly.

2. Reread pp. 1–4, pausing to build background knowledge or model comprehension. Use the questions below to check comprehension.

3. Have students reread pp. 1–4 in pairs.

4. Repeat the steps for pp. 5–8 of the Reader.

■ **After Reading** Use the exercises on the inside back cover of each Reader and invite students to share their writing. In a whole-group discussion, ask students, How did kids around the country help the kids who were affected by Hurricane Katrina? Record their answers on the board and invite them to point to pictures in the book to support their answers.

ELD Reader Beginning/Intermediate

■ **p. 1:** What happened in August of 2005? (A strong hurricane hit parts of the United States.)

■ **p. 4:** What did the kids of "Kids Who Care" do to help the victims of Hurricane Katrina? (sold lemonade)

Writing What do you think was the most interesting thing kids did to help the hurricane victims? Find the sentence in the book that tells about it. Copy the sentence. Then read it aloud to your partner.

ELL Reader Advanced/Advanced High

■ **pp. 2–3:** Where did some of the victims of Hurricane Katrina go after the storm? (Many people moved to other states.)

■ **p. 4:** Why did some kids in different parts of the country set up lemonade stands? (to raise money for the victims of Hurricane Katrina)

Study Guide Distribute copies of the ELL Reader Study Guide (*ELL Handbook,* p. 76). Scaffold comprehension of compare and contrast by helping students look back through the Reader in order to fill in the graphic organizer. Review their responses together. (**Answers** See *ELL Handbook,* pp. 209–212.)

Objectives
• Express opinions, ideas, and feelings ranging from communicating iangle words and short phrases to participating in extended discussions on a variety of social and grade-appropriate academic topics.
• Demonstrate comprehension of increasingly complex English by participating in shared reading, retelling or summarizing material, responding to questions, and taking notes commensurate with content area and grade level needs.

 eReaders

Conventions
Action and Linking Verbs

■ **Preteach** An action verb describes an action, such as *run, jump, hit, kick,* and *skip. The player kicked the ball.* A linking verb connects the subject to another word that names or describes the subject. These are linking verbs: *am, is, are, was, were, have, has, had, been, become, seems. You were kicking.*

■ **Practice** Write several subjects on the board. Help students make sentences with each. Have them use the pattern in English, *noun/verb*, for both action and linking verbs. Display their sentences, circle the appropriate verb, and mark it as an action or linking verb. Have students point out the pattern.

 Beginning/Intermediate Help students identify the action or linking verb in each of the following sentences:

The rain is warm.
Tram ran to the park.
John is raising his hand.

Advanced/Advanced High Display an image that shows action. Write three action verbs and three linking verbs that relate to the image. Have students work in pairs to make up sentences that contain the verbs.

■ **Reteach** Show students pictures of people performing various actions. Allow students to choose one of the pictures they would like to talk about. Display sentences about that picture. For example:

The girl wears a read sweater. She is happy.

Identify the action verb and tlinking verb in each sentence.

■ **Practice** Have students generate sentences about one of the pictures. Sentences should contain either action verbs or linking verbs. Have pairs edit sentences for correct verb tense.

 Beginning/Intermediate Have students work in pairs to create their sentences. Have them write one sentence using an action verb and one using a linking verb.

Advanced/Advanced High Have students work independently to write four sentences—two with an action verb and two with a linking verb. Have them circle the action verb in each sentence.

Objectives
• Speak using a variety of grammatical structures, sentence lengths, sentence types, and connecting words with increasing accuracy and ease as more English is acquired.
• Spell familiar English words with increasing accuracy, and employ English spelling patterns and rules with increasing accuracy as more English is acquired.

Content Objectives
• Decode and use action and linking verbs.
• Correctly write sentences with action and linking verbs.

Language Objectives
• Recognize patterns in English.
• Understand English structures in classroom materials.
• Write sentences with action and linking verbs.
• Edit writing for verb tenses.

 Transfer Skills

Linking Verbs The linking verbs *have* and *had* may be familiar to Spanish-speaking students. The Spanish verb *haber* is similarly.

Grammar Jammer

For more practice with verbs, use the Grammar Jammer for this target skill. See the Grammar Jammer Routine (*ELL Handbook,* p. 478).

Mini-Lesson: Verb in Writing

Reinforce the language structure of action and linking verbs. Usually, the verbs come after the nouns that do the action. Have students read pp. 254–255 of the Student Edition. As they read, they should find both action and linking verbs. Have them identify where the verbs are written in the sentences.

Content Objectives

- Identify poetic techniques in a text.

Language Objectives

- Speak using a variety of sentence lengths.
- Describe with detail and specificity.
- Use poetic techniques to write sentences.
- Share feedback for editing and revising.

Language Opportunity: Describing

Tell students that poems are often written to describe, so they include descriptive language with specific details. Have them turn to p. 252 in the Student Edition as you read the prompt. Point out the third item in the checklist: poems include vivid language. Ask students to orally describe an event in their lives, using details and specificity as they express thoughts and feelings with vivid language.

ELL *English Language Learners*

Poetic Techniques

■ **Introduce** Display the model and read it aloud. Remind students that writers use poetic techniques to produce a certain effect. *Listen to this sentence: The wild wind whistled and wailed. What did you notice about most of the words in that sentence? (They start with w.)* Underline the *w*'s in the sentence and explain that alliteration is a poetic device that repeats the same beginning sounds. Read the second sentence in the model and point out that the word *chug* really sounds like what a train does. *This poetic technique is called onomatopoeia. Words such as buzz, snap,* and *hiss are words that sound like real sounds.*

Writing Model
The wild wind whistled and wailed.
The train chugged along the track.

■ **Practice** Write these incomplete sentences on the board. Work together to finish the sentences using the poetic techniques of alliteration and onomatopoeia.

The _____ river rushed over the _____. (Possible answers: roaring, rocks)

The snake _____ at the frog. (Possible answer: hissed)

■ **Write** Have students write sentences about their favorite animal using the poetic techniques of alliteration and onomatopoeia. Point out that poems have phrases and sentences of varying lengths to make them sound good when read aloud. Have students say sentences of varying lengths aloud to see how they sound before adding them to their poems.

Leveled Support

Beginning Have students write the name of the animal at the top of their paper. Then have them draw details about the animal. Tell students to circle the first letter of the animal's name to help them come up with a sentence that uses alliteration. Also discuss the sound the animal makes. Then have students dictate to you a sentence or two that uses onomatopoeia. Write out their sentences and have students copy them.

Intermediate Have students work together in pairs, using poetic techniques to write one or two sentences about an animal. They may write alliterative sentences that use the first letter of the animal's name or sentences that use the sound that the animal makes.

Advanced/Advanced High Have students write their sentences independently. Then have pairs exchange papers and provide feedback for revising and editing.

Objectives

- Write using a variety of grade-appropriate sentence lengths, patterns, and connecting words to combine phrases, clauses, and sentences in increasingly accurate ways as more English is acquired.
- Narrate, describe, and explain with increasing specificity and detail to fulfill content area writing needs as more English is acquired.

Customize Your Writing

Weekly Writing Focus
Writing Forms and Patterns

- Instruction focuses on a different **product** each week.
- Mini-lessons and models help students learn key features and **organizational patterns**.

Grade 5 Products tall tale, personal narrative, historical fiction, persuasive essay, poetry, expository composition, and so on

Grade 5 Organization Patterns letter, sequence, poetic forms, main idea and details, narrative, and so on

Daily Writing Focus
Quick Writes for Fluency

- **Writing on Demand** Use the Quick Write routine for **writing on demand**.
- The Quick Write **prompt and routine** extend skills and strategies from daily writing lessons.

Unit Writing Focus
Writing Process ①②③④⑤

- Six **writing process** lessons provide structure to move students through the steps of the writing process.
- One-week and two-week pacing allows lessons to be used in **Writing Workshop**.

Steps of the Writing Process Plan and Prewrite, Draft, Revise, Edit, Publish and Present

Grade 5 Writing Process Products personal narrative, comic book, compare and contrast essay, cause-and-effect essay, persuasive essay, research report

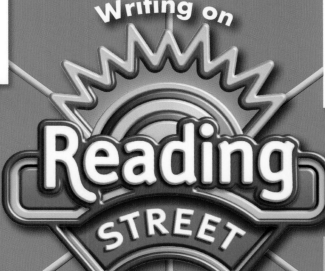

Writing on Reading STREET

MINI-LESSON

- Daily 10-minute mini-lessons focus instruction on the **traits** and **craft** of good writing.
- Instruction focuses on one writing trait and one writer's craft skill every week.

Traits focus/ideas, organization, voice, word choice, sentences, conventions

Craft drafting strategies, revising strategies, editing strategies

Read Like a Writer

- Use **mentor text** every week as a model to exemplify the traits of good writing.
- **Interact with text** every week to learn the key features of good writing.

Mentor Text Examine literature in the Student Edition.

 INTERACT with TEXT Underline, circle, and highlight model text in the *Reader's and Writer's Notebook*.

Write Guy
Jeff Anderson

Need Writing Advice?

Writing instruction is all about creating effective writers. We don't want to crush the inner writer in a child by over-correcting and over-editing. What makes effective writing instruction? Children need to write, write, write! But is that enough? Probably not. All kinds of instruction and guidance go into making an effective writer.

The Write Guy offers advice on teacher and peer conferencing, focusing on writing traits, revising strategies, editing strategies, and much, much more.

Customize Your Writing

Sometimes you want to spend more time on writing—perhaps you do a **Writing Workshop**.
This one- or two-week plan for the unit level writing projects can help.

1 Week Plan	Day 1	Day 2	Day 3	Day 4	Day 5
① Plan and Prewrite	■	■			
② Draft			■		
③ Revise				■	
④ Edit					■
⑤ Publish					■

2 Week Plan	Day 1	Day 2	Day 3	Day 4	Day 5	Day 6	Day 7	Day 8	Day 9	Day 10
① Plan and Prewrite	■	■	■	■						
② Draft					■	■	■			
③ Revise								■		
④ Edit									■	
⑤ Publish										■

Grade 5 Unit Writing Projects

Internet Guy
Don Leu

Unit Writing Project 1–21st Century Project

Unit 1 Podcasting

Unit 2 E-Newsletter

Unit 3 Story Exchange

Unit 4 E-Pen Pals

Unit 5 Community Interviews

Unit 6 Photo Description

Unit Writing Project 2–Writing Process

Unit 1 Personal Narrative

Unit 2 Comic Book/Graphic Novel

Unit 3 Compare and Contrast Essay

Unit 4 Cause-and-Effect Essay

Unit 5 Persuasive Essay

Unit 6 Research Report

E-Newsletter

Introduce genre and key features

Writing Project Create an e-newsletter with editorial articles about what it means to do the right thing.

Purpose Enhance skills in Internet research as well as using applications for word processing and design.

Audience Student, peers, teacher, family

In this workshop, we will create an e-newsletter with stories about what it means to do the right thing. We will use the Internet to find news articles about people who did the right or the wrong thing and write our opinions about them. Then we will design a newsletter that we can share with our friends and family.

Key Features of an E-Newsletter

- includes factual articles and editorial opinions relating to the same topic or theme
- provides interesting details and comments for readers to consider
- may include illustrations and photographs to make articles clearer
- is designed to appeal to a specific audience
- is written, designed, or published electronically

Academic Vocabulary

Newsletter A newsletter is a small newspaper written for a specific audience.

News article A news article gives facts about an event of importance to the world.

Editorial An editorial expresses the writer's opinion about something in the news.

Differentiated Instruction

 Strategic Intervention

Introduce the e-newsletter Show students examples of child-friendly newsletters. Point out the themes or main ideas of several articles and have students identify important facts in each. Show how illustrations and photos make articles more interesting.

Teacher Tip

Explore Examples Locate several "child-friendly" newsletters online to show as models in class. Using a projector, display appropriate results. Point out design elements and key features to students.

 Plan and Prewrite

MINI-LESSON

Read Like a Writer

■ **Examine Model Text** Display or read aloud a news article and one or more editorial letters or columns that comment on its subject. A news story gives facts about something that has happened. Editorial writing expresses thoughts and opinions about the event. Discuss the main facts of the story and the opinions of the editorial writing you shared. You are going to write a newsletter with articles and editorial columns. Your newsletter will include factual summaries of news stories you have read and columns expressing your opinion about them.

■ **Explore Model Text** Let's look at an example of a summary and editorial that you might find in a newsletter. This is the kind of column that you will write. Display and read aloud to students the article summary and editorial on 21st Century Transparency TC4. Ask them to identify important facts in the article summary and the main points in the writer's editorial about the article. Be sure students understand that the summary is to include only important facts, and the editorial is to express opinions.

21st Century Transparency TC4, TR DVD

Using a Search Engine

Think Aloud A search engine is a useful tool that allows us to search for information on the World Wide Web. We can find news articles by entering keywords into the search field. The search engine will find Web sites that use those keywords. We want to find stories by and for kids.

■ Display the home page of a search engine on a projector. Enter *"news stories for kids"* into the search field and read through the first five results. Discuss with students which descriptions suggest the most useful sites for finding appropriate child-oriented news articles. Have students write down the key phrase and one or two other keywords for their search.

Differentiated Instruction

 Strategic Intervention

Analyzing Text for a Specific Theme If students struggle to choose an article to summarize and write about, have them explain in their own words what it means to "do the right thing." As they review online news stories they have selected, have them answer these questions about each:
What was done?
What made this the right [or wrong] thing to do?

Teacher Tip

Student Safety Online Refer to your district's guidelines for Internet use before having students begin their online searches. If you are able to extend searches beyond children's news sites, limit children to the web sites and archives of local newspapers.

ELL

English Language Learners
Build Vocabulary If students do not know some words in the model on TC4, such as *equipment* or *caring*, define the words and use them in sentences. Explain the meanings of idiomatic uses such as *came up with* and *make a difference*.

Objectives
• Evaluate online sources.
• Learn to bookmark Web sites.
• Review the *5Ws* and *How*.

1 **Plan and Prewrite**
PREWRITE

MINI-LESSON

Evaluating Sources

Display a Web site that offers news for kids. I see that this Web site is a good place to find articles. Now I want to evaluate whether it has reliable information. Help students discern reliability of sites by asking the following questions:

• Is this site from a respected institution such as a museum or educational organization?
• Is the domain name *.edu*, *.org*, or *.gov*?
• Is the information on the site up-to-date? When was the site last updated?
• Does the information seem fair and factual?

Accessing links

Model for students the way to access the various features on the news site. Click on one or two links to appropriate articles, display the articles on a projector, and show students how to scan an article for important facts.

Point out the link, if present, for displaying a print-ready copy of the article. Have students access their chosen Web site and locate a news article they want to use. Remind students that they should choose an article that illustrates doing (or not doing) the right thing. Instruct them to print out a copy of the story.

Bookmarking sites

Encourage students to keep a record of the keywords and phrases that they used to access their news source site. Have them use their Internet browser's "bookmarks" or "favorites" function to save the site. If they copy and paste relevant information into a document that they can refer to later, remind them to save the URL (Web address) as well. Encourage students to share the best sites with their small group members.

Organize ideas	Have students write the questions *Who? What? Where? Why? When?* and *How?* on the left margin of a sheet of paper, leaving several lines of space after each question. These are often called the *5 Ws* and *How.* Ask them to read their articles and write its main facts beside the relevant questions.
Getting started	Have students look at their *5 Ws* and *How* sheet and write a topic sentence for their summary. Then they can write sentences that provide a brief account of the original story.
Examine model text	Display 21st Century Transparency TC4 and review the summary box of "We Can Make a Difference in the World."

Think Aloud This student started with a sentence that tells the main action of the article. The sentences that follow explain how this action came about and details about what resulted because of it. The summary includes the most important details from the article.

21st Century Transparency
TC4, TR DVD

Objectives
- Organize research and ideas.
- Write a first draft of an editorial.
- Revise a draft of an editorial.

2 Draft

Organize ideas
Display 21st Century Transparency TC5, "Editorial Response to Article" and model how to complete it. Explain your thinking as you list reasons for your opinion. Place a file containing a copy of the transparency on students' desktops. They can open the file and use a word processing application to enter their responses. Alternatively, you can distribute copies of the transparency for students to hand-write their notes.

21st Century Transparency TC5, TR DVD

Getting started
Have students look at their completed forms and write an introduction to their editorial. Then they can refer to their reasons and call to action to write additional paragraphs for their editorial. Have students conclude their editorial by asking readers to take action or explaining the importance of an action.

Examine model text
Display 21st Century Transparency TC4 and review the editorial titled "We Can Make a Difference in the World."

 Think Aloud This student's editorial began with an interesting paragraph that told what was important in the article and how she felt about it. The paragraph that follows gives reasons why the microbank project was the right thing to do. The final paragraph asks students to take up a similar project.

21st Century Transparency TC4, TR DVD

Develop draft
Display or read the checklist below for students. Remind students that their draft should capture their ideas; it will not be error-free. Suggest that students write an attention-grabbing title for their editorial at this time.

Use Your Own Words

✔ Information such as articles on a Web site is copyrighted by the author! Be sure to use your words, not theirs, in your writing. Using someone else's words without proper citation is called plagiarism.

✔ You can paraphrase or summarize the information you find on the Web sites that you use.

Revise

Revising for Clarity

- One way to revise editorial writing is to be sure it has a clear statement of the writer's opinion about the subject. Read these examples with students:

  Position unclear   It is usually good to help people in need. Many people have needs, especially poor people. If they could get help, it would change their lives. Our school does lots of projects. I wonder if we could try something like this?

  Position clear   When we can help those in need to a better life, we should. I think our school should take on a project like this to make a difference in the world.

  Discuss with students how the clear position statements use definite phrases such as *we should* and *I think our school should* and state specific actions to be taken.

Peer conferencing Have students print out a copy of their revised summary and editorial drafts. Organize small groups and have members of each group exchange their drafts for peer revision. Ask them to write revision suggestions for both the summary and the editorial. Have students consider these suggestions as they revise their writing.

Revise drafts Earlier we wrote drafts of our article summaries and editorials. Now we will revise our drafts. When we revise, we incorporate comments from peer conferencing and try to make our writing clearer and more interesting. Summaries contain only important facts, and editorials state an opinion clearly and give logical reasons.

Corrective feedback **If...** students have difficulty writing clear position statements,

then... share several letters to the editor from a local newspaper, help students pinpoint the position statement in each, and discuss its wording.

Differentiated Instruction

A **Advanced**
Apply Revising Skills As they revise their work, have students look for ways to improve their editorials by elaborating by including evidence and examples.

SI **Strategic Intervention**
Opinion versus Fact Define statements of fact and statements of opinion. Have students distinguish facts as statements one can prove:
Statement of fact: *Jorge is eleven years old.*
Statement of Opinion: *Jorge is the smartest student.*

Have students write their own statements of fact and opinion and test each other. Have them use sentence frames to respond:
I know it is true because ___.
It is an opinion because ___.

Teacher Tip

Plagiarism and the Internet Remind students that they may not copy text directly from a book or the Internet. They should paraphrase or restate text they find on a Web page when writing their articles.

Objectives

- Edit a revised draft using computer tools and proofreading to correct errors in grammar, mechanics, and spelling.
- Use the Internet to search for images and illustrations to enhance newsletter text.

4 Edit

MINI-LESSON

Using the Computer to Edit

■ The grammar and spelling checker is a useful tool to identify errors in your writing, but it can make mistakes, and it can miss errors. Carefully read each suggestion that the checker makes before you accept it to be sure that the correction is appropriate.

■ The spelling checker will catch many spelling errors, but if you use a real but incorrect word, it does not see the error. Type the following sentence in a word processing program and display it on a projector:

There community thinks helping others is a good idea, to.

Use the spelling checker to check the sentence. The spelling checker did not catch the incorrect words because they are actual words even though they are used incorrectly. What words do we need? How should they be spelled? Change "There" to "Their" and "to" to "too."

■ Have students practice editing the following sentences, first by using the grammar and spelling checker and then by themselves.

The students raise money and lone it to pore women.

They have shone that kids can change things for the better.

I think that hour school should tack on a project like this.

Edit drafts Ask students to edit their own drafts. After they use the grammar and spelling checker, have them print out their article and read it sentence by sentence. Ask them to check their drafts for spelling, grammar, punctuation, and capitalization.

Corrective feedback If... students have difficulty finding errors in their revised drafts, then... have them read the draft from end to beginning, sentence by sentence, and have them read for only one type of error at a time.

Publish and Present

 MINI-LESSON

Finding Images on the Internet

■ Display the home page of an Internet search engine on a projector. We can add photos and illustrations to our newsletter to make it more interesting for readers. We can look for pictures on the Internet. This search engine will help us find pictures that illustrate our theme of doing the right thing.

■ I want to find a picture of women in poor countries who have benefited from microbank loans. If available, choose the option for searching images in the search engine. Type the key phrases *microbank loans + women's businesses* into the search field. Display the results on the projector. Click on an option or image that is appropriate and display the site or image.

■ Have students search for appropriate images for their articles. Show students how to copy and save images onto their computer desktop using a file name they can easily identify. Have them store the images in a separate folder so they will be easily accessible when it is time to publish the e-newsletter.

Objectives
- Use a design program to lay out articles in newsletter format.
- Present an e-newsletter with news summaries and editorial columns.

 ## 5 Publish and Present

Options for presenting

You may choose to have students use one or both of the following methods for presenting their newsletter:

Print out a hard copy of the newsletter to take home to families and to display in the classroom.	Convert the newsletter file to a Portable Document Format (PDF). The PDF can be downloaded to a school Web site and made available to other classes in your school. For a larger audience, it can be uploaded to an educational file-sharing site.

Lay out the newsletter

Now that we have written and revised our article summaries and editorials about someone who did the right thing, it is time to put them together to create our e-newsletter. We will use a design program to format our text and the pictures we found into a presentation that is fun and easy to read. Help students decide on a logical order and arrangement of pieces on each page of the newsletter. Assist students in resizing images and flowing text into columns that may need to continue onto another page.

Give each student an opportunity to use a design application to lay out text and images. Assist students in resizing photographs and illustrations and in flowing text into multiple columns, as needed. Point out that some articles may need to continue on a second page if their text will not fit on one page. Help students combine their pages into one complete document. Print a final copy on a color printer to display in the classroom.

Customize Literacy in Your Classroom

Table of Contents
for Customize Literacy

Customize Literacy is organized into different sections, each one designed to help you organize and carry out an effective literacy program. Each section contains strategies and support for teaching comprehension skills and strategies. *Customize Literacy* also shows how to use weekly text sets of readers in your literacy program.

Weekly Text Sets
to Customize Literacy

The following readers can be used to enhance your literacy instruction.

	Concept Literacy Reader	Below-Level Reader	On-Level Reader	Advanced Reader	ELD Reader	ELL Reader
Unit 2 WEEK 1	*Beach Safety*	*The Oceans' Treasures*	*Sea Life*	*Our Essential Oceans*	*Hidden Treasures*	*Hidden Treasures*
Unit 2 WEEK 2	*William Carney: An American Hero*	*From Slave to Soldier*	*A Spy in Disguise*	*The Most Dangerous Woman in America*	*Making a Difference in Denmark*	*Making a Difference in Denmark*
Unit 2 WEEK 3	*César Chávez: Friend of Farm Workers*	*China: Today and Yesterday*	*Abuela's Gift*	*Moving to Mali*	*Kids Helping Kids*	*Kids Helping Kids*

Customize Literacy in Your Classroom

Instruction in comprehension skills and strategies provides readers with avenues to understanding a text. Through teacher modeling and guided, collaborative, and independent practice, students become independent thinkers who employ a variety of skills and strategies to help them make meaning as they read.

Mini-Lessons for Comprehension Skills and Strategies

Envision It! A Comprehension Handbook

Unit 1	Literary Elements, Cause and Effect, Fact and Opinion, Summarize, Inferring, Text Structure
Unit 2	Compare and Contrast, Sequence, Author's Purpose, Visualize, Story Structure, Monitor and Clarify, Background Knowledge
Unit 3	Sequence, Main Idea and Supporting Details, Fact and Opinion, Graphic Sources, Predict and Set Purpose, Important Ideas
Unit 4	Draw Conclusions, Generalize, Graphic Sources, Questioning, Monitor and Clarify
Unit 5	Literary Elements, Graphic Sources, Author's Purpose, Cause and Effect, Generalize, Inferring, Summarize
Unit 6	Draw Conclusions, Main Idea and Supporting Details, Compare and Contrast, Fact and Opinion, Sequence, Text Structure, Questioning

Envision It! Visual Skills Handbook

Author's Purpose
Categorize and Classify
Cause and Effect
Compare and Contrast
Draw Conclusions
Fact and Opinion
Generalize
Graphic Sources
Literary Elements
Main Idea and Details
Sequence

Envision It! Visual Strategies Handbook

Background Knowledge
Important Ideas
Inferring
Monitor and Clarify
Predict and Set Purpose
Questioning
Story Structure
Summarize
Text Structure
Visualize

Anchor Chart Anchor charts are provided with each strategy lesson. These charts incorporate the language of strategic thinkers. They help students make their thinking visible and permanent and provide students with a means to clarify their thinking about how and when to use each strategy. As students gain more experience with a strategy, the chart may undergo revision.

See pages 101–126 in the *First Stop on Reading Street* Teacher's Edition for additional support as you customize literacy in your classroom.

Good Readers DRA2 users will find additional resources in the *First Stop on Reading Street* Teacher's Edition on pages 104–105.

Contents

Pacing Guide

This chart shows the instructional sequence from *Scott Foresman Reading Street* for Grade 5. You can use this pacing guide as is to ensure you are following a comprehensive scope and sequence. Or, you can adjust the sequence to match your calendar, curriculum map, or testing schedule.

Grade 5

REVIEW WEEK

READING	UNIT 1 Week 1	Week 2	Week 3	Week 4	Week 5	UNIT 2 Week 1	Week 2
Comprehension Skill	Character and Plot	Cause and Effect	Theme and Setting	Fact and Opinion	Cause and Effect	Compare and Contrast	Sequence
Comprehension Strategy	Monitor and Clarify	Summarize	Inferring	Questioning	Text Structure	Visualize	Inferring
Vocabulary Strategy/Skill	Context Clues/Homographs	Context Clues/Homonyms	Dictionary/Glossary/Unknown Words	Context Clues/Antonyms	Context Clues/Multiple-Meaning Words	Context Clues/Unfamiliar Words	Dictionary/Glossary/Unknown Words
Fluency	Expression	Rate	Expression	Phrasing/Punctuation	Accuracy	Expression	Accuracy
Spelling/Word Work	Short Vowel VCCV, VCV	Long Vowel VCV	Long Vowel Digraphs	Adding -ed, -ing	Contractions	Digraphs th, sh, ch, ph	Irregular Plurals

REVIEW WEEK

	UNIT 4 Week 1	Week 2	Week 3	Week 4	Week 5	UNIT 5 Week 1	Week 2
Comprehension Skill	Draw Conclusions	Generalize	Graphic Sources	Generalize	Draw Conclusions	Character and Plot	Graphic Sources
Comprehension Strategy	Questioning	Predict and Set Purpose	Important Ideas	Story Structure	Visualize	Background Knowledge	Inferring
Vocabulary Skill/Strategy	Word Structure/Endings	Context Clues/Unfamiliar Words	Context Clues/Synonyms	Context Clues/Unfamiliar Words	Word Structure/Suffixes	Word Structure/Greek and Latin Roots	Dictionary/Glossary/Unknown Words
Fluency	Phrasing	Accuracy	Rate	Expression	Phrasing	Expression	Expression
Spelling/Word Work	Words from Many Cultures	Prefixes sub-, over-, out-, under-, super-	Homophones	Suffixes -ible, -able	Negative Prefixes	Multisyllabic Words	Related Words

Customize Literacy

 Are you the adventurous type? Want to use some of your own ideas and materials in your teaching? But you worry you might be leaving out some critical instruction kids need? **Customize Literacy** can help. **"**

REVIEW WEEK

UNIT 3

Week 3	Week 4	Week 5	Week 1	Week 2	Week 3	Week 4	Week 5
Compare and Contrast	Author's Purpose	Author's Purpose	Sequence	Main Idea/Details	Fact and Opinion	Main Idea/Details	Graphic Sources
Story Structure	Monitor and Clarify	Background Knowledge	Summarize	Visualize	Predict and Set Purpose	Text Structure	Important Ideas
Word Structure/Greek and Latin Roots	Context Clues/Unfamiliar Words	Word Structure/Endings -s, -ed, -ing	Context Clues/Multiple-Meaning Words	Word Structure/Greek and Latin Roots	Context Clues/Homonyms	Context Clues/Antonyms	Word Structure/Prefixes
Expression	Phrasing	Rate	Expression	Rate	Phrasing	Rate	Accuracy
Vowel Sounds with r	Final Syllables -en, -an, -el, -le, -il	Final Syllables -er, -ar, -or	Words with schwa	Compound Words	Consonant Sounds /j/, /ks/, /sk/, /s/	One Consonant or Two	Prefixes un-, de-, dis-

REVIEW WEEK

UNIT 6

Week 3	Week 4	Week 5	Week 1	Week 2	Week 3	Week 4	Week 5
Author's Purpose	Cause and Effect	Generalize	Draw Conclusions	Main Idea/Details	Compare and Contrast	Fact and Opinion	Sequence
Monitor and Clarify	Summarize	Questioning	Important Ideas	Text Structure	Story Structure	Predict and Set Purpose	Background Knowledge
Context Clues/Multiple-Meaning Words	Context Clues/Unfamiliar Words	Word Structure/Prefixes	Dictionary/Glossary/Unknown Words	Word Structure/Endings	Word Structure/Suffixes	Word Structure/Unfamiliar Words	Context Clues/Homographs
Accuracy	Phrasing	Rate	Accuracy	Phrasing/Punctuation Clues	Rate	Phrasing	Expression
Greek Word Parts	Latin Roots	Greek Word Parts	Suffixes -ous, -sion, -ion, -ation	Final Syllable -ant, -ent, -ance, -ence	Latin Roots	Related Words	Easily Confused Words

Pacing Guide

Grade 5

LANGUAGE ARTS

UNIT 1

	Week 1	Week 2	Week 3	Week 4	Week 5
Speaking and Listening	Interview	Storytelling	How-to Demonstration	Sportscast	Job Ad
Grammar	Four Kinds of Sentences	Subjects and Predicates	Independent and Dependent Clauses	Compound and Complex Sentences	Common, Proper, and Collective Nouns
Weekly Writing	Directions	Tall Tale	Invitation	Newsletter Article	Expository Composition
Trait of the Week	Organization	Voice	Focus/Ideas	Word Choice	Organization/ Paragraphs
Writing	Podcast/Personal Narrative				

REVIEW WEEK

UNIT 2

	Week 1	Week 2
Speaking and Listening	Talk Show	Informational Speech
Grammar	Regular and Irregular Plural Nouns	Possessive Nouns
Weekly Writing	Description	Informal Letter
Trait of the Week	Sentences	Voice

REVIEW WEEK

UNIT 4

	Week 1	Week 2	Week 3	Week 4	Week 5
Speaking and Listening	How-to Demonstration	Persuasive Speech	Description	Give Advice	Interview
Grammar	Subject and Object Pronouns	Pronouns and Antecedents	Possessive Pronouns	Indefinite and Reflexive Pronouns	Using *Who* and *Whom*
Weekly Writing	Picture Book	Friendly Letter	Formal Letter	Narrative Poetry	Autobiographical Sketch
Trait of the Week	Focus/Ideas	Sentences	Conventions	Word Choice	Voice
Writing	E-Pen Pals/Cause-and-Effect Essay				

UNIT 5

	Week 1	Week 2
Speaking and Listening	Dramatization	Newscast
Grammar	Contractions and Negatives	Adjectives and Articles
Weekly Writing	Rhyming Poem	Notes
Trait of the Week	Word Choice	Focus/Ideas

Customize Literacy

REVIEW WEEK

UNIT 3

Week 3	Week 4	Week 5
Readers' Theater	Panel Discussion	Documentary
Action and Linking Verbs	Main and Helping Verbs	Subject-Verb Agreement
Poem	Personal Narrative	Historical Fiction
Organization/ Poetic Structure	Word Choice	Word Choice

E-Newsletter/Comic Book Graphic Novel

Week 1	Week 2	Week 3	Week 4	Week 5
Play Review	Newscast	Introducing a Special Person	Give Directions	Advertisement
Past, Present, and Future Tenses	Principal Parts of Regular Verbs	Principal Parts of Irregular Verbs	Troublesome Verbs	Prepositions and Prepositional Phrases
Play	Persuasive Speech	Ad Brochure	Description	Expository Text
Word Choice	Focus/Ideas	Word Choice	Word Choice	Organization

Story Exchange/Compare and Contrast Essay

REVIEW WEEK

UNIT 6

Week 3	Week 4	Week 5
Storytelling	Discussion	Debate
This, That, These, and Those	Comparative and Superlative Adjectives	Adverbs
Biographical Sketch	Letter to the Editor	Summary
Sentences	Voice	Focus/Ideas

Interview/Persuasive Essay

Week 1	Week 2	Week 3	Week 4	Week 5
Debate	Interview	Storytelling	Newscast	Readers' Theater
Modifiers	Conjunctions	Commas	Quotations and Quotation Marks	Punctuation
Journal Entry	Mystery	Parody	Review	Personal Narrative
Voice	Focus/Ideas	Voice	Organization/ Paragraphs	Voice

Photo Description/Research Report

Teaching Record Chart

This chart shows the critical comprehension skills and strategies you need to cover. Check off each one as you provide instruction.

Reading/Comprehension	DATES OF INSTRUCTION		
Compare and contrast the themes or moral lessons of several works of fiction from various cultures.			
Describe the phenomena explained in origin myths from various cultures.			
Explain the effect of a historical event or movement on the theme of a work of literature.			
Analyze how poets use sound effects (e.g., alliteration, internal rhyme, onomatopoeia, rhyme scheme) to reinforce meaning in poems.			
Analyze the similarities and differences between an original text and its dramatic adaptation.			
Describe incidents that advance the story or novel, explaining how each incident gives rise to or foreshadows future events.			
Explain the roles and functions of characters in various plots, including their relationships and conflicts.			
Explain the different forms of third-person points of view in stories.			
Identify the literary language and devices used in biographies and autobiographies, including how authors present major events in a person's life.			
Evaluate the impact of sensory details, imagery, and figurative language in literary text.			
Read independently for a sustained period of time and summarize or paraphrase what the reading was about, maintaining meaning and logical order (e.g., generate a reading log or journal; participate in book talks).			
Draw conclusions from the information presented by an author and evaluate how well the author's purpose was achieved.			
Summarize the main ideas and supporting details in a text in ways that maintain meaning and logical order.			

Tired of using slips of paper or stickies to make sure you teach everything you need to? Need an easier way to keep track of what you have taught, and what you still need to cover? **Customize Literacy** *can help.*

Reading/Comprehension	DATES OF INSTRUCTION		
Determine the facts in a text and verify them through established methods.			
Analyze how the organizational pattern of a text (e.g., cause-and-effect, compare-and-contrast, sequential order, logical order, classification schemes) influences the relationships among the ideas.			
Use multiple text features and graphics to gain an overview of the contents of text and to locate information.			
Synthesize and make logical connections between ideas within a text and across two or three texts representing similar or different genres.			
Identify the author's viewpoint or position and explain the basic relationships among ideas (e.g., parallelism, comparison, causality) in the argument.			
Recognize exaggerated, contradictory, or misleading statements in text.			
Interpret details from procedural text to complete a task, solve a problem, or perform procedures.			
Interpret factual or quantitative information presented in maps, charts, illustrations, graphs, time lines, tables, and diagrams.			
Establish purposes for reading a text based on what students hope to accomplish by reading the text.			
Ask literal, interpretive, and evaluative questions of a text.			
Monitor and adjust comprehension using a variety of strategies.			
Make inferences about a text and use evidence from the text to support understanding.			
Summarize and paraphrase text in ways that maintain meaning and logical order within a text and across texts.			
Make connections between and across multiple texts.			

Student Edition p. EI•6

Compare and Contrast

Objectives:
- Students define *compare* and *contrast*.
- Students identify some clue words that can help them see comparisons.
- Students can identify comparisons even when clue words are not used.
- Students make comparisons between text and prior knowledge and ideas.

What is it? **Comparing** and **contrasting** means finding likenesses and/or differences between two or more people, places, things, or ideas. At Grade 5, students are using clue words such as *like, but, unlike,* and *as* to help identify likenesses and differences in text, but they are also seeing likenesses and differences in text without clue words. They understand that looking for comparisons can help them remember what they read. They begin to compare text with their own prior knowledge and ideas.

How Good Readers Use the Skill Comparing and contrasting are basic reasoning devices. We try to understand an unknown using the known—i.e., a likeness or difference. At first, students notice likenesses and differences. Older students begin to use clue words as signals for comparisons. They learn about similes and metaphors, which are literary comparisons. Students also learn that authors sometimes use comparison and contrast as a way to organize their writing.

Texts for Teaching

Student Edition
- *At the Beach: Abuelito's Story,* 5.1, pages 182–193
- *The Ch'i-lin Purse,* 5.1, pages 236–249
- *King Midas and the Golden Touch,* 5.2, pages 376–393

Leveled Readers
- See pages 24–29 for a list of Leveled Readers.

Mini-Lesson 1

Teach the Skill
Use the **Envision It!** lesson on page EI•6 to visually review compare and contrast.

Remind students that:
- to **compare** means to tell how things are the same or almost the same.
- to **contrast** means to tell how things are different.
- they can group things by comparing and contrasting.

Practice
Have students visualize two vehicles, such as a bicycle and a bus. Draw a Venn diagram (two overlapping circles) on the board with these labels: *Bicycle, Both Vehicles, Bus.* Work together to list qualities that are unique to each and then list the qualities the two vehicles share. Help get students started by asking: How are the two vehicles alike? How are they different? Students can name shape, size, number of wheels, purpose, and so on.
If... students have difficulty identifying likenesses and differences of two vehicles in their mind,
then... show pictures and have them begin with color, shape, and size.

Apply
As students read on their own, have them think about how places and people they read about are alike and different.

Writing
Students can write a compare/contrast paragraph using the information in the diagram.

Customize Literacy

Mini-Lesson 2

Teach the Skill

Use the Envision It! lesson on page EI•6 to visually review compare and contrast.

Remind students that:

- to **compare** means to tell how things are the same or almost the same.
- to **contrast** means to tell how things are different.
- some comparison/contrast texts have no clue words and you need to figure out the comparison on your own.
- they can compare what they read to their own experiences.

Practice

Write the following paragraph on the board and read it with students. Juan and Jamie are in the same grade. Juan goes to North School, but Jamie goes to West School. They like sports, although neither plays on a team yet. Juan likes baseball and hopes to make the team in the spring, while Jamie prefers soccer. Unlike Juan, however, Jamie practices every day. Circle the words *but, neither, while,* and *unlike.* Explain that these are clues to comparisons. Reread the sentences together and then complete a Venn diagram. Ask: Did you find other likenesses and differences that weren't preceded by clue words? How did you figure it out? (reading carefully)

If... students have difficulty identifying likenesses,

then... have them ask themselves: *Are they alike in this way? Are they different?*

Apply

As students read on their own, have them compare what they read to what they already know.

Writing

Students can write a paragraph comparing two people using some clue words.

Mini-Lesson 3

Teach the Skill

Use the Envision It! lesson on page EI•6 to visually review compare and contrast.

Remind students that:

- to **compare** means to tell how things are the same or almost the same.
- to **contrast** means to tell how things are different.
- clue words in text can help them see when an author is comparing or contrasting people, places, things, or ideas.
- some comparison/contrast texts have no clue words and you need to figure out the comparison on your own.

Practice

With students, think of two things to compare. As a class, create a Venn diagram, deciding the specific qualities for each thing and the qualities they share. Have partners write sentences using the qualities. Review clue words that will help their readers see comparisons.

Words for Comparing	Words for Contrasting
like alike similarly also in addition same as well as	unlike on the other hand but however different instead of

Have partners share their sentences. Talk about how finding likenesses and differences (comparisons and contrasts) as they read will help them better understand what they read.

If... students have difficulty writing sentences with clue words,

then... provide sentence starters, for example, *The king loved gold, but the queen loved _____.*

Apply

As students read on their own, have them make charts or diagrams to note comparisons and contrasts.

Writing

Students can turn their sentences into a paragraph or short story.

Objectives:

- Students identify sequence relationships and events, including those that occur simultaneously and in flashbacks.
- Students put events in correct chronological order.

Sequence

What is it? **Sequence** means the order in which things happen. Sequence can also mean the steps we follow to make or do something. Understanding sequence, or time relationships, is important in understanding certain genres, such as historical fiction and biography. Social studies and science texts use sequence to describe events and processes. At Grade 5, when clue words are not used to explicitly point out sequence, readers need to think about the order in which events occur.

Student Edition p. EI•13

How Good Readers Use the Skill Students experience time relationships every day. Teachers can build on these experiences and help students connect them to reading. At first, students understand sequence as what happens first, next, and last in a selection. Students can then move on to use clue words to decipher more complicated sequence relationships, such as flashbacks and simultaneous events.

Texts for Teaching

Student Edition
- *Hold the Flag High,* 5.1, pages 208–219
- *The Fabulous Perpetual Motion Machine,* 5.1, pages 330–343
- *Sweet Music in Harlem,* 5.2, pages 440–457

Leveled Readers
- See pages 24–29 for a list of Leveled Readers.

Mini-Lesson 1

Teach the Skill

Use the **Envision It!** lesson on page EI•13 to visually review sequence.

Remind students that:

- **sequence** means the order in which things happen. It can also be the steps we take to do or make something.
- **clue words** such as *first, last,* and *after* can help students figure out order.

Practice

Write the following sentences in random order on the board and have students put them in sequential order using clue words such as *first, next, then,* and so on. Students might use other words that indicate time as well, such as *last night* or *Monday.*

I made supper for everyone.
I got out a jar of sauce and a box of pasta.
I boiled the pasta and heated up the sauce.
I scooped ice cream for everyone.
We all did the dishes.

If... students have difficulty identifying sequence relationships,
then... use just two sentence and work with them to decide which action would come first.

Apply

As students read the assigned text, have them complete a sequence graphic organizer to order events.

Writing

Students can write about an activity or event using clue words.

 **Mini-Lesson 2**

Teach the Skill

Use the Envision It! lesson on page EI•13 to visually review sequence.

Remind students that:

- **sequence** means the order in which things happen. It can also be the steps we take to do or make something.
- **clue words** such as *first, last*, and *after* can help students figure out order.
- not all selections that are in time order have clue words.
- clue words such as *while*, *meanwhile*, and *during* signal events that are happening simultaneously.

Practice

Read aloud the following passage and have students listen for three events that happen in sequence and two events that happen simultaneously. Remind students that they may need to use their common sense and prior knowledge to determine sequence, as every event may not include a clue word.

Last night the kids made supper for everyone. I got the ingredients out of the fridge and lined them up. Meanwhile, Jarod set the table. I started the water boiling for pasta. This would take longer than heating the sauce. While the pasta boiled and the sauce bubbled, Jarod and I made a salad. After dinner, Jarod and I washed the dishes. As a treat, Dad took everyone out for dessert.

If... students have difficulty identifying sequence relationships, **then...** chunk the text and have them point out clue words that identify events in each chunk.

Apply

As students read the assigned text, have them complete a sequence graphic organizer.

Writing

Using appropriate clue words, students can write about two events that happen at the same time.

 **Mini-Lesson 3**

Teach the Skill

Use the Envision It! lesson on page EI•13 to visually review sequence.

Remind students that:

- **sequence** means the order in which things happen. It can also be the steps we take to do or make something.
- not all selections that are in time order have clue words.
- clue words such as *while, meanwhile*, and *during* signal events that are happening simultaneously
- sometimes events are told out of order and readers must look at verb tenses for clues to sequence.

Practice

Read aloud the following passage and have students listen for the order of events. Record their responses.

The story we read today brought another incident to mind. I was just eight when I got my first guitar, but this was still years after I had been taking piano lessons. I started those lessons shortly after turning five. The guitar sat in my closet until one day when my piano teacher brought her guitar to my lesson. We played a duet! I started playing the guitar that day and haven't stopped.

If... students have difficulty identifying sequence relationships, **then...** provide the graphic organizer for additional practice.

Apply

As students read the assigned text, have them complete a sequence graphic organizer.

Writing

Students can use what they learned about clue words to revise descriptions or personal narratives.

Instruction

Visualize

Mini-Lesson

Objectives:
- Students use their own experiences and details from the text to visualize.
- Students visualize to activate prior knowledge.
- Students create mental images to better comprehend what they read.

Texts for Teaching

Student Edition
- *At the Beach*, 5.1, pages 182–195
- *Leonardo's Horse*, 5.1, pages 360–377
- *The Gymnast*, 5.2, pages 142–151

Leveled Readers
- See pages 24–29 for a list of Leveled Readers.

Student Edition p. EI•25

Understand the Strategy

Visualizing means creating pictures in the mind. These pictures are created by combining what readers already know with descriptive words in a text. Visualizing involves all the senses, not just sight.

Teach

Use the **Envision It!** lesson on page EI•25 to visually review visualizing with students.

Remind students that authors use descriptive language to help us "place" events in a story, to understand characters, to picture events, and so on. Use a piece of text that describes an event to model making pictures in your mind. The chart below has some examples based on a passage about children in Iceland who rescue baby pufflings.

Details from Text	What I Visualize
Thousands of puffins nest on rocky coasts of Iceland.	I hear a lot of squawking. I think the ground is slippery with bird droppings.
The baby birds need to get to the sea, but city lights confuse them. Some die.	I feel the dampness of the sea. I can feel the rocky ground.
Children come out at night to help the pufflings get to the water.	I see little birds running crazily. I see shadows made by moonlight.

Practice

Supply students with a text and have them work in pairs to visualize. Then bring the groups together and talk about the pictures they made in their minds as they read. Make sure students identify details from text that helped them visualize.

If... students have difficulty visualizing,

then... model, describing the pictures you form as you read.

Apply

Remind students to make pictures as they read. Encourage them to take notes on a graphic organizer.

Anchor Chart

Anchor charts help students make their thinking visible and permanent. With an anchor chart, the group can clarify their thinking about how to use a strategy. Display anchor charts so readers can use them as they read. They may wish or need to review and edit the charts as they gain more experience with strategies. Here is a sample chart for visualizing.

Visualize

1. Preview to get an idea of what you will be reading.

2. Get ready to visualize. Read to see how the author tells you what places and people are like.

3. Think about what you already know. If the author says a whale is as big as a bus, make a picture in your mind of a whale next to a school bus.

4. Ask yourself questions as you read to put yourself in the story. Think about the words the author uses and try to put them together in a picture in your mind.

5. Make a chart or a web to write down details that help you make a picture.

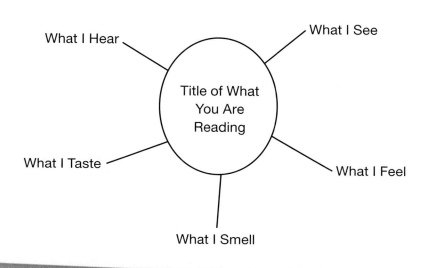

What I Hear

What I See

Title of What You Are Reading

What I Taste

What I Feel

What I Smell

Anchor Chart

Story Structure

Mini-Lesson

Objectives:
- Students recognize that stories have characters, setting, and plot.
- Students understand that stories usually include a problem, some rising action, a climax, and a resolution.
- Students ask questions to help them determine story structure.

Texts for Teaching

Student Edition
- *The Ch'i-lin Purse,* 5.1, pages 236–249
- *The Stormi Giovanni Club,* 5.2, pages 110–125
- *King Midas and the Golden Touch,* 5.2, pages 376–393

Leveled Readers
- See pages 24–29 for a list of Leveled Readers.

Understand the Strategy

Story structure refers to how a story is arranged. This means understanding the basic elements of a story—characters, setting, and plot—and how the author presents them. Recognizing story structure helps readers understand, recall, and appreciate stories.

Student Edition p. EI•22

Teach

Use the Envision It! lesson on page EI•22 to visually review story structure with students.

Remind students that understanding the elements of a story can help them comprehend it better. Reread or retell a familiar story and complete a story sequence chart. Use the terms *character, setting,* and *plot* as you do.

Story Sequence Chart

Beginning Problem/Conflict	
Middle Rising Action Climax	
End Resolution	

Practice

Supply students with a short piece of fiction and a story sequence chart. Read the selection together and call attention to the story elements. Then have students reread the piece and work in pairs to fill in the chart. Bring the group together and discuss their ideas. Ask: What problem does the character face? What were the most important events leading to the resolution? Was the problem resolved? What did the character learn?

If... students have difficulty recognizing story structure,

then... chunk the text for them and have them record events in that chunk. Emphasize that a plot is made up of several events.

Apply

Ask students to use a story sequence chart when they read on their own to determine problem/conflict, rising action, and resolution of a story.

Anchor Chart

Anchor charts help students make their thinking visible and permanent. With an anchor chart, the group can clarify their thinking about how to use a strategy. Display anchor charts so readers can use them as they read. They may wish or need to review and edit the charts as they gain more experience with strategies. Here is a sample chart for figuring out story structure.

Story Structure

1. Look over the story before you start to read. Ask:
What will this be about?
Do I recognize any characters?
What is going on in the pictures?

2. Try to figure out who is telling the story. If it is a narrator, the story will be told in third person. If it is being told by a character, it will be told in first person.

3. Try to figure out the problem or the conflict. Ask:
What is the main character trying to do?
What does he or she want?

4. Keep track of what happens in the story. Write down the events on a Story Sequence Chart.

5. Watch how the events build up throughout the story.

6. Decide what the climax of the story is. It is usually the most exciting part or when the most important thing happens to a character.

Anchor Chart

7. Look for the resolution of the story. Ask yourself:
Does the character solve his or her problem?
Does the character get what he or she wants?

8. Think about what the character might do next.

Using Multiple Strategies

Good readers use multiple strategies as they read. You can encourage students to read strategically through good classroom questioning. Use questions such as these to help students apply strategies during reading.

Answer Questions

- Who or what is this question about?
- Where can you look to find the answer to this question?

Ask Questions

- What do you want to know about _____?
- What questions do you have about the _____ in this selection? Use the words *who, what, when, where, why,* and *how* to ask your questions.
- Do you have any questions after reading?

Graphic Organizers

- What kind of graphic organizer could you use to help you keep track of the information in this selection?

Monitor and Clarify

- Does the story or article make sense?
- What don't you understand about what you read?
- Do you need to reread, review, read on, or check a reference source?
- Do you need to read more slowly or more quickly?
- What is a _____? Where could you look to find out?

Predict/Confirm Predictions

- What do you think this story or article will be about? Why do you think as you do?
- What do you think you will learn from this selection?
- Do the text features help you predict what will happen?
- Based on what has happened so far, what do you think will happen next?
- Is this what you thought would happen?
- How does _____ change what you thought would happen?

Preview

- What do the photographs, illustrations, or graphic sources tell about the selection?
- What do you want to find out? What do you want to learn?

Background Knowledge

- What do you already know about _____?
- Have you read stories or articles by this author before?
- How is this selection like others that you have read?
- What does this remind you of?
- How does your background knowledge help you understand _____?
- Did the text match what you already knew? What new information did you learn?

Story Structure

- Who are the characters in this story? the setting?
- What is the problem in this story? How does the problem get solved?
- What is the point of this story?

Summarize

- What two or three important ideas have you read so far?
- How do the text features relate to the important ideas?
- Is there a graphic organizer that can help you organize the information before you summarize?

Text Structure

- How has the author organized the writing?
- What clues tell you that the text is structured _____?

Visualize

- When you read this, what do you picture in your mind?
- What do you hear, see, or smell?
- What do you think _____ looks like? Why do you think as you do?

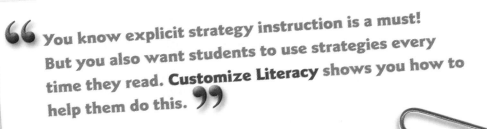

" You know explicit strategy instruction is a must! But you also want students to use strategies every time they read. **Customize Literacy** shows you how to help them do this. **"**

Glossary of Literacy Terms

This glossary lists academic language terms that are related to literacy.
They are provided for your information and professional use.

A

alliteration	the repetition of a consonant sound in a group of words, especially in poetry
allusion	a word or phrase that refers to something else the reader already knows from history, experience, or reading
animal fantasy	a story about animals that talk and act like people
answer questions	a reading strategy in which readers use the text and prior knowledge to answer questions about what they are reading
antonym	a word that means the opposite of another word
ask questions	a reading strategy in which readers ask themselves questions about the text to help make sense of what they read
author's point of view	the author's opinion on the subject he or she is writing about
author's purpose	the reason the author wrote the text
autobiography	the story of a real person's life written by that person

B

background knowledge	the information and experience that a reader brings to a text
biography	the story of a real person's life written by another person

C

cause	why something happens
character	a person, an animal, or a personified object in a story
chronological order	events in a selection, presented in the order in which they occurred
classify and categorize	put things, such as pictures or words, into groups
climax	the point in a story at which conflict is confronted
compare	tell how things are the same
comprehension	understanding of text being read—the ultimate goal of reading
comprehension strategy	a conscious plan used by a reader to gain understanding of text. Comprehension strategies may be used before, during, or after reading.
conclusion	a decision or opinion arrived at after thinking about facts and details and using prior knowledge
conflict	the problem or struggle in a story
context clue	the words, phrases, or sentences near an unfamiliar word that give the reader clues to the word's meaning
contrast	tell how things are different

Instruction

details small pieces of information

dialect form of a language spoken in a certain region or by a certain group of people that differs from the standard form of that language

D

dialogue written conversation

diary a day-to-day record of one's activities and thoughts

draw conclusions arrive at decisions or opinions after thinking about facts and details and using prior knowledge

effect what happens as the result of a cause

E

etymology an explanation of the origin and history of a word and its meaning

exaggeration a statement that makes something seem larger or greater than it actually is

expository text text that contains facts and information. Also called *informational text*.

fable a story, usually with animal characters, that is written to teach a moral, or lesson

F

fact piece of information that can be proved to be true

fairy tale a folk story with magical characters and events

fantasy a story that could not really happen

fiction writing that tells about imaginary people, things, and events

figurative language the use of language that gives words a meaning beyond their usual definitions in order to add beauty or force

flashback an interruption in the sequence of events of a narrative to include an event that happened earlier

folk tale a story that has been passed down by word of mouth

foreshadowing the use of hints or clues about what will happen later in a story

generalize make a broad statement or rule after examining particular facts

graphic organizer a drawing, chart, or web that illustrates concepts or shows how ideas relate to each other. Readers use graphic organizers to help them keep track of and understand important information and ideas as they read. Story maps, word webs, Venn diagrams, and KWL charts are graphic organizers.

G

graphic source a chart, diagram, or map within a text that adds to readers' understanding of the text

H

historical fiction	realistic fiction that takes place in the past. It is an imaginary story based on historical events and characters.
humor	writing or speech that has a funny or amusing quality
hyperbole	an exaggerated statement not meant to be taken literally, such as *I'm so hungry I could eat a horse.*

I

idiom	a phrase whose meaning differs from the ordinary meaning of the words. *A stone's throw* is an idiom meaning "a short distance."
imagery	the use of language to create beautiful or forceful pictures in the reader's mind
inference	conclusion reached on the basis of evidence and reasoning
inform	give knowledge, facts, or news to someone
informational text	writing that contains facts and information. Also called *expository text.*
interview	a face-to-face conversation in which someone responds to questions
irony	a way of speaking or writing in which the ordinary meaning of the words is the opposite of what the speaker or writer is thinking; a contrast between what is expected and what actually happens

J

jargon	the language of a special group or profession

L

legend	a story coming down from the past about the great deeds of a hero. Although a legend may be based on historical people and events, it is not regarded as historically true.
literary elements	the characters, setting, plot, and theme of a narrative text

main idea	the big idea that tells what a paragraph or a selection is mainly about; the most important idea of a text
metacognition	an awareness of one's own thinking processes and the ability to monitor and direct them to a desired goal. Good readers use metacognition to monitor their reading and adjust their reading strategies.
metaphor	a comparison that does not use *like* or *as*, such as *a heart of stone*
meter	the pattern of beats or accents in poetry
monitor and clarify	a comprehension strategy by which readers actively think about understanding their reading and know when they understand and when they do not. Readers use appropriate strategies to make sense of difficult words, ideas, or passages.
mood	the atmosphere or feeling of a written work
moral	the lesson or teaching of a fable or story
motive	the reason a character in a narrative does or says something
mystery	a story about mysterious events that are not explained until the end, so as to keep the reader in suspense
myth	a story that attempts to explain something in nature

M

narrative	a story, made up or true, that someone tells or narrates
narrator	the character in a selection who tells the story
nonfiction	writing that tells about real things, real people, and real events

N

onomatopoeia	the use of words that sound like their meanings, such as *buzz* and *hum*
opinion	someone's judgment, belief, or way of thinking
oral vocabulary	the words needed for speaking and listening
outcome	the resolution of the conflict in a story

O

paraphrase	retell the meaning of a passage in one's own words
personification	a figure of speech in which human traits or actions are given to animals or inanimate objects, as in *The sunbeam danced on the waves.*
persuade	convince someone to do or to believe something
photo essay	a collection of photographs on one theme, accompanied by text
play	a story that is written to be acted out for an audience

P

Instruction

P

plot	a series of related events at the beginning, middle, and end of a story; the action of a story
poem	an expressive, imaginative piece of writing often arranged in lines having rhythm and rhyme. In a poem, the patterns made by the sounds of the words have special importance.
pourquoi tale	a type of folk story that explains why things in nature came to be. *Pourquoi* is a French word meaning "why."
predict	tell what a selection might be about or what might happen in a text. Readers use text features and information to predict. They confirm or revise their predictions as they read.
preview	look over a text before reading it
prior knowledge	the information and experience that a reader brings to a text. Readers use prior knowledge to help them understand what they read.
prop	an item, such as an object, picture, or chart, used in a performance or presentation

R

reading vocabulary	the words we recognize or use in print
realistic fiction	a story about imaginary people and events that could happen in real life
repetition	the repeated use of some aspect of language
resolution	the point in a story where the conflict is resolved
rhyme	to end in the same sound(s)
rhythm	a pattern of strong beats in speech or writing, especially poetry
rising action	the buildup of conflicts and complications in a story

S

science fiction	a story based on science that often tells what life in the future might be like
semantic map	a graphic organizer, often a web, used to display words or concepts that are meaningfully related
sensory language	the use of words that help the reader understand how things look, sound, smell, taste, or feel
sequence	the order of events in a selection or the order of the steps in which something is completed
sequence words	clue words such as *first*, *next*, *then*, and *finally* that signal the order of events in a selection

S

setting	where and when a story takes place
simile	a comparison that uses *like* or *as*, as in *as busy as a bee*
speech	a public talk to a group of people made for a specific purpose
stanza	a group of lines in a poem
steps in a process	the order of the steps in which something is completed
story map	a graphic organizer used to record the literary elements and the sequence of events in a narrative text
story structure	how the characters, setting, and events of a story are organized into a plot
summarize	give the most important ideas of what was read. Readers summarize important information in the selection to keep track of what they are reading.
supporting detail	piece of information that tells about the main idea
symbolism	the use of one thing to suggest something else; often the use of something concrete to stand for an abstract idea

T

tall tale	a humorous story that uses exaggeration to describe impossible happenings
text structure	the organization of a piece of nonfiction writing. Text structures of informational text include cause/effect, chronological, compare/contrast, description, problem/solution, proposition/support, and ask/answer questions.
theme	the big idea or author's message in a story
think aloud	an instructional strategy in which a teacher verbalizes his or her thinking to model the process of comprehension or the application of a skill
tone	author's attitude toward the subject or toward the reader
topic	the subject of a discussion, conversation, or piece of text

V

visualize	picture in one's mind what is happening in the text. Visualizing helps readers imagine the things they read about.

Section 3 Matching Books and Readers

Leveled Readers Skills Chart

Scott Foresman Reading Street provides more than six hundred leveled readers.
Each one is designed to:

- Practice critical skills and strategies
- Build vocabulary and concepts
- Build fluency
- Develop a lifelong love of reading

Grade 5

Title	Level*	DRA Level	Genre	Comprehension Strategy
Jenna and the High Dive	N	30	Realistic Fiction	Monitor and Clarify
Dangerous Storms	N	30	Expository Nonfiction	Summarize
Our Village	N	30	Historical Fiction	Inferring
Rube Foster and the Chicago American Giants	N	30	Nonfiction	Questioning
The Golden Spike	O	34	Expository Nonfiction	Text Structure
The Ocean's Treasures	O	34	Expository Nonfiction	Visualize
From Slave to Soldier	O	34	Historical Fiction	Inferring
China: Today and Yesterday	O	34	Expository Nonfiction	Story Structure
A Visit to the Navajo Nation	O	34	Expository Nonfiction	Monitor and Clarify
Paul Revere's Ride	P	38	Narrative Nonfiction	Background Knowledge
George Ferris's Wheel	P	38	Expository Nonfiction	Summarize
The Designs of Da Vinci	P	38	Biography	Visualize
Paleontology: Digging for Dinosaurs and More	P	38	Nonfiction	Predict and Set Purpose
The Root of the Blues	P	38	Narrative Nonfiction	Text Structure
The Magic of Makeup	P	38	Expository Nonfiction	Important Ideas
The Long Trip Home	Q	40	Realistic Fiction	Monitor and Clarify
Storm Chasing Challenges	Q	40	Expository Nonfiction	Summarize
Toby's California Vacation	Q	40	Realistic Fiction	Inferring
Famous Women in Sports	Q	40	Biography	Questioning
Playing the Game	Q	40	Realistic Fiction	Questioning
The Land of Plenty	Q	40	Historical Fiction	Predict and Set Purpose
Surviving the Elements	Q	40	Expository Nonfiction	Important Ideas
Moving	Q	40	Realistic Fiction	Story Structure
Let the Games Begin	Q	40	Expository Nonfiction	Visualize
Giant Pumpkin on the Loose	Q	40	Fiction	Background Knowledge
A Railroad Over the Sierra	R	40	Expository Nonfiction	Text Structure
Sea Life	R	40	Expository Nonfiction	Visualize
A Spy in Disguise	R	40	Nonfiction	Inferring
Abuela's Gift	R	40	Realistic Fiction	Story Structure
Helping Others	R	40	Nonfiction	Monitor and Clarify

* Suggested Guided Reading Level. Use your knowledge of students' abilities to adjust levels as needed.

The chart here and on the next few pages lists titles of leveled readers appropriate for students in Grade 5. Use the chart to find titles that meet your students' interest and instructional needs. The books in this list were leveled using the criteria suggested in *Matching Books to Readers* and *Leveled Books for Readers, Grades 3–6* by Irene C. Fountas and Gay Su Pinnell. For more on leveling, see the *Reading Street Leveled Readers Leveling Guide*.

Target Comprehension Skill	Additional Comprehension Instruction	Vocabulary
Character and Plot	Graphic Sources	Homographs/Context Clues
Cause and Effect	Draw Conclusions	Context Clues/Homonyms
Setting and Theme	Author's Purpose	Dictionary/Glossary/Unfamiliar Words
Fact and Opinion	Generalize	Context Clues/Antonyms
Cause and Effect	Graphic Sources	Context Clues/Multiple Meanings
Compare and Contrast	Graphic Sources	Unfamiliar Words/Context Clues
Sequence	Draw Conclusions	Dictionary/Glossary/Unfamiliar Words
Compare and Contrast	Draw Conclusions	Word Structure/Greek and Latin Roots
Author's Purpose	Main Idea and Details	Context Clues/Unfamiliar Words
Author's Purpose	Draw Conclusions	Word Structure/Endings
Sequence	Generalize	Context Clues/Multiple Meanings
Main Idea and Details	Compare and Contrast	Word Structure/Greek and Latin Roots
Fact and Opinion	Cause and Effect	Context Clues/Homonyms
Main Idea and Details	Author's Purpose	Context Clues/Antonyms
Graphic Sources	Main Idea and Details	Word Structure/Prefixes
Character and Plot	Problem and Solution	Word Structure/Suffixes
Cause and Effect	Draw Conclusions	Context Clues/Homonyms
Setting and Theme	Generalize	Dictionary/Glossary/Unfamiliar Words
Fact and Opinion	Compare and Contrast	Context Clues/Antonyms
Draw Conclusions	Theme	Word Structure/Endings
Generalize	Plot	Context Clues/Unfamiliar Words
Graphic Sources	Main Idea and Details	Context Clues/Synonyms
Generalize	Theme	Context Clues/Unfamiliar Words
Draw Conclusions	Graphic Sources	Word Structure/Suffixes
Character and Plot	Author's Purpose	Word Structure/Greek and Latin Roots
Cause and Effect	Draw Conclusions	Context Clues/Multiple Meanings
Compare and Contrast	Main Idea and Details	Unfamiliar Words/Context Clues
Sequence	Generalize	Dictionary/Glossary/Unfamiliar Words
Compare and Contrast	Theme	Word Structure/Greek and Latin Roots
Author's Purpose	Main Idea and Details	Context Clues/Unfamiliar Words

Matching Books & Readers

Leveled Readers Skills Chart *Continued*

Grade 5 Title	Level*	DRA Level	Genre	Comprehension Strategy
Titanic: The "Unsinkable" Ship	R	40	Narrative Nonfiction	Inferring
Aim High: Astronaut Training	R	40	Expository Nonfiction	Monitor and Clarify
The Inside Story of Earth	R	40	Expository Nonfiction	Summarize
The California Gold Rush	R	40	Expository Nonfiction	Questioning
A Happy Accident	R	40	Realistic Fiction	Important Ideas
Paul Revere/American Revolutionary War	S	40	Narrative Nonfiction	Background Knowledge
Build a Perpetual Motion Machine	S	40	Expository Nonfiction	Summarize
The Italian Renaissance and Its Artists	S	40	Expository Nonfiction	Visualize
Searching for Dinosaurs	S	40	Expository Nonfiction	Predict and Set Purpose
Blues Legends	S	40	Biography	Text Structure
Computers in Filmmaking	S	40	Nonfiction	Important Ideas
Saving an American Symbol	S	40	Expository Nonfiction	Text Structure
Ancient Gold from the Ancient World	S	40	Expository Nonfiction	Story Structure
The Flight Over the Ocean	S	40	Narrative Nonfiction	Predict and Set Purpose
Jazz, Jazz, Jazz	S	40	Narrative Nonfiction	Background Knowledge
Journey to the New World	T	50	Historical Fiction	Questioning
Wilma Rudolph: Running to Win	T	50	Biography	Predict and Set Purpose
Changing for Survival: Bird Adaptations	T	50	Expository Nonfiction	Important Ideas
The New Kid at School	T	50	Narrative Nonfiction	Story Structure
Strange Sports with Weird Gear	T	50	Expository Nonfiction	Visualize
Bill Lucks Out	T	50	Realistic Fiction	Background Knowledge
Explore with Science	U	50	Expository Nonfiction	Inferring
Sailing the Stars	U	50	Expository Nonfiction	Monitor and Clarify
The Journey Through the Earth	U	50	Science Fiction	Summarize
The United States Moves West	U	50	Expository Nonfiction	Questioning
Driven to Change	U	50	Expository Nonfiction	Important Ideas
The Kudzu Invasion	U	50	Expository Nonfiction	Text Structure
The Signs	V	50	Realistic Fiction	Monitor and Clarify
Weather Forecasting	V	50	Expository Nonfiction	Summarize
The Medicine Harvest	V	50	Historical Fiction	Inferring

* Suggested Guided Reading Level. Use your knowledge of students' abilities to adjust levels as needed.

You know the theory behind leveled books: they let you match books with the interest and instructional levels of your students. You can find the right reader for every student with this chart. 99

Target Comprehension Skill	Additional Comprehension Instruction	Vocabulary
Graphic Sources	Cause and Effect	Dictionary/Glossary/Unfamiliar Words
Author's Purpose	Graphic Sources	Context Clues/Multiple Meanings
Cause and Effect	Fact and Opinion	Context Clues/Unfamiliar Words
Generalize	Main Idea and Details	Word Structure/Prefixes
Draw Conclusions	Graphic Sources	Dictionary/Glossary/Unfamiliar Words
Author's Purpose	Cause and Effect	Word Structure/Endings
Sequence	Draw Conclusions	Context Clues/Multiple Meanings
Main Idea and Details	Generalize	Word Structure/Greek and Latin Roots
Fact and Opinion	Compare and Contrast	Context Clues/Homonyms
Main Idea and Details	Author's Purpose	Context Clues/Antonyms
Graphic Sources	Main Idea and Details	Word Structure/Prefixes
Main Idea and Details	Cause and Effect	Word Structure/Endings
Compare and Contrast	Draw Conclusions	Word Structure/Suffixes
Fact and Opinion	Graphic Sources	Context Clues/Unfamiliar Words
Sequence	Fact and Opinion	Context Clues/Homographs
Draw Conclusions	Plot	Word Structure/Endings
Generalize	Author's Purpose	Context Clues/Unfamiliar Words
Graphic Sources	Main Idea and Details	Context Clues/Synonyms
Generalize	Cause and Effect	Context Clues/Unfamiliar Words
Draw Conclusions	Compare and Contrast	Word Structure/Suffixes
Character and Plot	Cause and Effect	Word Structure/Greek and Latin Roots
Graphic Sources	Cause and Effect	Dictionary/Glossary/Unfamiliar Words
Author's Purpose	Sequence	Context Clues /Multiple Meanings
Cause and Effect	Character and Plot	Context Clues/Unfamiliar Words
Generalize	Fact and Opinion	Word Structure/Prefixes
Draw Conclusions	Main Idea and Details	Dictionary/Glossary/Unfamiliar Words
Main Idea and Details	Generalize	Word Structure/Endings
Character and Plot	Author's Purpose	Homographs/Context Clues
Cause and Effect	Author's Purpose	Context Clues/Homonyms
Theme and Setting	Draw Conclusions	Dictionary/Glossary/Unfamiliar Words

Matching Books & Readers

Leveled Readers Skills Chart *Continued*

Grade 5 Title	Level*	DRA Level	Genre	Comprehension Strategy
The Journey of African American Athletes	V	50	Biography	Questioning
The Land of Opportunity	V	50	Narrative Nonfiction	Summarize
Our Essential Oceans	V	50	Expository Nonfiction	Visualize
The Golden Journey	V	50	Historical Fiction	Story Structure
Stop That Train!	V	50	Narrative Nonfiction	Predict and Set Purpose
Grandma Betty's Banjo	V	50	Realistic Fiction	Background Knowledge
The Most Dangerous Woman in America	W	60	Nonfiction	Inferring
Moving to Mali	W	60	Realistic Fiction	Story Structure
The Talker	W	60	Nonfiction	Ask Questions
The National Guard: Today's Minutemen	W	60	Expository Nonfiction	Background Knowledge
Philo and His Invention	W	60	Nonfiction	Summarize
Art's Inspiration	W	60	Expository Nonfiction	Visualize
What's New With Dinosaur Fossils?	W	60	Expository Nonfiction	Predict and Set Purpose
The Blues Evolution	X	60	Narrative Nonfiction	Text Structure
Special Effects in Hollywood	X	60	Expository Nonfiction	Important Ideas
Cheaper, Faster, and Better	X	60	Expository Nonfiction	Questioning
Operation Inspiration	X	60	Realistic Fiction	Predict and Set Purpose
Can Humans Make a Home in Outer Space?	X	60	Expository Nonfiction	Important Ideas
Nathaniel Comes to Town	X	60	Realistic Fiction	Story Structure
What Makes Great Athletes?	X	60	Expository Nonfiction	Visualize
The Sandwich Brigade	X	60	Realistic Fiction	Background Knowledge
Space Travel Inventions	X	60	Expository Nonfiction	Inferring
Astronauts and Cosmonauts	Y	60	Expository Nonfiction	Monitor and Clarify
The Shaping of the Continents	Y	60	Expository Nonfiction	Summarize
From Territory to Statehood	Y	60	Expository Nonfiction	Questioning
How the Wolves Saved Yellowstone	Y	60	Expository Nonfiction	Important Ideas
Mixed-Up Vegetables	Y	60	Expository Nonfiction	Text Structure
Precious Goods: From Salt to Silk	Y	60	Expository Nonfiction	Story Structure
Traveling by Plane	Y	60	Narrative Nonfiction	Predict and Set Purpose
Unexpected Music	Y	60	Expository Nonfiction	Background Knowledge

* Suggested Guided Reading Level. Use your knowledge of students' abilities to adjust levels as needed.

You know the theory behind leveled books: they let you match books with the interest and instructional levels of your students. You can find the right reader for every student with this chart. "

Target Comprehension Skill	Additional Comprehension Instruction	Vocabulary
Fact and Opinion	Fact and Opinion	Context Clues/Antonyms
Cause and Effect	Generalize	Context Clues/Multiple Meanings
Compare and Contrast	Author's Purpose	Unfamiliar Words/Context Clues
Compare and Contrast	Character	Word Structure/Suffixes
Fact and Opinion	Generalize	Context Clues/Unfamiliar Words
Sequence	Compare and Contrast	Context Clues/Homographs
Sequence	Graphic Sources	Dictionary/Glossary/Unfamiliar Words
Compare and Contrast	Character and Setting	Word Structure/Greek and Latin Roots
Fact and Opinion	Main Idea and Details	Context Clues/Unfamiliar Words
Author's Purpose	Main Idea and Details	Word Structure/Endings
Sequence	Generalize	Context Clues/Multiple Meanings
Main Idea and Details	Draw Conclusions	Word Structure/Greek and Latin Roots
Fact and Opinion	Draw Conclusions	Context Clues/Homonyms
Main Idea and Details	Cause and Effect	Context Clues/Antonyms
Graphic Sources	Sequence	Word Structure/Prefixes
Draw Conclusions	Cause and Effect	Word Structure/Endings
Generalize	Compare and Contrast	Context Clues/Unfamiliar Words
Graphic Sources	Main Idea and Details	Context Clues/Synonyms
Generalize	Theme and Plot	Context Clues/Unfamiliar Words
Draw Conclusions	Sequence	Word Structure/Suffixes
Character and Plot	Theme	Word Structure/Greek and Latin Roots
Graphic Sources	Generalize	Dictionary/Glossary/Unfamiliar Words
Author's Purpose	Compare and Contrast	Context Clues/Multiple Meanings
Cause and Effect	Graphic Sources	Context Clues/Unfamiliar Words
Generalize	Sequence	Word Structure/Prefixes
Draw Conclusions	Author's Purpose	Dictionary/Glossary/Unfamiliar Words
Main Idea and Details	Compare and Contrast	Word Structure Endings
Compare and Contrast	Draw Conclusions	Word Structure/Suffixes
Fact and Opinion	Setting	Context Clues/Unfamiliar Words
Sequence	Draw Conclusions	Context Clues/Homographs

Matching Books & Readers

What Good Readers Do

You can use the characteristics and behaviors of good readers to help all your students read better. But what are these characteristics and behaviors? And how can you use them to foster good reading behaviors for all your students? Here are some helpful tips.

Good Readers enjoy reading! They have favorite books, authors, and genres. Good readers often have a preference about where and when they read. They talk about books and recommend their favorites.

Develop this behavior by giving students opportunities to respond in different ways to what they read. Get them talking about what they read, and why they like or dislike it.

This behavior is important because book sharing alerts you to students who are somewhat passive about reading or have limited literacy experiences. Book sharing also helps you when you select books for the class.

Good Readers select books they can read.

Develop this behavior by providing a range of three or four texts appropriate for the student and then letting the student choose.

This behavior is important because students gain control over reading when they can choose from books they can read. This helps them become more independent in the classroom.

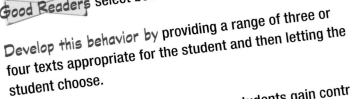

Good Readers read independently for longer periods of time.

Develop this behavior by taking note of the level of support students need during guided reading. Use this information to gauge independent reading time accordingly.

This behavior is important because students become better readers when they spend time reading many texts at their independent level.

Customize Literacy

 Want to improve student performance by fostering good reading behaviors? Customize Literacy can help.

Matching Books & Readers

Good Readers use text features to help them preview and set purposes.

Develop this behavior by having students use the title and illustrations in fiction texts or the title, contents, headings, and other graphic features in nonfiction texts to make predictions about what they will be reading.

This behavior is important because previewing actually makes reading easier! Looking at features and sampling the text enables readers to predict and set expectations for reading.

Good Readers predict and ask questions before and while they read.

Develop this behavior by asking questions. After reading a passage, ask students what they think will happen next in a fiction text. Have them ask a question they think will be answered in a nonfiction text and read on to see if it is.

This behavior is important because when students predict and ask questions as they read, they are engaged. They have a purpose for reading and a basis for monitoring their comprehension.

 Good Readers read meaningful phrases aloud with appropriate expression.

Develop this behavior by giving students lots of opportunities to read orally. As they read, note students' phrasing, intonation, and attention to punctuation and give help as needed.

This behavior is important because reading fluently in longer, meaningful phrases supports comprehension and ease in reading longer, more complex texts.

Good Readers read aloud at an appropriate reading rate with a high percent of accuracy.

Develop this behavior by timing students' oral reading to calculate their reading rates. You can also record students' miscues to determine a percent of accuracy. This will help identify problems.

This behavior is important because when students read fluently texts that are "just right," they find reading more enjoyable. A fluent reader is able to focus more on constructing meaning and is more likely to develop a positive attitude toward reading.

Good Readers use effective strategies and sources of information to figure out unknown words.

Develop this behavior by teaching specific strategies for figuring out unknown words, such as sounding out clusters of letters, using context, reading on, and using references.

This behavior is important because when readers have a variety of strategies to use, they are more able to decode and self-correct quickly. Readers who do these things view themselves as good readers.

CH-
QU-
ST-

Good Readers construct meaning as they read and then share or demonstrate their understanding.

Develop this behavior by having students retell what they read or write a summary of what they read in their own words.

This behavior is important because the ability to retell or write a summary is essential for success in reading. It shows how well a student has constructed meaning.

Good Readers locate and use what is explicitly stated in a text.

Develop this behavior by asking questions that require students to go back into the text to find explicitly stated information.

This behavior is important because the ability to recall, locate, and use specific information stated in a text enables readers to respond to literal questions, as well as to support opinions and justify their responses.

Good Readers make connections.

Develop this behavior by asking questions to help students make connections: *What does this remind you of? Have you ever read or experienced anything like this?*

This behavior is important because making connections helps readers understand and appreciate a text. Making connections to self, the world, and other texts supports higher-level thinking.

Good Readers interpret what they read by making inferences.

Develop this behavior by asking questions to help students tell or write about what they think was implied in the text: *Why do you think that happened? What helped you come to that conclusion?*

This behavior is important because the ability to go beyond the literal meaning of a text enables readers to gain a deeper understanding. When students make inferences, they use background knowledge, their personal knowledge, and the text to grasp the meaning of what is implied by the author.

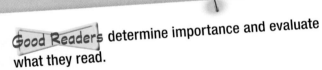

Good Readers determine importance and evaluate what they read.

Develop this behavior by always having students identify what they think is the most important message, event, or information in a text.

This behavior is important because readers must be able to sort out important from interesting information. The ability to establish and/ or use criteria and provide support when making judgments is an important critical thinking skill.

Good Readers support their responses using information from a text and/or their own background knowledge.

Develop this behavior by always asking students to give the reason(s) they identified an event, message, or idea as most important.

This behavior is important because the ability to justify one's response is important for all learners. It enables others to know the basis for a decision and provides an opening for further discussion.

Matching Books & Readers

Conversation Starters

Asking Good Questions When students read interesting and thought-provoking books, they want to share! You can encourage students to think critically about what they read. Use questions such as the following to assess comprehension as well as evoke good class/group discussions.

Author's Purpose

- Why did the author write this piece?

- How does figuring out the author's purpose help you decide how to read the text?

Cause and Effect

- Why did these events happen? How might they have been different if the causes had been different?

- Are there several causes that result in a single effect?

- Is there a single cause that has several effects?

Compare and Contrast

- What clue words show the author is comparing and/or contrasting in this article?

- How are the fictional characters and events in this story like and/or different from real people and events you know of?

Draw Conclusions

- Based on what you have read, seen, or experienced, what can you conclude about this event in the selection?

- This story seems to be a fantasy. Why might you conclude this?

- What words help you draw conclusions about the relationship between the characters?

Fact and Opinion

- What clue word or words signal that this is a statement of opinion?

- How could this statement of fact be proved true or false?

Generalize

- What generalization can you make about the story or the characters in it? What examples lead to that generalization?

- What details, facts, and logic does the author use to support this generalization?

- Is this a valid or a faulty generalization? Explain your ideas.

Graphic Sources

- How does the author use graphic sources (chart, maps, illustrations, time lines, and so on) to support ideas and opinions?

- This selection has many graphic sources. Which one or ones best help you understand the events or ideas in the selection? Why?

Literary Elements: Character, Setting, Plot, Theme

- Describe the main character at the beginning of the story and at the end of the story. How and why does he or she change?

- How is the setting important to the story? How might the story be different if its time or its place were different?

- What does the main character want at the beginning of the story? How does the main character go about trying to achieve this?

- A plot has a conflict, but the conflict isn't always between two characters. What is the conflict in this story? How is it resolved?

- In a few sentences, what is the plot of the story?

- What is the theme of the story? Use details from the story to support your statement.

Main Idea and Details

- What is the main idea of this paragraph or article? What are some details?

- The author makes this particular statement in the article. What details does the author provide to support that statement?

Sequence

- How is the sequence of events important in the text?

- Is the order of events important in this story? Why or why not?

- Based on what has already happened, what will most likely happen next?

Connecting Science and Social Studies

Scott Foresman Reading Street Leveled Readers are perfect for covering, supporting, or enriching science and social studies content. Using these books ensures that all students can access important concepts.

Grade 5 Leveled Readers

Science

Earth and Space Science

Nonfiction Books

- *Aim High: Astronaut Training*
- *Astronauts and Cosmonauts*
- *Can Humans Make a Home in Outer Space?*
- *Cheaper, Faster, and Better*
- *Dangerous Storms*
- *Explore with Science*
- *The Inside Story of Earth*
- *Sailing the Stars*
- *The Shaping of the Continents*
- *Space Travel Inventions*
- *Storm Chasing Challenges*
- *Traveling by Plane*
- *Weather Forecasting*

Fiction Books

- *The Journey Through the Earth*
- *The Signs*

Life Science

Nonfiction Books

- *Changing for Survival: Bird Adaptations*
- *Driven to Change*
- *How the Wolves Saved Yellowstone*
- *The Kudzu Invasion*
- *Mixed-Up Vegetables*
- *Our Essential Oceans*
- *Paleontology: Digging for Dinosaurs and More*
- *Sea Life*
- *Searching for Dinosaurs*
- *Surviving the Elements: Animals and Their Environments*
- *What's New with Dinosaur Fossils?*

Fiction Books

- *The Long Trip Home*
- *Toby's California Vacation*

Physical Science

Nonfiction Books

- *George Ferris's Wheel*
- *The Magic of Makeup: Going Behind the Mask*
- *Philo and His Invention*
- *The Search to Build a Perpetual Motion Machine*

Fiction Books

- *A Happy Accident*
- *Jenna and the High Dive*

Grade 5 Leveled Readers

Social Studies

Citizenship

Nonfiction Books
- Helping Others
- The National Guard: Today's Minutemen
- The New Kid at School

Fiction Books
- Bill Lucks Out
- Giant Pumpkin on the Loose
- The Sandwich Brigade

Culture

Nonfiction Books
- Art's Inspiration
- China: Today and Yesterday
- Computers in Filmmaking: Very Special Effects
- The Root of the Blues
- Special Effects in Hollywood
- Strange Sports with Weird Gear
- The Talker
- Unexpected Music
- A Visit to the Navajo Nation

Fiction Books
- Abuela's Gift
- Grandma Betty's Banjo
- The Medicine Harvest
- Moving
- Moving to Mali

Culture

- Nathaniel Comes to Town
- Operation Inspiration
- Our Village
- Playing the Game

Economics

Nonfiction Books
- Ancient Gold from the Ancient World
- The Oceans' Treasures
- Precious Goods: From Salt to Silk

History

Nonfiction Books
- The Blues Evolution
- The California Gold Rush
- The Flight Over the Ocean: Yesterday and Today
- From Territory to Statehood
- The Golden Spike
- The Italian Renaissance and Its Artists
- Jazz, Jazz, Jazz
- The Land of Opportunity
- Let the Games Begin: History of the Olympics
- The Most Dangerous Woman in America

History

- Paul Revere and the American Revolutionary War
- Paul Revere's Ride
- A Railroad Over the Sierra
- Rube Foster and the Chicago American Giants
- Saving an American Symbol
- A Spy in Disguise
- Stop That Train!
- Titanic: The "Unsinkable" Ship
- The United States Moves West
- What Makes Great Athletes?

Fiction Books
- From Slave to Soldier
- The Golden Journey
- Journey to the New World
- The Land of Plenty

More Great Titles

Biography
- Blues Legends
- The Designs of Da Vinci
- Famous Women in Sports
- The Journey of African American Athletes
- Wilma Rudolph: Running to Win

Connecting Science and Social Studies

Need more choices? Look back to Grade 4.

Grade 4 Leveled Readers

Science

Earth and Space Science

Nonfiction Books
- *Danger: The World Is Getting Hot!*
- *Darkness Into Light*
- *Day for Night*
- *Earth's Closest Neighbor*
- *Let's Explore Antarctica!*
- *Looking For Changes*
- *The Mysteries of Space*
- *One Giant Leap*
- *Orbiting the Sun*
- *Putting a Stop to Wildfires*
- *Severe Weather: Storms*
- *Storm Chasers*
- *Wondrously Wild Weather*

Fiction Books
- *Exploring the Moon*
- *Flash Flood*
- *Life on Mars: The Real Story*
- *Stuart's Moon Suit*
- *Surviving Hurricane Andrew*
- *To the Moon!*

Life Science

Nonfiction Books
- *Birds Take Flight*
- *Come Learn About Dolphins*
- *Dolphins: Mammals of the Sea*
- *Florida Everglades: Its Plants and Animals*
- *The Gray Whale*
- *How Does Echolocation Work?*
- *Migration Relocation*
- *Mini Microbes*
- *Mysterious Monsters*
- *Plants and Animals in Antarctica*
- *Saving Trees Using Science*
- *Sharing Our Planet*
- *What in the World Is That?*

Life Science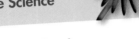

Fiction Books
- *The Missing Iguana Mystery*
- *Protecting Wild Animals*
- *The Salamander Stumper*
- *Top Hat Tompkins, the Detective*

Grade 4 Leveled Readers

Social Studies

Citizenship

Nonfiction Books
- Equality in American Schools
- Danger! Children at Work
- Dogs on the Job

Fiction Books
- Mountain Rescue
- The Super Secret Surprise Society

Culture

Nonfiction Books
- The Black Ensemble Theater
- The Diné
- From Spain to America
- What It Takes to Stage a Play

Fiction Books
- A Book of Their Own
- A New Home
- Birthday Surprise
- Cheers for the Cheetahs
- The Grizzly Bear Hotshots
- Living with Grandpa Joseph
- The Show Must Go On!
- Something to Do
- To Be a Star

Economics

Nonfiction Books
- The Alaskan Pipeline
- Ranches in the Southwest
- Ranching in the Great American Desert
- Two Powerful Rivers

Fiction Books
- The Seahaven Squids Host a Pet Wash

History

Nonfiction Books
- Becoming a Melting Pot
- The Civil Rights Movement
- Code Breakers: Uncovering German Messages
- Let's Get to Know the Incas
- The Long Journey West
- Meet the Maya
- The Navajo Code Talkers
- Pompeii, the Lost City
- The Rosetta Stone: The Key to Ancient Writing
- The Sauk and Fox Native Americans
- Speaking in Code
- The Story of Libraries
- Thor Heyerdahl's Incredible Raft
- We Shall Overcome
- The Women's Movement

History

Fiction Books
- Bessie Coleman
- The Incredible Alexander Graham Bell

Geography

Nonfiction Books
- America's National Parks
- Maine, Now and Then
- A Trip to Capital Hill
- The Wonders of Western Geography

Fiction Books
- From Sea to Shining Sea

Government

Nonfiction Books
- The Power of the People
- The United States Government

More Great Titles

Biography
- Amazing Female Athletes
- Jim Thorpe
- John Muir
- The Legacy of César Chávez
- Lewis and Clark and the Corps of Discovery

Matching Books & Readers

Connecting Science and Social Studies

Need more choices? Look ahead to Grade 6.

Grade 6 Leveled Readers

Science

Earth and Space Science

Nonfiction Books

- *Earth and Its Place in Space*
- *Electricity*
- *Elements in Our Universe*
- *Exploring Mars*
- *Exploring the World Below*
- *Global Warming*
- *The Hidden Worlds of Caves*
- *The History of Green Power*
- *It's About Time!*
- *Living Greener*
- *Riches from Our Earth*
- *Swimming Safely in the Ocean*
- *Wonders Down Under*

Earth and Space Science

Fiction Books

- *The Domes on Mars*
- *Moon Kids, Earth Kids*
- *Moonman Markie*
- *The Rip Current Rescue*
- *Rock Canyon Challenge*
- *Sea's Visit: A Tale From Nigeria*
- *Tom Rides Out the Quake*

Life Science

Nonfiction Books

- *Animals of the Arctic*
- *Archaeology in China*
- *The Battle over the Rain Forests*
- *A Biome of the World: The Taiga*
- *The Debate over Zoos: Captive or Free?*
- *Ecosystems of Rain Forests*
- *Faithful Four-Footed Friends*
- *The Great Apes*
- *Life in the Arctic Circle*
- *Speaking for Wolves*
- *The Price of Knowledge: The Interaction of Animals and Scientists*
- *Saving Feathered Friends*

Fiction Books

- *Egg Watching*
- *Twilight of the Wolves*
- *The Very Special Gift*

Grade 6 Leveled Readers

Social Studies

Citizenship

Fiction Books

- *The Best Community Service Project Ever*

Culture

Nonfiction Books

- *Armchair Archaeology*
- *Cuban Americans*
- *From China to America: My Story*
- *Living and Growing in China*
- *Tribes of the Amazon Rain Forest*
- *Viva America! Cubans in the United States*

Fiction Books

- *Adams's Hippo Lesson*
- *Chess Is for Fun*
- *How Anansi Captured the Story of the Rain*
- *Jeff and Jack*
- *Jenna the Scatterbrain*
- *Lady Red Rose and the Woods*
- *Monkey Tales*
- *Our New Life in the Big City*
- *Pedro's Flute*
- *Sally's Summer with Her Grandparents*
- *A Small-Town Summer*
- *When Julie Got Lost*

History

Nonfiction Books

- *Ancient Greece, Modern Culture*
- *Ancient Life Along the Nile*
- *The Aztec Empire*
- *The Chinese Struggle to America: An Immigration History*
- *Colonization and Native Peoples*
- *Defying Death and Time: Mummies*
- *Discovering Classical Athens*
- *The Freedoms of Speech and Assembly in the United States*
- *Greetings from the Four Corners!*
- *How Did Ancient Greece Become So Great?*
- *Immigrants of Yesterday and Today*
- *A Migrant Music: Jazz*
- *The Movements of Citizens*
- *Pulling Down the Walls: The Struggle of African American Performers*
- *The Race to the Bottom of the World*
- *Restless Humanity*
- *Robert Abbott's Dream: The Chicago Defender and the Great Migration*
- *The Secrets of the Past*
- *Spanish Conquests of the Americas*
- *The Struggle for Higher Education*

History

- *Uncovering the Secrets of Ancient Egypt*

Fiction Books

- *The Doaks of Montana*
- *From Youngsters to Old Timers*
- *Grizzled Bill's New Life*
- *Lucky Chuck and His Least Favorite Cousin*
- *The Noble Boy and the Brick Maker*
- *Sir Tom*
- *Sleepyville Wakes Up*
- *Timmy Finds His Home*

Geography

Nonfiction Books

- *The Mining Debate*
- *Mystery of the Ancient Pueblo*
- *The Quests for Gold*

Fiction Books

- *The Adventures in Matunaland*

More Great Titles

Biography

- *20th Century African American Singers*
- *From Oscar Micheaux to the Oscars*
- *Inventors at Work*

Planning Teacher Study Groups

Adventurous teachers often have good ideas for lessons. A teacher study group is a great way to share ideas and get feedback on the best way to connect content and students. Working with other teachers can provide you with the support and motivation you need to implement new teaching strategies. A teacher study group offers many opportunities to collaborate, support each other's work, share insights, and get feedback.

Think About It

A weekly or monthly teacher study group can help support you in developing your expertise in the classroom. You and a group of like-minded teachers can form your own study group. What can this group accomplish?

- Read and discuss professional articles by researchers in the field of education.

- Meet to share teaching tips, collaborate on multi-grade lessons, and share resources.

- Develop lessons to try out new teaching strategies. Meet to share experiences and discuss how to further improve your teaching approach.

Let's Meet!

Forming a study group is easy. Just follow these four steps:

1. **Decide on the size of the group.** A small group has the advantage of making each member feel accountable, but make sure that all people have the ability to make the same commitment!

2. **Choose teachers to invite to join your group.** Think about who you want to invite. Should they all teach the same grade? Can you invite teachers from other schools? Remember that the more diverse the group, the more it benefits from new perspectives.

3. **Set goals for the group.** In order to succeed, know what you want the group to do. Meet to set goals. Rank goals in order of importance and refer often to the goals to keep the group on track.

4. **Make logistical decisions.** This is often the most difficult. Decide where and when you will meet. Consider an online meeting place where group members can post discussion questions and replies if people are not able to meet.

What Will We Study? Use the goals you set to help determine what your group will study. Consider what materials are needed to reach your goals, and how long you think you will need to prepare for each meeting.

How Will It Work? Think about how you structure groups in your classroom. Then use some of the same strategies.

- **Assign a group facilitator.** This person is responsible for guiding the meeting. This person comes prepared with discussion questions and leads the meeting. This could be a rotating responsibility dependent on experience with various topics. This person might be responsible for providing the materials.

- **Assign a recorder.** Have someone take notes during the meeting and record group decisions.

- **Use the jigsaw method.** Not everyone has time to be a facilitator. In this case, divide the text and assign each portion to a different person. Each person is responsible for leading the discussion on that particular part.

Meet Again Make a commitment to meet for a minimum number of times. After that, the group can reevaluate and decide whether or not to continue.

" Have some great teaching tips to share? Want to exchange ideas with your colleagues? Build your own professional community of teachers. **Customize Literacy** gets you started. "

Building Community

Trial Lessons

Use your colleagues' experiences to help as you think about new ways to connect content and students. Use the following plan to create a mini-lesson. It should last twenty minutes. Get the support of your colleagues as you try something new and then reflect on what happened.

Be Creative! As you develop a plan for a mini-lesson, use these four words to guide planning: *purpose*, *text*, *resources*, and *routine*.

- **Purpose:** Decide on a skill or strategy to teach. Define your purpose for teaching the lesson.

- **Text:** Develop a list of the materials you could use. Ask your colleagues for suggestions.

- **Resources:** Make a list of the available resources, and consider how to use those resources most effectively. Consider using the leveled readers listed on pages CL24–CL29 and CL36–CL41 of Customize Literacy.

- **Routine:** Choose an instructional routine to structure your mini-lesson. See the mini-lessons in Customize Literacy for suggestions.

Try It! Try out your lesson! Consider audio- or videotaping the lesson for later review. You may wish to invite a colleague to sit in as you teach. Make notes on how the lesson went.

How Did It Go? Use the self-evaluation checklist on page CL45 as you reflect on your trial lesson. This provides a framework for later discussion.

Discuss, Reflect, Repeat Solicit feedback from your teacher study group. Explain the lesson and share your reflections. Ask for suggestions on ways to improve the lesson. Take some time to reflect on the feedback. Modify your lesson to reflect what you have learned. Then try teaching the lesson again.

Checklist for Teacher Self-Evaluation

How Well Did I ...

	Very Well	Satisfactory	Not Very Well
Plan the lesson?			
Select the appropriate level of text?			
Introduce the lesson and explain its objectives?			
Review previously taught skills?			
Directly explain the new skills being taught?			
Model the new skills?			
Break the material down into small steps?			
Integrate guided practice into the lesson?			
Monitor guided practice for student understanding?			
Provide feedback on independent practice?			
Maintain an appropriate pace?			
Assess student understanding of the material?			
Stress the importance of applying the skill as they read?			
Maintain students' interest?			
Ask questions?			
Handle student questions and responses?			
Respond to the range of abilities?			

Building Community

Books for Teachers

Students aren't the only ones who need to read to grow. Here is a brief list of books that you may find useful to fill your reading teacher basket and learn new things.

A Professional Bibliography

Afflerbach, P. "Teaching Reading Self-Assessment Strategies." *Comprehension Instruction: Research-Based Best Practices.* The Guilford Press, 2002.

Bear, D. R., M. Invernizzi, S. Templeton, and F. Johnston. *Words Their Way.* Merrill Prentice Hall, 2004.

Beck, I. L., and M. G. McKeown. *Improving Comprehension with Questioning the Author: A Fresh and Expanded View of a Powerful Approach.* Scholastic, 2006.

Beck, I., M. G. McKeown, and L. Kucan. *Bringing Words to Life: Robust Vocabulary Instruction.* The Guilford Press, 2002.

Blachowicz, C. and P. Fisher. "Vocabulary Instruction." *Handbook of Reading Research,* vol. III. Lawrence Erlbaum Associates, 2000.

Blachowicz, C. and D. Ogle. *Reading Comprehension: Strategies for Independent Learners.* The Guilford Press, 2008.

Block, C. C. and M. Pressley. "Best Practices in Comprehension Instruction." *Best Practices in Literacy Instruction.* The Guilford Press, 2003.

Daniels, H. *Literature Circles.* 2nd ed. Stenhouse Publishers, 2002.

Dickson, S. V., D. C. Simmons, and E. J. Kame'enui. "Text Organization: Instructional and Curricular Basics and Implications." *What Reading Research Tells Us About Children with Diverse Learning Needs: Bases and Basics.* Lawrence Erlbaum Associates, 1998.

Diller, D. *Making the Most of Small Groups: Differentiation for All.* Stenhouse Publishers, 2007.

Duke, N. and P. D. Pearson. "Effective Practices for Developing Reading Comprehension." *What Research Has to Say About Reading Instruction,* 3rd ed. Newark, DE: International Reading Association, 2002.

Fillmore, L. W. and C. E. Snow. *What Teachers Need to Know About Language.* Office of Educational Research and Improvement, U.S. Department of Education, 2000.

Fountas, I. C. and G. S. Pinnell. *Guiding Readers and Writers Grades 3–6: Teaching Comprehension, Genre, and Content Literacy.* Heinemann, 2001.

Guthrie, J. and E. Anderson. "Engagement in Reading: Processes of Motivated Strategic, Knowledgeable, Social Readers." *Engaged Reading: Processes, Practices, and Policy Implications.* Teachers College Press, 1999.

Harvey, S. and A. Goudvis. *Strategies That Work: Teaching Comprehension to Enhance Understanding.* 2nd ed. Stenhouse Publishers, 2007.

Keene, E. O. and S. Zimmerman. *Mosaic of Thought.* 2nd ed. Heinemann, 2007.

Leu Jr., D. J. "The New Literacies: Research on Reading Instruction with the Internet and Other Digital Technologies." *What Research Has to Say About Reading Instruction,* 3rd ed. International Reading Association, 2002.

McKeown, M. G. and I. L. Beck. "Direct and Rich Vocabulary Instruction." *Vocabulary Instruction: Research to Practice.* The Guilford Press, 2004.

McTighe, J. and K. O'Conner. "Seven Practices for Effective Learning." *Educational Leadership,* vol. 63, no. 3 (November 2005).

Nagy, W. E. *Teaching Vocabulary to Improve Reading Comprehension.* International Reading Association, 1998.

National Reading Panel. *Teaching Children to Read.* National Institute of Child Health and Human Development, 1999.

Ogle, D. and C. Blachowicz. "Beyond Literature Circles: Helping Students Comprehend Information Texts." *Comprehension Instruction: Research-Based Practices.* The Guilford Press, 2001.

Pressley, M. *Reading Instruction That Works: The Case for Balanced Teaching,* 3rd ed. The Guilford Press, 2005.

Stahl, S. A. "What Do We Know About Fluency?" *The Voice of Evidence in Reading Research.* Paul H. Brookes, 2004.

Taylor, B. M., P. D. Pearson, D. S. Peterson, and M. C. Rodriguez. "The CIERA School Change Framework: An Evidence-Based Approach to Professional Development and School Reading Improvement." *Reading Research Quarterly,* vol. 40, no. 1 (January/February/March 2005).

Valencia, S. W. and M. Y. Lipson. "Thematic Instruction: A Quest for Challenging Ideas and Meaningful Learning." *Literature-Based Instruction: Reshaping the Curriculum.* Christopher-Gordon Publishers, 1998.

Building Community

Oral Vocabulary for

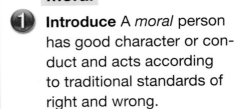
At the Beach

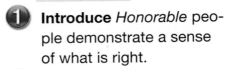 **Oral Vocabulary Routine**

frank

1. **Introduce** People who are *frank* are not afraid to say what they think.

2. **Demonstrate** Lee's father was *frank* about how much it would cost to fix the car.

3. **Apply** Discuss with students times when they feel they were *frank* with someone. When is it good to be *frank*?

honorable

1. **Introduce** *Honorable* people demonstrate a sense of what is right.

2. **Demonstrate** The policeman's *honorable* actions earned him a medal from the community.

3. **Apply** Have students discuss *honorable* actions or motives. Why is it important to be *honorable*?

moral

1. **Introduce** A *moral* person has good character or conduct and acts according to traditional standards of right and wrong.

2. **Demonstrate** Will is a *moral* person, and when he found the bag of money, he took it to the police station.

3. **Apply** Discuss with students what they think it means to show good morals.

oath

1. **Introduce** An *oath* is a statement in which a person swears that something is true.

2. **Demonstrate** I gave an *oath* that I would tell the truth.

3. **Apply** Talk with students about times when people take an *oath,* such as in a courtroom.

guilt

1. **Introduce** *Guilt* is the feeling of having done something wrong.

2. **Demonstrate** The evidence against them proved their *guilt.* Even though no one had seen Nate hit the ball through the window, his *guilt* made him knock on the door and confess.

3. **Apply** Have students discuss times when they might have felt *guilty* about something.

justice

1. **Introduce** *Justice* is the quality of being fair and right.

2. **Demonstrate** A courthouse is a place where the law is used to uphold *justice.*

3. **Apply** Have students talk about how laws are important to uphold *justice.*

Hold the Flag High

Amazing Words Oral Vocabulary Routine

 DAY 1

poses

① **Introduce** Someone *poses* when he or she is pretending to be someone they aren't.

② **Demonstrate** My sister *poses* as a rock star and dances in front of a mirror.

③ **Apply** Have volunteers act out historical figures and have the class guess who each actor *poses* as.

officers

① **Introduce** An *officer* is someone who commands other people in the armed forces.

② **Demonstrate** The *officer* had his troops make a ten-mile hike as part of their training.

③ **Apply** Discuss with students the different ranks of officers in the armed forces (e.g., major, captain, general, and admiral).

 DAY 2

maneuver

① **Introduce** *Maneuver* means to plan something skillfully or to use clever tricks to accomplish something.

② **Demonstrate** He used a series of *maneuvers* to get us to use his plan.

③ **Apply** Discuss with students situations in which they could employ a *maneuver* to accomplish something.

 DAY 3

trembling

① **Introduce** *Trembling* means "moving gently with a quick, shaking motion."

② **Demonstrate** The leaves *trembled* in the breeze. Gus *trembled* with fear when he heard the thunder claps.

③ **Apply** Discuss with students situations that might make them tremble.

 DAY 4

audacity

① **Introduce** *Audacity* means boldness or reckless daring.

② **Demonstrate** He had the *audacity* to barge into the classroom in the middle of a test.

③ **Apply** Have students talk about situations in life, in movies, or on television in which they have seen people or actors act with *audacity*.

brazen

① **Introduce** A *brazen* person acts shamelessly.

② **Demonstrate** Bullies often act in a *brazen* manner.

③ **Apply** Discuss with students how the similarities and differences between the words audacity and brazen.

The Ch'i-lin Purse

 Amazing Words Oral Vocabulary Routine

DAY 1

favor

1. **Introduce** A *favor* is an act of kindness.
2. **Demonstrate** The *favors* that meant the most came from volunteers who gave their time. Laura did Callie a huge *favor* by helping her with her homework.
3. **Apply** Have students talk about *favors* they have done for others or others have done for them.

panic

1. **Introduce** To *panic* is to have such great fear that you lose control of yourself.
2. **Demonstrate** I *panicked* when I got stuck inside the elevator.
3. **Apply** Have students discuss situations that might cause people to *panic*.

distress

1. **Introduce** *Distress* means "great pain or suffering."
2. **Demonstrate** The loss of the kitten caused Maggie much *distress*.
3. **Apply** Discuss other situations that may cause *distress*.

DAY 2

nurture

1. **Introduce** *Nurture* means to bring up or care for.
2. **Demonstrate** Chuck and Jen *nurtured* the baby bird until it was able to fly away.
3. **Apply** Have students discuss how they would *nurture* a pet, such as a dog or a cat.

DAY 3

aid

1. **Introduce** *Aid* means to give support to someone or to help people.
2. **Demonstrate** The Red Cross *aids* victims of natural disasters and other catastrophes.
3. **Apply** Ask students to identify groups within the community that provide *aid* to others.

DAY 4

social worker

1. **Introduce** A *social worker* is someone who works toward the betterment of social conditions in a community.
2. **Demonstrate** The *social worker* provided recreational activities for students and their families who were going through difficult times.
3. **Apply** Point out that many *social workers* have gone to school to learn different ways to help people who are having misfortunes or are disadvantaged.

UNIT 2 Acknowledgments

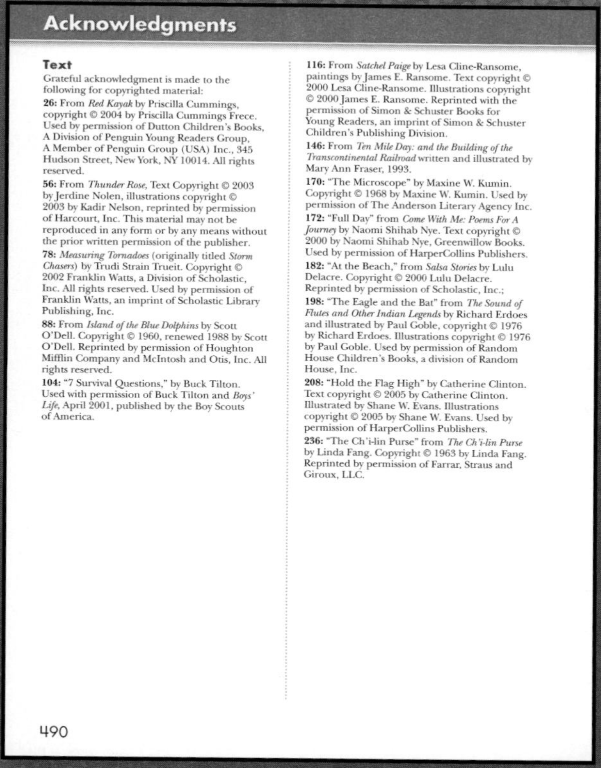

Acknowledgments

Text

Grateful acknowledgment is made to the following for copyrighted material:

26: From *Red Kayak* by Priscilla Cummings, copyright © 2004 by Priscilla Cummings Frece. Used by permission of Dutton Children's Books, A Division of Penguin Young Readers Group, A Member of Penguin Group (USA) Inc., 345 Hudson Street, New York, NY 10014. All rights reserved.

56: From *Thunder Rose,* Text Copyright © 2003 by Jerdine Nolen, illustrations copyright © 2003 by Kadir Nelson, reprinted by permission of Harcourt, Inc. This material may not be reproduced in any form or by any means without the prior written permission of the publisher.

78: *Measuring Tornadoes* (originally titled *Storm Chasers*) by Trudi Strain Trueit. Copyright © 2002 Franklin Watts, a Division of Scholastic, Inc. All rights reserved. Used by permission of Franklin Watts, an imprint of Scholastic Library Publishing, Inc.

88: From *Island of the Blue Dolphins* by Scott O'Dell. Copyright © 1960, renewed 1988 by Scott O'Dell. Reprinted by permission of Houghton Mifflin Company and McIntosh and Otis, Inc. All rights reserved.

104: "7 Survival Questions," by Buck Tilton. Used with permission of Buck Tilton and *Boys' Life,* April 2001, published by the Boy Scouts of America.

116: From *Satchel Paige* by Lesa Cline-Ransome, paintings by James E. Ransome. Text copyright © 2000 Lesa Cline-Ransome. Illustrations copyright © 2000 James E. Ransome. Reprinted with the permission of Simon & Schuster Books for Young Readers, an imprint of Simon & Schuster Children's Publishing Division.

146: From *Ten Mile Day: and the Building of the Transcontinental Railroad* written and illustrated by Mary Ann Fraser, 1993.

170: "The Microscope" by Maxine W. Kumin. Copyright © 1968 by Maxine W. Kumin. Used by permission of The Anderson Literary Agency Inc.

172: "Full Day" from *Come With Me: Poems For A Journey* by Naomi Shihab Nye. Text copyright © 2000 by Naomi Shihab Nye, Greenwillow Books. Used by permission of HarperCollins Publishers.

182: "At the Beach," from *Salsa Stories* by Lulu Delacre. Copyright © 2000 Lulu Delacre. Reprinted by permission of Scholastic, Inc.;

198: "The Eagle and the Bat" from *The Sound of Flutes and Other Indian Legends* by Richard Erdoes and illustrated by Paul Goble, copyright © 1976 by Richard Erdoes. Illustrations copyright © 1976 by Paul Goble. Used by permission of Random House Children's Books, a division of Random House, Inc.

208: "Hold the Flag High" by Catherine Clinton. Text copyright © 2005 by Catherine Clinton. Illustrated by Shane W. Evans. Illustrations copyright © 2005 by Shane W. Evans. Used by permission of HarperCollins Publishers.

236: "The Ch'i-lin Purse" from *The Ch'i-lin Purse* by Linda Fang. Copyright © 1963 by Linda Fang. Reprinted by permission of Farrar, Straus and Giroux, LLC.

490

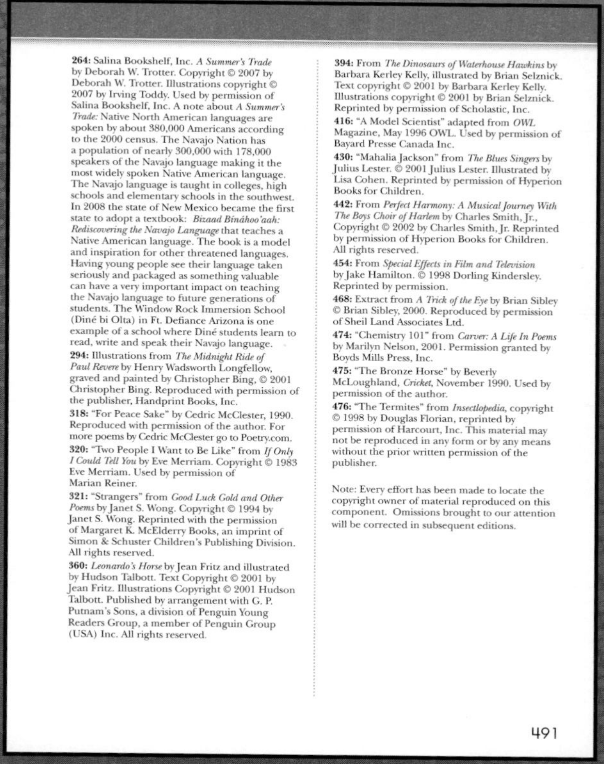

264: Salina Bookshelf, Inc. *A Summer's Trade* by Deborah W. Trotter. Copyright © 2007 by Deborah W. Trotter. Illustrations copyright © 2007 by Irving Toddy. Used by permission of Salina Bookshelf, Inc. A note about *A Summer's Trade:* Native North American languages are spoken by about 380,000 Americans according to the 2000 census. The Navajo Nation has a population of nearly 300,000 with 178,000 speakers of the Navajo language making it the most widely spoken Native American language. The Navajo language is taught in colleges, high schools and elementary schools in the southwest. In 2008 the state of New Mexico became the first state to adopt a textbook: *Bizaad Bináhoo'aah: Rediscovering the Navajo Language* that teaches a Native American language. The book is a model and inspiration for other threatened languages. Having young people see their language taken seriously and packaged as something valuable can have a very important impact on teaching the Navajo language to future generations of students. The Window Rock Immersion School (Diné bi Olta) in Ft. Defiance Arizona is one example of a school where Diné students learn to read, write and speak their Navajo language.

294: Illustrations from *The Midnight Ride of Paul Revere* by Henry Wadsworth Longfellow, graved and painted by Christopher Bing, © 2001 Christopher Bing. Reproduced with permission of the publisher, Handprint Books, Inc.

318: "For Peace Sake" by Cedric McClester, 1990. Reproduced with permission of the author. For more poems by Cedric McClester go to Poetry.com.

320: "Two People I Want to Be Like" from *If Only I Could Tell You* by Eve Merriam. Copyright © 1983 Eve Merriam. Used by permission of Marian Reiner.

321: "Strangers" from *Good Luck Gold and Other Poems* by Janet S. Wong. Copyright © 1994 by Janet S. Wong. Reprinted with the permission of Margaret K. McElderry Books, an imprint of Simon & Schuster Children's Publishing Division. All rights reserved.

360: *Leonardo's Horse* by Jean Fritz and illustrated by Hudson Talbott. Text Copyright © 2001 by Jean Fritz. Illustrations Copyright © 2001 Hudson Talbott. Published by arrangement with G. P. Putnam's Sons, a division of Penguin Young Readers Group, a member of Penguin Group (USA) Inc. All rights reserved.

394: From *The Dinosaurs of Waterhouse Hawkins* by Barbara Kerley Kelly, illustrated by Brian Selznick. Text copyright © 2001 by Barbara Kerley Kelly. Illustrations copyright © 2001 by Brian Selznick. Reprinted by permission of Scholastic, Inc.

416: "A Model Scientist" adapted from *OWL* Magazine, May 1996 OWL. Used by permission of Bayard Presse Canada Inc.

430: "Mahalia Jackson" from *The Blues Singers* by Julius Lester. © 2001 Julius Lester. Illustrated by Lisa Cohen. Reprinted by permission of Hyperion Books for Children.

442: From *Perfect Harmony: A Musical Journey With The Boys Choir of Harlem* by Charles Smith, Jr., Copyright © 2002 by Charles Smith, Jr. Reprinted by permission of Hyperion Books for Children. All rights reserved.

454: From *Special Effects in Film and Television* by Jake Hamilton. © 1998 Dorling Kindersley. Reprinted by permission.

468: Extract from *A Trick of the Eye* by Brian Sibley © Brian Sibley, 2000. Reproduced by permission of Sheil Land Associates Ltd.

474: "Chemistry 101" from *Carver: A Life In Poems* by Marilyn Nelson, 2001. Permission granted by Boyds Mills Press, Inc.

475: "The Bronze Horse" by Beverly McLoughland, *Cricket,* November 1990. Used by permission of the author.

476: "The Termites" from *Insectlopedia,* copyright © 1998 by Douglas Florian, reprinted by permission of Harcourt, Inc. This material may not be reproduced in any form or by any means without the prior written permission of the publisher.

Note: Every effort has been made to locate the copyright owner of material reproduced on this component. Omissions brought to our attention will be corrected in subsequent editions.

491

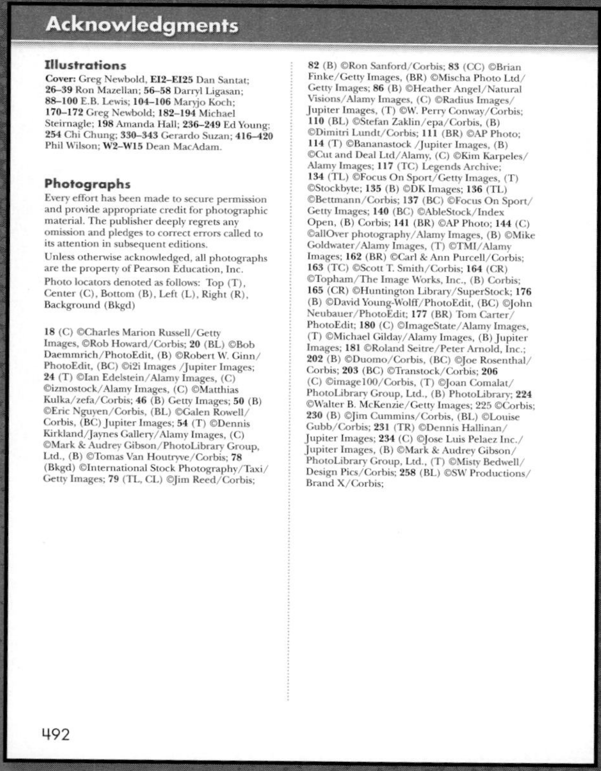

Acknowledgments

Illustrations

Cover: Greg Newbold, **EI2–EI25** Dan Santat; **26–39** Ron Mazellan; **56–58** Darryl Ligasan; **88–100** E.B. Lewis; **104–106** Maryjo Koch; **170–172** Greg Newbold; **182–194** Michael Steirnagle; **198** Amanda Hall; **236–249** Ed Young; **254** Chi Chung; **330–343** Gerardo Suzan; **416–420** Phil Wilson; **W2–W15** Dean MacAdam.

Photographs

Every effort has been made to secure permission and provide appropriate credit for photographic material. The publisher deeply regrets any omission and pledges to correct errors called to its attention in subsequent editions.

Unless otherwise acknowledged, all photographs are the property of Pearson Education, Inc.

Photo locators denoted as follows: Top (T), Center (C), Bottom (B), Left (L), Right (R), Background (Bkgd)

18 (C) ©Charles Marion Russell/Getty Images, ©Rob Howard/Corbis; **20** (BL) ©Bob Daemmrich/PhotoEdit, (B) ©Robert W. Ginn/PhotoEdit, (BC) ©i2i Images /Jupiter Images; **24** (T) ©Ian Edelstein/Alamy Images, (C) ©izmostock/Alamy Images, (C) ©Matthias Kulka/zefa/Corbis; **46** (B) Getty Images; **50** (B) ©Eric Nguyen/Corbis, (BL) ©Galen Rowell/Corbis, (BC) Jupiter Images; **54** (T) ©Dennis Kirkland/Jaynes Gallery/Alamy Images, (C) ©Mark & Audrey Gibson/PhotoLibrary Group, Ltd., (B) ©Tomas Van Houtryve/Corbis; **78** (Bkgd) ©International Stock Photography/Taxi/Getty Images; **79** (TL, CL) ©Jim Reed/Corbis; **82** (B) ©Ron Sanford/Corbis; **83** (CC) ©Brian Finke/Getty Images, (BR) ©Mischa Photo Ltd/Getty Images; **86** (B) ©Heather Angel/Natural Visions/Alamy Images, (C) ©Radius Images/Jupiter Images, (T) ©W. Perry Conway/Corbis; **110** (BL) ©Stefan Zaklin/epa/Corbis, (B) ©Dimitri Lundt/Corbis; **111** (BR) ©AP Photo; **114** (T) ©Bananastock /Jupiter Images, (B) ©Cut and Deal Ltd/Alamy, (C) ©Kim Karpeles/Alamy Images; **117** (TC) Legends Archive; **134** (TL) ©Focus On Sport/Getty Images, (T) ©Stockbyte; **135** (B) ©DK Images; **136** (TL) ©Bettmann/Corbis; **137** (BC) ©Focus On Sport/Getty Images; **140** (BC) ©AbleStock/Index Open, (B) Corbis; **141** (BR) ©AP Photo; **144** (C) ©allOver photography/Alamy Images, (B) ©Mike Goldwater/Alamy Images, (T) ©TMI/Alamy Images; **162** (BR) ©Carl & Ann Purcell/Corbis; **163** (TC) ©Scott T. Smith/Corbis; **164** (CR) ©Topham/The Image Works, Inc., (B) Corbis; **165** (CR) ©Huntington Library/SuperStock; **176** (B) ©David Young-Wolff/PhotoEdit, (BC) ©John Neubauer/PhotoEdit; **177** (BR) Tom Carter/PhotoEdit; **180** (C) ©ImageState/Alamy Images, (T) ©Michael Gilday/Alamy Images, (B) Jupiter Images; **181** ©Roland Seitre/Peter Arnold, Inc.; **202** (B) ©Duomo/Corbis, (BC) ©Joe Rosenthal/Corbis; **203** (BC) ©Transtock/Corbis; **206** (C) ©image100/Corbis, (T) ©Joan Comalat/PhotoLibrary Group, Ltd., (B) PhotoLibrary; **224** ©Walter B. McKenzie/Getty Images; 225 ©Corbis; **230** (B) ©Jim Cummins/Corbis, (BL) ©Louise Gubb/Corbis; **231** (TR) ©Dennis Hallinan/Jupiter Images; **234** (C) ©Jose Luis Pelaez Inc./Jupiter Images, (B) ©Mark & Audrey Gibson/PhotoLibrary Group, Ltd., (T) ©Misty Bedwell/Design Pics/Corbis; **258** (BL) ©SW Productions/Brand X/Corbis;

492

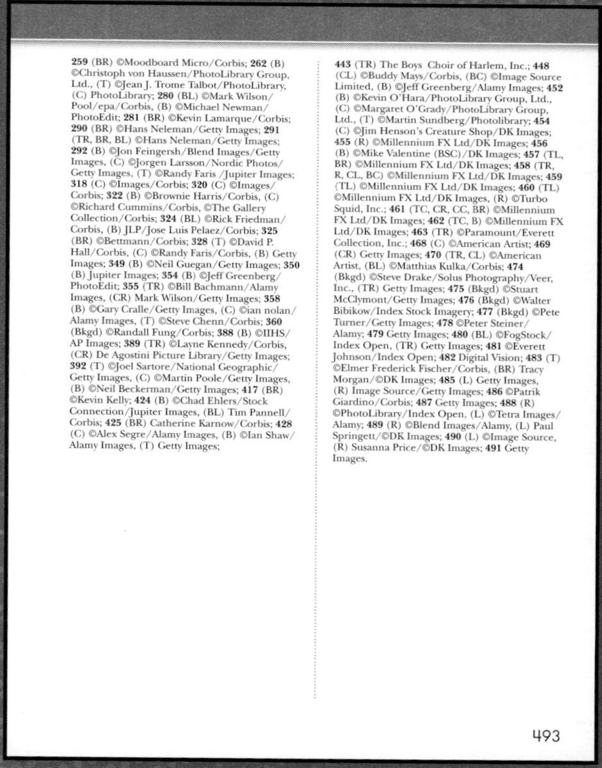

259 (BR) ©Moodboard Micro/Corbis; **262** (B) ©Christoph von Haussen/PhotoLibrary Group, Ltd., (T) ©Jean J. Trome Talbot/PhotoLibrary, (C) PhotoLibrary; **280** (BL) ©Mark Wilson/Pool/epa/Corbis, (B) ©Michael Newman/PhotoEdit; **281** (BR) ©Kevin Lamarque/Corbis; **290** (BR) ©Hans Neleman/Getty Images; **291** (TR, BR, BL) ©Hans Neleman/Getty Images; **292** (B) ©Jon Feingersh/Blend Images/Getty Images, (C) ©Jorgen Larsson/Nordic Photos/Getty Images, (T) ©Randy Faris /Jupiter Images; **318** (C) ©Images/Corbis; **320** (C) ©Images/Corbis; **322** (B) ©Brownie Harris/Corbis, (C) ©Richard Cummins/Corbis, ©The Gallery Collection/Corbis; **324** (BL) ©Rick Friedman/Corbis, (B) JLP/Jose Luis Pelaez/Corbis; **325** (BR) ©Bettmann/Corbis; **328** (T) ©David P. Hall/Corbis, (C) ©Randy Faris/Corbis, (B) Getty Images; **349** (B) ©Neil Guegan/Getty Images; **350** (B) Jupiter Images; **354** (B) ©Jeff Greenberg/PhotoEdit; **355** (TR) ©Bill Bachmann/Alamy Images, (CR) Mark Wilson/Getty Images; **358** (B) ©Gary Cralle/Getty Images, (C) ©ian nolan/Alamy Images, (T) ©Steve Chenn/Corbis; **360** (Bkgd) ©Randall Fung/Corbis; **388** (B) ©IIHS/AP Images; **389** (TR) ©Layne Kennedy/Corbis, (CR) De Agostini Picture Library/Getty Images; **392** (T) ©Joel Sartore/National Geographic/Getty Images, (C) ©Martin Poole/Getty Images, (B) ©Neil Beckerman/Getty Images; **417** (BR) ©Kevin Kelly; **424** (B) ©Chad Ehlers/Stock Connection/Jupiter Images, (BL) Tim Pannell/Corbis; **425** (BR) Catherine Karnow/Corbis; **428** (C) ©Alex Segre/Alamy Images, (B) ©Ian Shaw/Alamy Images, (T) Getty Images; **443** (TR) The Boys Choir of Harlem, Inc.; **448** (CL) ©Buddy Mays/Corbis, (BC) ©Image Source Limited, (B) ©Jeff Greenberg/Alamy Images; **452** (B) ©Kevin O'Hara/PhotoLibrary Group, Ltd., (C) ©Margaret O'Grady/PhotoLibrary Group, Ltd., (T) ©Martin Sundberg/Photolibrary; **454** (C) ©Jim Henson's Creature Shop/DK Images; **455** (R) ©Millennium FX Ltd/DK Images; **456** (B) ©Mike Valentine (BSC)/DK Images; **457** (TL, BR) ©Millennium FX Ltd/DK Images; **458** (TR, R, CL, BC) ©Millennium FX Ltd/DK Images; **459** (TL) ©Millennium FX Ltd/DK Images; **460** (TL) ©Millennium FX Ltd/DK Images, (R) ©Turbo Squid, Inc.; **461** (TC, CR, CC, BR) ©Millennium FX Ltd/DK Images; **462** (TC, B) ©Millennium FX Ltd/DK Images; **463** (TR) ©Paramount/Everett Collection, Inc.; **468** (C) ©American Artist; **469** (CR) Getty Images; **470** (TR, CL) ©American Artist, (BL) ©Matthias Kulka/Corbis; **474** (Bkgd) ©Steve Drake/Solus Photography/Veer, Inc., (TR) Getty Images; **475** (Bkgd) ©Stuart McClymont/Getty Images; **476** (Bkgd) ©Walter Bibikow/Index Stock Imagery; **477** (Bkgd) ©Pete Turner/Getty Images; **478** ©Peter Steiner/Alamy; **479** Getty Images; **480** (BL) ©FogStock/Index Open, (TR) Getty Images; **481** ©Everett Johnson/Index Open; **482** Digital Vision; **483** (T) ©Elmer Frederick Fischer/Corbis, (BR) Tracy Morgan/©DK Images; **485** (L) Getty Images, (R) Image Source/Getty Images; **486** ©Patrik Giardino/Corbis; **487** Getty Images; **488** (R) ©PhotoLibrary/Index Open, (L) ©Tetra Images/Alamy; **489** (R) ©Blend Images/Alamy, (L) Paul Springett/©DK Images; **490** (L) ©Image Source, (R) Susanna Price/©DK Images; **491** Getty Images.

493

Teacher's Edition

Text

KWL Strategy: The KWL Interactive Reading Strategy was developed and is used by permission of Donna Ogle, National-Louis University, Skokie, Illinois, co-author of *Reading Today and Tomorrow,* Holt, Rinehart & Winston Publishers, 1988. (See also the *Reading Teacher,* February 1986, pp. 564–570.)

Understanding by Design quotes: Wiggins, G. & McTighe, J. (2005). *Understanding by Design.* Alexandria, VA: Association for Supervision and Curriculum Development.

Illustrations

Cover Greg Newbold

Running Head Linda Bronson

Photographs

Every effort has been made to secure permission and provide appropriate credit for photographic material. The publisher deeply regrets any omission and pledges to correct errors called to its attention in subsequent editions.

Unless otherwise acknowledged, all photographs are the property of Pearson Education, Inc.

Teacher Notes

Teacher Resources

Looking for Teacher Resources and other important information?

In the **First Stop** on Reading Street

Teacher Resources
Looking for Teacher Resources and other important information?

In the **First Stop**
on Reading Street